T0281396

iOS Code Testing

Test-Driven Development and
Behavior-Driven Development
with Swift

Abhishek Mishra

Apress®

iOS Code Testing: Test-Driven Development and Behavior-Driven Development with Swift

Abhishek Mishra
Milton Keynes, United Kingdom

ISBN-13 (pbk): 978-1-4842-2688-9   ISBN-13 (electronic): 978-1-4842-2689-6
DOI 10.1007/978-1-4842-2689-6

Library of Congress Control Number: 2017945747

Cover image designed by Freepik

Managing Director: Welmoed Spahr
Editorial Director: Todd Green
Acquisitions Editor: Aaron Black
Development Editor: James Markham
Technical Reviewer: Chaim Krause
Coordinating Editor: Jessica Vakili
Copy Editor: Karen Jameson
Compositor: SPi Global
Indexer: SPi Global
Artist: SPi Global

Distributed to the book trade worldwide by Springer Science+Business Media New York, 233 Spring Street, 6th Floor, New York, NY 10013. Phone 1-800-SPRINGER, fax (201) 348-4505, e-mail orders-ny@springer-sbm.com, or visit www.springeronline.com. Apress Media, LLC is a California LLC and the sole member (owner) is Springer Science + Business Media Finance Inc (SSBM Finance Inc). SSBM Finance Inc is a **Delaware** corporation.

For information on translations, please e-mail rights@apress.com, or visit http://www.apress.com/rights-permissions.

Apress titles may be purchased in bulk for academic, corporate, or promotional use. eBook versions and licenses are also available for most titles. For more information, reference our Print and eBook Bulk Sales web page at http://www.apress.com/bulk-sales.

Any source code or other supplementary material referenced by the author in this book is available to readers on GitHub via the book's product page, located at www.apress.com/978-1-4842-2688-9. For more detailed information, please visit http://www.apress.com/source-code.

Printed on acid-free paper

*To my wife Sonam, for her love and support through
all the years we've been together.*

To my daughter Elana, for bringing joy and happiness into our lives.

Contents at a Glance

About the Author xv

About the Technical Reviewer xvii

Acknowledgments xix

■Chapter 1: Introduction to Test-Driven Development 1

■Chapter 2: Writing Your First Set of Unit Tests with Xcode 13

■Chapter 3: The MVVM Architectural Pattern.............................. 43

■Chapter 4: Applying TDD to the Model...................................... 61

■Chapter 5: Applying TDD to View Controllers 101

■Chapter 6: Applying TDD to Collection View Controllers 161

■Chapter 7: Testing URLSession 211

■Chapter 8: Working with Legacy Code...................................... 257

■Chapter 9: Continuous Integration... 283

■Chapter 10: Introduction to Behavior-Driven Development 317

■Chapter 11: Installing Quick... 329

■Chapter 12: Applying TDD and BDD Techniques 351

■Chapter 13: Testing the User Interface 407

Index.. 433

Contents

About the Author xv

About the Technical Reviewer xvii

Acknowledgments xix

■Chapter 1: Introduction to Test-Driven Development 1

What Is Test-Driven Development? 1

TDD Terminology 2

Subject under Test 2

Unit Test 2

State Verification Test 3

Interaction Test 3

Negative Test 4

Test Suite 6

Assertions 7

Instantiating Classes for Testing 9

Principles of Test-Driven Development 10

Test First 10

Red – Green – Refactor 10

Write the Minimum Amount of Code 11

Remove Duplication 11

Summary 11

Notes 11

■**Chapter 2: Writing Your First Set of Unit Tests with Xcode** **13**

Downloading and Installing Xcode 14

Creating a New Project with Unit Test Support 15

Adding Support for Unit Tests to an Existing Project............................ 16

A Tour of Xcode 18

The Project Navigator 18

Test Case Classes 20

The Test Navigator 23

Viewing Test Reports 25

Code Coverage Reports 25

Building the Cookie Factory App 26

Building the Cookie Class 28

Building the CookieController Class 32

Updating the View Controller Class 39

Viewing Code Coverage Data... 40

Summary.. 41

■**Chapter 3: The MVVM Architectural Pattern**.................................. **43**

The MVC Architectural Pattern 43

The Model-ViewController Architectural Pattern................................. 44

Model-ViewController Testability Issues... 45

The Model-View-ViewModel Architectural Pattern.............................. 46

Advantages of MVVM.. 47

ViewModel Instantiation 48

Isolated View Controller... 48

Table View Controllers 49

Navigation Controller-Based Apps 50

Summary.. 60

▓**Chapter 4: Applying TDD to the Model**.. **61**

Creating the Xcode Project.. 62

Building the Model Layer... 64

 The AccountOwner Class..64

 Creating the First Name Validator Class 70

 Creating the Last Name Validator Class..76

 Creating the Email Address Validator Class 82

Integrating the Validator Classes into the AccountOwner Class............ 85

The Transaction Class... 94

The BankAccount Class... 95

Testing Core Data 98

Summary.. 99

▓**Chapter 5: Applying TDD to View Controllers** **101**

Application Architecture 102

Creating the Xcode Project.. 103

Building the User Interface Layer 104

 Building the Login View Controller Scene...106

 Building the Signup View Controller Scene 110

 Creating a Segue Between the Login Scene and the Signup Scene 113

Building the Model Layer... 115

 The LoginModel Class...115

 The SignupModel Class 116

Building the ViewModel Layer 118

 The LoginViewModel Class..118

 View Model – View Controller Binding...123

 The SignupViewModel Class 143

Connecting the View Controller to the View Model 147

    Binding the Login View Controller Class to the View Model 147

    Binding the Signup View Controller Class to the View Model 157

    Transitioning from the Login View Controller to the Signup View Controller 160

Summary 160

Chapter 6: Applying TDD to Collection View Controllers 161

Application Architecture 162

Creating the Xcode Project 162

Adding Resources to the Project 164

Building the User Interface Layer 165

    Creating New Classes 166

    Building the Collection View Controller Scene 167

    Adding a Section Header Accessory View 169

    Building the Collection View Cell 172

Building the Model Layer 177

    The Photo Class 178

    The City Class 180

    The Album Class 181

Building the ViewModel Layer 182

    The CollectionViewModel Class 183

    The CollectionViewCellViewModel Class 200

    The CollectionViewSectionHeaderViewModel Class 202

Binding the View Layer to the View Model 203

    Binding the Collection View Controller Class to the View Model 204

    Binding the CollectionViewCell Class to the View Model 207

    Binding the CollectionViewSectionHeader Class to the View Model 208

Summary 209

■Chapter 7: Testing URLSession 211

Strategies for Testing the Networking Layer 213

Preparing the PhotoBook Project 214

Remote Content Specification 216

Configuring Application Transport Security 216

Building the Networking Layer 217

    Creating the ServiceController Class 222

    Creating the MockURLSession Class 224

    Creating the MockURLSessionDataTask Class 226

Updating the Model Layer 227

    Updating the Album Class 228

    Updating the Photo Class 239

Updating the View Model Layer 249

    Updates to the Collection View Model 249

    Updates to the Collection View Cell View Model 251

Updating the View Layer 252

    Updates to the Collection View Controller 252

    Updates to the Collection View Cell 253

Summary 256

■Chapter 8: Working with Legacy Code 257

Splitting a Large Class 257

Adding Functionality to an Existing Class 265

    Encapsulate Using Classes and Methods 265

    Rename and Replace 270

    Decorators 271

Decoupling Classes Using Protocols 277

Using Dependency Injection to Create More Testable Code 279

Summary 282

Notes 282

■**Chapter 9: Continuous Integration** **283**

Installing macOS Server 284

Launching macOS Server 285

Setting Up Access for Team Members 289

Starting Xcode Server 290

Configuring Xcode Server 293

Xcode Version 294

Apple Developer Teams 294

Development Devices 295

Repositories 295

Creating a New Git Repository on Xcode Server 296

Configuring Xcode 298

Adding Xcode Server Credentials to Xcode 298

Create a New Xcode Project and Host Its Repository on Xcode Server 301

Clone an Existing Local Repository to Xcode Server 302

Clone a Git Repository from Xcode Server 304

Cloning a Git Repository from GitHub 305

Creating and Integrating Bots 306

Create a Bot 306

Integrate a Bot 315

Summary 316

■**Chapter 10: Introduction to Behavior-Driven Development** **317**

What Is Behavior Driven Development 317

The Difference between BDD and TDD 318

Business Requirements and User Scenarios 318

From User Scenarios to BDD Tests 319

Anatomy of a Quick Test Case 321

Advantages and Disadvantages of BDD 326

Summary 327

■Chapter 11: Installing Quick 329

Adding Quick to an Xcode Project 329

Adding Quick to an Xcode Project Using CocoaPods 329

Adding Quick to an Xcode Project Using Carthage 335

Adding Quick to an Xcode Project Using Git Submodules 342

Summary 349

■Chapter 12: Applying TDD and BDD Techniques 351

Reviewing the Business Requirements 351

High-Level Application Architecture 355

Creating the Xcode Project 357

Adding Resources to the Project 359

Building the User Interface Layer 360

Writing BDD Tests with Quick 368

Examining the BDD Test for Scenario Number 3 374

Examining the BDD Test for Scenario Number 4 375

Examining the BDD Test for Scenario Number 5 376

Examining the BDD Test for Scenario Number 6 377

Examining the BDD Test for Scenario Number 7 377

Examining the BDD Test for Scenario Number 8 378

Examining the BDD Test for Scenario Number 9 379

Creating Stub Objects 380

Adding The Restaurant Data File to the Project 382

Examining the Remaining Compilation Errors 383

Building the Model Layer 384

Building the ViewModel Layer 387

    The SearchViewModel Class 387

    The RestaurantTableViewModel Class 393

    The RestaurantTableViewCellViewModel Class 395

View Controller to View Model Bindings 400

Summary 405

■Chapter 13: Testing the User Interface 407

Adding Support for UI Testing to Your Project 408

New Projects 408

Existing Projects 410

UI Test Classes 411

Creating New Test Classes 415

Changes to XCTest to Support UI Testing 416

XCUIApplication 416

XCUIDevice 418

    XCUIElement, XCUIElementAttributes 418

XCUIElementAttributes 420

XCUIElementQuery and XCUIElementTypeQueryProvider 421

Assertions 424

UI Recording 426

Waiting Before Asserting 426

Putting It All Together 427

Summary 432

Index 433

About the Author

Abhishek Mishra has been active in the IT industry for over 19 years and has extensive experience with a wide range of programming languages and platforms.

He is the author of iPhone and iPad App – 24 Hour Trainer, Swift iOS – 24 Hour Trainer, and the technical reviewer of Professional iOS Programming.

He holds a Masters degree in Computer Science from the University of London and currently provides consultancy services to Barclays Bank PLC in London as a Solutions Architect.

His previous clients have included British Sky Broadcasting, Centrica, Expedia., Kantar Media, and Havas Media. He lives with his wife and daughter in London.

About the Technical Reviewer

Chaim Krause is first, and foremost, a #Geek. Other hashtags used to define him are (in no particular order) #autodidact, #maker, #gamer, #raver, #teacher, #adhd, #edm, #wargamer, #privacy, #liberty, #civilrights, #computers, #developer, #software, #dogs, #cats, #opensource, #techicaleditor, #author, #polymath, #polyglot, #american, #unity3d, #javascript, #smartwatch, #linux, #energydrinks, #midwesterner, #webmaster, #robots, #sciencefiction, #sciencefact, #universityofchicago, #politicalscience, and #bipolar. He can always be contacted at chaim@chaim.com and goes by the Nom de Net of Tinjaw.

Acknowledgments

This book would not have been possible without the support of the team at Apress including Aaron Black and Jessica Vakili. I would also like to thank Chaim Krause for taking the time to read the entire manuscript and his keen eye for detail. It has been my privilege to work with you. Thank you.

CHAPTER 1

■ ■ ■

Introduction to Test-Driven Development

Well over a billion apps have been developed for the iOS platform since its inception. Most of the early apps were rather simple and often developed by a single developer. Over the years, iOS apps have become increasingly complex pieces of software that often involve large, distributed teams of developers working in Agile environments with complex build and release pipelines.

Modern apps often perform several complex operations including (but not limited to) presenting a complex user interface, multithreading, storing data in local databases, interfacing with multiple sensors, media recording and playback, and consuming RESTful web API's.

With such a complex interplay between components of an app and several thousand lines of source code spread across several hundred classes, how do we know for certain that the code we have written does what we think it does? How do we know that our code can handle edge scenarios? And finally, how do we know that we have built the right software that meets business requirements? The answer to the first two questions is addressed by the practice of unit testing, and Behavior-Driven Development (BDD) addresses the answer to the question of building the right software in the first place. BDD is covered in Chapter 10. In this chapter and the next one you will learn about unit testing, and the related discipline of Test-Driven Development (TDD).

What Is Test-Driven Development?

Test Driven Development (TDD) has its roots in a programming paradigm called Extreme Programming[1] (XP), created by Kent Beck in 1996. The use of the word "extreme" signifies a radical departure from standard programming practices of that time.

TDD is designed to provide developers with a tangible way to prove that the code they have written does what they think it does, and to provide some confidence that the new code that has been written does not cause any potential side effects with existing code.

© Abhishek Mishra 2017
A. Mishra, *iOS Code Testing*, DOI 10.1007/978-1-4842-2689-6_1

Central to the TDD approach is the concept that a developer not only writes actual code to carry out the app's functionality but also tests code that ensures his application's code does what it is supposed to do. The test code is not shipped with the product.

While writing test code in addition to code that carries out the app's intended functionality is indeed extra work, it should be seen as an up-front investment toward improving the quality of the product that ships to customers. A team that practices TDD techniques will, over time, observe a reduction in the number of regression defects.

■ **Note**   TDD is often used interchangeably with the term Unit Test; however, these two terms are not the same thing. TDD is an approach to software development where the test code is written first: in essence, the tests drive development.

A unit test is just a piece of test code viewed in isolation. A unit test is one of the by-products of adopting a TDD approach.

However, the mere existence of one or more unit tests does not necessarily imply that the developer followed a TDD approach. The unit tests could, for instance, have been fitted retrospectively to existing code.

If you find working on large problems overwhelming, you may find TDD to be a useful technique to break down a problem into smaller ones, use tests to solve the smaller problems, and in the process end up solving the larger problem. You will soon realize that large problems are not as overwhelming once you approach them with a TDD mindset.

TDD Terminology

This section examines some of the common terminology associated with Test-Driven Development.

Subject under Test

This is usually a piece of code, or unit of functionality you wish to test. In most situations the subject under test is usually a single method of a Swift class. However, you may encounter scenarios where a small group of methods or classes are being tested together. In such cases, the subject under test usually represents a complete functionality or user journey. The subject under test is sometimes also known as the system under test.

Unit Test

This is the piece of code that tests the subject under test. A unit test is also known as a "test case." Unit tests work by calling the subject under test under controlled conditions, and verifying some kind of expected behavior. It is common for an application to have hundreds of unit tests with each test testing a very small piece of the functionality.

Individual unit tests are implemented as independent methods of a Swift class that derives from an XCTestCase. This Swift class is also commonly referred to as a test class.

In most cases you will create one test class for each class you wish to test. The XCTestCase class is part of the XCTest framework, and the framework must be imported with an import statement. The following code listing contains a simple test class with one unit test:

```
import XCTest
@testable import LoginService

class LoginServiceTests: XCTestCase {

    func testExample() {

        // insert test code here.
    }

}
```

■ **Note**   The code that forms these unit tests is not part of the code base that will ship to the clients. Unit tests are typically executed every time a developer attempts to create a build, with the build being created only if all tests pass.

The method signature of a unit test is similar to that of a method that takes no arguments and does not return a value. However, the name of a unit test method always begins with the keyword "test." There are usually strict naming conventions followed for unit test methods; these will be discussed in the next lesson.

State Verification Test

A state verification test is a type of unit test that calls methods on an object (subject under test) and verifies the state of the object after calling the method. Such tests do not care about implementation detail and will continue to pass even if the internal workings of the methods being tested are changed in the future. State verification tests usually rely on assertions to carry out the actual verification. Assertions are covered later in this lesson.

Interaction Test

An interaction test is a type of unit test that attempts to verify a specific sequence of interactions between objects when a method is called. Such tests are also known as behavior verification tests. Interaction tests do not necessarily have to involve multiple objects. You could also use an interaction test to verify the sequence of calls to methods of the same object.

In a complex object-oriented system, a single object may need to interact with several other objects when a method is called. When it comes to interaction tests, the subject under test is still a single class, and not the entire group of classes. One typically instantiates the subject under test and uses special mock or stub versions of all the other objects involved in the scope of the interaction test. Mock and stub objects are covered later in this lesson.

■ **Note**   Since interaction tests verify the behavior of a group of classes, they are inherently more fragile than state verification tests. For instance, a change in the order in which methods are called could easily break an interaction test. One way to make interaction tests less brittle is by reducing the number of classes covered by the scope of the test.

Negative Test

A negative unit test is one that verifies something did not happen. This can be useful in some cases. However, one must never solely rely on negative tests. This is because while a negative test can verify that something did not happen, it is immune to any number of things that did happen. The code base could change considerably without have a single negative test fail. If all your unit tests were negative tests, then your tests collectively are providing limited value.

Negative unit tests in Swift are almost always state verification tests. Although it is possible to create negative unit tests that are interaction tests, the relevant setup required is quite complicated and often outweighs the value of writing the negative test.

As an example of a negative unit test in action, consider the following Swift class that could be used to represent a bank account:

```
enum AccountType {
    case currentAccount
    case savingsAccount
}

class BankAccount {

    var accountName:String
    var accountNumber:String
    var accountType:AccountType
    private var transactions:[Transaction]

    init(accountName:String,
         accountNumber:String,
         accountType:AccountType) {

        self.accountName = accountName
        self.accountNumber = accountNumber
        self.accountType = accountType
        self.transactions = [Transaction]()
    }
```

```
func addTransaction(_ transaction:Transaction) {
    transactions.append(transaction)
}

func accountBalance() -> Float {
    var balance:Float = 0
    for transaction in self.transactions {
        if transaction.isCredit {
            balance = balance + transaction.amount
        } else {
            balance = balance + transaction.amount
        }
    }

    return balance
}
}
```

Individual transactions within a BankAccount object are represented using Transaction objects. The definition of a simple Transaction class is presented next:

```
class Transaction {

    var description:String
    var amount:Float
    var isCredit:Bool

    init(description:String,
         amount:Float,
         isCredit:Bool) {

        self.description = description
        self.amount = amount
        self.isCredit = isCredit
    }

}
```

With these two classes in mind, a negative unit test could be used to verify that a call to the addTransaction() method of the BankAccount class does not change the account name. This test could be written as follows:

```
func testAddTransaction_DoesNotChangeAccountName() {

    let bankAccount = BankAccount(accountName: "John Smith",
                                  accountNumber: "14918",
                                  accountType: .savingsAccount)
```

```
let transaction = Transaction(description: "Salary",
                              amount: 100.0,
                              isCredit: true)

bankAccount.addTransaction(transaction)

XCTAssertTrue(bankAccount.accountName.compare("John Smith") ==
.orderedSame,
              "Call to addTransaction should have no effect on
              account name.")
}
```

Assertions haven't been covered yet, but they will be shortly. This test ensures that the value of the accountName variable of the BankAccount instance does not change when addTransaction is called.

Test Suite

A test suite is simply a collection of test case files. Test suites usually have their own group in the Xcode project explorer and are included in a separate build target from the rest of the application's code (Figure 1-1).

Figure 1-1. *Separate Folder Groups for Test Suites in Xcode*

A single Xcode project can have multiple test suites, for example, one test suite may contain unit tests, and another may contain interaction tests. In the next lesson, you will learn to configure Xcode build schemes to include specific test suites as part of the build process.

Assertions

Assertions are the bread and butter of both state verification and interaction tests. An assertion represents a failure of a unit test. Typically, your unit test will call a method on an object, and this method may perform a number of activities such as returning a value, changing some values in the object, or calling out to other methods.

If you know the expected result of the method you are calling, you can build a unit test that calls the method with known inputs and expects a specific result. If the result of calling the method does not match the expected value, the test will indicate failure by firing an assertion.

The standard unit-testing framework that ships with Xcode is called XCTest and contains several macros to help create assertions within a unit test. Table 1-1 lists some of these macros.

Table 1-1. *XCTest Assertion Macros*

Macro	Description
XCTAssert(expression, message)	Generates a failure if the expression evaluates to false. An optional string message may be provided to indicate the reason for failure.
XCTAssertEqualObjects(expression1, expression2, message)	Generates a failure when expression1 is not equal to expression 2, where both expression 1 and expression 2 are objects. Both objects involved must implement Equatable. An optional string message may be provided to indicate the reason for failure.
XCTAssertNotEqualObjects(expression1, expression2, message)	Generates a failure when expression1 is equal to expression 2, where both expression 1 and expression 2 are objects. Both objects involved must implement Equatable. An optional string message may be provided to indicate the reason for failure.
XCTAssertEqual(expression1, expression2, message)	Generates a failure when expression1 is not equal to expression 2. This test is for primitive data types. An optional string message may be provided to indicate the reason for failure.
XCTAssertNotEqual(expression1, expression2, message)	Generates a failure when expression1 is equal to expression 2. Both expression1 and expression 2 are primitive data types. An optional string message may be provided to indicate the reason for failure.
XCTAssertNil (expression, message)	Generates a failure when the expression is not nil. An optional string message may be provided to indicate the reason for failure.

(continued)

Table 1-1. (*continued*)

Macro	Description
XCTAssertNotNil(expression, message)	Generates a failure when the expression is nil. An optional string message may be provided to indicate the reason for failure.
XCTAssertTrue (expression, message)	Generates a failure when the expression evaluates to false. Identical to XCTAssert(), provided to create more readable tests. An optional string message may be provided to indicate the reason for failure.
XCTAssertFalse (expression, message)	Generates a failure when the expression evaluates to true. An optional string message may be provided to indicate the reason for failure.

The following code snippet lists a unit test that will fail using the XCTAssertTrue macro. Figure 1-2 is a snapshot of the Xcode test navigator showing a failed test.

```
func testNumber1IsGreaterThanNumber2() {
    let number1 = 9218
    let number2 = 673666
    XCTAssertTrue(number1 > number2,
                "number1 should be greater than number2")
}
```

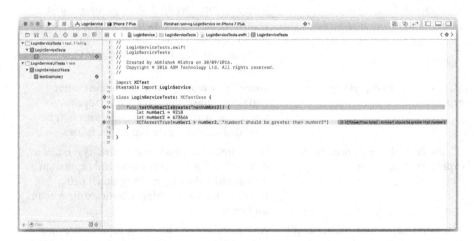

Figure 1-2. *Failed Unit Test*

This test fails because the test expects number1 to be greater than number2. Fixing it is a simple matter of editing the value of number1 to be greater than number2:

```
func testNumber1IsGreaterThanNumber2() {
    let number1 = 921800
    let number2 = 673666
    XCTAssertTrue(number1 > number2,
                    "number1 should be greater than number2")
}
```

This particular test obviously does not have much utility; it does not call any methods on other objects, or change the state of an object. It is only presented to serve as an example of how assertions work.

Instantiating Classes for Testing

Instantiating classes in isolation can sometimes get very tricky. A class's initializer may require several parameters, each of which may be objects themselves. The problem is compounded if one of the dependent classes you are instantiating requires access to a system resource such as a network connection, file, or database.

To be able to write meaningful and succinct unit tests, you need to be able to instantiate your subject under test without having to worry too much about building its dependencies.

The most common solution to the problem of instantiating an object's dependencies is to create fake "stunt double" versions of the dependencies. For this approach to work, these fake objects should look like the real object, and be much easier to instantiate. These fake objects could, for instance, implement the same protocols as the objects they are trying to emulate and perform harmless functionality within method implementations.

Such objects could easily be used as dependencies for the class under test, and allow you to create meaningful tests. Two types of fake objects are commonly found with unit tests:

- Stub object. A stub object (also known as a stub), is a fake object that can be used in place of a real dependency, is significantly easier to instantiate, and provides harmless method implementations of the object it is trying to emulate.

- Mock object. A mock object (also known as a mock), is similar to a stub. However, the key difference is that a mock is used in a test assertion, or asserted against.

For example, if you were writing a test that calls a method on object A and expects a different method on object B to be called by object A, then object B is a mock object because your test method expects a method to be called on object B. Any other objects C, D, E that may have been instantiated to assist writing the test, but are not the target of your test's expectations will be called stubs.

Principles of Test-Driven Development

In this section you will learn about some of the key principles of TDD. These principles are applicable regardless of the programming language, target platform, or IDE choice.

Test First

For unit tests to truly drive development, they need to be written before the code that they will test. In fact, one of the key principles of TDD is that the tests are written first, and the developer then focuses on writing the minimum amount of code needed to make all tests pass. When tests are written first, the resulting software tends to be more modularized because developers are forced to think of the software in terms of small components that are built independently and interact with each other.

The tests collectively define the acceptance criteria of the project. If you have a comprehensive suite of tests, the code is considered ready as soon as all tests pass and no further changes to the code base are required. In practice, a developer writes a single test, and then runs it to check if it fails. The developer then proceeds to write the code to make this one test pass. This is an iterative process, and over time a comprehensive set of tests is created by the developer, which serves as both the acceptance criteria as well as living documentation for the code base.

Once all tests pass, the feature in question is deemed to be complete. This process is iterative, with each iteration creating new tests and code to make these tests pass.

It is not necessary for the same developer to write both the subject under test as well as the unit tests. In fact, it is quite common for a senior developer to use unit tests to specify the behavior of a class for a junior developer. Given these tests, the junior developer can implement the class and knows his work is done when all the unit tests pass.

Red – Green – Refactor

The test first principle requires you to write tests up front. If you were to follow this principle and write a test for code that does not yet exist, chances are that the test will not compile, or it will compile and it will fail.

This stage of development that involves creating a failing test that encapsulates the expected outcome of the system under test is called the Red stage. The color red has to do with the use of the red color by popular IDE's like Xcode and Visual Studio to indicate failed tests in a summary view.

No one likes a failing test. Once you have created a failing test, then the next step is to fix the failing test by writing the minimum amount of code to make the test pass. This second stage is called the Green stage. The color green has to do with its use by popular IDE's to indicate passing tests in a summary view.

Reaching the green stage may involve both creating new code as well as modifying existing code. The coding effort focuses on making the bare minimum change to fix the test. To put it another way, something that is "good enough" will be fine.

It is quite common to find that in order to fix one failing test, you need to create a new class, or method, and begin a test first approach to this sub problem, thus creating a series of failing tests. This is perfectly normal and will all be resolved once you have fixed the innermost layer of tests.

After having successfully fixed a set of failing tests, you may look at the code you have written and decide that it needs refactoring. The final stage of the red-green-refactor approach is about optionally refactoring the code that was written in the second stage while ensuring that you do not break any existing tests.

Write the Minimum Amount of Code

This practice requires that you do not write any code that is not needed. When you are in the process of building a method to satisfy a failing test, it is tempting to add extra parameters to the method, or create an additional method anticipating future needs. This practice must be avoided, and you really must then always make sure you have tests covering the momentarily superfluous functionality that you have built.

Remove Duplication

This is an activity that you will find yourself undertaking as part of a refactoring exercise. The idea is to remove duplicate functionality from your classes. Always remember to have a set of unit tests in place before you begin refactoring so that you can be sure that you are not changing the behavior of the class.

It is also common to apply this principle to the tests themselves. Over time as the number of unit tests in your project increases, you will find yourself refactoring the tests themselves, removing common functionality between tests into its own independent test.

Summary

In this chapter you have been introduced to the idea of Test-Driven Development, the difference between TDD and Unit Tests, different types of unit tests, assertions, and general principles of TDD. In the next chapter you will explore some of these topics in more detail.

Note

1. Extreme Programming Explained, Kent Beck, 1999. Addison Wesley. ISBN: 0201616416.

CHAPTER 2

Writing Your First Set of Unit Tests with Xcode

In this chapter you will download Xcode and learn to use it to create a simple app using test-driven development techniques. The app you will build will use the Single View Application template and allow the user to create different types of cookies by tapping on buttons in the user interface. The app will present a running total of each type of cookie created as well as the total number of cookies created. Figure 2-1 depicts the user interface of the finished application.

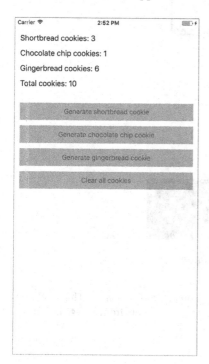

Figure 2-1. *The CookieFactory App in the iOS Simulator*

© Abhishek Mishra 2017
A. Mishra, *iOS Code Testing*, DOI 10.1007/978-1-4842-2689-6_2

The aim of this chapter is to get you familiar with the process of creating unit tests, running them, and viewing results. Therefore, the tests that you create in this chapter will not be exhaustive, and some portions of code will be left untested at the end of the chapter. Chapters 3, 4, and 5 of this book discuss specific topics such as the MVVM application architecture, testing model objects, and testing view controllers.

The complete source code for the app can be downloaded anonymously from github using the following URL:

```
https://github.com/asmtechnology/Lesson02.iOSTesting.2017.Apress.git
```

If you are an experienced developer you may wish to skip reading the contents of this chapter and examine the final project directly.

Downloading and Installing Xcode

If you have not done so already, use the Mac App Store to download and install the latest version of Xcode for your Mac (see Figure 2-2).

Figure 2-2. *Xcode page in the Mac App Store Application*

As of writing this chapter, Xcode 8 is the latest version of Mac OS X Sierra. The Xcode app is over 10Gb in size and the download process can take anywhere from 15 – 45 minutes depending on your Internet connection speed.

Creating a New Project with Unit Test Support

When creating new iOS application projects, you have the option to create projects with builit-in support for unit testing. Start the process of creating a new Xcode project by launching Xcode and selecting the File ➤ New ➤ Project menu item.

You will be asked to choose a template for your new project. Xcode 8 allows you to build projects for the iOS, macOS, tvOS, and watchOS platforms and provides a selection of templates for each platform (see Figure 2-3).

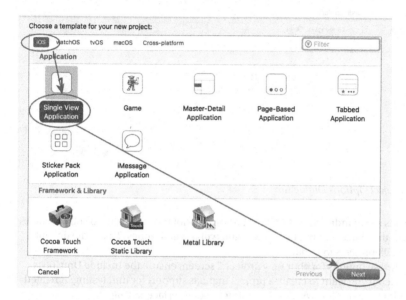

Figure 2-3. *iOS Project Template Dialog Box*

Select a suitable iOS template and click on Next. In this section, I am going to use the iOS Single View Application Template, which is one of the most commonly used iOS application templates.

After selecting the project template, you will be presented with an options dialog where you can select some options to customize certain aspects of the template (Figure 2-4).

15

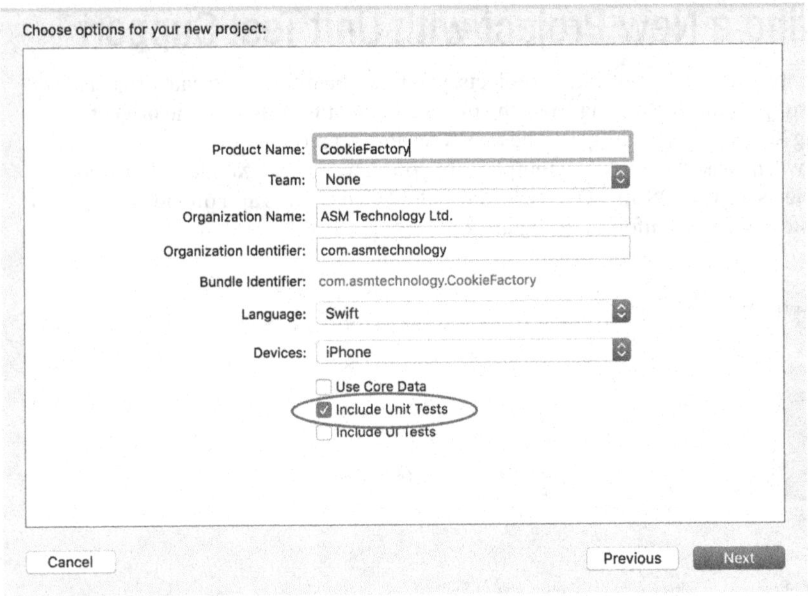

Figure 2-4. *Project Options Dialog Box*

Some fields are mandatory, so the Next button will not be enabled until you fill them. The projects in this book are built using Swift and will target iPhones. This is the default setup for new iOS projects in Xcode.

In the "Choose options for your new project:" screen, ensure the Include Unit Tests option is selected if you want to create a project that has support for unit testing. A related option called Include UI Tests will add support for user interface testing.

Click the Next button and save the project in a suitable folder on your Mac's hard disk. The project that you have created will have an additional build target setup specifically for unit testing as well as a sample unit test file with boilerplate code.

After creating a new project Xcode by default, Xcode opens the project for you. Close the Xcode project for now. The next section discusses the process involved in adding support for unit testing to an existing project.

Adding Support for Unit Tests to an Existing Project

To add support for unit tests to an existing iOS application project, open the project in Xcode and select the File ➤ New ➤ Target menu item. Select the iOS Unit Testing Bundle option in the target template dialog box (Figure 2-5).

Figure 2-5. *Target Template Dialog Box*

After selecting the target template, you will be presented with an options dialog where you can select some options to customize certain aspects of the template (see Figure 2-6).

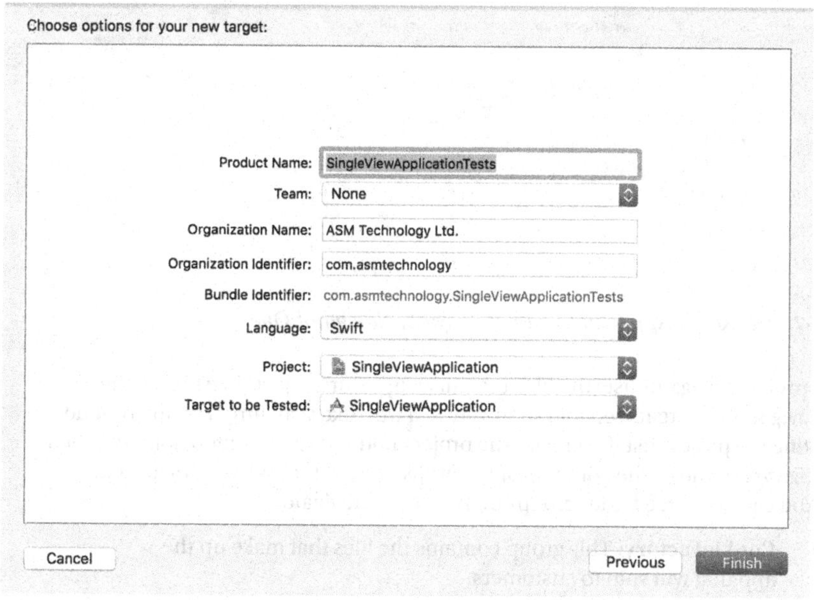

Figure 2-6. *Target Options Dialog Box*

In most cases you can simply accept the default values for the options and click Finish. A special build target (called a test target) will be added to your project preconfigured to support unit tests. In addition to the test target, a sample unit test file with boilerplate code will be added to your project.

A Tour of Xcode

Before you can begin to write unit tests in Xcode, you need to become familiar with some of the areas of the Xcode user interface that deal with unit tests. As you write more tests, you are likely to use one or more sections of the user interface discussed here. To start with, open the CookieFactory project in Xcode.

The Project Navigator

The project navigator is located on the left-hand side of the Xcode user interface (see Figure 2-7). If the project navigator is not visible, use the View ➤ Navigators ➤ Show Project Navigator menu item.

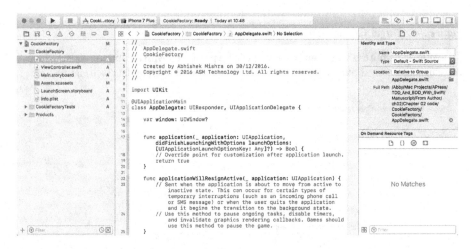

Figure 2-7. *The Xcode Application with the Project Navigator Open*

The project navigator lists the files that make up your project. The files in the project navigator are organized hierarchically in a tree-like structure with the root node representing the project itself. Beneath the project node sits a number of folders called groups. Figure 2-8 shows the contents of the project navigator for the CookieFactory project. You can see three folder groups in the project navigator:

- **CookieFactory:** This group contains the files that make up the app that will ship to customers.

- **CookieFactoryTests:** This group contains the files that contain the test code, and any resources needed by the test code. The files in this group are not included in the app that will ship to customers.

- **Products:** This group contains the final build products.

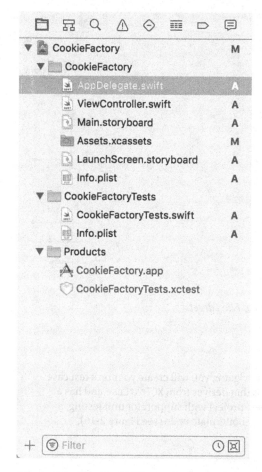

Figure 2-8. *The CookieFactory Project in the Project Navigator*

Files can be moved around in the project navigator using drag-and-drop operations. You my be tempted to think that the act of creating/moving a file under the test group will automatically imply that the file will not be part of the product that is shipped to the customer.

This is not the case; groups just serve as an aid to unclutter and organize a list of files in the project. Whether or not the file will be included with the app that is shipped to customers depends on the build target(s) that the file is included in. A new iOS project with unit test support will have two build targets; a file can be a member of either, neither, or both targets.

You can select a file in the project navigator and use the file inspector to view/change the build targets to which the file belongs (see Figure 2-9). To show the file inspector, use the View ➤ Utilities ➤ Show File Inspector menu item.

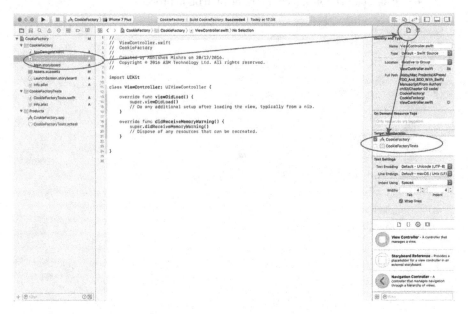

Figure 2-9. *Using the File Inspector to Set Up File Targets*

Test Case Classes

Under the test folder group of the project navigator, you will create your unit test case classes. A unit test case class is a Swift class that derives from XCTestCase and has a number of methods. When you create a new project with support for unit testing, a default test case class is created for you with boilerplate code (see Figure 2-10).

Figure 2-10. Default Test Case File and Target Membership

Test case classes contain test code, that is, code that will test your main application's code. Test case classes may contain five types of methods:

- **Setup method:** This method is called setUp() and is called once before each test method is executed in the test class. It is commonly used to put any common setup code used across multiple unit tests.

- **Teardown method:** This method is called tearDown() and is called after each test method is executed in the test class.

- **Test methods:** These methods encapsulate individual unit tests and their names all begin with the word "test."

- **Performance testing methods:** These methods encapsulate individual performance tests and their names all begin with "testPerformance."

- **Swift methods:** A test case class, like any other Swift class, can have its own methods. In a test case class, methods that do not encapsulate unit tests are usually written to contain support logic and will be called from a unit test.

Besides the default test case file that was created with the project, you can create additional test case files using the File ➤ New ➤ File menu item and choosing the iOS Unit Test Case File template (see Figure 2-11).

21

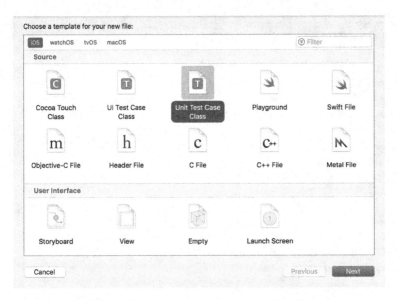

Figure 2-11. *File Template Dialog Box*

When a new test case file is created, Xcode provides a boilerplate setup and teardown methods and a couple of empty unit test methods to help you get started. Listing 2-1 lists a new unit test case class created by Xcode.

Listing 2-1. CookieFactoryTests.swift

```
import XCTest

class CookieFactoryTests: XCTestCase {

    override func setUp() {
        super.setUp()
        // Put setup code here. This method is called before the invocation
        of each test method in the class.
    }

    override func tearDown() {
        // Put teardown code here. This method is called after the
        invocation of each test method in the class.
        super.tearDown()
    }

    func testExample() {
        // This is an example of a functional test case.
        // Use XCTAssert and related functions to verify your tests produce
        the correct results.
    }
```

```
func testPerformanceExample() {
    // This is an example of a performance test case.
    self.measure {
        // Put the code you want to measure the time of here.
    }
}
```

}

The Test Navigator

The test navigator is an area of the Xcode user interface that displays a hierarchical view of all the test case files in the test target and all the unit tests within these test case files (see Figure 2-12).

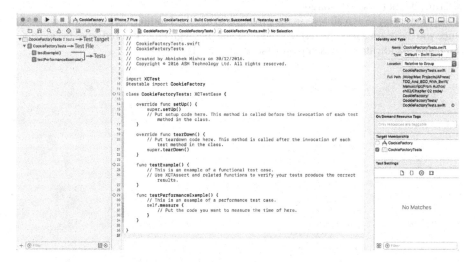

Figure 2-12. *Xcode Test Navigator*

To show the test navigator, use the View ➤ Navigators ➤ Show Test Navigator menu item. If you hover your mouse pointer over a unit test you will see a button appear toward the right of the test name; clicking on that button will run the selected test (see Figure 2-13).

Figure 2-13. *Unit Tests within the Xcode Test Navigator*

You will also see the same button appear when you hover your mouse pointer over the name of a test case file and the test target. In the former situation, clicking on the button will run all unit tests in the test case file sequentially, and in the latter situation, it will run all unit tests in the target.

Another way to run all tests in the project is to use the Product ➤ Test menu item. Once you have run a test, the test navigator will display a green tick or red cross beside the test name to indicate success or failure (see Figure 2-14).

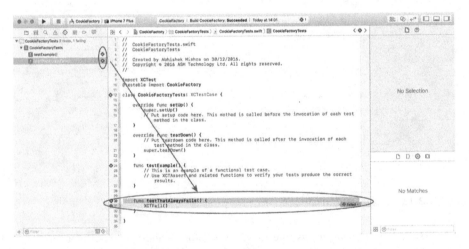

Figure 2-14. *Passed and Failed Unit Tests*

Clicking on the name of the test in the test navigator will open up the code for the test in the source editor. It is important to note that the test code is also code and must be able to compile before the tests can be executed. If your project has compilation errors in either the test code or the code being tested, you will need to fix these before the tests can run.

Viewing Test Reports

You can use the report navigator to access a report of all tests in the project (see Figure 2-15). To show the report navigator use the View ➤ Navigators ➤ Show Report Navigator.

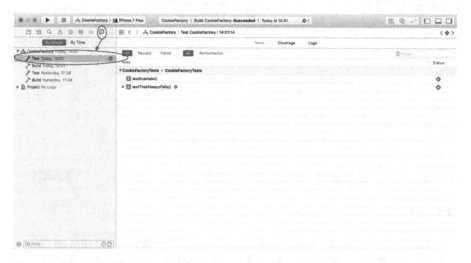

Figure 2-15. *Xcode Test Report Navigator*

The report navigator can be used to access project logs and build reports as well as test reports. Click on the latest test activity node in the list of reports to view the test report.

Code Coverage Reports

A code coverage report can be used to get a measure of the number of lines of source code that are executed after a group of tests have run. Code coverage reports are not enabled by default in Xcode 8. To enable code coverage reports, access the scheme settings dialog box by using the Product ➤ Scheme ➤ Edit Scheme menu item (see Figure 2-16).

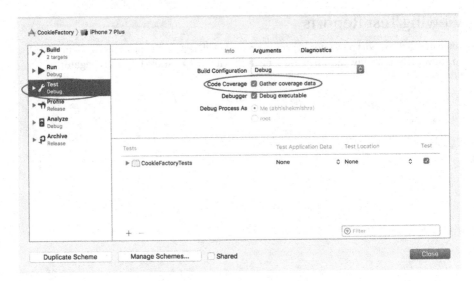

Figure 2-16. *Xcode Scheme Settings*

Click on the Test action, enable the Gather Coverage Data option, and click on Close. Code coverage reports can also be accessed via the report navigator. To generate code coverage reports, Xcode will have to collect data as your tests are being executed. Each subsequent run of your test code will update the coverage report although you may need to run your tests a couple of times before initial coverage reports are available.

Building the Cookie Factory App

In the previous section you were introduced to the different aspects of the Xcode user interface that pertain to unit testing. In this section you add features to the CookieFactory project that you have created earlier. The user interface for the finished app has been presented in Figure 2-1.

Each time the user taps on one of the buttons, a cookie of a specific type is created and appropriate labels are updated on the user interface.

To get started, ensure the CookieFactory project is opened in Xcode and the application's main storyboard file is open for editing. Add four buttons and four labels to the default scene of the application's storyboard and position them to resemble Figure 2-17.

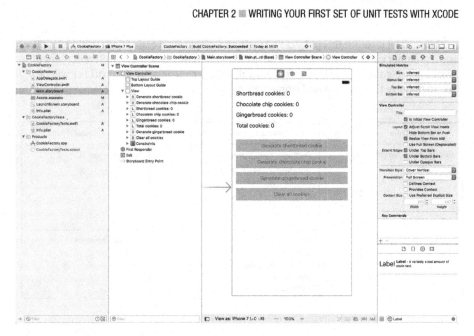

Figure 2-17. *View Controller Scene from the Main Storyboard File*

Create outlets and actions in the ViewController.swift file and connect them to their respective user interface elements as described in Table 2-1.

Table 2-1. *View Controller Outlets and Actions*

Name	Type	User Interface Element
`@IBOutlet weak var shortbreadCookies: UILabel!`	IBOutlet	Shortbread cookie label.
`@IBOutlet weak var chocolateChipCookies: UILabel!`	IBOutlet	Chocolate chip cookie label.
`@IBOutlet weak var gingerbreadCookies: UILabel!`	IBOutlet	Gingerbread cookie label.
`@IBOutlet weak var totalCookies: UILabel!`	IBOutlet	Total cookie label.
`@IBAction func onGenerate ShortbreadCookies(_ sender: Any)`	IBAction	Touch Up Inside event of the Generate Shortbread Cookie button.
`@IBAction func onGenerate ChocolateChipCookies(_ sender: Any)`	IBAction	Touch Up Inside event of the Generate Chocolate chip Cookie button.
`@IBAction func onGenerate GingerbreadCookies(_ sender: Any)`	IBAction	Touch Up Inside event of the Generate Gingerbread Cookie button.
`@IBAction func onClearAllCookies (_ sender: Any)`	IBAction	Touch Up Inside event of the Clear All Cookies button.

The model layer for this project will contain a single class called Cookie, which will have a member variable type that can be used to differentiate between different types of cookies (see Figure 2-18). A dedicated controller class called CookieController will be used to manage the creation and storage of cookies.

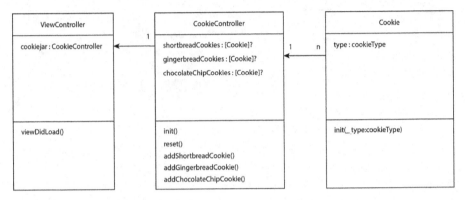

Figure 2-18. *Model Layer*

In a more complex application, you may want to move the responsibility of creating cookies out of the CookieController class and into its own factory class.

The view controller will make calls to relevant methods of CookieController class and update the text in the labels.

Building the Cookie Class

Delete the CookieFactoryTests.swift file under the CookieFactoryTests group that was created by Xcode when you created the project.

Create a new Unit Test Case file called CookieTests.swift under the CookieFactoryTestsGroup, and ensure that the file is a member of the CookieFactory test target (see Figure 2-19).

Figure 2-19. *The default CookieTests.Swift File*

Replace the contents of the CookieTests.swift file with the code in Listing 2-2.

Listing 2-2. CookieTests.swift

```
import XCTest

class CookieTests: XCTestCase {

    override func setUp() {
        super.setUp()
    }

    override func tearDown() {
        super.tearDown()
    }

    func testInit_GingerbreadCookieType_DoesNotReturnNil() {
        let cookie = Cookie(.gingerbread)
        XCTAssertNotNil(cookie)
    }

    func testInit_ShortbreadCookieType_DoesNotReturnNil() {
        let cookie = Cookie(.shortbread)
        XCTAssertNotNil(cookie)
    }
```

```swift
func testInit_ChocolateChipCookieType_DoesNotReturnNil() {
    let cookie = Cookie(.chocolateChip)
    XCTAssertNotNil(cookie)
}

func testInit_GingerbreadCookieType_SetsCookieTypeIvarCorrectly() {
    let cookie = Cookie(.gingerbread)
    XCTAssertEqual(cookie.type, .gingerbread)
}

func testInit_ShortbreadCookieType_SetsCookieTypeIvarCorrectly() {
    let cookie = Cookie(.shortbread)
    XCTAssertEqual(cookie.type, .shortbread)
}

func testInit_ChocolateChipCookieType_SetsCookieTypeIvarCorrectly() {
    let cookie = Cookie(.chocolateChip)
    XCTAssertEqual(cookie.type, .chocolateChip)
}

}
```

You will receive several compiler errors at this point because the Cookie class does not exist yet. Observe how the tests have defined the desired interface of the Cookie class. In this particular case, the tests mandate the following:

- The Cookie class must have an initializer that accepts a type identifier.

- The Cookie class must have an instance variable called type.

- The Type identifier can have one of three possible values: .chocolateChip, .gingerbread, and .shortbread.

Create a new Swift class called Cookie under the CookieFactory group and update its contents to match Listing 2-3.

Listing 2-3. Cookie.swift

```swift
import Foundation

enum cookieType {
    case shortbread
    case gingerbread
    case chocolateChip
}
```

```
class Cookie : NSObject {
    var type:cookieType

    init(_ type:cookieType) {
        self.type = type
        super.init()
    }
}
```

Ensure that Cookie.swift is a member of both the main and test targets. This is because you intend to use CookieClass.swift in both the app that you are building as well as the unit tests (see Figure 2-20).

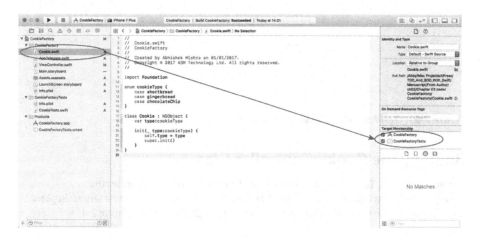

Figure 2-20. *Inspecting the Target Membership of the Cookie.swift file*

Save the file and use the Product ➤ Test menu item to run all tests. You should see all tests pass (see Figure 2-21).

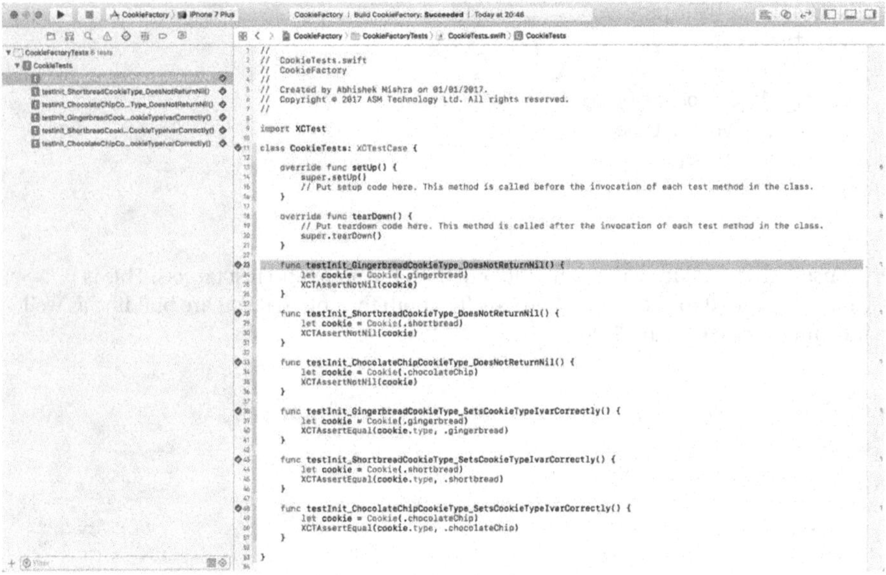

Figure 2-21. *Test Inspector Showing All Tests Passing*

Building the CookieController Class

Create a new Unit Test Case file called CookieControllerTests.swift under the
CookieFactoryTests group, and ensure that the file is a member of the test target. Replace
the contents of the CookieControllerTests.swift file with the code in Listing 2-4.

Listing 2-4. CookieControllerTests.swift

```
import XCTest

class CookieControllerTests: XCTestCase {

    override func setUp() {
        super.setUp()
    }

    override func tearDown() {
        super.tearDown()
    }

}
```

```swift
// MARK: Initializer tests
extension CookieControllerTests {

    func testInit_GingerbreadCookieArray_IsNotNil() {
        let cookieJar = CookieController()
        XCTAssertNotNil(cookieJar.gingerbreadCookies)
    }

    func testInit_ShortbreadCookieArray_IsNotNil() {
        let cookieJar = CookieController()
        XCTAssertNotNil(cookieJar.shortbreadCookies)
    }

    func testInit_ChocolateChipCookieArray_IsNotNil() {
        let cookieJar = CookieController()
        XCTAssertNotNil(cookieJar.shortbreadCookies)
    }

    func testInit_GingerbreadCookieCount_IsZero() {
        let cookieJar = CookieController()
        XCTAssertEqual(cookieJar.gingerbreadCookies!.count, 0)
    }

    func testInit_ShortbreadCookieCount_IsZero() {
        let cookieJar = CookieController()
        XCTAssertEqual(cookieJar.shortbreadCookies!.count, 0)
    }

    func testInit_ChocolateChipCookieCount_IsZero() {
        let cookieJar = CookieController()
        XCTAssertEqual(cookieJar.chocolateChipCookies!.count, 0)
    }
}

// MARK: addGingerbreadCookie tests
extension CookieControllerTests {

    func testAddGingerbreadCookie_Increments_NumberOfGingerbreadCookies_ByOne() {
        let cookieJar = CookieController()

        let numberOfCookies = cookieJar.gingerbreadCookies!.count
        cookieJar.addGingerbreadCookie()

        let expectedNumberOfCookies = numberOfCookies + 1
        XCTAssertEqual(cookieJar.gingerbreadCookies!.count,
        expectedNumberOfCookies)
    }
```

```swift
    func testAddGingerbreadCookie_DoesNotIncrement_NumberOfShortbreadCookies() {
        let cookieJar = CookieController()

        let numberOfCookies = cookieJar.shortbreadCookies!.count
        cookieJar.addGingerbreadCookie()

        XCTAssertEqual(cookieJar.shortbreadCookies!.count, numberOfCookies)
    }

    func testAddGingerbreadCookie_DoesNotIncrement_NumberOfChocolateChipCookies() {
        let cookieJar = CookieController()

        let numberOfCookies = cookieJar.chocolateChipCookies!.count
        cookieJar.addGingerbreadCookie()

        XCTAssertEqual(cookieJar.chocolateChipCookies!.count, numberOfCookies)
    }

}

// MARK: addShortbreadCookie tests
extension CookieControllerTests {

    func testAddShortbreadCookie_Increments_NumberOfShortbreadCookies_ByOne() {
        let cookieJar = CookieController()

        let numberOfCookies = cookieJar.shortbreadCookies!.count
        cookieJar.addShortbreadCookie()

        let expectedNumberOfCookies = numberOfCookies + 1
        XCTAssertEqual(cookieJar.shortbreadCookies!.count, expectedNumberOfCookies)
    }

    func testAddShortbreadCookie_DoesNotIncrement_NumberOfGingerbreadCookies() {
        let cookieJar = CookieController()

        let numberOfCookies = cookieJar.gingerbreadCookies!.count
        cookieJar.addShortbreadCookie()

        XCTAssertEqual(cookieJar.gingerbreadCookies!.count, numberOfCookies)
    }

    func testAddShortbreadCookie_DoesNotIncrement_NumberOfChocolateChipCookies() {
        let cookieJar = CookieController()

        let numberOfCookies = cookieJar.chocolateChipCookies!.count
        cookieJar.addShortbreadCookie()
```

```
        XCTAssertEqual(cookieJar.chocolateChipCookies!.count, numberOfCookies)
    }

}

// MARK: addChocolateChipCookie tests
extension CookieControllerTests {

    func testAddChocolateChipCookie_Increments_NumberOfChocolateChipCookies_ByOne() {
        let cookieJar = CookieController()

        let numberOfCookies = cookieJar.chocolateChipCookies!.count
        cookieJar.addChocolateChipCookie()

        let expectedNumberOfCookies = numberOfCookies + 1
        XCTAssertEqual(cookieJar.chocolateChipCookies!.count, expectedNumberOfCookies)
    }

    func testAddChocolateChipCookie_DoesNotIncrement_NumberOfShortbreadCookies() {
        let cookieJar = CookieController()

        let numberOfCookies = cookieJar.shortbreadCookies!.count
        cookieJar.addChocolateChipCookie()

        XCTAssertEqual(cookieJar.shortbreadCookies!.count, numberOfCookies)
    }

    func testAddChocolateChipCookie_DoesNotIncrement_NumberOfGingerbreadCookies() {
        let cookieJar = CookieController()

        let numberOfCookies = cookieJar.gingerbreadCookies!.count
        cookieJar.addChocolateChipCookie()

        XCTAssertEqual(cookieJar.gingerbreadCookies!.count, numberOfCookies)
    }

}

// MARK: Reset tests
extension CookieControllerTests {

    func testReset_GingerbreadCookieArray_WithZeroElements_RemainsEmpty() {
        let cookieJar = CookieController()
        cookieJar.reset()
        XCTAssertEqual(cookieJar.gingerbreadCookies!.count, 0)
    }
```

```swift
func testReset_ShortbreadCookieArray_WithZeroElements_RemainsEmpty() {
    let cookieJar = CookieController()
    cookieJar.reset()
    XCTAssertEqual(cookieJar.shortbreadCookies!.count, 0)
}

func testReset_ChocolateChipCookieArray_WithZeroElements_RemainsEmpty() {
    let cookieJar = CookieController()
    cookieJar.reset()
    XCTAssertEqual(cookieJar.chocolateChipCookies!.count, 0)
}

func testReset_GingerbreadCookieArray_WithElements_BecomesEmpty() {
    let cookieJar = CookieController()

    cookieJar.addGingerbreadCookie()
    cookieJar.reset()

    XCTAssertEqual(cookieJar.gingerbreadCookies!.count, 0)
}

func testReset_ShortbreadCookieArray_WithElements_BecomesEmpty() {
    let cookieJar = CookieController()

    cookieJar.addShortbreadCookie()
    cookieJar.reset()

    XCTAssertEqual(cookieJar.shortbreadCookies!.count, 0)
}

func testReset_ChocolateChipCookieArray_WithElements_BecomesEmpty() {
    let cookieJar = CookieController()

    cookieJar.addChocolateChipCookie()
    cookieJar.reset()

    XCTAssertEqual(cookieJar.chocolateChipCookies!.count, 0)
}
}
```

You will receive several compiler errors at this point because the CookieController class does not exist yet. These tests define the following desired characteristics for the CookieController class:

- The CookieController class must have an initializer that does not accept any parameters.

- The CookieController class must have three arrays, one for each type of cookie.

- The CookieController class must have a method called addGingerbreadCookie(), which when called will add one gingerbread cookie to the relevant array.

- The CookieController class must have a method called addShortbreadCookie(), which when called will add one shortbread cookie to the relevant array.

- The CookieController class must have a method called addChocolateChipCookie(), which when called will add one chocolate chip cookie to the relevant array.

- The CookieController class must have a method called reset(), which when called will clear all the arrays.

I have used class extensions to group tests for each method. The only advantage this provides is readability; feel free to move all the tests from extensions to the main class if you prefer. You may also have noticed that I have used long descriptive names for test methods. You should try to create descriptive names that describe the name of the method being tested, the initial conditions, and expected output.

Create a new Swift class called CookieController under the CookieFactory group and update its contents to match Listing 2-5.

Listing 2-5. CookieController.swift

```swift
import Foundation

class CookieController : NSObject {

    var shortbreadCookies:[Cookie]?
    var gingerbreadCookies:[Cookie]?
    var chocolateChipCookies:[Cookie]?

    override init() {
        self.shortbreadCookies = [Cookie]()
        self.gingerbreadCookies = [Cookie]()
        self.chocolateChipCookies = [Cookie]()
        super.init()
    }

    func reset() {
        self.shortbreadCookies?.removeAll()
        self.gingerbreadCookies?.removeAll()
        self.chocolateChipCookies?.removeAll()
    }
}
```

```
func addShortbreadCookie() -> Void {
    let cookie = Cookie(.shortbread)
    shortbreadCookies?.append(cookie)
}

func addGingerbreadCookie() -> Void {
    let cookie = Cookie(.gingerbread)
    gingerbreadCookies?.append(cookie)
}

func addChocolateChipCookie() -> Void {
    let cookie = Cookie(.chocolateChip)
    chocolateChipCookies?.append(cookie)
}
}
```

Save the file and use the Product ➤ Test menu item to run all tests. You should see all tests pass (see Figure 2-22).

Figure 2-22. *Test Inspector Showing All Tests Passing*

Updating the View Controller Class

You have now built both the Cookie and the CookieFactory classes using test-driven development techniques. It is now time to integrate the CookieFactory class into the view controller.

While you can use test-driven techniques to perform the integration, to keep things simple in this lesson, I have opted to not use TDD techniques on the view controller class. Applying TDD techniques to view controllers is described at length in Chapter 5.

Update the contents of the ViewController.swift file to match Listing 2-6.

Listing 2-6. ViewController.swift

```swift
import UIKit

class ViewController: UIViewController {

    var cookiejar:CookieController?

    @IBOutlet weak var totalCookies: UILabel!
    @IBOutlet weak var gingerbreadCookies: UILabel!
    @IBOutlet weak var shortbreadCookies: UILabel!
    @IBOutlet weak var chocolateChipCookies: UILabel!

    override func viewDidLoad() {
        super.viewDidLoad()
        cookiejar = CookieController()
        refreshUI()
    }

    override func didReceiveMemoryWarning() {
        super.didReceiveMemoryWarning()
    }

    @IBAction func onGenerateGingerbreadCookies(_ sender: Any) {
        cookiejar?.addGingerbreadCookie()
        refreshUI()
    }

    @IBAction func onGenerateChocolateChipCookies(_ sender: Any) {
        cookiejar?.addChocolateChipCookie()
        refreshUI()
    }

    @IBAction func onGenerateShortbreadCookies(_ sender: Any) {
        cookiejar?.addShortbreadCookie()
        refreshUI()
    }
```

```
@IBAction func onClearAllCookies(_ sender: Any) {
    cookiejar?.reset()
    refreshUI()
}

private func refreshUI() -> Void {
    let totalGinger = cookiejar!.gingerbreadCookies!.count
    let totalShort = cookiejar!.shortbreadCookies!.count
    let totalChocolate = cookiejar!.chocolateChipCookies!.count
    let total = totalGinger + totalShort + totalChocolate

    gingerbreadCookies.text = "Gingerbread cookies: \(totalGinger)"
    shortbreadCookies.text = "Shortbread cookies: \(totalShort)"
    chocolateChipCookies.text = "Chocolate chip cookies: \(totalChocolate)"
    totalCookies.text = "Total cookies: \(total)"
}

}
```

Save the project and run it on the simulator using the Product ➤ Run menu item. After you have had a chance to try out the application and verify that it is working, you may want to dig a little deeper to find out how effective the unit tests have been.

One way to gauge the effectiveness of unit tests is to use a code coverage report. This report will give you information on the number of lines of application code that were executed by test code.

The next section looks at Xcode's code coverage reporting tools. Before you can view code coverage reports, you must ensure that you have executed your unit tests at least once.

Code coverage data is deleted when you close Xcode. If you reopen a project in Xcode, you will need to run all unit tests using the Prodct ➤ Test menu item so that Xcode can generate code coverage data.

Viewing Code Coverage Data

If you have enabled code coverage reports in the scheme settings dialog box, you will see the code coverage ribbon appear to the right side of the source code editor. Click on the CookieFactory.swift file in the project navigator and observe the numbers in the code coverage ribbon (see Figure 2-23).

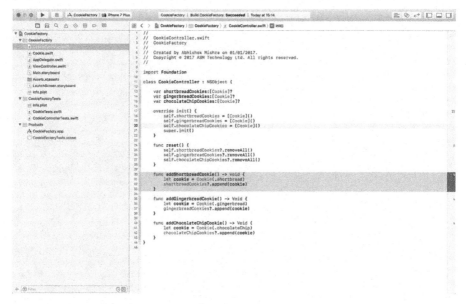

Figure 2-23. *Xcode Code Coverage Information*

You will notice that the code coverage ribbon lists a number beside each of the methods of the CookieFactory class. The number indicates the number of times the method was called when you ran your test suite.

Hovering your mouse pointer over a number in the code coverage ribbon will highlight the associated method in red or green. A green highlight means that the method has been called at least once by your tests, and a red highlight means that the method is not currently being covered by your test suite.

Code coverage is a useful tool to get an idea of the parts of your production code that are covered by your tests, but must be used with caution. Many development teams try to achieve high code coverage by writing meaningless tests, or tests that cover iOS framework code. It is better to have fewer and more meaningful tests than a large number of tests that are difficult to maintain or understand by new members of the team.

Summary

This chapter has introduced you to sections of the Xcode user interface that deal with unit testing. You have also built a simple single view application using basic TDD techniques and have learned to examine code coverage reports.

The next chapter will discuss the MVVM architectural pattern and how applications that are built using this pattern are easier to test.

■ ■ ■

CHAPTER 3

The MVVM Architectural Pattern

This chapter will examine a commonly used architectural pattern called Model-View-Controller (MVC), its iOS equivalent Model–ViewController (M-VC), and the testability issues that arise when using this common pattern. You will then be introduced to a new architectural pattern called Model, View, ViewModel (MVVM) and the advantages of this pattern from a code reusability and testability perspective.

To avoid confusion in the chapter, I spell out "Model-ViewController" when discussing the iOS version and the abbreviation "MVC" when referring to a common pattern.

The MVC Architectural Pattern

The Model-View-Controller is one of the most common application architectural patterns in use today, across a variety of programming languages (Java, .NET, Objective-C, Swift). It was designed to help developers implement user interfaces on computers and aims to separate the representation of data from the manner in which it is presented to the user. Figure 3-1 depicts the standard MVC pattern.

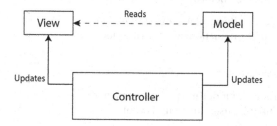

Figure 3-1. Standard Model-View-Controller Pattern

© Abhishek Mishra 2017
A. Mishra, *iOS Code Testing*, DOI 10.1007/978-1-4842-2689-6_3

This pattern has three key components (sometimes called layers):

- **Model:** The model component handles the storage of data used by the application and accepts commands to read or update the data from the controller. It could be a single class or a group of related classes.

- **View:** The view component reads data from the model and handles the rendering/presentation of the model. The view can be thought to be the visual representation of the model, and it can selectively present certain parts of the model.

- **Controller:** The controller component sits in between the model and the view, handles user input, updates the model, and updates the view as necessary. Business logic and networking code resides in one or more controllers, and controllers can communicate with other controllers. In other words, controllers make the brain of the application.

The Model-ViewController Architectural Pattern

Cocoa Touch, UIKit, and other Apple frameworks provide all the necessary infrastructure to implement the Model-ViewController architecture in iOS Apps:

- **Model:** Can be any NSObject subclass, or even an NSManagedObjectModel subclass.

- **View:** Can be any UIView subclass, for example, UILabel, UIButton, and UIScrollView.

- **Controller:** Can be any NSObject subclass.

However, Apple has also created the concept of a "View Controller" that combines both the view and controller into a single class. In fact, view controllers are so common that many developers new to iOS development don't realize that it is possible to create controllers independently.

Figure 3-2 shows what the Model-ViewController architectural pattern looks like in a typical iOS application, with the view controller owning both the model and the view. The roles of the three components are summarized below:

- **View:** Responsible for rendering the model, requests data from the view controller, passes user interaction events to the view controller.

- **Model:** Responsible for storing data.

- **View controller:** Reads from the model and provides data to the view, updates the model, handles user interaction events.

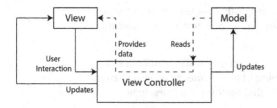

Figure 3-2. *The Model-View-Controller Pattern*

However, since the view and the view controller are tightly coupled, with the view controller owning the view, the architectural pattern begins to resemble Figure 3-3. In fact, it is extremely rare for a view to be paired with different view controllers.

Figure 3-3. *Interaction between View, View Controller, and Model objects*

If you have been developing iOS applications for a few months, you will soon realize that in terms of lines of code, view controllers are often the largest files in the project. This is due to the fact that view controllers commonly act as delegates, data sources, contain networking code, contain view management logic, and make network calls, etc. View controllers also commonly implement multiple protocols, which results in controller logic being mixed up with the code that supports protocols. These bloated view controllers are often called "Massive View Controllers."

Some of the logic in massive view controllers belongs in the view controller, but a lot of it is presentation, model transformation, and networking logic, which should ideally go in a separate helper objects/controllers.

Model-ViewController Testability Issues

While testing the model layer of the model-view controller, pattern does not present any significant challenge; testing the view controller, on the other hand, presents a few issues:

- **Difficult to instantiate:** Instantiating a view controller under a test may not be trivial; all IBOutlets will need to be stubbed using appropriate subclasses. You will need to include the XIB or storyboard in the test target, and potentially end up instantiating a complex stack of UI layer objects like navigation controllers, and table views. Adding storyboards to the test target, just to be able to instantiate a view controller, will make your tests very fragile and you may end up questioning the value of the tests themselves.

- **Difficult to mock:** Due to the tightly coupled nature of the code in a view controller, it is often difficult to test a single method in isolation.

- **Testing the UI layer in a unit test:** Unit tests should not test the UI layer; a view controller blurs the lines between code that performs UI logic and code that performs business logic.

The Model-View-ViewModel Architectural Pattern

The Model-View-ViewModel (MVVM) architectural pattern was developed by Microsoft to help developers build XAML-based WPF applications, but as you will soon learn, MVVM can be easily adapted to be used within iOS/Swift applications. MVVM is an expansion of MVC where we formally couple the view and the controller, but move all the presentation logic out of the controller into a new object called the view model.

Within an iOS/Swift context, the role of the view is fulfilled by the view+view controller combination (see Figure 3-4).

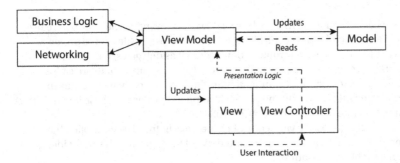

Figure 3-4. *Model-View View-Model pattern on iOS*

The roles of the three components are summarized below:

- **Model:** Responsible for storing data, maintains two-way communication with the view model.

- **View/View controller:** Represents the view part of the pattern, and handles user interaction events. Maintains two-way communication with the view model.

- **View model:** Handles presentation logic, maintains two-communication with both the model and the view/view controller. Handles communication with other controllers that may provide specific functionality like complex business logic, and network requests.

Microsoft's original MVVM pattern makes extensive use of XAML bindings to link the three principle components of this pattern. On iOS/Swift applications, there are two options available to link the principal components of this pattern:

- **Using Swift protocols:** The principal components of the pattern interact with each other through a well-defined set of protocols. Each component implements the relevant set of protocols.

- **Using ReactiveCocoa/RxSwift:** Third-party libraries have now emerged that allow Swift developers to apply reactive-programming principles to create bindings between the principal components of the pattern.

■ **Note**   Reactive programming is outside the scope of this book. All examples in this book use the protocol-based approach.

Advantages of MVVM

This section lists some of the key advantages of the MVVM pattern over the M-VC pattern:

- The MVVM pattern moves code out of a single view controller class and distributes this code over a more granular set of classes; this reduces the size of any individual class and therefore addresses the massive view controller problem.

- The view/view controller component is loosely coupled with the model; and with the view model, developers in a team can build these components independently and concurrently. It is also significantly easier to accommodate UI changes without having any significant impact on either the model, or the view model layers.

- When implemented properly, there should be no direct reference to UIKit in the view model. The view and the view model are loosely coupled. This makes it easy to instantiate view models in test cases. A suitable mock or stub view needs only to implement the relevant protocols required by the view.

- Decoupling the view layer from the view-model layer gives the advantage that the view layer can be implemented using different UI technologies. The view model and model code can, for instance, be reused in a MacOS application by simply substituting the view layer.

- MVVM being based on loosely coupled classes increases testability. A class in one layer can be instantiated independently of the other layers. Using protocols to define the contracts between participating classes makes the task of stubbing/mocking dependences significantly easier.

- MVVM promotes separation of concerns between objects. When objects are not tightly coupled, the resulting code is more change resistant and easier to maintain over the long term.

ViewModel Instantiation

There are various strategies that you can use to instantiate view models. This section examines a few common scenarios that you will encounter while creating iOS apps with the MVVM pattern.

Isolated View Controller

In case you are dealing with an isolated view controller, a common strategy is to instantiate the view model inside the viewDidLoad() method of the view controller class. The following code snippet demonstrates this strategy:

```
class CountriesViewController: UIViewController {

    private var viewModel:CountriesViewModel?

    override func viewDidLoad() {
        super.viewDidLoad()

        self.viewModel = CountriesViewModel(view: self,
                        title:"Select a country")
    }
}
```

A few noteworthy points about this strategy:

- The view controller owns the view model via a strong private var.

- The view model is injected with a reference to the view/view controller in the initializer. The view model will hold a weak reference to the view/view controller.

- The view model's initializer can also be used to inject other parameters that are required to set it up.

Chapter 5 will examine techniques to create isolated view controller-based applications using TDD techniques and the MVVM pattern.

Table View Controllers

When you are dealing with a table view controller, the view model for the table view controller will provide information on the number of rows and sections. The view model can also be used to maintain the index of the currently selected cell. But where does the data within each cell come from?

Each table view cell is also a view in its own right, and the MVVM pattern must be applied to the individual table view cells as well as the enclosing table view. You could potentially use the same view model for both the table view as well as individual cells, but this approach overloads the view model with multiple responsibilities.

A better approach is to use different view models for the table view and the individual table view cells. This approach keeps the size of each view model small, as each view model is only going to be response responsible for a single view, and not child views.

Instantiating the view model for the table view controller is a simple matter of putting a few lines of code in the viewDidLoad() method of the table view controller. How and when does one instantiate view models for the individual cells?

A good approach is to build a factory method within the view model of the table view controller, and use this factory method to get view models for the individual cells.

The factory method can encapsulate the nitty gritty of creating a view model for a cell, and giving the cell view model a relevant model object. The factory method could also be moved out of the table view controller's view model into its own class, in which case you are using a dedicated object for a view model construction.

An ideal place to call the view model factory (either method or object), would be within the tableView(_ tableView:, cellForRowAt:)method of the table view controller. This approach is demonstrated in the following snippet:

```
override func tableView(_ tableView: UITableView, cellForRowAt indexPath:
IndexPath) -> UITableViewCell {
        let cell = tableView.dequeueReusableCell(withIdentifier:
        "CountryCell", for: indexPath) as? CountriesTableViewCell

        guard let viewModel = tableViewModel,
            let countriesTableViewCell = cell else {
            return UITableViewCell()
        }

        let cellViewModel =
            viewModel.cellViewModel(forIndexPath: indexPath)
        countriesTableViewCell.viewModel = cellViewModel

        return countriesTableViewCell
}
```

In this snippet a custom UITableViewCell instance is obtained by using the dequeRe usableCell(withIdentifier:, for) method of the table view:

```
let cell = tableView.dequeueReusableCell(withIdentifier: "CountryCell",
for: indexPath) as? CountriesTableViewCell
```

A factory method called cellViewModel(forIndexPath:) is called on the table view controller's view model:

```
let cellViewModel = viewModel.cellViewModel(forIndexPath: indexPath)
```

This method returns a view model for the table view cell, which is then assigned to a property of the table view cell, before returning the cell:

```
countriesTableViewCell.viewModel = cellViewModel
return countriesTableViewCell
```

This snippet assumes that the table view cell will own the cell view model.

Navigation Controller-Based Apps

Master-detail apps are quite common on iOS. These applications are usually implemented using a table view controller within a navigation controller. When a user taps on a cell in the table view, a push segue is triggered to slide the detail view from the right. The detail view controller that appears usually displays information that is related to the cell that was tapped in the table view.

When building such an application using the MVVM pattern, it should be quite obvious by now that the table view controller (master view) will have its own view model, and the detail view controller that is subsequently pushed onto the navigation stack will also have its own view model.

The challenge in this case is building the detail view model with the correct model object so that the detail view will contain the correct information.

As in the previous section, you can use the factory method approach to instantiate either, or both view models. The factory method will need to be called from the prepare(for segue: UIStoryboardSegue, sender: Any?) method of the master table view controller class.

You will also need to ensure that the master view model is capable of tracking the selected cell index. This is so that the appropriate detail model can be linked to the detail view model.

This approach can also be applied to collection view controllers as collection view controllers are similar in many respects to table view controllers. Chapter 6 covers the topic of building MVVM-based collection view controllers using TDD techniques.

Listings 3-1 – 3-5 demonstrate how the MVVM pattern can be applied to a table view controller. The listings collectively form parts of an application that displays a list with the names of a few common colors. When a user selects a color from this list, a detail view, painted with the selected color is presented (see Figure 3-5).

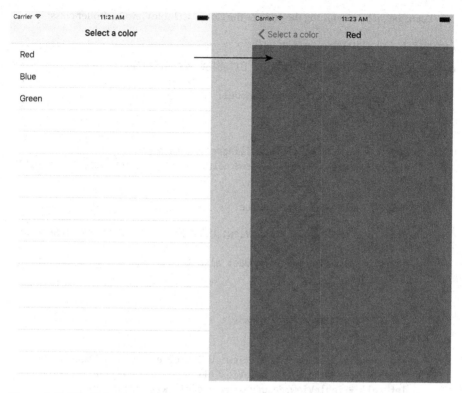

Figure 3-5. *The ColorList App*

The complete source code for the project, along with unit tests, can be downloaded anonymously from github using the following URL:

https://github.com/asmtechnology/Lesson03.iOSTesting.2017.Apress.git

There are five key classes involved in this snippet:

- **ColorListTableViewController:** This is a subclass of UITableViewController and presents the user with a list of colors.

- **ColorDetailViewController:** This is a subclass of UIViewController and is displayed when the user selects a color from the list of colors.

- **ColorTableViewModel:** This is the view model for the color list table view controller class.

- **ColorDetailViewModel:** This is the view model for the color detail view controller class.

- **Color:** Represents the model for this project.

For the purpose of brevity, protocols are not listed in this snippet. You can, however, download the project and examine the protocols in detail.

Let us begin by examining the code or the ColorListTableViewController class:

Listing 3-1. ColorListTableViewController

```swift
class ColorListTableViewController: UITableViewController {

    private var viewModel:TableViewModel?

    override func viewDidLoad() {
        super.viewDidLoad()
        self.clearsSelectionOnViewWillAppear = false
        self.viewModel = ColorTableViewModel(view: self, title:"Select a color")
    }

    // MARK: - Table view data source

    override func tableView(_ tableView: UITableView, numberOfRowsInSection
    section: Int) -> Int {
        guard let viewModel = viewModel else {
            return 0
        }

        return viewModel.numberOfRows()
    }

    override func tableView(_ tableView: UITableView, cellForRowAt
    indexPath: IndexPath) -> UITableViewCell {
        let cell = tableView.dequeueReusableCell(withIdentifier:
        "ColorListttCell", for: indexPath) as? ColorListTableViewCell

        guard let viewModel = viewModel,
            let colorListTableViewCell = cell else {
                return UITableViewCell()
        }

        let detailViewModel = viewModel.cellViewModel(forIndexPath:
        indexPath)
        colorListTableViewCell.viewModel = detailViewModel
        return colorListTableViewCell
    }

    override func tableView(_ tableView: UITableView, didSelectRowAt
    indexPath: IndexPath) {
        guard let viewModel = viewModel else {
            return
        }

        viewModel.selectRow(atIndexPath:indexPath)
        self.performSegue(withIdentifier: "colorDetailSegue", sender: nil)
    }
```

```
override func prepare(for segue: UIStoryboardSegue, sender: Any?) {
    guard let identifier = segue.identifier, let viewModel = viewModel
    else {
        return
    }

    if identifier.compare("colorDetailSegue") != .orderedSame {
        return
    }

    if let colorDetailViewController = segue.destination as?
    ColorDetailViewController,
        let destinationViewModel = viewModel.viewModelForSelectedRow() {

        destinationViewModel.setView(delegate: colorDetailViewController)
        colorDetailViewController.viewModel = destinationViewModel
    }

    }
}
```

In Listing 3-1, the table view controller owns the table view model. The view model is an instance of ColorTableViewModel and is instantiated within the viewDidLoad method of the table view controller:

```
override func viewDidLoad() {
    super.viewDidLoad()
    self.clearsSelectionOnViewWillAppear = false
    self.viewModel = ColorTableViewModel(view: self, title:"Select a color")
}
```

The tableView(_ tableView:, cellForRowAt:) -> UITableViewCell method creates table view cells, and passes a view model into each table view cell. The view model for each cell is created using a factory method called cellViewModel(forIndexPath) -> CellViewModel? provided by ColorTableViewModel.

```
override func tableView(_ tableView: UITableView, cellForRowAt indexPath:
IndexPath) -> UITableViewCell {
    let cell = tableView.dequeueReusableCell(withIdentifier:
    "ColorListtCell", for: indexPath) as? ColorListTableViewCell

    guard let viewModel = viewModel,
        let colorListTableViewCell = cell else {
            return UITableViewCell()
    }
```

```
        let detailViewModel = viewModel.cellViewModel(forIndexPath: indexPath)
        colorListTableViewCell.viewModel = detailViewModel
        return colorListTableViewCell
    }
```

Tapping on a cell in the table view records the index position of the selected cell in the view model, and performs a segue to animate the detail view controller onto the screen:

```
override func tableView(_ tableView: UITableView, didSelectRowAt indexPath:
IndexPath) {
    guard let viewModel = viewModel else {
        return
    }

    viewModel.selectRow(atIndexPath:indexPath)
    self.performSegue(withIdentifier: "colorDetailSegue", sender: nil)
}
```

■ **Note**   You do not need to call `performSegue(withIdentifier:, sender:)` if you have created a segue from the table view cell to the detail view controller in the story board. If, however, the segue has been created from the table view controller to the detail view controller, then you will need to call `performSegue(withIdentifier:, sender:)` to trigger the segue.

The code to generate a view model for the detail view controller, as well as assign the view model to a property of the detail view controller, can be found in the prepare(for, sender:) method:

```
override func prepare(for segue: UIStoryboardSegue, sender: Any?) {
        guard let identifier = segue.identifier, let viewModel = viewModel
        else {
            return
        }

        if identifier.compare("colorDetailSegue") != .orderedSame {
            return
        }

        if let colorDetailViewController = segue.destination as?
        ColorDetailViewController,
            let destinationViewModel = viewModel.viewModelForSelectedRow() {

            destinationViewModel.setView(delegate: colorDetailViewController)
            colorDetailViewController.viewModel = destinationViewModel
        }

    }
}
```

Let us now examine the ColorDetailViewController class:

Listing 3-2. ColorDetailViewController

```swift
class ColorDetailViewController: UIViewController {

    var viewModel:ColorDetailViewModel?

    override func viewDidAppear(_ animated: Bool) {
        if let viewModel = viewModel {
            viewModel.viewDidAppear(animated)
        }
    }

}

extension ColorDetailViewController : ColorDetailViewControllerDelegate {
    func setNavigationTitle(_ title:String) -> Void {
        self.title = title
    }

    func setBackgroundColor(red:Float, blue:Float, green:Float, alpha:Float) ->
    Void {
        self.view.backgroundColor = UIColor(red: CGFloat(red), green:
        CGFloat(green), blue: CGFloat(blue), alpha: CGFloat(alpha))
    }
}
```

This is a very small and straightforward class. It holds a strong reference to a
view model, and gives the view model a chance to handle presentation logic in the
viewDidAppear() method:

```swift
override func viewDidAppear(_ animated: Bool) {
    if let viewModel = viewModel {
        viewModel.viewDidAppear(animated)
    }
}
```

In response to this event, the view model will change the background color and title
of the view via a set of delegate methods implemented by the view controller.
Let us now examine the code for the ColorTableViewModel class:

```swift
func setNavigationTitle(_ title:String) -> Void {
    self.title = title
}

func setBackgroundColor(red:Float, blue:Float, green:Float, alpha:Float) -> Void {
    self.view.backgroundColor = UIColor(red: CGFloat(red), green:
    CGFloat(green), blue: CGFloat(blue), alpha: CGFloat(alpha))
}
```

Listing 3-3. ColorListTableViewModel

```
class ColorTableViewModel: NSObject {

    var tableTitle:String

    fileprivate var coulorData:[Color]
    fileprivate var selectedIndexPath:IndexPath?
    fileprivate weak var view:ColorListTableViewControllerDelegate?

    init (view:ColorListTableViewControllerDelegate?, title:String) {
        self.view = view
        self.tableTitle = title

        self.coulorData = []

        if let redModel = Color(name: "Red", red: 1.0, green: 0.0, blue:
        0.0, alpha: 1.0),
            let blueModel = Color(name: "Blue", red: 0.0, green: 0.0, blue:
            1.0, alpha: 1.0),
            let greenModel = Color(name: "Green", red: 0.0, green: 1.0,
            blue: 0.0, alpha: 1.0) {
            self.coulorData.append(redModel)
            self.coulorData.append(blueModel)
            self.coulorData.append(greenModel)

        }
    }
}

extension ColorTableViewModel : TableViewModel {

    func setView(delegate:AnyObject?) -> Void {
        self.view = delegate as? ColorListTableViewControllerDelegate
    }

    func numberOfRows() -> Int {
        return coulorData.count
    }

    func cellViewModel(forIndexPath indexPath:IndexPath) -> CellViewModel? {
        let row = indexPath.row
        if row < 0 || row >= self.coulorData.count {
            return nil
        }

        let cellText = coulorData[row].name
        return TableViewCellViewModel(view:nil, cellText: cellText)
    }
```

```
func selectRow(atIndexPath indexPath:IndexPath) {
    self.selectedIndexPath = indexPath
}

func viewModelForSelectedRow() -> ColorDetailViewModel? {
    guard let selectedIndexPath = selectedIndexPath else {
        return nil
    }

    if selectedIndexPath.row < 0 || selectedIndexPath.row >= coulorData.
    count {
        return nil
    }

    return ColorDetailViewModel(view:nil, model:coulorData[selectedIndex
    Path.row])
}

func viewDidAppear(_ animated: Bool) {
    guard let view = view else {
        return
    }
    view.setNavigationTitle(tableTitle)
}

func model(forIndexPath indexPath:IndexPath) -> AnyObject? {
    let row = indexPath.row
    if row < 0 || row >= self.coulorData.count {
        return nil
    }

    return coulorData[row] as AnyObject
}

}
```

The code in Listing 3-3 handles the presentational aspects of the table view, as well as building view models for cells and the detail view controller. The ColorListTableViewModel instance holds a weak reference to the view layer as well as a strong reference to an array of model objects. This array represents the model layer for this application:

```
fileprivate weak var view:ColorListTableViewControllerDelegate?

fileprivate var coulorData:[Color]
```

Let us now examine the code for the ColorDetailViewModel class:

Listing 3-4. ColorDetailViewMoel

```
import Foundation

class ColorDetailViewModel : NSObject {
    weak var view:ColorDetailViewControllerDelegate?
    var model:Color?

    init(view:ColorDetailViewControllerDelegate?, model:Color?) {
        self.view = view
        self.model = model
        super.init()
    }
}

extension ColorDetailViewModel : ViewModel {
    func viewDidAppear(_ animated: Bool) {
        if let view = self.view, let model = self.model {
            view.setBackgroundColor(red: model.red, blue: model.blue, green:
            model.green, alpha: model.alpha)

            view.setNavigationTitle(model.name)
        }
    }

    func setView(delegate:AnyObject?) -> Void {
        self.view = delegate as? ColorDetailViewControllerDelegate
    }
}
```

The code in Listing 3-4 represents the view model for the detail view controller. The view model holds a weak reference to the view layer, as well as a strong reference to a model object. The model object is an instance of a Color class.

```
weak var view:ColorDetailViewControllerDelegate?

var model:Color?
```

The view model's viewDidAppear event is wired to be called by the matching event of the view controller call. The view model uses this event to set the background color and title of the view:

```
func viewDidAppear(_ animated: Bool) {
    if let view = self.view, let model = self.model {
        view.setBackgroundColor(red: model.red, blue: model.blue, green:
        model.green, alpha: model.alpha)

        view.setNavigationTitle(model.name)
    }
}
```

Let us examine the code for the Color class next:

Listing 3-5. Color.swift

```
import Foundation

class Color {
    private static let zero = Float(floatLiteral: 0.0)
    private static let one = Float(floatLiteral: 1.0)

    var name:String
    var red:Float
    var green:Float
    var blue:Float
    var alpha:Float

    init?(name:String, red:Float, green:Float, blue:Float, alpha:Float) {
        if (red < Color.zero || red > Color.one) {
            return nil
        }

        if (green < Color.zero || green > Color.one) {
            return nil
        }

        if (blue < Color.zero || blue > Color.one) {
            return nil
        }

        if (alpha < Color.zero || alpha > Color.one) {
            return nil
        }

        self.name = name
        self.red = red
        self.green = green
        self.blue = blue
        self.alpha = alpha
    }
}
```

The code in Listing 3-5 represents a single model object. The model object contains attributes to describe the name of the color as well as individual R, G, B, and A component values:

```
var name:String
var red:Float
var green:Float
var blue:Float
var alpha:Float
```

59

Summary

In this chapter you have learned about the ubiquitous Model-View-Controller (MVC) pattern and its iOS equivalent Model-ViewController (M-VC) pattern. Applications built using the M-VC pattern tend to have massive view controller classes that are very difficult to test.

You have also been introduced to Microsoft's alternative to the MVC pattern, known as the Model-View-ViewModel (MVVM) pattern. This pattern has its roots in WPF/XAML applications but can be easily adapted and used in iOS applications.

Applications built with the MVVM pattern are significantly easier to test than applications built using the MVC or M-VC patterns.

CHAPTER 4

■ ■ ■

Applying TDD to the Model

This chapter will examine the process of building the model layer of an app using TDD techniques. Since this chapter focuses on the model layer, you will not be building a user interface or any presentation logic.

Testing the components of the model layer of an application is just as important as testing other components in the app. In a very simple app, the model layer may consist of a single class that has a few instance variables. Even in this simplified scenario, unit tests can be used to establish that the model class has the member variables that other parts of the application expect it to have.

In more complex apps, the model layer may consist of several classes with complex relationships and responsibilities. Individual classes within the model layer may perform data transformation, persistence, and validation. In such scenarios, unit tests help establish (and maintain) the relationships between the classes, and provide a measure of confidence that the transformation, persistence, and validation logic are working as expected.

The model layer that is presented in this chapter is designed to represent a bank account along with a set of transactions in that account. We will create classes to represent bank accounts, individuals who own the account, and transactions within the account. Figure 4-1 depicts the class diagram of the model layer.

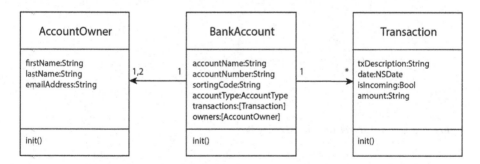

Figure 4-1. *Model Layer Classes*

A brief description of the classes that make up the model layer follows:

- **BankAccount:** Represents a single bank account. A bank account object can represent either a savings account or a current account.

© Abhishek Mishra 2017
A. Mishra, *iOS Code Testing*, DOI 10.1007/978-1-4842-2689-6_4

- **Transaction:** Represents a single transaction. A transaction object can represent either money coming into the account or money leaving the account.

- **AccountOwner:** Represents an individual (or entity) that owns the bank account. An account may have up to two owners.

The complete source code for the app can be downloaded anonymously from github using the following URL:

```
https://github.com/asmtechnology/Lesson04.iOSTesting.2017.Apress.git
```

Creating the Xcode Project

Launch Xcode and create a new iOS project based on the Single View Application template (see Figure 4-2).

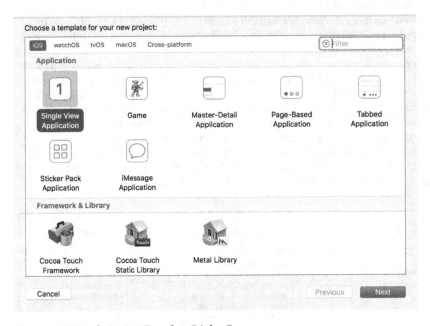

Figure 4-2. *Xcode Project Template Dialog Box*

Use the following options while creating the new project (see Figure 4-3):

- **Product Name:** BankAccount

- **Team:** None

- **Organization Name:** Provide a suitable name

- **Organization Identifier:** Provide a suitable identifier

- **Language:** Swift

- **Devices:** iPhone

- **Use Core Data:** Unchecked

- **Include Unit Tests:** Checked

- **Include UI Tests:** Unchecked

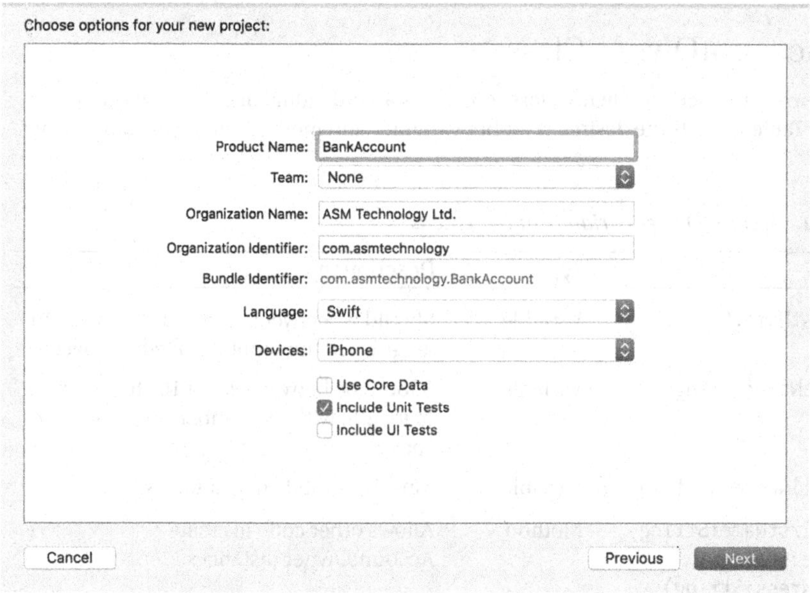

Figure 4-3. Xcode Project Options Dialog Box

■ **Note**   Even though we have used the Single View Application Template while creating this project, there will be no user interface/presentation code added into the project. In Chapter 6, you will build an app to display bank account details, and a list of transactions in a collection view. The project in Chapter 6 will build on the files created in this chapter.

Save the project to a suitable location on your computer and click Create. Since this project will contain several new classes, it will be a good idea to place class files under appropriate groups within the project navigator.

Create a group called Model in the Xcode project navigator. You will create model layer specific classes within this group.

Building the Model Layer

There are three model classes that we need to build:

- AccountOwner
- Transaction
- BankAccount

Each of these will be built using TDD techniques in subsequent sections of this chapter.

The AccountOwner Class

An instance of the AccountOwner class represents an individual or entity that owns an account. Table 4-1 lists the desired member variables and methods of the AccountOwner class.

Table 4-1. *AccountOwner variables and methods.*

Item	Type	Description
var firstName:String	Variable	Should be between 2 and 10 characters in length, with no numbers or white space.
var lastName:String	Variable	Should be between 2 and 10 characters in length, with no numbers or white space.
var emailAddress:String	Variable	Must be a valid email address.
init?(firstName:String, lastName:String, emailAddress:String)	Method	Allows other code to create AccountOwner instances.

Create a new iOS Unit Test Case class called AccountOwnerTests under the BankAccountTests group of the project explorer (see Figure 4-4).

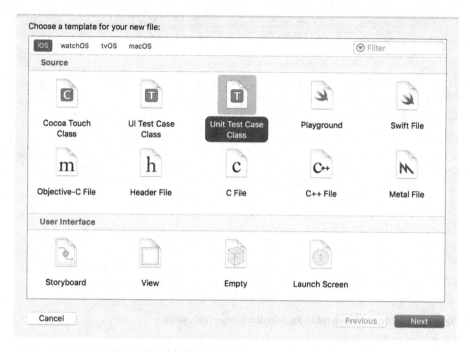

Choose a template for your new file:

iOS   watchOS   tvOS   macOS   ⊚ Filter

Source

C	**T**	**T**	swift	swift
Cocoa Touch Class	UI Test Case Class	Unit Test Case Class	Playground	Swift File
m	**h**	**c**	**C++**	**M**
Objective-C File	Header File	C File	C++ File	Metal File

User Interface

Storyboard	View	Empty	Launch Screen

Cancel   Previous   **Next**

Figure 4-4. Xcode File Template Dialog Box

Select the AccountOwnerTests.swift file in the project explorer and use the file
inspector to ensure that the file is included in the BankAccountTests target and not the
BankAccount target (see Figure 4-5). If the file inspector is not visible, View ➤ Utilities ➤
Show File Inspector menu item.

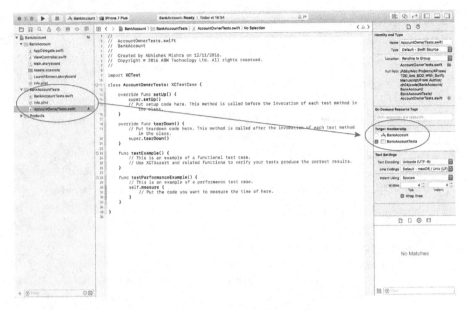

Figure 4-5. *Target Membership for AccountOwnerTests.swift*

A test case file contains a couple of empty stub methods called testExample and testPerformanceExample. These methods are there to help you get started writing your tests. We will not be using these stub methods in this chapter, so feel free to delete them.

Create a new unit test method called testAccountOwner_ValidFirstName_ ValidLastName_ValidEmail_CanBeInstantiated() and add the following code to the method body:

```
func testAccountOwner_ValidFirstName_ValidLastName_ValidEmail_
CanBeInstantiated() {
    let accountOwner = AccountOwner(firstName: validFirstName,
                                    lastName: validLastName,
                                    emailAddress: validEmailAddress)

    XCTAssertNotNil(accountOwner)
}
```

Add the following private constant declarations to the top of the AccountOwnerTests.swift file:

```
private let validFirstName = "Andrew"
private let validLastName = "Hill"
private let validEmailAddress = "a.hill@abcfinancial.com"

private let invalidFirstName = "A"
private let invalidLastName = "h"
private let invalidEmailAddress = "abcfinancial.com"

private let emptyString = ""
```

These constants represent a set of valid and invalid first names, last names, and email addresses, and will be used within the test cases in this class. It is a good practice to declare all the constants used in test cases at the top of the file that contains the test cases, and not create ad hoc constants within test cases.

You will notice that this code fails to compile; that is because the AccountOwner class has not been created yet. Failure to compile test code is in this case being treated as a test failure.

To fix this failure, create a new class called AccountOwner under the Model group in the project navigator, and update its implementation to match the following code snippet:

```
import Foundation

class AccountOwner: NSObject {

    init?(firstName:String, lastName:String, emailAddress:String) {
        super.init()
    }

}
```

Save the file and run all unit tests using the Product ➤ Test menu item. You will see that all unit tests have passed (see Figure 4-6).

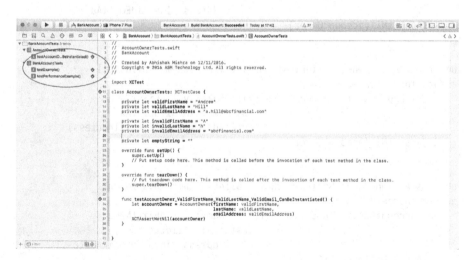

Figure 4-6. *Xcode Test Navigator*

We need a few more test cases for the AccountOwner class. You can choose to build up the features of the AccountOwner class one test at a time, or write a few tests up front and then write features in the AccountOwner class to make a small group of tests pass, and repeat as necessary.

Add the code from Listing 4-1 to the AccountOwnerTests class to create a few additional tests.

67

Listing 4-1. AccountOwnerTests.swift

```swift
func testAccountOwner_InvalidFirstName_ValidLastName_ValidEmail_
CanNotBeInstantiated() {
    let accountOwner = AccountOwner(firstName: invalidFirstName,
                                    lastName: validLastName,
                                    emailAddress: validEmailAddress)
    XCTAssertNil(accountOwner)
}

func testAccountOwner_InvalidFirstName_InvalidLastName_ValidEmail_
CanNotBeInstantiated() {
    let accountOwner = AccountOwner(firstName: invalidFirstName,
                                    lastName: invalidLastName,
                                    emailAddress: validEmailAddress)
    XCTAssertNil(accountOwner)
}


func testAccountOwner_InvalidFirstName_InvalidLastName_InvalidEmail_
CanNotBeInstantiated() {
    let accountOwner = AccountOwner(firstName: invalidFirstName,
                                    lastName: invalidLastName,
                                    emailAddress: invalidEmailAddress)
    XCTAssertNil(accountOwner)
}

func testAccountOwner_ValidFirstName_InvalidLastName_ValidEmail_
CanNotBeInstantiated() {
    let accountOwner = AccountOwner(firstName: validFirstName,
                                    lastName: invalidLastName,
                                    emailAddress: validEmailAddress)
    XCTAssertNil(accountOwner)
}

func testAccountOwner_ValidFirstName_ValidLastName_InvalidEmail_
CanNotBeInstantiated() {
    let accountOwner = AccountOwner(firstName: validFirstName,
                                    lastName: validLastName,
                                    emailAddress: invalidEmailAddress)
    XCTAssertNil(accountOwner)
}

func testAccountOwner_ValidFirstName_InvalidLastName_InvalidEmail_
CanNotBeInstantiated() {
    let accountOwner = AccountOwner(firstName: validFirstName,
                                    lastName: invalidLastName,
                                    emailAddress: invalidEmailAddress)
    XCTAssertNil(accountOwner)
}
```

```swift
func testAccountOwner_EmptyFirstName_ValidLastName_ValidEmail_
CanNotBeInstantiated() {
    let accountOwner = AccountOwner(firstName: emptyString,
                                    lastName: validLastName,
                                    emailAddress: validEmailAddress)
    XCTAssertNil(accountOwner)
}

func testAccountOwner_ValidFirstName_EmptyLastName_ValidEmail_
CanNotBeInstantiated() {
    let accountOwner = AccountOwner(firstName: validFirstName,
                                    lastName: emptyString,
                                    emailAddress: validEmailAddress)
    XCTAssertNil(accountOwner)
}

func testAccountOwner_ValidFirstName_ValidLastName_EmptyEmail_
CanNotBeInstantiated() {
    let accountOwner = AccountOwner(firstName: validFirstName,
                                    lastName: validLastName,
                                    emailAddress: emptyString)
    XCTAssertNil(accountOwner)
}
```

The code in Listing 4-1 adds nine new test cases, each of which relate to instantiating AccountOwner objects. These nine test cases collectively ensure that an AccountOwner object can not be instantiated if the first name, last name, or e-mail address is invalid.

This time you will notice that there are no compiler warnings after you have added these nine new test cases. However, when you run all tests by using the Product ➤ Test menu item, you will notice that all these new test cases fail (see Figure 4-7).

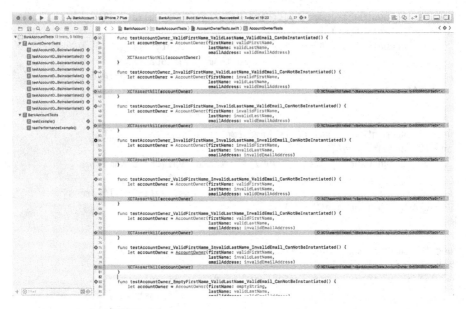

Figure 4-7. *Failing Unit Tests*

Fixing these tests require us to define a set of rules that will be used to validate user names, passwords, and email addresses. We will then create classes that encapsulate these rules, and integrate calls to instances of these validation classes into an initializer method in the AccountOwner class.

We'll create the following validation classes using TDD techniques next:

- First name

- Last name

- Email address

Creating the First Name Validator Class

For the purposes of the project being developed in this chapter, let us assume the following validation criteria are to be applied to the first name:

- Should be between 2 and 10 characters in length.

- Should not include numbers.

- Should not include white space.

Let us first create a set of tests for a class called FirstNameValidator. The FirstNameValidator class does not exist yet, hence these tests will not compile. However, the tests we are about to write ensure that the FirstNameValidator class will encapsulate all the validation criteria listed above in a method called validate().

Create a new iOS Unit Test Case class called FirstNameValidatorTests under the BankAccountTests group of the project explorer and ensure the FirstNameValidatorTests. swift file is included in the BankAccountTests target and not the BankAccount target.

Replace the contents of the FirstNameValidatorTests.swift file with Listing 4-2.

Listing 4-2. FirstNameValidatorTests.swift

```swift
import XCTest

class FirstNameValidatorTests: XCTestCase {

    fileprivate let emptyString = ""

    fileprivate let singleCharachterName = "a"
    fileprivate let twoCharachterName = "ab"
    fileprivate let tenCharachterName = "abcdefghij"
    fileprivate let elevenCharachterName = "abcdefghijk"

    fileprivate let nameWithWhitespace = "abc def"

    fileprivate let nameWithDigit0 = "abc00"
    fileprivate let nameWithDigit1 = "abc11"
    fileprivate let nameWithDigit2 = "abc22"
    fileprivate let nameWithDigit3 = "abc33"
    fileprivate let nameWithDigit4 = "abc44"
    fileprivate let nameWithDigit5 = "abc55"
    fileprivate let nameWithDigit6 = "abc66"
    fileprivate let nameWithDigit7 = "abc77"
    fileprivate let nameWithDigit8 = "abc88"
    fileprivate let nameWithDigit9 = "abc99"

    override func setUp() {
        super.setUp()
        // Put setup code here. This method is called before the invocation
        of each test method in the class.
    }

    override func tearDown() {
        // Put teardown code here. This method is called after the
        invocation of each test method in the class.
        super.tearDown()
    }
}

// MARK: Empty string validation
extension FirstNameValidatorTests {
```

```swift
    func testValidate_EmptyString_ReturnsFalse() {
        let validator = FirstNameValidator()
        XCTAssertFalse(validator.validate(emptyString), "string can not be
        empty.")
    }

}

// MARK: String length validation
extension FirstNameValidatorTests {

    func testValidate_InputLessThanTwoCharachtersInLength_ReturnsFalse() {
        let validator = FirstNameValidator()
        XCTAssertFalse(validator.validate(singleCharachterName), "string can
        not have less than 2 characters.")
    }

    func testValidate_InputGreaterThanTenCharachtersInLength_ReturnsFalse() {
        let validator = FirstNameValidator()
        XCTAssertFalse(validator.validate(elevenCharachterName), "string can
        not have more than 11 characters.")
    }

    func testValidate_InputTwoCharachtersInLength_ReturnsTrue() {
        let validator = FirstNameValidator()
        XCTAssertTrue(validator.validate(twoCharachterName), "string with 2
        charachters should have been valid.")
    }

    func testValidate_InputTenCharachtersInLength_ReturnsTrue() {
        let validator = FirstNameValidator()
        XCTAssertTrue(validator.validate(tenCharachterName), "string with 10
        charachters should have been valid.")
    }
}

// MARK: white space validation
extension FirstNameValidatorTests {

    func testValidate_InputWithWhitespace_ReturnsFalse() {
        let validator = FirstNameValidator()
        XCTAssertFalse(validator.validate(nameWithWhitespace), "string can
        not have white space.")
    }

}
```

```swift
// MARK: Numeric digit validation
extension FirstNameValidatorTests {

    func testValidate_InputWithDigit0_ReturnsFalse() {
        let validator = FirstNameValidator()
        XCTAssertFalse(validator.validate(nameWithDigit0), "string can not
        have digit 0 in it.")
    }

    func testValidate_InputWithDigit1_ReturnsFalse() {
        let validator = FirstNameValidator()
        XCTAssertFalse(validator.validate(nameWithDigit1), "string can not
        have digit 1 in it.")
    }

    func testValidate_InputWithDigit2_ReturnsFalse() {
        let validator = FirstNameValidator()
        XCTAssertFalse(validator.validate(nameWithDigit2), "string can not
        have digit 2 in it.")
    }

    func testValidate_InputWithDigit3_ReturnsFalse() {
        let validator = FirstNameValidator()
        XCTAssertFalse(validator.validate(nameWithDigit3), "string can not
        have digit 3 in it.")
    }

    func testValidate_InputWithDigit4_ReturnsFalse() {
        let validator = FirstNameValidator()
        XCTAssertFalse(validator.validate(nameWithDigit4), "string can not
        have digit 4 in it.")
    }

    func testValidate_InputWithDigit5_ReturnsFalse() {
        let validator = FirstNameValidator()
        XCTAssertFalse(validator.validate(nameWithDigit5), "string can not
        have digit 5 in it.")
    }

    func testValidate_InputWithDigit6_ReturnsFalse() {
        let validator = FirstNameValidator()
        XCTAssertFalse(validator.validate(nameWithDigit6), "string can not
        have digit 6 in it.")
    }
```

```
    func testValidate_InputWithDigit7_ReturnsFalse() {
        let validator = FirstNameValidator()
        XCTAssertFalse(validator.validate(nameWithDigit7), "string can not
        have digit 7 in it.")
    }

    func testValidate_InputWithDigit8_ReturnsFalse() {
        let validator = FirstNameValidator()
        XCTAssertFalse(validator.validate(nameWithDigit8), "string can not
        have digit 8 in it.")
    }

    func testValidate_InputWithDigit9_ReturnsFalse() {
        let validator = FirstNameValidator()
        XCTAssertFalse(validator.validate(nameWithDigit9), "string can not
        have digit 9 in it.")
    }

}
```

The tests in Listing 4-2 assume that the validator class will implement a method called validate() that will return true or false. When you approach a problem with TDD techniques, your tests will define the interface of the class that will be built to make the tests pass.

You may also have noticed that class extensions have been used to group similar tests. This is a commonly used approach to segregate a large number of tests in a single class.

You will once again notice that the tests we have just written do not compile. This is because the FirstNameValidator class has not been created yet.

To make the test code compile, create a new class called FirstNameValidator under the Model group in the project navigator, and update its implementation to match Listing 4-3.

Listing 4-3. FirstNameValidator.swift

```
import Foundation

class FirstNameValidator: NSObject {

    func validate(_ value:String) -> Bool {
        if ((value.characters.count < 2) || (value.characters.count > 10)) {
            return false
        }

        let whitespace = Set(" ".characters)
        if (value.characters.filter {whitespace.contains($0)}).count > 0 {
            return false
        }

        let numbers = Set("0123456789".characters)
        if (value.characters.filter {numbers.contains($0)}).count > 0 {
            return false
        }
```

```
guard let regexValidator = try? NSRegularExpression(pattern:
"([A-Za-z'])", options: .caseInsensitive) else {
    return false
}

if regexValidator.numberOfMatches(in: value,
                                  options: NSRegularExpression.
                                  MatchingOptions.reportCompletion,
                                  range: NSMakeRange(0, value.
                                  characters.count)) > 0 {
    return true
}

return false
}

}
```

This code in Listing 4-3 declares the FirstNameValidator class as a subclass of NSObject, with a single method called validate that returns a Boolean. Save the file and run all unit tests using the Product ➤ Test menu item. All the tests around FirstNameValidator should pass; however you should still see test failures around the AccountOwner class (see Figure 4-8).

Figure 4-8. *Xcode Test Navigator with Passing and Failing Tests*

These failing tests are fine for now and will be made to pass once we build the other validator objects and integrate these validator objects with the AccountOwner class.

Creating the Last Name Validator Class

The last name validator class will be very similar to the first name validator class created in the previous section. For the purposes of the project being developed in this chapter, let us assume the following validation criteria are to be applied to the last name:

- Should be between 2 and 10 characters in length.

- Should not include numbers.

- Should not include white space.

- Should not include any punctuation or special characters except for the ' character (as in O'Hara). Special characters in this context include arithmetic symbols, underscores, logical symbols, and parentheses.

Create a new iOS Unit Test Case class called LastNameValidatorTests under the BankAccountTests group of the project explorer and ensure the new file is included in the test target.

Replace the contents of the LastNameValidatorTests.swift file with Listing 4-4.

Listing 4-4. LastNameValidatorTests.swift

```
import XCTest

class LastNameValidatorTests: XCTestCase {

    fileprivate let emptyString = ""

    fileprivate let singleCharachterName = "a"
    fileprivate let twoCharachterName = "ab"
    fileprivate let tenCharachterName = "abcdefghij"
    fileprivate let elevenCharachterName = "abcdefghijk"

    fileprivate let nameWithWhitespace = "abc def"
    fileprivate let nameWithSingleQuote = "abc'def"

    fileprivate let nameWithUnsupportedSpecialCharacters =
    "_+-.,!@#$%^&*();\\/|<>\""

    fileprivate let nameWithDigit0 = "abc00"
    fileprivate let nameWithDigit1 = "abc11"
    fileprivate let nameWithDigit2 = "abc22"
    fileprivate let nameWithDigit3 = "abc33"
    fileprivate let nameWithDigit4 = "abc44"
    fileprivate let nameWithDigit5 = "abc55"
```

```swift
    fileprivate let nameWithDigit6 = "abc66"
    fileprivate let nameWithDigit7 = "abc77"
    fileprivate let nameWithDigit8 = "abc88"
    fileprivate let nameWithDigit9 = "abc99"

    override func setUp() {
        super.setUp()
        // Put setup code here. This method is called before the invocation
        of each test method in the class.
    }

    override func tearDown() {
        // Put teardown code here. This method is called after the
        invocation of each test method in the class.
        super.tearDown()
    }
}

// MARK: Empty string validation
extension LastNameValidatorTests {

    func testValidate_EmptyString_ReturnsFalse() {
        let validator = LastNameValidator()
        XCTAssertFalse(validator.validate(emptyString), "string can not be
        empty.")
    }

}

// MARK: String length validation
extension LastNameValidatorTests {

    func testValidate_InputLessThanTwoCharachtersInLength_ReturnsFalse() {
        let validator = LastNameValidator()
        XCTAssertFalse(validator.validate(singleCharachterName), "string can
        not have less than 2 characters.")
    }

    func testValidate_InputGreaterThanTenCharachtersInLength_ReturnsFalse() {
        let validator = LastNameValidator()
        XCTAssertFalse(validator.validate(elevenCharachterName), "string can
        not have more than 11 characters.")
    }

    func testValidate_InputTwoCharachtersInLength_ReturnsTrue() {
        let validator = LastNameValidator()
```

```swift
        XCTAssertTrue(validator.validate(twoCharachterName), "string with 2
        charachters should have been valid.")
    }

    func testValidate_InputTenCharachtersInLength_ReturnsTrue() {
        let validator = LastNameValidator()
        XCTAssertTrue(validator.validate(tenCharachterName), "string with 10
        charachters should have been valid.")
    }
}

// MARK: white space validation
extension LastNameValidatorTests {

    func testValidate_InputWithWhitespace_ReturnsFalse() {
        let validator = LastNameValidator()
        XCTAssertFalse(validator.validate(nameWithWhitespace), "string can
        not have white space.")
    }

}

// MARK: special charachter validation
extension LastNameValidatorTests {

    func testValidate_InputWithSingleQuote_ReturnsTrue() {
        let validator = LastNameValidator()
        XCTAssertTrue(validator.validate(nameWithSingleQuote), "string with
        single quote should have been valid.")
    }

    func testValidate_InputWithSpecialCharacters_ReturnsFalse() {
        let validator = LastNameValidator()
        XCTAssertFalse(validator.validate(nameWithUnsupportedSpecialCharacters),
        "string can not have special characters.")
        }

}

// MARK: Numeric digit validation
extension LastNameValidatorTests {

    func testValidate_InputWithDigit0_ReturnsFalse() {
        let validator = LastNameValidator()
        XCTAssertFalse(validator.validate(nameWithDigit0), "string can not
        have digit 0 in it.")
    }
```

```swift
func testValidate_InputWithDigit1_ReturnsFalse() {
    let validator = LastNameValidator()
    XCTAssertFalse(validator.validate(nameWithDigit1), "string can not
    have digit 1 in it.")
}

func testValidate_InputWithDigit2_ReturnsFalse() {
    let validator = LastNameValidator()
    XCTAssertFalse(validator.validate(nameWithDigit2), "string can not
    have digit 2 in it.")
}

func testValidate_InputWithDigit3_ReturnsFalse() {
    let validator = LastNameValidator()
    XCTAssertFalse(validator.validate(nameWithDigit3), "string can not
    have digit 3 in it.")
}

func testValidate_InputWithDigit4_ReturnsFalse() {
    let validator = LastNameValidator()
    XCTAssertFalse(validator.validate(nameWithDigit4), "string can not
    have digit 4 in it.")
}

func testValidate_InputWithDigit5_ReturnsFalse() {
    let validator = LastNameValidator()
    XCTAssertFalse(validator.validate(nameWithDigit5), "string can not
    have digit 5 in it.")
}

func testValidate_InputWithDigit6_ReturnsFalse() {
    let validator = LastNameValidator()
    XCTAssertFalse(validator.validate(nameWithDigit6), "string can not
    have digit 6 in it.")
}

func testValidate_InputWithDigit7_ReturnsFalse() {
    let validator = LastNameValidator()
    XCTAssertFalse(validator.validate(nameWithDigit7), "string can not
    have digit 7 in it.")
}

func testValidate_InputWithDigit8_ReturnsFalse() {
    let validator = LastNameValidator()
    XCTAssertFalse(validator.validate(nameWithDigit8), "string can not
    have digit 8 in it.")
}
```

```swift
func testValidate_InputWithDigit9_ReturnsFalse() {
    let validator = LastNameValidator()
    XCTAssertFalse(validator.validate(nameWithDigit9), "string can not
    have digit 9 in it.")
}

}
```

It is worth noting that the code in Listing 4-4 uses a single test case to handle all special characters:

```swift
func testValidate_InputWithSpecialCharacters_ReturnsFalse() {
    let validator = LastNameValidator()
    XCTAssertFalse(validator.validate(nameWithUnsupportedSpecialCharacters),
    "string can not have special characters.")
}
```

You can, if you wish, create one test case per special character. If you are using your test cases as documentation for the LastNameValidator class, then having one test case per special character will create more explicit documentation at the cost of increasing the number of test cases.

These new test cases will not compile because the LastNameValidator class has not been created yet. Create a new class called LastNameValidator under the Model group in the project navigator, and update its implementation to match Listing 4-5.

Listing 4-5. LastNameValidator.swift

```swift
import Foundation

class LastNameValidator: NSObject {

    func validate(_ value:String) -> Bool {
        if ((value.characters.count < 2) || (value.characters.count > 10)) {
            return false
        }

        let whitespace = Set(" ".characters)
        if (value.characters.filter {whitespace.contains($0)}).count > 0 {
            return false
        }

        let numbers = Set("0123456789".characters)
        if (value.characters.filter {numbers.contains($0)}).count > 0 {
            return false
        }

        let specialCharacters = Set("_+-.,!@#$%^&*();\\/|<>\"".characters)
        if (value.characters.filter {specialCharacters.contains($0)}).count > 0 {
            return false
        }
```

```
guard let regexValidator = try? NSRegularExpression(pattern:
"([A-Za-z'])", options: .caseInsensitive) else {
    return false
}

if regexValidator.numberOfMatches(in: value,
                                  options: NSRegularExpression.
                                  MatchingOptions.reportCompletion,
                                  range: NSMakeRange(0, value.
                                  characters.count)) > 0 {
    return true
}

return false
}

}
```

The code in Listing 4-5 declares the LastNameValidator class as a subclass of
NSObject, with a single class method called validate that returns a Boolean. Save the
file and run all unit tests using the Product ➤ Test menu item. All the tests around
LastNameValidator should pass (see Figure 4-9).

Figure 4-9. *All Tests in LastNameValidator.swift Pass*

Creating the Email Address Validator Class

Create a new iOS Unit Test Case class called EmailAddressValidatorTests under the BankAccountTests group of the project explorer, and ensure the new file is included in the test target.

Replace the contents of the EmailAddressValidatorTests.swift file with Listing 4-6.

Listing 4-6. EmailAddressValidatorTests.swift

```swift
import XCTest

class EmailAddressValidatorTests: XCTestCase {

    fileprivate let emptyString = ""

    fileprivate let validEmailAddress1 = "a@b.com"
    fileprivate let validEmailAddress2 = "a@b.co.uk"
    fileprivate let validEmailAddress3 = "a@b.io"
    fileprivate let validEmailAddress4 = "andrew.shaw@byteowl.io"

    fileprivate let invalidEmailAddress1 = "ab.com"
    fileprivate let invalidEmailAddress2 = "abcom"
    fileprivate let invalidEmailAddress3 = "a@b@com"

    override func setUp() {
        super.setUp()
        // Put setup code here. This method is called before the invocation
        of each test method in the class.
    }

    override func tearDown() {
        // Put teardown code here. This method is called after the
        invocation of each test method in the class.
        super.tearDown()
    }
}

// MARK: Empty string validation
extension EmailAddressValidatorTests {

    func testValidate_EmptyString_ReturnsFalse() {
        let validator = EmailAddressValidator()
        XCTAssertFalse(validator.validate(emptyString), "string can not be
        empty.")
    }

}
```

```swift
// MARK: invalid email-addresses
extension EmailAddressValidatorTests {

    func testValidate_InvalidEmailAddress1_ReturnsFalse() {
        let validator = EmailAddressValidator()
        XCTAssertFalse(validator.validate(invalidEmailAddress1),
        "/(invalidEmailAddress1) is not a valid e-mail address.")
    }

    func testValidate_InvalidEmailAddress2_ReturnsFalse() {
        let validator = EmailAddressValidator()
        XCTAssertFalse(validator.validate(invalidEmailAddress2),
        "/(invalidEmailAddress2) is not a valid e-mail address.")
    }

    func testValidate_InvalidEmailAddress3_ReturnsFalse() {
        let validator = EmailAddressValidator()
        XCTAssertFalse(validator.validate(invalidEmailAddress3),
        "/(invalidEmailAddress3) is not a valid e-mail address.")
    }

}

// MARK: valid email-addresses
extension EmailAddressValidatorTests {

    func testValidate_ValidEmailAddress1_ReturnsTrue() {
        let validator = EmailAddressValidator()
        XCTAssertTrue(validator.validate(validEmailAddress1),
        "/(validEmailAddress1) is a valid e-mail address.")
    }

    func testValidate_ValidEmailAddress2_ReturnsTrue() {
        let validator = EmailAddressValidator()
        XCTAssertTrue(validator.validate(validEmailAddress2),
        "/(validEmailAddress2) is a valid e-mail address.")
    }

    func testValidate_ValidEmailAddress3_ReturnsTrue() {
        let validator = EmailAddressValidator()
        XCTAssertTrue(validator.validate(validEmailAddress3),
        "/(validEmailAddress3) is a valid e-mail address.")
    }

    func testValidate_ValidEmailAddress4_ReturnsTrue() {
        let validator = EmailAddressValidator()
        XCTAssertTrue(validator.validate(validEmailAddress4),
        "/(validEmailAddress4) is a valid e-mail address.")
    }

}
```

These new test cases will not compile because the EmailAddressValidator class has not been created yet. Create a new class called EmailAddressValidator under the Model group in the project navigator, and update its implementation to match Listing 4-7.

Listing 4-7. EmailaddressValidator.swift

```swift
import Foundation

class EmailAddressValidator: NSObject {

    func validate(_ value:String) -> Bool {
        if (value.characters.count < 6) {
            return false
        }

        let whitespace = Set(" ".characters)
        if (value.characters.filter {whitespace.contains($0)}).count > 0 {
            return false
        }

        let numbers = Set("0123456789".characters)
        if (value.characters.filter {numbers.contains($0)}).count > 0 {
            return false
        }

        let specialCharacters = Set("+,!#$%^&*();\\/|<>\"".characters)
        if (value.characters.filter {specialCharacters.contains($0)}).count
        > 0 {
            return false
        }

        guard let regexValidator = try? NSRegularExpression(pattern: "([A-Z0-
9._%+-]+@[A-Z0-9.-]+\\.[A-Z]{2,4})", options: .caseInsensitive) else {
            return false
        }

        if regexValidator.numberOfMatches(in: value,
                                options: NSRegularExpression.
                                MatchingOptions.reportCompletion,
                                range: NSMakeRange(0, value.
                                characters.count)) > 0 {
            return true
        }

        return false
    }

}
```

This snippet declares the EmailAddressValidator class as a subclass of NSObject, with a single class method called validate that returns a Boolean. Save the file and run all unit tests using the Product ➤ Test menu item.

All test cases for the FirstNameValidator, LastNameValidator, and EmailAddressValidator class should now pass. In the next section, you will integrate these components into the AccountOwner class.

Integrating the Validator Classes into the AccountOwner Class

The AccountOwner class has a failable initializer that takes three parameters: a first name, last name, and email address. This initializer should return nil if any of its three parameters are invalid.

```
init?(firstName:String, lastName:String, emailAddress:String) {
    super.init()
}
```

We have already built classes to validate first names, last names, and email addresses. We need to now integrate these classes into the initializer of AccountOwner. Integrating these validator classes into AccountOwner's init? method implies three things:

1. Validator objects for the first name, last name, and email address need to be injected into the AccountOwner class.

2. The validate method on the individual validator objects will be called when the AccountOwner's init? method is called.

3. The validate method on the validator object will be called with the correct value that was provided into AccountOwner's init? method.

There are various techniques we can use to inject dependencies into a class, and these techniques have been covered in Chapter 2. In this case, I will inject the validator classes as parameters into AccountOwner's initializer.

Modify the init? method in AccountOwner.swift to match the following snippet:

```
init?(firstName:String, lastName:String, emailAddress:String,
    firstNameValidator:FirstNameValidator?=nil,
    lastNameValidator:LastNameValidator? = nil,
    emailAddressValidator:EmailAddressValidator? = nil) {

    super.init()
}
```

I have added three optional parameters to the initializer, each with a default value of nil. The reason I have done this is so that I can inject mock objects into the initializer when called from a test case, and use real objects when called otherwise.

You need to make sure this small refactoring effort has not broken any tests that were previously passing. Save the file and run all unit tests using the Product ➤ Test menu item. You will observe that no new tests are broken as a result of this refactoring.

Now that we have the means to inject our validators into AccountOwner, let us inject a mock first name validator object and write a test that ensures that the validate method on the mock object is called when an AccountOwner object is instantiated.

Add the following test case to the AccountOwnerTest.swift file:

```
func testAccountOwner_ValidFirstName_ValidLastName_ValidEmailAddress_
ValidFirstNameValidator_CallsValidateOnValidator() {

    let expectation = self.expectation(description: "Expected validate to be
    called on validator.")

    let mockFirstNameValidator = MockFirstNameValidator(expectation,
    expectedValue:validFirstName)

    let _ = AccountOwner(firstName: validFirstName,

                    lastName: validLastName,
                    emailAddress: validEmailAddress,
                    firstNameValidator:mockFirstNameValidator)

    self.waitForExpectations(timeout: 1.0, handler: nil)
}
```

This test case first creates an XCTestExpectation instance

```
let expectation = self.expectation(description: "Expected validate to be
called on validator.")
```

The test case then instantiates a mock first name validator object. This mock validator is an instance of a class called MockFirstNameValidator (which will be built shortly).

```
let mockFirstNameValidator = MockFirstNameValidator(expectation,
expectedValue:validFirstName)
```

Recall that the validator objects that have been created previously all have a single validate method:

```
class func validate(_ value:String) -> Bool
```

The mock validator is given a reference to the expectation object as well as the string we expect will be injected into the validate method by AccountOwner's init? method. The mock validator object will fulfill the expectation when its validate method is called with the expected value.

The test case then instantiates an AccountOwner with a valid first name, last name, email address, and first name validator.

```
let _ = AccountOwner(firstName: validFirstName,
                     lastName: validLastName,
                     emailAddress: validEmailAddress,
                     firstNameValidator:mockFirstNameValidator)
```

Finally, the test case waits for up to one second for the test expectation to be fulfilled.

```
self.waitForExpectations(timeout: 1.0, handler: nil)
```

Create a new group in the project explorer under the BankAccountTests group, called Mocks. Create a new class called MockFirstNameValidator under the Mocks group in the project navigator (see Figure 4-10). This new class does not need to be a member of the BankAccount target, as it is only used in the unit test target.

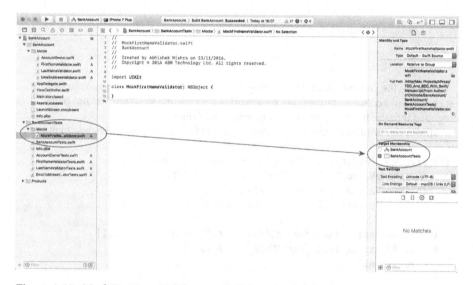

Figure 4-10. *MockFirstNameValidator.swift Target Membership*

Update the implementation of the MockFirstNameValidator class to match Listing 4-8.

Listing 4-8. MockFirstNameValidator.swift

```
import Foundation
import XCTest

class MockFirstNameValidator: FirstNameValidator {

    private var expectation:XCTestExpectation?
    private var expectedValue:String?
```

```
init(_ expectation:XCTestExpectation, expectedValue:String) {
    self.expectation = expectation
    self.expectedValue = expectedValue
    super.init()
}

override func validate(_ value:String) -> Bool {

    if let expectation = self.expectation,
        let expectedValue = self.expectedValue {
        if value.compare(expectedValue) == .orderedSame {
            expectation.fulfill()
        }
    }

    return super.validate(value)
}
}
```

Save the file and run all unit tests using the Product ➤ Test menu item. Your new test case should compile, but will not pass. This is because the validator has not been integrated into the init? method of the AccountOwner object.

Modify the implementation of the init? method of the AccountOwner class to match:

```
init?(firstName:String, lastName:String, emailAddress:String,
    firstNameValidator:FirstNameValidator? = nil,
    lastNameValidator:LastNameValidator? = nil,
    emailAddressValidator:EmailAddressValidator? = nil) {

    let validator1 = firstNameValidator ?? FirstNameValidator()
    if validator1.validate(firstName) == false {
        return nil
    }

    super.init()
}
```

Save the file and run all unit tests using the Product ➤ Test menu item. Your new test case will now pass (see Figure 4-11).

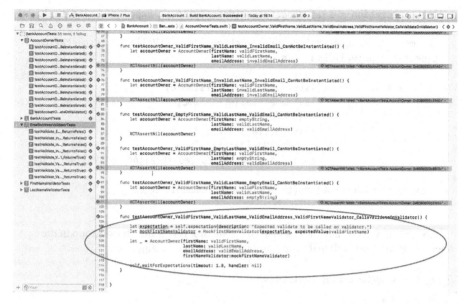

Figure 4-11. *Xcode Test Navigator with Passing and Failing Tests*

This new test case that you have just completed verifies that the first name validator object integrates correctly with the AccountOwner object.

Now, let us create a couple of additional test cases to verify the integration of the last name and email address validator objects with the AccountOwner object. Add the following two additional test cases to the AccountOwnerTests.swift file:

```swift
func testAccountOwner_ValidFirstName_ValidLastName_ValidEmailAddress_
ValidLastNameValidator_CallsValidateOnValidator() {

    let expectation = self.expectation(description: "Expected validate to be
    called on validator.")
    let mockLastNameValidator = MockLastNameValidator(expectation,
    expectedValue:validLastName)

    let _ = AccountOwner(firstName: validFirstName,
                    lastName: validLastName,
                    emailAddress: validEmailAddress,
                    firstNameValidator:nil,
                    lastNameValidator:mockLastNameValidator)

    self.waitForExpectations(timeout: 1.0, handler: nil)
}

func testAccountOwner_ValidFirstName_ValidLastName_ValidEmailAddress_
ValidEmailAddressValidator_CallsValidateOnValidator() {
```

```
    let expectation = self.expectation(description: "Expected validate to be
    called on validator.")
    let mockEmailAddressValidator = MockEmailAddressValidator(expectation,
    expectedValue:validEmailAddress)

    let _ = AccountOwner(firstName: validFirstName,
                         lastName: validLastName,
                         emailAddress: validEmailAddress,
                         firstNameValidator:nil,
                         lastNameValidator:nil,
                         emailAddressValidator:mockEmailAddressValidator)

    self.waitForExpectations(timeout: 1.0, handler: nil)
}
```

Create a new class called MockLastNameValidator under the Mocks group in the project navigator and update its implementation to match Listing 4-9.

Listing 4-9. MockLastNameValidator.swift

```
import Foundation
import XCTest

class MockLastNameValidator: LastNameValidator {

    private var expectation:XCTestExpectation?
    private var expectedValue:String?

    init(_ expectation:XCTestExpectation, expectedValue:String) {
        self.expectation = expectation
        self.expectedValue = expectedValue
        super.init()
    }

    override func validate(_ value:String) -> Bool {

        if let expectation = self.expectation,
            let expectedValue = self.expectedValue {
            if value.compare(expectedValue) == .orderedSame {
                expectation.fulfill()
            }
        }

        return super.validate(value)
    }
}
```

Create a new class called MockEmailAddressValidator under the Mocks group in the project navigator and update its implementation to match Listing 4-10.

Listing 4-10. MockEmailAddressValidator.swift

```swift
import Foundation
import XCTest

class MockEmailAddressValidator: EmailAddressValidator {

    private var expectation:XCTestExpectation?
    private var expectedValue:String?

    init(_ expectation:XCTestExpectation, expectedValue:String) {
        self.expectation = expectation
        self.expectedValue = expectedValue
        super.init()
    }

    override func validate(_ value:String) -> Bool {

        if let expectation = self.expectation,
            let expectedValue = self.expectedValue {
            if value.compare(expectedValue) == .orderedSame {
                expectation.fulfill()
            }
        }

        return super.validate(value)
    }

}
```

Modify the implementation of the init? method of the AccountOwner class to match:

```swift
import Foundation

class AccountOwner: NSObject {

    var firstName:String?
    var lastName:String?
    var emailAddress:String?

    init?(firstName:String, lastName:String, emailAddress:String,
        firstNameValidator:FirstNameValidator? = nil,
        lastNameValidator:LastNameValidator? = nil,
        emailAddressValidator:EmailAddressValidator? = nil) {
```

```
        let validator1 = firstNameValidator ?? FirstNameValidator()
        if validator1.validate(firstName) == false {
            return nil
        }

        let validator2 = lastNameValidator ?? LastNameValidator()
        if validator2.validate(lastName) == false {
            return nil
        }

        let validator3 = emailAddressValidator ?? EmailAddressValidator()
        if validator3.validate(emailAddress) == false {
            return nil
        }

        super.init()
    }
}
```

Save the file and run all unit tests using the Product ➤ Test menu item. You will notice that all tests written so far now pass, including the test in AccountOwner tests that have been failing up until this point (see Figure 4-12).

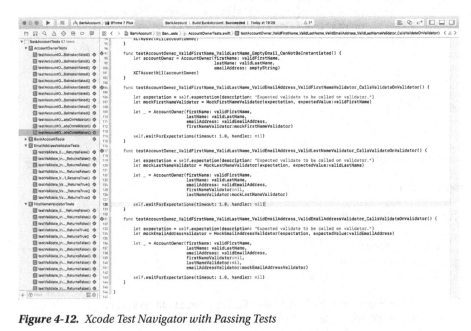

Figure 4-12. Xcode Test Navigator with Passing Tests

The AccountOwner class is almost ready, but for one small missing feature: the values of first name, last name, and email address that are provided in the initializer, if, should be copied over to instance variables.

Add the following three additional test cases to the AccountOwnerTests.swift file:

```swift
func testAccountOwner_ValidFirstName_ValidLastName_ValidEmailAddress_
CopiesFirstNameToIVAR() {

    let accountOwner = AccountOwner(firstName: validFirstName,
                        lastName: validLastName,
                        emailAddress: validEmailAddress)

    let isEqual = accountOwner!.firstName.compare(validFirstName) ==
    .orderedSame
    XCTAssertTrue(isEqual)
}

func testAccountOwner_ValidFirstName_ValidLastName_ValidEmailAddress_
CopiesLastNameToIVAR() {

    let accountOwner = AccountOwner(firstName: validFirstName,
                            lastName: validLastName,
                            emailAddress: validEmailAddress)

    let isEqual = accountOwner!.lastName.compare(validLastName) ==
    .orderedSame
    XCTAssertTrue(isEqual)
}

func testAccountOwner_ValidFirstName_ValidLastName_ValidEmailAddress_
CopiesEmailAddressToIVAR() {

    let accountOwner = AccountOwner(firstName: validFirstName,
                            lastName: validLastName,
                            emailAddress: validEmailAddress)

    let isEqual = accountOwner!.emailAddress.compare(validEmailAddress) ==
    .orderedSame
    XCTAssertTrue(isEqual)
}
```

Declare the following variables in the AccountOwner class:

```swift
var firstName:String
var lastName:String
var emailAddress:String
```

Add the following lines of code to the implementation of the init? method of the AccountOwner class:

```
self.firstName = firstName
self.lastName = lastName
self.emailAddress = emailAddress
```

Save the file and run all unit tests using the Product ➤ Test menu item. You will notice that all tests pass. This concludes the development of the AccountOwner class. In the next section we will develop the Transaction class using TDD techniques.

The Transaction Class

A Transaction object represents a sum of money either entering or leaving the bank account. Table 4-2 lists the desired member variables and methods of the Transaction class:

Table 4-2. *Transaction variables and methods*

Item	Type	Description
var txDescription:String	Variable	Contains a textual description of the transaction. Should be up to 20 characters in length, cannot be empty.
var date:NSDate	Variable	Represents a valid date.
var isIncoming:Bool	Variable	True if the transaction represents a sum of money being credited into the account.
var amount:String	Variable	Represents the transaction amount. Can only include numbers and the period (.) character.
init?(description:String, date:NSDate, isIncoming:Bool, amount:String)	Method	Allows other code to create Transaction instances.

The approach to developing the Transaction class will be very similar to the AccountOwner class. You will need to create tests that test verify the behavior of the initializer and any validator objects. In this particular case, validator objects will be needed for the description and the amount. There is no need to validate the isIncoming property. You may wish to add some validation around the range of dates that may be allowed.

The complete Transaction class is provided in Listing 4-11. If you would like to examine the code for the tests and the validator objects, download the finished project anonymously from github using the following URL:

```
https://github.com/asmtechnology/Lesson04.iOSTesting.2017.Apress.git
```

Listing 4-11. Transaction.swift

```swift
import Foundation

class Transaction: NSObject {

    var txDescription:String
    var date:NSDate
    var isIncoming:Bool
    var amount:String

    init?(txDescription:String, date:NSDate, isIncoming:Bool, amount:String,
        descriptionValidator:TransactionDescriptionValidator? = nil,
        amountValidator:AmountValidator? = nil) {

        let validator1 = descriptionValidator ?? TransactionDescriptionValidator()
        if validator1.validate(txDescription) == false {
            return nil
        }

        let validator2 = amountValidator ?? AmountValidator()
        if validator2.validate(amount) == false {
            return nil
        }

        self.txDescription = txDescription
        self.date = date
        self.isIncoming = isIncoming
        self.amount = amount
    }

}
```

The BankAccount Class

A BankAccount object represents a current or savings bank account in the context of our app. Table 4-3 lists the desired member variables and methods of the BankAccount class.

Table 4-3. *Transaction variables and methods*

Item	Type	Description
`var accountName:String`	Variable	Contains a textual description of the account. Should be up to 20 characters in length, cannot be empty. Special characters are allowed.
`var accountNumber:String`	Variable	Contains a numeric account number, must be a 9-digit number, no white space or special characters are permitted.
`var sortingCode:String`	Variable	Contains a six digit number that identifies a branch. No white space or special characters are permitted. Must begin with either 40 or 49.
`var accountType:AccountType`	Variable	An enumerated value that represents the account type. Can be either currentAccount or savingsAccount.
`var transactions:[Transaction]`	Variable	An array of transactions.
`var owners:[AccountOwner]`	Variable	An array of account owners. A bank account must have at least one owner, and can have up to 2 account owners.
`init?(accountName:String, accountNumber:String, sortingCode:String, accountType:AccountType, owners:[AccountOwner])`	Method	Allows other code to create BankAccount instances.

The approach to developing the BankAccount class will be very similar to the AccountOwner class. You will need to create tests that test verify the behavior of the initializer and any validator objects. In this particular case, validator objects will be needed for the accountName, accountNumber, and sortingCode properties.

The complete BankAccount class is provided in Listing 4-12. If you would like to examine the code for the tests and the validator objects, download the finished project anonymously from github using the following URL:

```
https://github.com/asmtechnology/Lesson04.iOSTesting.2017.Apress.git
```

Listing 4-12. BankAccount.swift

```
import Foundation

enum AccountType {
    case currentAccount
```

```
        case savingsAccount
}

class BankAccount: NSObject {

    var accountName:String
    var accountNumber:String
    var sortingCode:String
    var accountType:AccountType
    var transactions:[Transaction]
    var owners:[AccountOwner]

    init?(accountName:String,
          accountNumber:String,
          sortingCode:String,
          accountType:AccountType,
          owners:[AccountOwner],
          accountNameValidator:AccountNameValidator? = nil,
          accountNumberValidator:AccountNumberValidator? = nil,
          sortingCodeValidator:SortingCodeValidator? = nil) {

        let validator1 = accountNameValidator ?? AccountNameValidator()
        if validator1.validate(accountName) == false {
            return nil
        }

        let validator2 = accountNumberValidator ?? AccountNumberValidator()
        if validator2.validate(accountNumber) == false {
            return nil
        }

        let validator3 = sortingCodeValidator ?? SortingCodeValidator()
        if validator3.validate(sortingCode) == false {
            return nil
        }

        if owners.count == 0 {
            return nil
        }

        self.accountName = accountName
        self.accountNumber = accountNumber
        self.sortingCode = sortingCode
        self.accountType = accountType
        self.owners = owners
        self.transactions = [Transaction]()
    }

}
```

Testing Core Data

The model objects built so far in this chapter all have one thing in common – they are all NSObject subclasses. This is quite common in many iOS Apps; however, an increasing number of apps are using object persistence frameworks like Core Data to both represent and persist the model data.

A detailed discussion of Core Data is outside the scope of this book. Testing the model layer is perhaps one of the biggest hurdles faced by developers who have used Core Data in the model layer.

Core Data is designed to persist your model objects along with their relationships into a database. For Core Data to be able to achieve its objectives, it introduces a plethora of classes such as NSManagedObject, NSManagedObjectContext, NSManagedObjectModel, NSPersistentStoreCoordintor, and also requires that you let Core Data manage the life cycle of your model objects.

With Core Data managing the life cycle of your model objects, you can not simply instantiate your model objects using a designated or convenience initializers; instead you need to request a managed object context to instantiate the object.

While the managed object context itself can be conveniently instantiated with a designated initializer, one of the parameters to this initializer is a persistent store coordinator that requires you to provide the path to a SQLite database file.

Instantiating persistent store coordinators in your applications code is a very common thing to do; however to instantiate one of these in a unit test case, you will need to include a database in the test target. Including a database in a test target is strictly frowned upon because tests that read and write from a database can easily create dependencies between test cases.

It is easy to imagine a test case writing some data into a database, and another reading some of the data. This type of behavior creates tight coupling between tests, the precise execution order of the tests become important, and the tests are not independent anymore. It is far worse when this type of behavior occurs inadvertently.

Fortunately Core Data has an often overlooked feature called in-memory stores that can be used within tests without including an SQLlite file in the test target. An in-memory store is a RAM-based database, and is commonly used to implement caching strategies. One of the key properties of an in-memory store is that they can be destroyed and re-created to an initial state with little performance overhead.

The following code snippet shows how you can create managed object context that uses an in-memory persistent store coordinator:

```
func inMemoryManagedObjectContext() -> NSManagedObjectContext? {

    guard let managedObjectModel = NSManagedObjectModel.
    mergedModel(from:[Bundle.main]) else {
        return nil
    }

    let persistentStoreCoordinator = NSPersistentStoreCoordinator(managedObj
    ectModel: managedObjectModel)
    do {
```

```
    try persistentStoreCoordinator.addPersistentStore(ofType:
    NSInMemoryStoreType,

                                        configurationName: nil,
                                        at: nil,
                                        options: nil)
} catch {
    print("Failed to create in-memory persistent store.")
    return nil
}

let managedObjectContext = NSManagedObjectContext(concurrencyType:
.mainQueueConcurrencyType)
managedObjectContext.persistentStoreCoordinator =
persistentStoreCoordinator

return managedObjectContext
}
```

You can make use of this method in your test case's setup method to create managed object context backed by an in-memory store. You can then use this managed object context to instantiate Core Data objects within your tests.

Summary

In this chapter you have created the model layer of an application using Test-Driven techniques. For each component of the model layer, you first created a set of test cases, and then built the corresponding model layer class to ensure the test cases pass.

You have also learned to create validator objects that validate the content of the model layer objects, and how to inject these validator objects as dependencies into model layer objects.

Finally, you learned to create mock objects in Swift and use the mock objects to verify the integration between model layer objects and injected validator objects.

CHAPTER 5

■ ■ ■

Applying TDD to View Controllers

This chapter will examine the process of building an iOS app based on the Single View Controller project template using TDD techniques. The app will have two view controllers that provide sign up and login screen functionality. This app will be built using the MVVM application architecture.

Figure 5-1 depicts the user interface of the finished application.

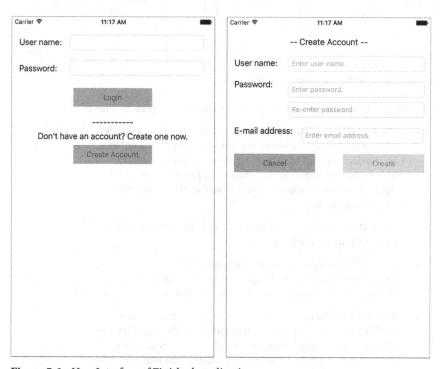

Figure 5-1. *User Interface of Finished application*

© Abhishek Mishra 2017
A. Mishra, *iOS Code Testing*, DOI 10.1007/978-1-4842-2689-6_5

The complete source code for the app can be downloaded anonymously from github using the following URL:

```
https://github.com/asmtechnology/Lesson05.iOSTesting.2017.Apress.git
```

Application Architecture

The application architecture consists of four distinct layers (see Figure 5-2).

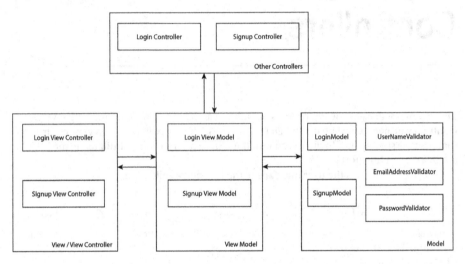

Figure 5-2. *LoginForm Application Architecture*

Following is a brief description of the layers and the component classes:

- **Model Layer:** Consists of the LoginModel and SignupModel classes, instances of which are used to store the data entered by the user on the Login and Signup screens respectively. This layer also contains three classes to handle field validation – UserNameValidator, PasswordValidator, and EmailAddressValidator.

- **View Model Layer:** Consists of the LoginViewModel and SignupViewModel classes.

- **View/View Controller Layer:** Consists of the LoginViewController and SignupViewController classes. These classes provide the user interface for the app.

- **Other Controllers Layer:** Consists of the LoginController and SignupController classes that carry out the actual process of login and signup. In this project, these classes are stub implementations. In a real-world scenario, you will write code in these classes to connect to your back-end web services and perform the necessary steps required to log in/sign up.

Creating the Xcode Project

Let us start by creating a new Xcode project. Launch Xcode and create a new iOS project based on the Single View Application template (see Figure 5-3).

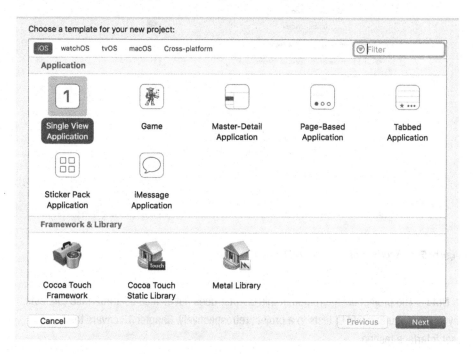

Figure 5-3. *Xcode Project Template Dialog Box*

Use the following options while creating the new project (see Figure 5-4):

- **Product Name:** LoginForm
- **Team:** None
- **Organization Name:** Provide a suitable name
- **Organization Identifier:** Provide a suitable identifier
- **Language:** Swift
- **Devices:** iPhone
- **Use Core Data:** Unchecked
- **Include Unit Tests:** Checked
- **Include UI Tests:** Unchecked

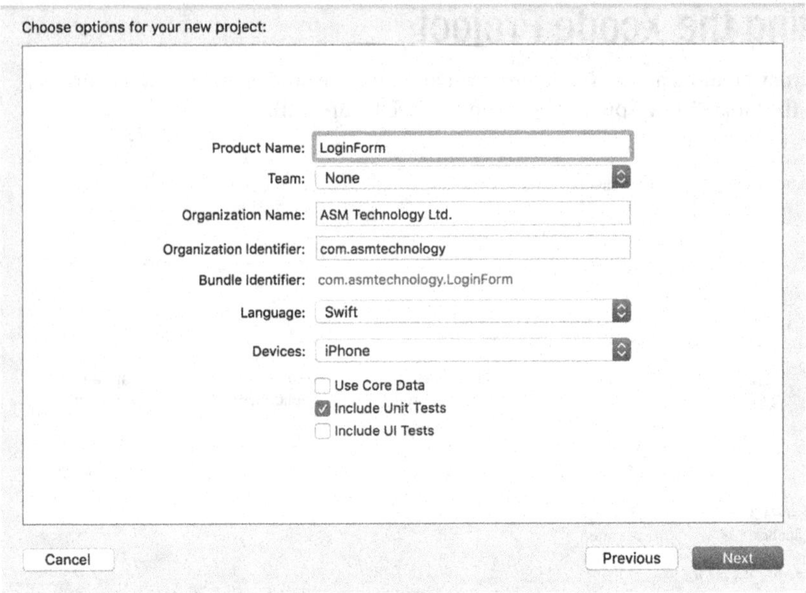

Figure 5-4. *Xcode Project Options Dialog Box*

■ **Note** The project being created in this chapter does not include user interface (UI) tests. If you wish, you can add UI tests to a project retrospectively. Chapter 13 covers the topic of user interface testing.

Save the project to a suitable location on your computer and click Create. Since this project will contain several new classes, it will be a good idea to place class files under appropriate groups within the project navigator.

Create the following groups in the Xcode project navigator, under the LoginForm folder:

- View

- Model

- ViewModel

- Protocols

Building the User Interface Layer

The user interface for this application consists of two storyboard scenes and a segue between the scenes (see Figure 5-5).

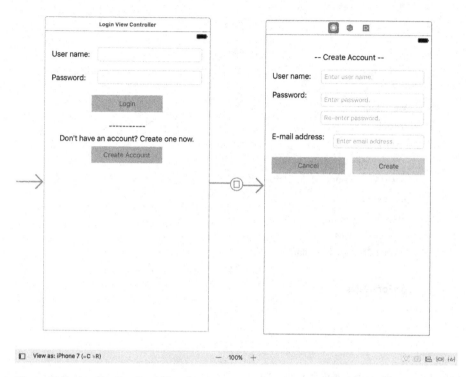

Figure 5-5. Application Storyboard

The new project that you have created has a default view controller that we will not use. Delete the ViewController.swift file from the project navigator, and create two new UIViewController subclasses under the View group called:

- LoginViewController, and

- SignupViewController.

The project navigator should resemble Figure 5-6.

Figure 5-6. LoginForm Project Navigator

Building the Login View Controller Scene

Open the Main.storyboard file and click on the default scene in the storyboard.
Use the Identity Inspector to change the class associated with the default scene to
LoginViewController (see Figure 5-7).

Figure 5-7. *Custom View Controller class setup in the Identity Inspector*

Add two text fields, two buttons, and four labels to the default storyboard scene and arrange them to resemble Figure 5-8. Create appropriate constraints for the elements to maintain this arrangement on different screen sizes.

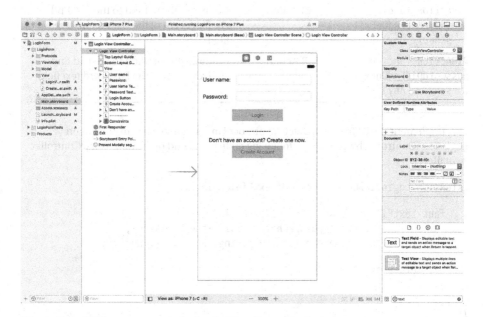

Figure 5-8. *UI Components on the Login View Controller Scene*

107

Using the storyboard, set up the LoginViewController class to act as the delegate for the two text fields. Table 5-1 lists the outlets and action methods that you need to create in the LoginViewController class along with their associated user interface elements.

Table 5-1. *Login view controller outlets and actions*

Name	Type	Description
@IBOutlet weak var userNameTextField: UITextField!	IB Outlet	Connect this outlet to the User name text field of the storyboard scene.
@IBOutlet weak var passwordTextField: UITextField!	IB Outlet	Connect this outlet to the Password text field of the storyboard scene.
@IBOutlet weak var loginButton: UIButton!	IB Outlet	Connect this outlet to the Login button of the storyboard scene.
@IBOutlet weak var createAccountButton: UIButton!	IB Outlet	Connect this outlet to the Create Account button of the storyboard scene.
@IBAction func login (_ sender: Any)	IB Action	Connect this method to the Touch Up Inside event of the Login button.
@IBAction func createAccount (_ sender: Any)	IB Action	Connect this method to the Touch Up Inside event of the Create Account button.
@IBAction func userNameDidEndOnExit (_ sender: Any)	IB Action	Connect this method to the Did End On Exit event of the User name text field.
@IBAction func passwordDidEndOnExit (_ sender: Any)	IB Action	Connect this method to the Did End On Exit event of the Password text field.

Implement the UITextFieldDelegate protocol in a separate class extension on LoginViewController by adding the following code to the end of the LoginViewController. swift file:

```
extension LoginViewController: UITextFieldDelegate {

    func textField(_ textField: UITextField,
                shouldChangeCharactersIn range: NSRange,
                replacementString string: String) -> Bool {

        return true
    }

}
```

The above snippet contains a bare-bones implementation of the textField(_, shouldChangeCharactersIn, replacementString) delegate method from UITextFieldDelegate. The code in LoginViewController.swift should now resemble Listing 5-1.

Listing 5-1. LoginViewController.swift

```swift
import UIKit

class LoginViewController: UIViewController {

    @IBOutlet weak var userNameTextField: UITextField!
    @IBOutlet weak var passwordTextField: UITextField!
    @IBOutlet weak var loginButton: UIButton!
    @IBOutlet weak var createAccountButton: UIButton!

    override func viewDidLoad() {
        super.viewDidLoad()

    }

    override func didReceiveMemoryWarning() {
        super.didReceiveMemoryWarning()
    }

    @IBAction func login(_ sender: Any) {

    }

    @IBAction func createAccount(_ sender: Any) {

    }

    @IBAction func userNameDidEndOnExit(_ sender: Any) {

    }

    @IBAction func passwordDidEndOnExit(_ sender: Any) {

    }
}

extension LoginViewController: UITextFieldDelegate {

    func textField(_ textField: UITextField,
                   shouldChangeCharactersIn range: NSRange,
                   replacementString string: String) -> Bool {

        return true
    }

}
```

Building the Signup View Controller Scene

Drag and drop a new view controller from the Object Library onto the storyboard, and place the new view controller scene beside the default storyboard scene.

Use the Identity Inspector to change the class associated with the new view controller scene to SignupViewController.

Add four text fields, four labels, and two buttons to the new storyboard scene and arrange them to resemble Figure 5-9. Create appropriate constraints for the elements to maintain this arrangement on different screen sizes.

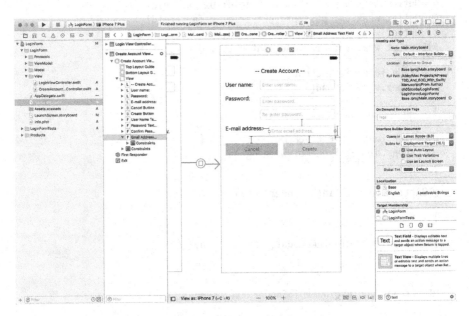

Figure 5-9. *UI Components on the Signup View Controller Scene*

Using the storyboard, set up the SignupViewController class to act as the delegate for the four text fields. Table 5-2 lists the outlets and action methods that must be created in the SignupViewController class along with their associated user interface elements.

Table 5-2. Signup view controller outlets and actions

Name	Type	Description
`@IBOutlet weak var userNameTextField: UITextField!`	IB Outlet	Connect this outlet to the User name text field of the storyboard scene.
`@IBOutlet weak var passwordTextField: UITextField!`	IB Outlet	Connect this outlet to the Password text field of the storyboard scene.
`@IBOutlet weak var confirmPasswordTextField: UITextField!`	IB Outlet	Connect this outlet to the Re-enter password text field of the storyboard scene.
`@IBOutlet weak var emailAddressTextField: UITextField!`	IB Outlet	Connect this outlet to the email address text field of the storyboard scene.
`@IBOutlet weak var createButton: UIButton!`	IB Outlet	Connect this outlet to the Create button of the storyboard scene.
`@IBOutlet weak var cancelButton: UIButton!`	IB Outlet	Connect this outlet to the Cancel button of the storyboard scene.
`@IBAction func create (_ sender: Any)`	IB Action	Connect this method to the Touch Up Inside event of the Create button.
`@IBAction func cancel(_ sender: Any)`	IB Action	Connect this method to the Touch Up Inside event of the Cancel button.
`@IBAction func userNameDidEndOnExit(_ sender: Any)`	IB Action	Connect this method to the Did End On Exit event of the User name text field.
`@IBAction func passwordDidEndOnExit(_ sender: Any)`	IB Action	Connect this method to the Did End On Exit event of the Password text field.
`@IBAction func confirmPasswordDidEndOnExit(_ sender: Any)`	IB Action	Connect this method to the Did End On Exit event of the Re-enter password text field.
`@IBAction func emailAddressDidEndOnExit(_ sender: Any)`	IB Action	Connect this method to the Did End On Exit event of the email address text field.

Implement the UITextFieldDelegate protocol in a separate class extension on SignupViewController by adding the following code to the end of the SignupViewController.swift file:

```
extension SignupViewController: UITextFieldDelegate {

    func textField(_ textField: UITextField,
                   shouldChangeCharactersIn range: NSRange,
                   replacementString string: String) -> Bool {

        return true
    }

}
```

The above snippet contains a bare-bones implementation of the textField(_, shouldChangeCharactersIn, replacementString) delegate method from UITextFieldDelegate. The code in SignupViewController.swift should now resemble Listing 5-2.

Listing 5-2. SignupViewController.swift

```
import UIKit

class SignupViewController: UIViewController {

    @IBOutlet weak var userNameTextField: UITextField!
    @IBOutlet weak var passwordTextField: UITextField!
    @IBOutlet weak var confirmPasswordTextField: UITextField!
    @IBOutlet weak var emailAddressTextField: UITextField!
    @IBOutlet weak var createButton: UIButton!
    @IBOutlet weak var cancelButton: UIButton!

    override func viewDidLoad() {
        super.viewDidLoad()
    }

    override func didReceiveMemoryWarning() {
        super.didReceiveMemoryWarning()
    }

    @IBAction func create(_ sender: Any) {

    }

    @IBAction func cancel(_ sender: Any) {

    }
```

```swift
@IBAction func userNameDidEndOnExit(_ sender: Any) {

}

@IBAction func passwordDidEndOnExit(_ sender: Any) {

}

@IBAction func confirmPasswordDidEndOnExit(_ sender: Any) {

}

@IBAction func emailAddressDidEndOnExit(_ sender: Any) {

}

}

extension SignupViewController: UITextFieldDelegate {

    func textField(_ textField: UITextField,
                   shouldChangeCharactersIn range: NSRange,
                   replacementString string: String) -> Bool {

        return true
    }

}
```

Creating a Segue Between the Login Scene and the Signup Scene

Create a Present Modally segue from the login view controller scene to the create account view controller scene of the storyboard. With the segue selected, switch to the Attributes Inspector and set the value of the Identifier attribute to presentCreate Account (see Figure 5-10).

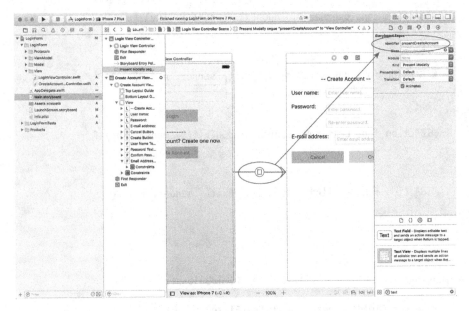

Figure 5-10. *Setting up the Identifier Attribute of a Segue*

This concludes the topic of building the user interface for the app. You may be wondering why TDD techniques have not been applied until this point in this project. There are a couple of reasons for this:

1. We are building the user interface of the app using storyboards, and wiring up outlets and actions through interface builder. Xcode does not provide any convenient method to build this part of the application using a test-first approach.

2. You could opt to build the user interface programmatically instead of using storyboards. However, there is very little benefit to be gained from building the user interface with TDD techniques.

3. The UI of an app can change frequently and can easily be tested using specialized UI test techniques or manual testing. Using a TDD-based approach to building the UI is wasted effort as you will need to modify your tests with every small UI change made to the app.

4. If you come from a "tests create living documentation for a project" mindset, then you will find it hard to justify how unit tests can create better documentation for the user interface of the app over a simple screen shot.

Building the Model Layer

There are two model classes that we need to build - LoginModel and SignupModel. In an app as simple as the one we are building you may be tempted to ask why do we need separate model classes at all? We could simply choose to use a simple dictionary of strings to represent the model.

The reason to have separate model classes is to accommodate a certain minimal level of data validation into the model. While the validation logic itself may be moved to a separate specialized validator object, such validator objects will conceptually reside in the model layer alongside the model objects.

The LoginModel Class

The LoginModel class contains properties that store the information the user has entered into the fields of the login screen of the app. When a user taps the login button on the user interface, the view model will build a LoginModel instance and pass this instance to a specialized controller class that handles login-specific logic. The specialized login controller class may perhaps connect to back-end services and log in using the credentials provided.

Using a dedicated model object to store the values entered by the user in the fields of the login screen decouples the logic in the login controller from the user interface. Table 5-3 lists the desired properties and methods of the LoginModel class.

Table 5-3. LoginModel Properties and Methods

Item	Type	Description
var userName:String	Variable	Should be between 2 and 10 characters in length, with no white space. Underscores are allowed. Special characters are not permitted.
var password:String	Variable	Should be between 6 and 10 characters in length, with no white space. Must have at least one uppercase letter, one lowercase letter, and one number.
init?(userName:String, password:String)	Method	Allows other code to create LoginModel instances.

The approach to developing the LoginModel class will be very similar to the model layer classes that were developed in Chapter 4. You will need to create tests that test verify the behavior of the initializer and any validator objects.

The complete LoginModel class is shown in Listing 5-3. If you would like to examine the code for the tests and the validator objects, download the finished project anonymously from github using the following URL:

```
https://github.com/asmtechnology/Lesson05.iOSTesting.2017.Apress.git
```

Listing 5-3. LoginModel.swift

```
import Foundation

class LoginModel: NSObject {

    var userName:String
    var password:String

    init?(userName:String, password:String,
          userNameValidator:UserNameValidator? = nil,
          passwordValidator:PasswordValidator? = nil) {

        let validator1 = userNameValidator ?? UserNameValidator()
        if validator1.validate(userName) == false {
            return nil
        }

        let validator2 = passwordValidator ?? PasswordValidator()
        if validator2.validate(password) == false {
            return nil
        }

        self.userName = userName
        self.password = password

        super.init()
    }
}
```

The SignupModel Class

The SignupModel class contains properties that store the information that the user has entered into the fields of the create account screen. When the user taps the create button on the user interface, the view model will build a SignupModel instance and pass this instance to a specialized controller class that contains signup logic. The specialized signup controller class may perhaps connect to back-end services and create a new account on a server-side database using the credentials provided. Table 5-4 lists the desired properties and methods of the SignupModel class.

Table 5-4. *SignupModel Properties and Methods*

Item	Type	Description
var userName:String	Variable	Should be between 2 and 10 characters in length, with no numbers or white space. Underscores are allowed. Special characters are not permitted.
var password:String	Variable	Should be between 2 and 10 characters in length, with no white space.
var emailAddress:String	Variable	Must be a valid email address.
init?(userName:String, password:String, emailAddress:String)	Method	Allows other code to create SignupModel instances.

The approach to developing the SignupModel class will be very similar to the model layer classes that were developed in Chapter 4. You will need to create tests that test verify the behavior of the initializer and any validator objects.

The complete SignupModel class is provided in Listing 5-4. If you would like to examine the code for the tests and the validator objects, download the finished project anonymously from github using the following URL:

```
https://github.com/asmtechnology/Lesson05.iOSTesting.2017.Apress.git
```

Listing 5-4. SignupModel.swift

```swift
import Foundation

class SignupModel: NSObject {

    var userName:String
    var password:String
    var emailAddress:String

    init?(userName:String, password:String, emailAddress:String,
        userNameValidator:UserNameValidator? = nil,
        passwordValidator:PasswordValidator? = nil,
        emailAddressValidator:EmailAddressValidator? = nil) {

        let validator1 = userNameValidator ?? UserNameValidator()
        if validator1.validate(userName) == false {
            return nil
        }

        let validator2 = passwordValidator ?? PasswordValidator()
        if validator2.validate(password) == false {
            return nil
        }
```

```
    let validator3 = emailAddressValidator ?? EmailAddressValidator()
    if validator3.validate(emailAddress) == false {
        return nil
    }

    self.userName = userName
    self.password = password
    self.emailAddress = emailAddress

    super.init()
  }

}
```

Building the ViewModel Layer

There are two view model classes that we need to build - LoginViewModel and SignupViewModel. These correspond to the LoginViewController and SignupViewController classes respectively. The view model will hold a strong reference to model layer objects and use protocols to establish an interface through which it can communicate with the view controller.

The LoginViewModel Class

The LoginViewModel class represents the view model between the LoginViewController class and the LoginModel class.

We will adopt a TDD approach to developing the login view model class. Create a new iOS Unit Test Case class called LoginViewModelTests under the LoginFormTests group of the project explorer (see Figure 5-11).

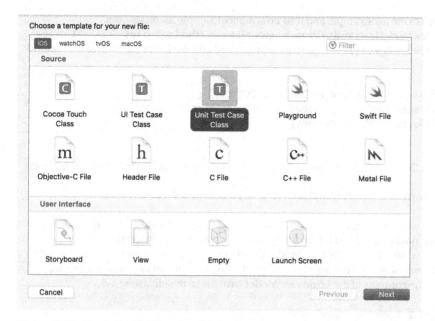

Figure 5-11. Xcode Project Template Dialog Box

Select the LoginViewModelTests.swift file in the project explorer and use the file inspector to ensure that the file is included in the LoginFormTests target and not the LoginForm target (see Figure 5-12). If the file inspector is not visible, View ➤ Utilities ➤ Show File Inspector menu item.

Figure 5-12. LoginViewModelTests Target Membership

Delete the testExample and testPerformanceExample methods from LoginViewModelTests.swift. Create a new unit test method called `testInit_ValidView_InstantiatesObject()`in a separate extension and add the following code to the method body:

```
func testInit_ValidView_InstantiatesObject() {
    let viewModel = LoginViewModel(view:mockLoginViewController!)
    XCTAssertNotNil(viewModel)
}
```

Add the following variable declaration to the top of the LoginViewModelTests class:

```
fileprivate var mockLoginViewController:MockLoginViewController?
```

You will notice that this code fails to compile; that is because the LoginViewModel class has not been created yet. To fix this failure, create a new class called LoginViewModel under the ViewModel group in the project navigator. Ensure the LoginViewModel class is a member of both the LoginForm and LoginFormTests target. Update the contents of the LoginViewModel.swift file to match Listing 5-5.

Listing 5-5. LoginViewModel.swift

```
import Foundation

class LoginViewModel: NSObject {

    weak var view:LoginViewControllerProtocol?

    init(view:LoginViewControllerProtocol) {
        super.init()
        self.view = view
    }

}
```

The initializer for the LoginViewModel class takes a reference to the view. Note that the type of the view parameter is LoginViewControllerProtocol and not LoginViewController.

The view model makes use of a protocol to create a loosely coupled relationship with the view. As far as the view model is concerned, any class that implements the LoginViewControllerProtocol protocol can be used as the view. This loose coupling with the view makes the view model easy to instantiate in a unit test, independent of a view controller.

Create a new Swift file called LoginViewControllerProtocol (see Figure 5-13) under the Protocols group of the project explorer, and ensure the new file is a member of both the LoginFormTests and LoginForm targets.

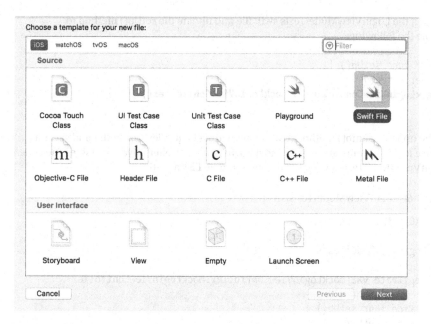

Figure 5-13. *Xcode File Template Dialog Box*

Update the code in LoginViewControllerProtocol to resemble the following:

```
import Foundation

protocol LoginViewControllerProtocol : class {

}
```

Create a new group called Mocks under the LoginFormTests group, and create a new Swift class called MockLoginViewController under the Mocks group. Ensure the MockLoginViewController.swift file is only a member of the LoginFormTests target.

Update the code in MockLoginViewController.swift to resemble the following:

```
import UIKit
import XCTest

class MockLoginViewController : LoginViewControllerProtocol {

}
```

Open the LoginViewModelTests.swift file and update the setUp() method to resemble the following:

```
override func setUp() {
    super.setUp()
    mockLoginViewController = MockLoginViewController()
}
```

The updated setup() method instantiates a MockLoginViewController and saves a reference to this new instance in the mockLoginViewController private variable. The code in LoginViewModelTests.swift should now resemble Listing 5-6.

Listing 5-6. LoginViewModelTests.swift

```
import XCTest

class LoginViewModelTests: XCTestCase {

    fileprivate var mockLoginViewController:MockLoginViewController?

    override func setUp() {
        super.setUp()
        mockLoginViewController = MockLoginViewController()
    }

    override func tearDown() {
        super.tearDown()
    }

}

// MARK: initialization tests
extension LoginViewModelTests {

    func testInit_ValidView_InstantiatesObject() {
        let viewModel = LoginViewModel(view:mockLoginViewController!)
        XCTAssertNotNil(viewModel)
    }

}
```

Save the file and run all unit tests using the Product ➤ Test menu item. You will see that the unit test you have added in LoginViewModelTests.swift has passed (see Figure 5-14).

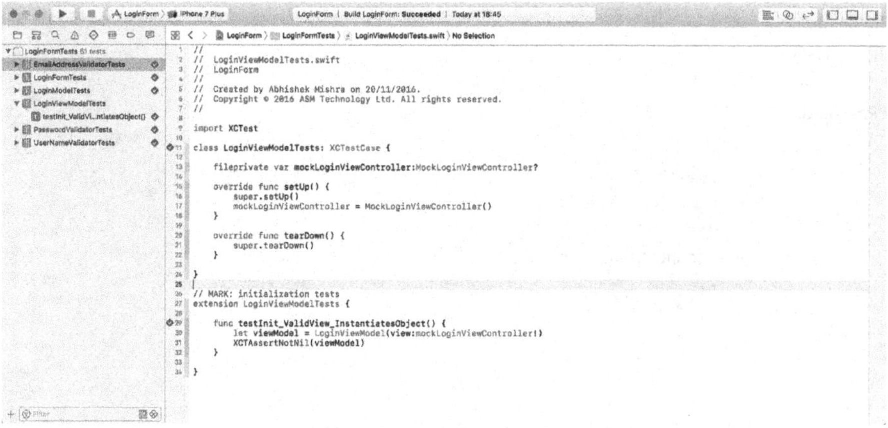

Figure 5-14. *Basic tests for the Login View Model*

The view model test created so far verifies that a view model can be instantiated; and in order to make this test pass you created a view model class, a protocol, and a mock class.

The next test you will write will verify that the view model saves a reference to the view that was injected into the initializer, in an instance variable. Create a new unit test method called testInit_ValidView_CopiesViewToIvar() under the previous test method and add the following code to the method body:

```
func testInit_ValidView_CopiesViewToIvar() {
    let viewModel = LoginViewModel(view:mockLoginViewController!)

    if let lhs = mockLoginViewController, let rhs = viewModel.view as?
    MockLoginViewController {
        XCTAssertTrue(lhs === rhs)
    }
}
```

Save the file and run all unit tests using the Product ➤ Test menu item. You will notice that all tests written so far continue to pass.

View Model – View Controller Binding

The login view model we have built so far does not do anything useful. You can instantiate it, but it has no methods that can be called. To work out what methods should be added to the view model, let us take a look at the user interface of the login view controller (see Figure 5-15).

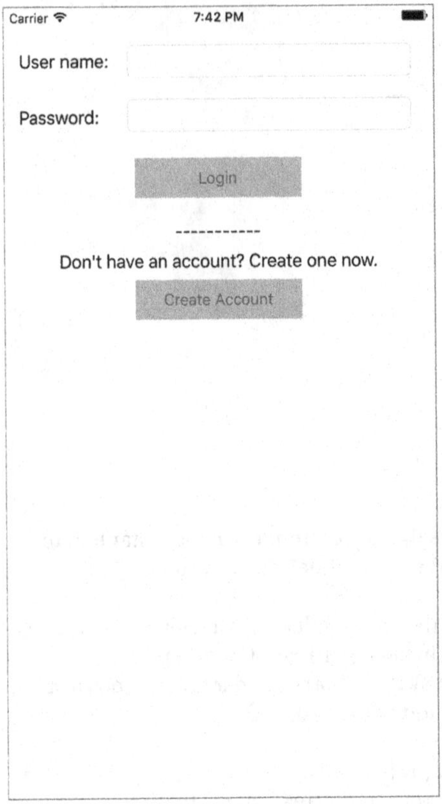

Figure 5-15. *User Interface of the Login View Controller*

You can see that the user interface of the login view controller consists of a couple of text fields and buttons. A user can use the text fields to specify his credentials and tap on the Login button, or the user can tap on the Create account button to go to a different screen of the app.

In order to make the view model useful for the view controller, you need to add methods to the view model that can be called from various life-cycle methods and event handlers in the view controller. Table 5-5 lists the methods we will add to the LoginViewModel class.

Table 5-5. *LoginViewModel Methods*

Item	Description
func performInitialViewSetup()	Should be called from the viewDidLoad() method of the view controller class. Resets user interface elements to their initial states.
func login(userName:String?, password:String?)	Called by the login view controller when the user taps on the Login button. Creates a LoginModel instance and displays an alert to the user.
func userNameDidEndOnExit()	Called by the login view controller when the didEndOnExit event is received by the user name text field. Dismisses the keyboard if it was visible.
func passwordDidEndOnExit()	Called by the login view controller when the didEndOnExit event is received by the password text field. Dismisses the keyboard if it was visible.
func userNameUpdated (_ value:String?)	Called by the login view controller as the user updates the text in the user name field. Calls a validator object to check if the text in the user name field is valid. If both the user name and password fields are valid, then the Login button will be enabled.
func passwordUpdated (_ value:String?)	Called by the login view controller as the user updates the text in the user name field. Calls a validator object to check if the text in the password field is valid. If both the user name and password fields are valid, then the Login button will be enabled.

The view model will also need to be able to update UI elements on the view controller to reflect changes in the application state or model data. Since the view model uses a protocol to bind with the view controller, you will need to add methods to the protocol that will allow the view model to request the view controller to update user interface elements. Table 5-6 lists the methods that will be added to LoginViewControllerProtocol.

Table 5-6. *LoginViewControllerProtocol Methods*

Item	Description
func clearUserNameField()	Called by the view model. The view controller should clear the contents of the user name field.
func clearPasswordField()	Called by the view model. The view controller should clear the contents of the password field.
func enableLoginButton (_ status:Bool)	Called by the view model. The view controller should enable or disable the Login button depending on the value of status.
func enableCreateAccountButton (_ status:Bool)	Called by the view model. The view controller should enable or disable the Create Account button depending on the value of status.
func hideKeyboard()	Called by the view model. The view controller should hide the keyboard if it is visible.

You will now add the desired methods to the LoginViewModel class using TDD techniques.

Building the performInitialViewSetup Method

The performInitialViewSetupMethod method should perform the following tasks:

- Clear the contents of the username field.
- Clear the contents of the password field.
- Disable the Login button.
- Enable the Create Account button.

Add the tests in Listing 5-7 to the bottom of the LoginViewModelTests.swift file:

Listing 5-7. Tests for the performInitialViewSetup method

```
// MARK: performInitialViewSetup tests
extension LoginViewModelTests {

    func testPerformInitialViewSetup_Calls_ClearUserNameField_OnViewController() {
        let expectation = self.expectation(description: "expected
        clearUserNameField() to be called")
        mockLoginViewController!.expectationForClearUserNameField = expectation

        let viewModel = LoginViewModel(view:mockLoginViewController!)
        viewModel.performInitialViewSetup()

        self.waitForExpectations(timeout: 1.0, handler: nil)
    }
```

```
func testPerformInitialViewSetup_Calls_ClearPasswordField_OnViewController() {
    let expectation = self.expectation(description: "expected
    clearPasswordField() to be called")
    mockLoginViewController!.expectationForClearPasswordField = expectation

    let viewModel = LoginViewModel(view:mockLoginViewController!)
    viewModel.performInitialViewSetup()

    self.waitForExpectations(timeout: 1.0, handler: nil)
}

func testPerformInitialViewSetup_DisablesLoginButton_OnViewController() {
    let expectation = self.expectation(description: "expected
    enableLoginButton(false) to be called")
    mockLoginViewController!.expectationForEnableLoginButton =
    (expectation, false)

    let viewModel = LoginViewModel(view:mockLoginViewController!)
    viewModel.performInitialViewSetup()

    self.waitForExpectations(timeout: 1.0, handler: nil)
}

func testPerformInitialViewSetup_EnablesCreateAccountButton_OnViewController() {
    let expectation = self.expectation(description: "expected
    enableCreateAccountButton(true) to be called")
    mockLoginViewController!.expectationForCreateAccountButton =
    (expectation, true)

    let viewModel = LoginViewModel(view:mockLoginViewController!)
    viewModel.performInitialViewSetup()

    self.waitForExpectations(timeout: 1.0, handler: nil)
}
}
```

Listing 5-7 adds four new test cases, one for each task that must be performed by performInitialViewSetup(). Since all four cases test parts of the same method, I have grouped them into in a class extension; however you can add all four test methods to the main test class definition instead of a separate extension.

To get this code to compile, you will need to make a few code changes to the project.

Add a few variable declarations and method implementations to the MockLoginViewController.swift file:

```
var expectationForClearUserNameField:XCTestExpectation?
var expectationForClearPasswordField:XCTestExpectation?
var expectationForEnableLoginButton:(XCTestExpectation, Bool)?
var expectationForCreateAccountButton:(XCTestExpectation, Bool)?
var expectationForHideKeyboard:XCTestExpectation?
```

```swift
func clearUserNameField() {
    self.expectationForClearUserNameField?.fulfill()
}

func clearPasswordField() {
    self.expectationForClearPasswordField?.fulfill()
}

func enableLoginButton(_ status:Bool) {
    if let (expectation, expectedValue) = self.expectationForEnableLoginButton {
        if status == expectedValue {
            expectation.fulfill()
        }
    }
}

func enableCreateAccountButton(_ status:Bool) {
    if let (expectation, expectedValue) = self.expectationForCreateAccountButton {
        if status == expectedValue {
            expectation.fulfill()
        }
    }
}
```

Add the following method implementation to the LoginViewModel.swift file:

```swift
func performInitialViewSetup() {
    view?.clearUserNameField()
    view?.clearPasswordField()
    view?.enableLoginButton(false)
    view?.enableCreateAccountButton(true)
}
```

Add the following method definitions to the LoginViewControllerProtocol.swift file:

```swift
func clearUserNameField()
func clearPasswordField()
func enableLoginButton(_ status:Bool)
func enableCreateAccountButton(_ status:Bool)
```

Add the following method implementations to the LoginViewController.swift file in a class extension:

```swift
extension LoginViewController : LoginViewControllerProtocol {

    func clearUserNameField() {
        self.userNameTextField.text = ""
    }
```

```swift
    func clearPasswordField() {
        self.passwordTextField.text = ""
    }

    func enableLoginButton(_ status:Bool) {
        self.loginButton.isEnabled = status
    }

    func enableCreateAccountButton(_ status:Bool) {
        self.loginButton.isEnabled = status
    }
}
```

Save the file and run all unit tests using the Product ➤ Test menu item. You will see that the unit tests you have added in LoginViewModelTests.swift have passed (see Figure 5-16).

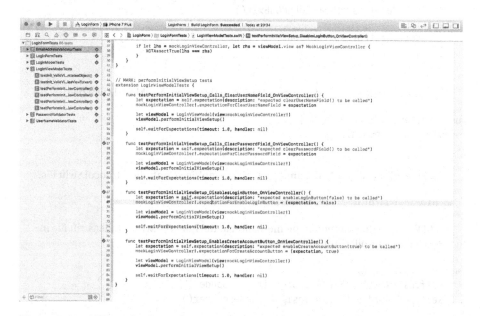

Figure 5-16. *All Tests for the performInitialViewSetup Method are Passing.*

Building the userNameDidEndOnExit Method

The userNameDidEndOnExit() method of the view model is called by the login view controller when the didEndOnExit event is received from the username text field. When this method is called, the view model asks the view controller to dismiss the keyboard if it was visible.

You may be tempted to skip the view model entirely in this scenario and simply place the code to dismiss the keyboard in the func userNameDidEndOnExit(_ sender: Any) action method of the view controller class. The proper use of the MVVM pattern requires you to remove presentation logic from the view controller and put it in the view model. Hiding the keyboard is presentation logic, and the view model dictates when the keyboard should be hidden.

Add the following code snippet to the bottom of the LoginViewModelTests.swift file:

```
// MARK: userNameDidEndOnExit tests
extension LoginViewModelTests {

    func testUserNameDidEndOnExit_Calls_HideKeyboard_OnViewController() {
        let expectation = self.expectation(description: "expected
        hideKeyboard() to be called")
        mockLoginViewController!.expectationForHideKeyboard = expectation

        let viewModel = LoginViewModel(view:mockLoginViewController!)
        viewModel.userNameDidEndOnExit()

        self.waitForExpectations(timeout: 1.0, handler: nil)
    }
}
```

Add the following method implementation to the LoginViewModel.swift file:

```
func userNameDidEndOnExit() {
    view?.hideKeyboard()
}
```

Add the following method definition to the LoginViewControllerProtocol.swift file:

```
func hideKeyboard()
```

Add the following method implementation to the LoginViewController.swift file in the LoginViewControllerProtocol extension:

```
func hideKeyboard() {
    self.userNameTextField.resignFirstResponder()
    self.passwordTextField.resignFirstResponder()
}
```

Add the following method implementation to the MockLoginViewController.swift file:

```
func hideKeyboard() {
    self.expectationForHideKeyboard?.fulfill()
}
```

Save the file and run all unit tests using the Product ➤ Test menu item. You will see that the unit tests you have added in LoginViewModelTests.swift have passed.

Building the passwordDidEndOnExit Method

The passwordDidEndOnExit() method of the view model is called by the login view controller when the didEndOnExit event is received from the password text field. When this method is called, the view model asks the view controller to dismiss the keyboard if it was visible.

Add the following code snippet to the bottom of the LoginViewModelTests.swift file:

```
// MARK: passwordDidEndOnExit tests
extension LoginViewModelTests {

    func testPasswordDidEndOnExit_Calls_HideKeyboard_OnViewController() {
        let expectation = self.expectation(description: "expected
        hideKeyboard() to be called")
        mockLoginViewController!.expectationForHideKeyboard = expectation

        let viewModel = LoginViewModel(view:mockLoginViewController!)
        viewModel.passwordDidEndOnExit()

        self.waitForExpectations(timeout: 1.0, handler: nil)
    }
}
```

Add the following method implementation to the LoginViewModel.swift file:

```
func passwordDidEndOnExit() {
    view?.hideKeyboard()
}
```

Save the file and run all unit tests using the Product ➤ Test menu item. You will see that the unit tests you have added in LoginViewModelTests.swift have passed.

Building the userNameUpdated Method

The userNameUpdated(_ value:String?) method of the view model is called by the login view controller when the user updates the contents of the username field.

When this method is called, the view model checks to see if the text entered by the user represents a valid username. If it does, and the content of the password text field is also valid, then the view model asks the view controller to enable the "Login" button.

Building this logic will require you to first write a series of tests. Add the tests in Listing 5-8 to the bottom of the LoginViewModelTests.swift file:

Listing 5-8. Tests for the userNameUpdated method

```
// MARK: userNameUpdated tests
extension LoginViewModelTests {

    func testUserNameUpdated_Calls_Validate_OnUserNameValidator() {
        let expectation = self.expectation(description: "expected validate()
        to be called")
```

```
        let viewModel = LoginViewModel(view:mockLoginViewController!)
        viewModel.userNameValidator = MockUserNameValidator(expectation,
        expectedValue: validUserName)

        viewModel.userNameUpdated(validUserName)

        self.waitForExpectations(timeout: 1.0, handler: nil)
    }

    func testUserNameUpdated_ValidUserName_PasswordValidated_
    EnablesLoginButton_OnViewController() {
        let expectation = self.expectation(description: "expected
        enableLogin(true) to be called")
        mockLoginViewController!.expectationForEnableLoginButton =
        (expectation, true)

        let viewModel = LoginViewModel(view:mockLoginViewController!)
        viewModel.passwordValidated = true
        viewModel.userNameUpdated(validUserName)

        self.waitForExpectations(timeout: 1.0, handler: nil)
    }

    func testUserNameUpdated_ValidUserName_PasswordNotValidated_
    DisablesLoginButton_OnViewController() {
        let expectation = self.expectation(description: "expected
        enableLogin(false) to be called")
        mockLoginViewController!.expectationForEnableLoginButton =
        (expectation, false)

        let viewModel = LoginViewModel(view:mockLoginViewController!)
        viewModel.passwordValidated = false

        viewModel.userNameUpdated(validUserName)

        self.waitForExpectations(timeout: 1.0, handler: nil)
    }

    func testUserNameUpdated_InvalidUserName_PasswordValidated_
    DisablesLoginButton_OnViewController() {
        let expectation = self.expectation(description: "expected
        enableLogin(false) to be called")
        mockLoginViewController!.expectationForEnableLoginButton =
        (expectation, false)

        let viewModel = LoginViewModel(view:mockLoginViewController!)
        viewModel.passwordValidated = true
```

```
        viewModel.userNameUpdated(invalidUserName)

        self.waitForExpectations(timeout: 1.0, handler: nil)
    }

    func testUserNameUpdated_InvalidUserName_PasswordNotValidated_
    DisablesLoginButton_OnViewController() {
        let expectation = self.expectation(description: "expected
        enableLogin(false) to be called")
        mockLoginViewController!.expectationForEnableLoginButton =
        (expectation, false)

        let viewModel = LoginViewModel(view:mockLoginViewController!)
        viewModel.passwordValidated = false

        viewModel.userNameUpdated(invalidUserName)

        self.waitForExpectations(timeout: 1.0, handler: nil)
    }
}
```

Add the following variable declarations to the LoginViewModelTests file:

```
fileprivate var validUserName = "abcdefghij"
fileprivate var invalidUserName = "a"
```

Add the following variable declarations to the LoginViewModel.swift file:

```
var userNameValidator:UserNameValidator?
var userNameValidated:Bool
var passwordValidated:Bool
```

Modify the implementation of the init(view:) method of the LoginViewModel.swift file to match:

```
init(view:LoginViewControllerProtocol) {
    self.userNameValidated = false
    self.passwordValidated = false

    super.init()

    self.view = view
}
```

Add the following method implementation to the LoginViewModel.swift file:

```swift
func userNameUpdated(_ value:String?) {

    guard let value = value else {
        view?.enableLoginButton(false)
        return
    }

    let validator = self.userNameValidator ?? UserNameValidator()
    userNameValidated = validator.validate(value)

    if userNameValidated == false {
        view?.enableLoginButton(false)
        return
    }

    if passwordValidated == false {
        view?.enableLoginButton(false)
        return
    }

    view?.enableLoginButton(true)
}
```

Save the file and run all unit tests using the Product ➤ Test menu item. You will see that the unit tests you have added in LoginViewModelTests.swift have passed.

Building the passwordUpdated Method

The passwordUpdated(_ value:String?) method of the view model is called by the login view controller when the user updates the contents of the password field.

When this method is called, the view model checks to see if the text entered by the user represents a valid password. If it does, and the content of the user name text field is also valid, then the view model asks the view controller to enable the "Login" button.

Add the tests in Listing 5-9 to the bottom of the LoginViewModelTests.swift file:

Listing 5-9. Tests for the passwordUpdated method

```swift
// MARK: passwordUpdated tests
extension LoginViewModelTests {

    func testPasswordUpdated_Calls_Validate_OnPasswordValidator() {
        let expectation = self.expectation(description: "expected validate()
        to be called")

        let viewModel = LoginViewModel(view:mockLoginViewController!)
        viewModel.passwordValidator = MockPasswordValidator(expectation,
        expectedValue: validPassword)
```

```
        viewModel.passwordUpdated(validPassword)

        self.waitForExpectations(timeout: 1.0, handler: nil)
    }

    func testPasswordUpdated_ValidPassword_UserNameValidated_
    EnablesLoginButton_OnViewController() {
        let expectation = self.expectation(description: "expected
        enableLogin(true) to be called")
        mockLoginViewController!.expectationForEnableLoginButton =
        (expectation, true)

        let viewModel = LoginViewModel(view:mockLoginViewController!)
        viewModel.userNameValidated = true
        viewModel.passwordUpdated(validPassword)

        self.waitForExpectations(timeout: 1.0, handler: nil)
    }

    func testPasswordUpdated_ValidPassword_UserNameNotValidated_
    DisablesLoginButton_OnViewController() {
        let expectation = self.expectation(description: "expected
        enableLogin(false) to be called")
        mockLoginViewController!.expectationForEnableLoginButton =
        (expectation, false)

        let viewModel = LoginViewModel(view:mockLoginViewController!)
        viewModel.userNameValidated = false

        viewModel.passwordUpdated(validPassword)

        self.waitForExpectations(timeout: 1.0, handler: nil)
    }

    func testPasswordUpdated_InvalidPassword_UserNameValidated_
    DisablesLoginButton_OnViewController() {
        let expectation = self.expectation(description: "expected
        enableLogin(false) to be called")
        mockLoginViewController!.expectationForEnableLoginButton =
        (expectation, false)

        let viewModel = LoginViewModel(view:mockLoginViewController!)
        viewModel.userNameValidated = true

        viewModel.passwordUpdated(invalidPassword)

        self.waitForExpectations(timeout: 1.0, handler: nil)
    }
```

```swift
    func testPasswordUpdated_InvalidPassword_UserNameNotValidated_
    DisablesLoginButton_OnViewController() {
        let expectation = self.expectation(description: "expected
        enableLogin(false) to be called")
        mockLoginViewController!.expectationForEnableLoginButton =
        (expectation, false)

        let viewModel = LoginViewModel(view:mockLoginViewController!)
        viewModel.userNameValidated = false

        viewModel.passwordUpdated(invalidPassword)

        self.waitForExpectations(timeout: 1.0, handler: nil)
    }
}
```

Add the following variable declarations to the LoginViewModelTests file:

```swift
fileprivate let validPassword = "D%io7AFn9Y"
fileprivate let invalidPassword = "a3$Am"
```

Add the following variable declaration to the LoginViewModel.swift file:

```swift
var passwordValidator:PasswordValidator?
```

Add the following method implementation to the LoginViewModel.swift file:

```swift
func passwordUpdated(_ value:String?) {

    guard let value = value else {
        view?.enableLoginButton(false)
        return
    }

    let validator = self.passwordValidator ?? PasswordValidator()
    passwordValidated = validator.validate(value)

    if passwordValidated == false {
        view?.enableLoginButton(false)
        return
    }

    if userNameValidated == false {
        view?.enableLoginButton(false)
        return
    }

    view?.enableLoginButton(true)
}
```

Save the file and run all unit tests using the Product ➤ Test menu item. You will see that the unit tests you have added in LoginViewModelTests.swift have passed.

Building the Login Method

The login(userName, password) method of the view model is called when the user taps on the Login button. The contents of the username and password text fields are passed into the login method. The login method will create a LoginModel object and call the doLogin method on an instance of a controller class that will encapsulate the logic needed to authenticate the user.

In a real-world application, this login controller class would contain logic to send a request to a back-end server. For the purposes of this chapter, however, we will build a bare-bones login controller class that uses hard-coded credentials to authenticate users.

Add the tests in Listing 5-10 to the bottom of the LoginViewModelTests.swift file:

Listing 5-10. Tests for the login method

```
// MARK: login tests
extension LoginViewModelTests {

    func testLogin_ValidParameters_Calls_doLogin_OnLoginController() {
        let expectation = self.expectation(description: "expected doLogin()
        to be called")

        let mockLoginController = MockLoginController(expectation,
        expectedUserName:validUserName, expectedPassword:validPassword)
        mockLoginController.shouldReturnTrueOnLogin = true

        let viewModel = LoginViewModel(view:mockLoginViewController!)
        viewModel.loginController = mockLoginController
        mockLoginController.loginControllerDelegate = viewModel

        viewModel.login(userName: validUserName, password: validPassword)

        self.waitForExpectations(timeout: 1.0, handler: nil)
    }

    func testLogin_ValidParameters_Calls_doLoginWithExpectedUserName_
    OnLoginController() {
        let expectation = self.expectation(description: "expected doLogin()
        to be called")

        let mockLoginController = MockLoginController(expectation,
        expectedUserName:validUserName, expectedPassword:validPassword)
        mockLoginController.shouldReturnTrueOnLogin = true
```

```
        let viewModel = LoginViewModel(view:mockLoginViewController!)
        viewModel.loginController = mockLoginController
        mockLoginController.loginControllerDelegate = viewModel

        viewModel.login(userName: validUserName, password: validPassword)

        self.waitForExpectations(timeout: 1.0, handler: nil)
    }

    func testLogin_ValidParameters_Calls_doLoginWithExpectedPassword_
    OnLoginController() {
        let expectation = self.expectation(description: "expected doLogin()
        to be called")

        let mockLoginController = MockLoginController(expectation,
        expectedUserName:validUserName, expectedPassword:validPassword)
        mockLoginController.shouldReturnTrueOnLogin = true

        let viewModel = LoginViewModel(view:mockLoginViewController!)
        viewModel.loginController = mockLoginController
        mockLoginController.loginControllerDelegate = viewModel

        viewModel.login(userName: validUserName, password: validPassword)

        self.waitForExpectations(timeout: 1.0, handler: nil)
    }

}
```

Note that these tests make use of a mock class called MockLoginController to stand in for the login controller and fulfill a test expectation when the doLogin() method is called on the mock class. Let us create the login controller and its mock class next.

Creating the Login Controller Class

We will create a bare-bones class to represent the login controller – a class that in a real-world example would encapsulate logic to authenticate the user with a back-end server.

We will not use TDD techniques while creating the login controller class. Create a new group in the Xcode project navigator called "Controllers," and under that group create a new Swift file called LoginController.swift. Ensure that the new file is a member of both the LoginForm and LoginFormTests targets (see Figure 5-17).

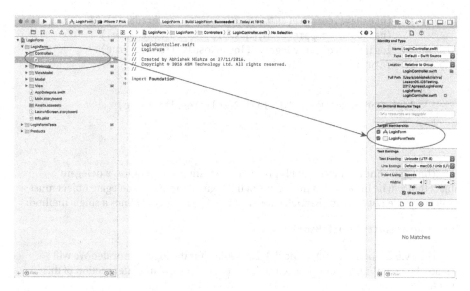

***Figure 5-17.** LoginController.swift Target Membership*

Update the contents of LoginController.swift to match the contents of Listing 5-11.

***Listing 5-11.** LoginController.swift*

```
import Foundation

protocol LoginControllerDelegate : class {
    func loginResult(result:Bool)
}

class LoginController : NSObject {

    let dummyUsername = "Alibaba"
    let dummyPassword = "Abracadabra"

    weak var loginControllerDelegate : LoginControllerDelegate?

    init(delegate:LoginControllerDelegate?) {
        self.loginControllerDelegate = delegate
        super.init()
    }

    func doLogin(model:LoginModel) {

        let userName = model.userName
        let password = model.password
```

```
    if ((userName.compare(dummyUsername) == .orderedSame) &&
        (password.compare(dummyPassword) == .orderedSame)) {
        loginControllerDelegate?.loginResult(result: true)
        return
    }

    loginControllerDelegate?.loginResult(result: false)
}

}
```

The login controller class that is presented in Listing 5-11 requires a delegate object that will be informed of the results of the login attempt. The delegate object must conform to the LoginControllerDelegate protocol. The protocol defines a single method:

```
func loginResult(result:Bool)
```

Thee view model will act as the delegate object for the login controller. We will update the LoginViewModel class to implement this protocol in a later section of this chapter.

Creating the Mock Login Controller Class

Create a new Swift file called MockLoginController.swift under the Mocks groups of the Xcode project navigator.Ensure that the new file is a member of the LoginFormTests target only (see Figure 5-18).

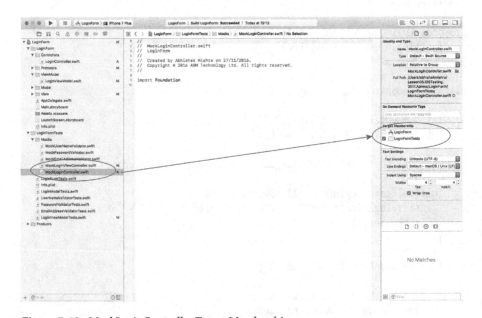

Figure 5-18. *MockLoginController Target Membership*

Update the contents of MockLoginController.swift to match the contents of Listing 5-12.

Listing 5-12. MockLoginController.swift

```swift
import Foundation
import XCTest

class MockLoginController : LoginController {

    private var expectation:XCTestExpectation?
    private var expectedUserName:String?
    private var expectedPassword:String?

    var shouldReturnTrueOnLogin:Bool

    init(_ expectation:XCTestExpectation, expectedUserName:String,
    expectedPassword:String) {
        self.expectation = expectation
        self.expectedUserName = expectedUserName
        self.expectedPassword = expectedPassword
        self.shouldReturnTrueOnLogin = false

        super.init(delegate:nil)
    }

    override func doLogin(model:LoginModel) {
        if let expectation = self.expectation,
            let expectedUserName = self.expectedUserName,
            let expectedPassword = expectedPassword {

            if ((model.userName.compare(expectedUserName) == .orderedSame) &&
                (model.password.compare(expectedPassword) == .orderedSame)){
                expectation.fulfill()
            }
        }

        loginControllerDelegate?.loginResult(result:shouldReturnTrueOnLogin)
    }

}
```

Updating the LoginViewModel Class

Add the following class extension to the LoginViewModel class:

```
extension LoginViewModel : LoginControllerDelegate {

    func loginResult(result: Bool) {
        // do someting with the result,
        // perhaps segue to a different screen of the app.
    }

}
```

This class extension ensures that the LoginViewModel class conforms to the LoginControllerDelegate protocol. Conformance requires that the login view model implements the loginResult(result:) method.

The body of the loginResult(result:) method is empty in this implementation. In a production application you may call a method on the view controller to segue to a different screen of the app.

Add the following variable declaration to the LoginViewModel class:

```
var loginController:LoginController?
```

Add the following method implementation to the LoginViewModel class:

```
func login(userName:String?, password:String?) {

    let controller = self.loginController ?? LoginController(delegate:self)

    if let userName = userName,
        let password = password,
        let model = LoginModel(userName: userName, password: password) {
        controller.doLogin(model: model)
    }
}
```

Save the file and run all unit tests using the Product ➤ Test menu item. You will see that all the unit tests you have added so far to this project have passed (see Figure 5-19).

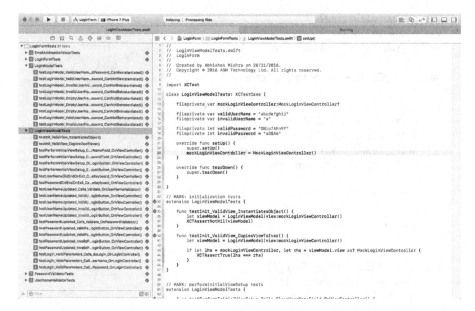

Figure 5-19. *All Login View Model Tests are Passing*

The SignupViewModel Class

The SignupViewModel class represents the view model between the SignupViewController class and the SignupModel class. The process of building the SignupViewModel class is identical to that of the LoginViewModel class.

The complete SignupViewModel class is presented in Listing 5-13. If you would like to examine the code for the tests and related mock objects, download the finished project anonymously from github using the following URL:

https://github.com/asmtechnology/Lesson05.iOSTesting.2017.Apress.git

Listing 5-13. SignupViewModel.swift

```
import Foundation

class SignupViewModel: NSObject {

    weak var view:SignupViewControllerProtocol?

    var userNameValidator:UserNameValidator?
    var passwordValidator:PasswordValidator?
    var emailAddressValidator:EmailAddressValidator?

    var userNameValidated:Bool
    var password1Validated:Bool
    var password2Validated:Bool
```

143

```swift
var password1:String?
var password2:String?
var passwordsAreIdentical:Bool

var signupController:SignupController?

init(view:SignupViewControllerProtocol) {
    self.userNameValidated = false
    self.password1Validated = false
    self.password2Validated = false
    self.passwordsAreIdentical = false

    super.init()

    self.view = view
}

func performInitialViewSetup() {
    view?.clearUserNameField()
    view?.clearPasswordField()
    view?.clearConfirmPasswordField()
    view?.enableCreateButton(false)
    view?.enableCancelButton(true)
}

func userNameDidEndOnExit() {
    view?.hideKeyboard()
}

func passwordDidEndOnExit() {
    view?.hideKeyboard()
}

func confirmPasswordDidEndOnExit() {
    view?.hideKeyboard()
}

func userNameUpdated(_ value:String?) {

    guard let value = value else {
        view?.enableCreateButton(false)
        return
    }

    let validator = self.userNameValidator ?? UserNameValidator()
    userNameValidated = validator.validate(value)
```

```
    if userNameValidated == false {
        view?.enableCreateButton(false)
        return
    }

    if password1Validated == true &&
        password2Validated == true &&
        passwordsAreIdentical == true {

        view?.enableCreateButton(true)
        return
    }

    view?.enableCreateButton(false)
}

func passwordUpdated(_ value:String?) {

    self.password1 = value

    guard let password1 = self.password1 else {
        view?.enableCreateButton(false)
        return
    }

    if let password2 = password2 {
        passwordsAreIdentical = password1.compare(password2) == .orderedSame
    } else {
        passwordsAreIdentical = false
    }

    let validator = self.passwordValidator ?? PasswordValidator()
    password1Validated = validator.validate(password1)

    if userNameValidated == false {
        view?.enableCreateButton(false)
        return
    }

    if password1Validated == true &&
        password2Validated == true &&
        passwordsAreIdentical == true {

        view?.enableCreateButton(true)
        return
    }

    view?.enableCreateButton(false)
}
```

```swift
    func confirmPasswordUpdated(_ value:String?) {

        self.password2 = value

        guard let password2 = self.password2 else {
            view?.enableCreateButton(false)
            return
        }

        if let password1 = password1 {
            passwordsAreIdentical = password1.compare(password2) == .orderedSame
        } else {
            passwordsAreIdentical = false
        }

        let validator = self.passwordValidator ?? PasswordValidator()
        password2Validated = validator.validate(password2)

        if userNameValidated == false {
            view?.enableCreateButton(false)
            return
        }

        if password1Validated == true &&
            password2Validated == true &&
            passwordsAreIdentical == true {

            view?.enableCreateButton(true)
            return
        }

        view?.enableCreateButton(false)
    }

    func signup(userName:String?, password:String?, emailAddress:String?) {

        let controller = self.signupController ?? SignupController(delegate:self)

        if let userName = userName,
            let password = password,
            let emailAddress = emailAddress,
            let model = SignupModel(userName: userName, password: password,
            emailAddress:emailAddress) {
            controller.doSignup(model: model)
        }
    }

}
```

```
extension LoginViewModel : SignupControllerDelegate {

    func signupResult(result: Bool) {
        // do someting with the result,
        // perhaps segue to a different screen of the app.
    }

}
```

Connecting the View Controller to the View Model

So far in this chapter, we have used a test-driven approach to build the model and view model layers for two view controllers. It is now time to make calls to the view models from the view controllers.

Should you adopt a test-driven approach to creating these bindings between the view controller and the view model? The answer is, "It depends on how valuable you feel these tests will be in the long run."

The whole point of the MVVM architectural pattern is to make the view controllers lightweight and easier to test. The view controller, however, is still tightly coupled with the view that is presented to the user, and can be difficult to instantiate in a test target.

In order to instantiate the view controller in a unit test you will need to stub the outlets in the view controller that will be involved in the test. The LoginForm project consists of two view controllers, each with their own view models. The view models have been built with the intention that the view controller will make calls to the view model at certain strategic points. The next sections of this chapter will examine the process of creating bindings between the view controller and the view model using test-driven techniques.

Binding the Login View Controller Class to the View Model

Table 5-7 lists the methods in the LoginViewController class along with their associated view model bindings.

Table 5-7. *Login view controller and view model bindings*

Login View Controller Method	Login View Model Method
func viewDidLoad()	func performInitialViewSetup()
@IBAction func login(_ sender: Any)	func login(userName:String?, password:String?)
@IBAction func userNameDidEndOnExit (_ sender: Any)	func userNameDidEndOnExit()
@IBAction func passwordDidEndOnExit (_ sender: Any)	func passwordDidEndOnExit()
func textField(_ textField: UITextField, shouldChangeCharactersIn range: NSRange, replacementString string: String) -> Bool	func userNameUpdated (_ value:String?) And func passwordUpdated (_ value:String?)

Create a new iOS Unit Test Case class called LoginViewControllerTests under the LoginFormTests group of the project explorer.

Delete the testExample and testPerformanceExample methods from LoginViewControllerTests.swift.

Calling the performInitialSetup Method of the View Model from the View Controller

Add the following test case to the LoginViewControllerTests.swift file:

```
func testViewDidLoad_Calls_PerformInitialSetup_OnViewModel() {

    let expectation = self.expectation(description: "expected
    performInitialViewSetup() to be called")

    let loginViewController = LoginViewController()

    let viewModel = MockLoginViewModel(view:loginViewController)
    viewModel.performInitialViewSetupExpectation = expectation

    loginViewController.viewModel = viewModel

    loginViewController.viewDidLoad()

    self.waitForExpectations(timeout: 1.0, handler: nil)
}
```

The aim of this test case is to ensure that the view model's performInitialViewSetup() method is called by the viewDidLoad method of the view controller. The test has be built around injecting a mock view model object into the view controller and fulfilling a test expectation when the performInitalViewSetup() method on the mock object is called.

Create a new class called MockLoginViewModel under the Mocks group in the project navigator. Ensure this new class is only included in the test target and update its implementation to match the contents of Listing 5-14.

Listing 5-14. MockLoginViewModel.swift

```swift
import Foundation
import XCTest

class MockLoginViewModel : LoginViewModel {

    var performInitialViewSetupExpectation:XCTestExpectation?
    var userNameDidEndOnExitExpectation:XCTestExpectation?
    var passwordDidEndOnExitExpectation:XCTestExpectation?
    var userNameUpdatedExpectation:(XCTestExpectation, expectedValue:String)?
    var passwordUpdatedExpectation:(XCTestExpectation, expectedValue:String)?
    var loginExpectation:(XCTestExpectation, expectedUserName:String,
    expectedPassword:String)?

    override func performInitialViewSetup() {
        performInitialViewSetupExpectation?.fulfill()
    }

    override func userNameDidEndOnExit() {
        userNameDidEndOnExitExpectation?.fulfill()
    }

    override func passwordDidEndOnExit() {
        passwordDidEndOnExitExpectation?.fulfill()
    }

    override func userNameUpdated(_ value:String?) {
        if let (expectation, expectedValue) = self.userNameUpdatedExpectation,
            let value = value {
            if value.compare(expectedValue) == .orderedSame {
                expectation.fulfill()
            }
        }
    }
}
```

```
    override func passwordUpdated(_ value:String?) {
        if let (expectation, expectedValue) = self.passwordUpdatedExpectation,
            let value = value {
            if value.compare(expectedValue) == .orderedSame {
                expectation.fulfill()
            }
        }
    }

    override func login(userName:String?, password:String?) {

        if let (expectation, expectedUserName, expectedPassword) = self.
        loginExpectation,
            let userName = userName,
            let password = password {
            if ((userName.compare(expectedUserName) == .orderedSame) &&
                (password.compare(expectedPassword) == .orderedSame)) {

                expectation.fulfill()
            }
        }
    }

}
```

You need to modify the LoginViewController class to allow you to inject the view model as a dependency. While testing, you will want to inject a mock or stub view model. In the release version of your app, you will want to create an instance of a real view model. Add the following variable declaration to the LoginViewController class:

```
var viewModel:LoginViewModel?
```

Update the implementation of the viewDidLoad() method of the LoginViewController class to match the following snippet:

```
override func viewDidLoad() {
    super.viewDidLoad()

    if self.viewModel == nil {
        self.viewModel = LoginViewModel(view: self)
    }

    self.viewModel?.performInitialViewSetup()
}
```

In this modified viewDidLoad implementation, you instantiate a view model if one hasn't been instantiated already and then call the performInitialViewSetup() method on the view model instance.

It is important to note that the view model instance is public, and we can therefore provide a mock view model instance from our tests.

Save the file and run all unit tests using the Product ➤ Test menu item. You will see that the unit test you have just created has passed (see Figure 5-20).

Figure 5-20. *All LoginViewControllerTests are Passing.*

Calling the userNameDidEndOnExit Method of the View Model from the View Controller

Add the following test case to the LoginViewControllerTests.swift file:

```
func testUserNameDidEndOnExit_Calls_UserNameDidEndOnExit_OnViewModel() {

    let expectation = self.expectation(description: "expected
    userNameDidEndOnExit() to be called")

    let loginViewController = LoginViewController()

    let viewModel = MockLoginViewModel(view:loginViewController)
    viewModel.userNameDidEndOnExitExpectation = expectation

    loginViewController.viewModel = viewModel

    loginViewController.userNameDidEndOnExit(self)

    self.waitForExpectations(timeout: 1.0, handler: nil)
}
```

151

The aim of this test case is to ensure that the view model's userNameDidEndOnExit() method is called by the userNameDidEndOnExit method of the view controller.

Update the implementation of the userNameDidEndOnExit method of the LoginViewController class to match:

```
@IBAction func userNameDidEndOnExit(_ sender: Any) {
    viewModel?.userNameDidEndOnExit()
}
```

Save the file and run all unit tests using the Product ➤ Test menu item. You will see that the unit test you have just created has passed.

Calling the passwordDidEndOnExit Method of the View Model from the View Controller

Add the following test case to the LoginViewControllerTests.swift file:

```
func testPasswordDidEndOnExit_Calls_PasswordDidEndOnExit_OnViewModel() {

    let expectation = self.expectation(description: "expected
    passwordDidEndOnExit() to be called")

    let loginViewController = LoginViewController()

    let viewModel = MockLoginViewModel(view:loginViewController)
    viewModel.passwordDidEndOnExitExpectation = expectation

    loginViewController.viewModel = viewModel

    loginViewController.passwordDidEndOnExit(self)

    self.waitForExpectations(timeout: 1.0, handler: nil)
}
```

The aim of this test case is to ensure that the view model's passwordDidEndOnExit() method is called by the passwordDidEndOnExit method of the view controller.

Update the implementation of the passwordDidEndOnExit method of the LoginViewController class to match:

```
@IBAction func passwordDidEndOnExit(_ sender: Any) {
    viewModel?.passwordDidEndOnExit()
}
```

Save the file and run all unit tests using the Product ➤ Test menu item. You will see that the unit test you have just created has passed.

Calling the Login Method of the View Model from the View Controller

Add the following test cases to the LoginViewControllerTests.swift file:

```
func testLogin_ValidUserNameAndPassword_Calls_Login_OnViewModel_
WithExpectedUserName() {

    let expectation = self.expectation(description: "expected login() to be called")

    let userNameTextFieldStub = UITextFieldStub(text:validUserName)
    let passwordTextFieldStub = UITextFieldStub(text:"")

    let loginViewController = LoginViewController()
    loginViewController.userNameTextField = userNameTextFieldStub
    loginViewController.passwordTextField = passwordTextFieldStub

    let viewModel = MockLoginViewModel(view:loginViewController)
    viewModel.loginExpectation = (expectation,
    expectedUserName:validUserName, expectedPassword:"")

    loginViewController.viewModel = viewModel

    loginViewController.login(self)

    self.waitForExpectations(timeout: 1.0, handler: nil)
}

func testLogin_ValidUserNameAndPassword_Calls_Login_OnViewModel_
WithExpectedPassword() {

    let expectation = self.expectation(description: "expected login() to be called")

    let userNameTextFieldStub = UITextFieldStub(text:"")
    let passwordTextFieldStub = UITextFieldStub(text:validPassword)

    let loginViewController = LoginViewController()
    loginViewController.userNameTextField = userNameTextFieldStub
    loginViewController.passwordTextField = passwordTextFieldStub

    let viewModel = MockLoginViewModel(view:loginViewController)
    viewModel.loginExpectation = (expectation, expectedUserName:"",
    expectedPassword:validPassword)

    loginViewController.viewModel = viewModel

    loginViewController.login(self)

    self.waitForExpectations(timeout: 1.0, handler: nil)
}
```

153

The aim of these test cases is to ensure that the view model's login() method is called by the login action method of the view controller. The view model's login method requires the username and password, both of which are read from UITextField instances in the view.

Since these values are read from text fields that are created using a storyboard, you will need to create stub text fields and set the values of the corresponding outlets manually.

In each of the above test cases, stub objects are created for the text fields and applied to the view controller's outlets, using code similar to the following snippet:

```
let userNameTextFieldStub = UITextFieldStub(text:"")
let passwordTextFieldStub = UITextFieldStub(text:validPassword)

let loginViewController = LoginViewController()
loginViewController.userNameTextField = userNameTextFieldStub
loginViewController.passwordTextField = passwordTextFieldStub
```

Create a new group called Stubs under the LoginFormTests group, and create a new Swift class called UITextFieldStub under the Stubs group. Ensure the UITextFieldStub. swift file is only a member of the LoginFormTests target.

Update the code in UITextFieldStub.swift to resemble the following:

```
import UIKit

class UITextFieldStub : UITextField {

    init(text:String) {
        super.init(frame: CGRect.zero)
        super.text = text
    }

    required init?(coder aDecoder: NSCoder) {
        super.init(coder: aDecoder)
    }
}
```

Add the following variable declaration to the LoginViewControllerTests class:

```
fileprivate var validUserName = "abcdefghij"
fileprivate let validPassword = "D%io7AFn9Y"
```

Update the implementation of the login action method of the LoginViewController class to match:

```
@IBAction func login(_ sender: Any) {
    viewModel?.login(userName: userNameTextField.text, password:
passwordTextField.text)
}
```

Save the file and run all unit tests using the Product ➤ Test menu item. You will see that the unit test you have just created has passed.

Calling the userNameUpdated and passwordUpdated Methods of the View Model from the View Controller

Add the following test cases to the LoginViewControllerTests.swift file:

```
func testTextFieldShouldChangeCharacters_userNameTextField_Calls_
UserNameUpdated_OnViewModel_WithExpectedUsername() {

    let expectation = self.expectation(description: "expected
    userNameUpdated() to be called")

    let userNameTextFieldStub = UITextFieldStub(text:validUserName)
    let passwordTextFieldStub = UITextFieldStub(text:validPassword)

    let loginViewController = LoginViewController()
    loginViewController.userNameTextField = userNameTextFieldStub
    loginViewController.passwordTextField = passwordTextFieldStub

    let viewModel = MockLoginViewModel(view:loginViewController)
    viewModel.userNameUpdatedExpectation = (expectation,
    expectedValue:validUserName)

    loginViewController.viewModel = viewModel

    let _ = loginViewController.textField(userNameTextFieldStub,
                                shouldChangeCharactersIn:
                                NSMakeRange(0, 1),
                                replacementString: "A")

    self.waitForExpectations(timeout: 1.0, handler: nil)
}

func testTextFieldShouldChangeCharacters_passwordTextField_Calls_
PasswordUpdated_OnViewModel_WithExpectedUsername() {

    let expectation = self.expectation(description: "expected
    passwordUpdated() to be called")

    let userNameTextFieldStub = UITextFieldStub(text:validUserName)
    let passwordTextFieldStub = UITextFieldStub(text:validPassword)

    let loginViewController = LoginViewController()
    loginViewController.userNameTextField = userNameTextFieldStub
    loginViewController.passwordTextField = passwordTextFieldStub
```

```
    let viewModel = MockLoginViewModel(view:loginViewController)
    viewModel.passwordUpdatedExpectation = (expectation,
    expectedValue:validPassword)

    loginViewController.viewModel = viewModel

    let _ = loginViewController.textField(passwordTextFieldStub,
                                 shouldChangeCharactersIn:
                                 NSMakeRange(0, 1),
                                 replacementString: "A")

    self.waitForExpectations(timeout: 1.0, handler: nil)
}
```

The aim of these test cases is to ensure that either the view model's userNameUpdated() method or the passwordUpdated() method is called by the textField(shouldChange CharactersIn, replacementString) method of the view controller.

Update the implementation of the textField(shouldChangeCharactersIn, replacementString) method of the LoginViewController class to match:

```
extension LoginViewController: UITextFieldDelegate {

    func textField(_ textField: UITextField,
                 shouldChangeCharactersIn range: NSRange,
                 replacementString string: String) -> Bool {

        if textField == self.userNameTextField {
            self.viewModel?.userNameUpdated(textField.text)
        }

        if textField == self.passwordTextField {
            self.viewModel?.passwordUpdated(textField.text)
        }

        return true
    }

}
```

Save the file and run all unit tests using the Product ➤ Test menu item. You will see that the unit tests you have just created have passed.

Binding the Signup View Controller Class to the View Model

Table 5-8 lists the methods in the SignupViewController class along with their associated view model bindings.

Table 5-8. *Signup view controller and view model bindings*

Signup View Controller Method	Signup View Model Method
func viewDidLoad()	func performInitialViewSetup()
@IBAction func login(_ sender: Any)	func login(userName:String?, password:String?)
@IBAction func userNameDidEndOnExit (_ sender: Any)	func userNameDidEndOnExit()
@IBAction func passwordDidEndOnExit (_ sender: Any)	func passwordDidEndOnExit()
func textField(_ textField: UITextField, shouldChangeCharactersIn range: NSRange, replacementString string: String) -> Bool	func userNameUpdated(_ value:String?) And func passwordUpdated(_ value:String?)

The complete SignupViewController class is presented in Listing 5-15. If you would like to examine the code for the tests, download the finished project anonymously from github using the following URL:

https://github.com/asmtechnology/Lesson05.iOSTesting.2017.Apress.git

Listing 5-15. SignupViewController.swift

```
import UIKit

class SignupViewController: UIViewController {

    @IBOutlet weak var userNameTextField: UITextField!
    @IBOutlet weak var passwordTextField: UITextField!
    @IBOutlet weak var confirmPasswordTextField: UITextField!
    @IBOutlet weak var emailAddressTextField: UITextField!
    @IBOutlet weak var createButton: UIButton!
    @IBOutlet weak var cancelButton: UIButton!

    var viewModel:SignupViewModel?
```

```swift
    override func viewDidLoad() {
        super.viewDidLoad()

        if self.viewModel == nil {
            self.viewModel = SignupViewModel(view: self)
        }

        self.viewModel?.performInitialViewSetup()
    }

    override func didReceiveMemoryWarning() {
        super.didReceiveMemoryWarning()
        // Dispose of any resources that can be recreated.
    }

    @IBAction func create(_ sender: Any) {
        viewModel?.signup(userName: userNameTextField.text, password:
        passwordTextField.text, emailAddress: emailAddressTextField.text)
    }

    @IBAction func cancel(_ sender: Any) {
        self.dismiss(animated: true, completion: nil)
    }

    @IBAction func userNameDidEndOnExit(_ sender: Any) {
        viewModel?.userNameDidEndOnExit()
    }

    @IBAction func passwordDidEndOnExit(_ sender: Any) {
        viewModel?.passwordDidEndOnExit()
    }

    @IBAction func confirmPasswordDidEndOnExit(_ sender: Any) {
        viewModel?.confirmPasswordDidEndOnExit()
    }

    @IBAction func emailAddressDidEndOnExit(_ sender: Any) {
        viewModel?.emailAddressDidEndOnExit()
    }

}

extension SignupViewController: UITextFieldDelegate {

    func textField(_ textField: UITextField,
                   shouldChangeCharactersIn range: NSRange,
                   replacementString string: String) -> Bool {
```

```swift
        if textField == self.userNameTextField {
            self.viewModel?.userNameUpdated(textField.text)
        }

        if textField == self.passwordTextField {
            self.viewModel?.passwordUpdated(textField.text)
        }

        if textField == self.confirmPasswordTextField {
            self.viewModel?.confirmPasswordUpdated(textField.text)
        }

        if textField == self.emailAddressTextField {
            self.viewModel?.emailAddressUpdated(textField.text)
        }

        return true
    }

}

extension SignupViewController : SignupViewControllerProtocol {

    func clearUserNameField() {
        self.userNameTextField.text = ""
    }

    func clearPasswordField() {
        self.passwordTextField.text = ""
    }

    func clearConfirmPasswordField() {
        self.confirmPasswordTextField.text = ""
    }

    func enableCancelButton(_ status:Bool) {
        self.cancelButton.isEnabled = status
    }

    func enableCreateButton(_ status:Bool) {
        self.createButton.isEnabled = status
    }

    func hideKeyboard() {
        self.userNameTextField.resignFirstResponder()
        self.passwordTextField.resignFirstResponder()
        self.confirmPasswordTextField.resignFirstResponder()
    }
}
```

Transitioning from the Login View Controller to the Signup View Controller

The final task remaining in this project is to transition from the login view controller to the signup view controller when the Create Account button is tapped on the login screen.

Earlier in this chapter, you created a segue called "presentCreateAccount" between the corresponding storyboard scenes.

Update the implementation of the createAccount() action method of LoginViewController to match the following snippet.

```
@IBAction func createAccount(_ sender: Any) {
    self.performSegue(withIdentifier: "presentCreateAccount", sender: self)
}
```

You may have noticed that I have not created any unit tests to test this transition. UI transitions are better tested using UI tests. UI Testing is covered in Chapter 13.

Summary

In this chapter you have learned to create view controllers using TDD techniques and the MVVM pattern. You started by creating the user interface and model layer objects. You then built the view models for the login and signup screens. Finally, you connected the view controller to the view model.

CHAPTER 6

■ ■ ■

Applying TDD to Collection View Controllers

This chapter will examine the process of building a collection view controller-based iOS app using TDD techniques. The app will have a single view controller that presents a list of pictures and will be built using the MVVM application architecture. Figure 6-1 depicts the user interface of the finished application.

Figure 6-1. *The PhotoBook Application*

© Abhishek Mishra 2017
A. Mishra, *iOS Code Testing*, DOI 10.1007/978-1-4842-2689-6_6

The complete source code for the app can be downloaded anonymously from github using the following URL:

```
https://github.com/asmtechnology/Lesson06.iOSTesting.2017.Apress.git
```

Application Architecture

The application architecture consists of three distinct layers (see Figure 6-2).

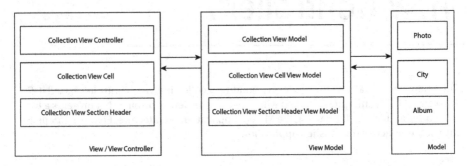

Figure 6-2. *PhotoBook Application Architecture*

A brief description of the layers and the component classes follows:

- **Model Layer:** Consists of the Photo, City, and Album classes that are used to hold the data that will be displayed to the user. Album is the top-level object and consist of multiple cities, with each city containing one or more photos that were taken in that city.

- **View Model Layer:** Consists of the CollectionViewModel, CollectionViewCellViewModel, and CollectionViewSectionHeaderViewModel classes.

- **View/View Controller Layer:** This layer contains the user interface of the project and consists of the CollectionViewController, CollectionViewCell, and CollectionViewSectionHeader classes.

Creating the Xcode Project

Launch Xcode and create a new iOS project based on the Single View Application template. Use the following options while creating the new project (see Figure 6-3):

- **Product Name:** PhotoBook
- **Team:** None
- **Organization Name:** Provide a suitable name

- **Organization Identifier:** Provide a suitable identifier
- **Language:** Swift
- **Devices:** iPhone
- **Use Core Data:** Unchecked
- **Include Unit Tests:** Checked
- **Include UI Tests:** Unchecked

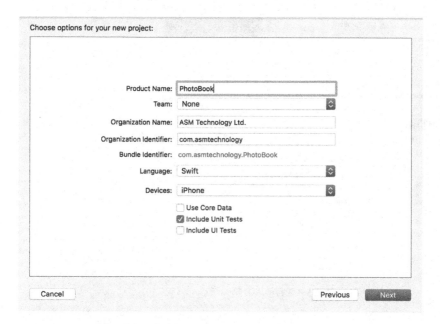

Figure 6-3. Xcode Project Options Dialog

> ■ **Note** The project being created in this chapter does not include user interface (UI) tests. If you wish, you can add UI tests to a project retrospectively. Chapter 13 covers the topic of user interface testing.

Save the project to a suitable location on your computer and click Create. Since this project will contain several new classes, it will be a good idea to place class files under appropriate groups within the project navigator.

Create the following groups in the Xcode project navigator:

- View
- Model
- ViewModel
- Protocols

Adding Resources to the Project

Delete the Assets.xcassets folder from the project navigator. Ensure that you select the Move to Trash option when prompted by Xcode.

Add the Albums.plist and the Assets.xcassets folder provided with this lesson's downloads into the project. While adding these new items, ensure the Copy Items if Needed option is checked in the import dialog box (see Figure 6-4).

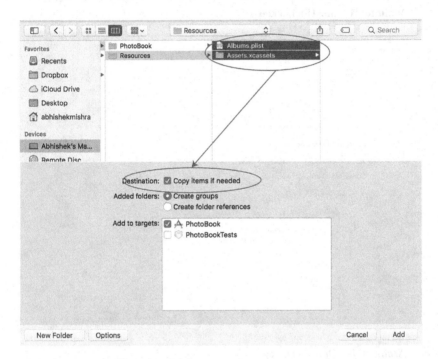

Figure 6-4. *Xcode File Import Dialog*

The asset bundle you have imported contains photos categorized under six cities, and each city is represented by a subfolder within the asset bundle (see Figure 6-5).

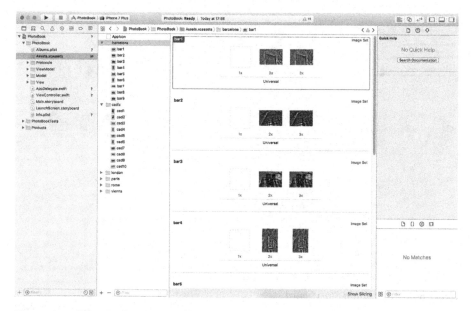

Figure 6-5. *PhotoBook Asset Bundle*

You may also have noticed that no 1X images have been provided for the assets. This is because this app is built for iPhone's only and the latest iOS version is not supported on non-retina iPhones.

Building the User Interface Layer

The user interface for this application consists of a single storyboard scene embedded within a navigation controller (see Figure 6-6).

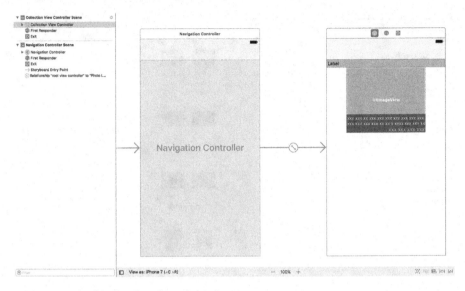

Figure 6-6. Application Storyboard

Creating New Classes

Delete the ViewController.swift file from the project navigator, and create the following Swift classes under the View group:

- A UICollectionViewController subclass called CollectionViewController.

- A UICollectionViewCell subclass called CollectionViewCell.

- A UICollectionReusableView subclass called CollectionViewSectionHeader.

Ensure these classes are included in both the PhotoBook and PhotoBookTests targets. The project navigator should resemble Figure 6-7.

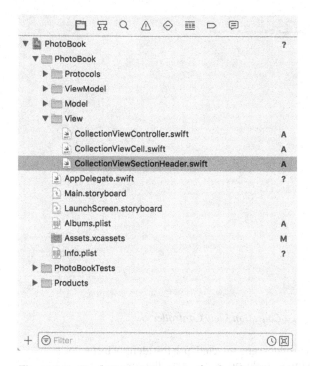

Figure 6-7. *Xcode Project Navigator for the PhotoBook Project*

Building the Collection View Controller Scene

Open the Main.storyboard file and delete the default scene in the storyboard. Drag and drop a Collection View Controller from the Object Library onto the storyboard scene (see Figure 6-8).

***Figure 6-8.** Storyboard Scene with a Collection View Controller*

With the collection view controller scene selected, use the Identity Inspector to change the class associated with the collection view controller scene to CollectionViewController (see Figure 6-9).

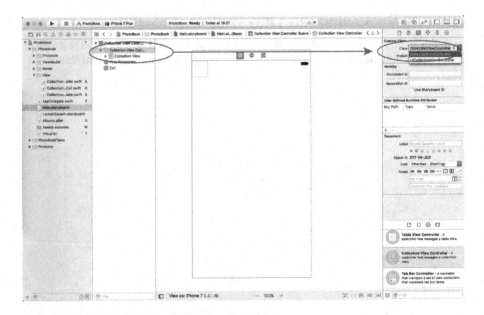

***Figure 6-9.** Custom Class Applied to Storyboard Scene*

With the collection view controller scene selected, switch to the Attributes Inspector and check the Is Initial View Controller option (see Figure 6-10).

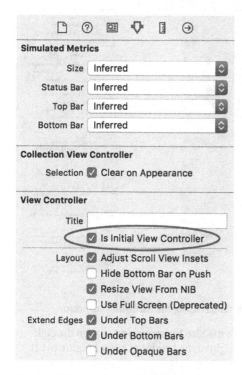

Figure 6-10. *Xcode Attributes Inspector*

Adding a Section Header Accessory View

Select the collection view within the collection view controller scene, and use the Attributes Inspector to enable the Section Header accessory view (see Figure 6-11).

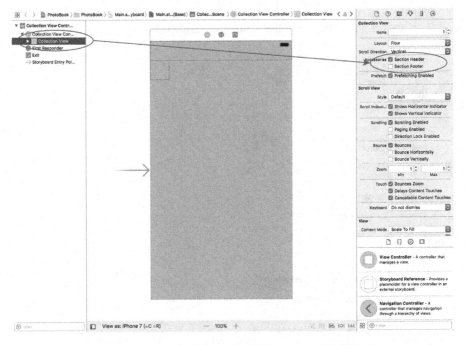

Figure 6-11. *Section Header Accessory View Enabled using the Attributes Inspector*

With the collection view selected, switch to the Size Inspector and change the cell size to width = 250, height = 200. Change the height of the header to 25 (see Figure 6-12).

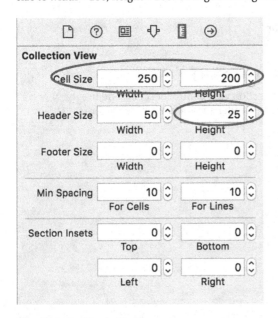

Figure 6-12. *Xcode Size Inspector*

Select the collection view header accessory view (this will be identified as the Collection Reusable View in the document outline), and use the Identity Inspector to change the class associated with the header accessory view to CollectionViewSectionHeader (see Figure 6-13).

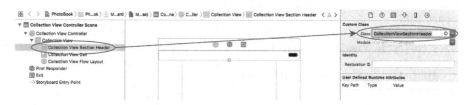

Figure 6-13. *Custom Class Setup for the Header Accessory View*

Use the Attributes Inspector to change the background color of the header accessory view to a shade of gray, and the value of the Identifier attribute to CollectionViewSectionHeader.

Drag and drop a label from the Object Library onto the header accessory view and position it to resemble Figure 6-14. Use appropriate constraints for the label to maintain this position on different screen sizes. Set the font size of the text in the label to 14 points. See Figure 6-14.

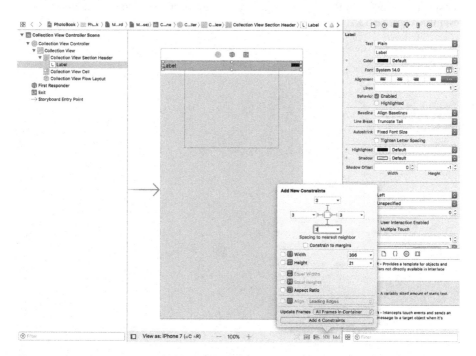

Figure 6-14. *Constraints on the Header Accessory View*

Using the Assistant Editor, create an outlet for the label in the
CollectionViewSectionHeader.swift file. Name this outlet title. The code in
CollectionViewSectionHeader.swift should resemble Listing 6-1.

Listing 6-1. CollectionViewSectionHeader.swift

```
import UIKit

class CollectionViewSectionHeader: UICollectionReusableView {

    @IBOutlet weak var title: UILabel!
}
```

Building the Collection View Cell

Go back to the storyboard, select the collection view cell, and use the Identity Inspector
to change the class associated with the collection view cell to CollectionViewCell.
Switch to the Attributes Inspector and change the value of the Identity attribute to
CollectionViewCell.

Using the Object Library, drag and drop an image view onto the empty collection
view cell. Use the Attributes Inspector to set the content mode of the image view
to Aspect Fill. Position the image view and set up appropriate layout constraints to
resemble Figure 6-15.

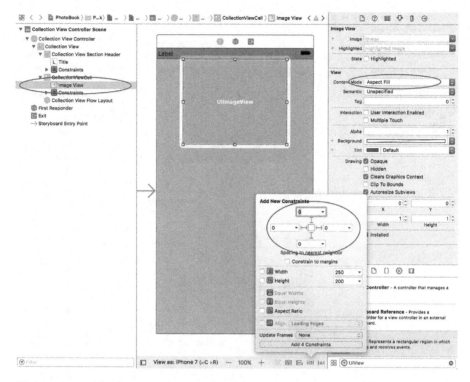

Figure 6-15. *Adding an Image View to the Collection View Cell*

Using the Object Library, drag and drop an empty view onto the collection view cell, on top of the image view. Use the Attributes Inspector to set the background color of the view to black with an opacity of 40%. Position the new view and set up appropriate layout constraints to resemble Figure 6-16.

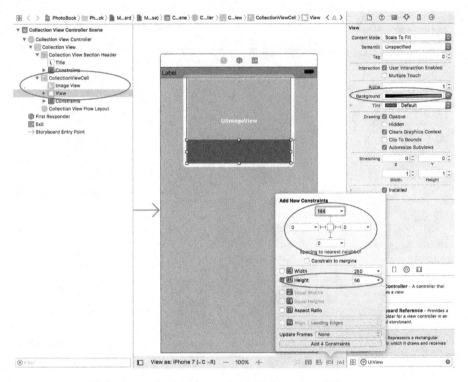

Figure 6-16. *Adding a Translucent View to the Collection View Cell*

Drag and drop two labels from the Object Library onto the new view you have just created. Make sure these two labels are encompassed by the view and place the labels one below the other (see Figure 6-17).

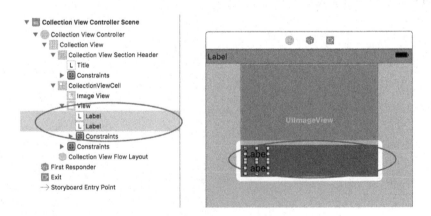

Figure 6-17. *Adding Labels to the Collection View Cell*

Using the Attributes Inspector, apply the following properties to the upper label:

- **Foreground Color:** White
- **Font Size:** 14 point
- **Number of Lines:** 2

Using the Pin constraints button, apply the following constraints to the upper label:

- **Left:** 2
- **Top:** 2
- **Bottom:** 2
- **Right:** 2
- **Constrain to Margins:** Unchecked
- **Update Frames:** None

Using the Attributes Inspector, apply the following properties to the lower label:

- **Foreground Color:** Blue
- **Font Size:** 17 point
- **Number of Lines:** 1
- **Text Alignment:** Right

Using the Pin constraints button, apply the following constraints to the lower label:

- **Left:** 2
- **Bottom:** 2
- **Right:** 2
- **Height:**15
- **Constrain to Margins:** Unchecked
- **Update Frames:** All Frames In Container

The storyboard should now resemble Figure 6-18.

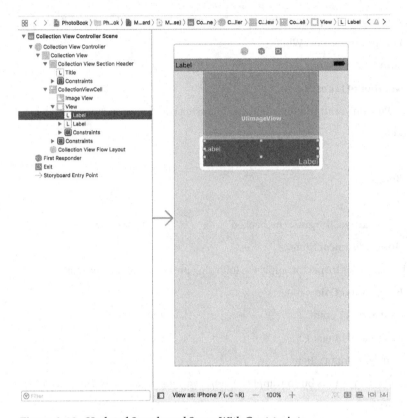

Figure 6-18. *Updated Storyboard Scene With Contstraints*

Using the Assistant Editor, create outlets for the image view and the labels in the CollectionViewCell.swift file, as per Table 6-1.

Table 6-1. *Collection View Cell Outlets*

User Interface Object	Outlet Name
Image View	imageView
Upper Label	captionLabel
Lower Label	shotDetailsLabel

The code in CollectionViewCell.swift should resemble Listing 6-2.

Listing 6-2. CollectionViewCell.swift

```
import UIKit

class CollectionViewCell: UICollectionViewCell {
```

```
@IBOutlet weak var imageView: UIImageView!
@IBOutlet weak var captionLabel: UILabel!
@IBOutlet weak var shotDetailsLabel: UILabel!

}
```

Select the collection view controller scene of the story board and embed it within a navigation controller using the Editor ➤ Embed In ➤ Navigation Controller menu item. The final storyboard should resemble Figure 6-19.

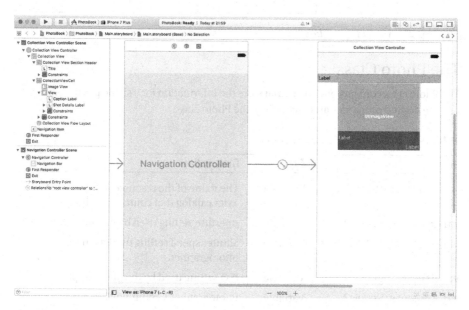

Figure 6-19. *Collection View Controller Scene Embeddded Within a Navigation Controller*

Building the Model Layer

There are three model classes that we need to build – Photo, City, and Album. The relationship between these classes is depicted in Figure 6-20. The Album object is the top-level model object. An Album object contains an array of City objects, and each City object contains an array of Photo objects. Photo objects store metadata for individual photos along with the name of a resource in the project's asset catalog from where the actual image can be loaded.

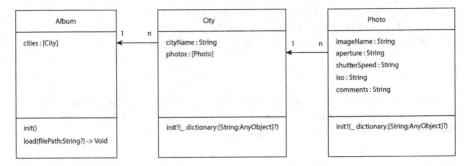

Figure 6-20. *Model Layer Classes*

The Photo Class

The Photo class contains properties that store the information for a single photo. Table 6-2 lists the desired properties and methods of the Photo class.

Table 6-2. *Photo Properties and Methods*

Item	Type	Description
var imageName:String?	Variable	The name of the resource in the project's asset catalog that contains the image.
var aperture:String?	Variable	Aperture setting used by the photographer.
var shutterSpeed:String?	Variable	Shutter speed setting used by the photographer.
var iso:String?	Variable	ISO setting used by the photographer.
var comments:String?	Variable	Photographer's comments.
init?(_ dictionary: [String : AnyObject]?)	Method	Allows other code to create Photo instances. Requires a dictionary with certain mandatory keys as input.

The init method will require a dictionary with all of the following mandatory keys to be present:

- imageName
- aperture
- shutterSpeed
- iso
- comment

The approach to developing the Photo class will be very similar to the model layer classes that were developed in Chapter 4. The tests will be around the behavior of the init method and how it handles missing keys in the dictionary.

The complete Photo class is shown in Listing 6-3. If you would like to examine the code for the tests, download the finished project anonymously from github using the following URL:

```
https://github.com/asmtechnology/Lesson06.iOSTesting.2017.Apress.git
```

Listing 6-3. Photo.swift

```swift
import Foundation

class Photo: NSObject {

    var imageName:String?
    var aperture:String?
    var shutterSpeed:String?
    var iso:String?
    var comments:String?

    let imageNameKey = "imageName"
    let apertureKey = "aperture"
    let shutterSpeedKey = "shutterSpeed"
    let isoKey = "iso"
    let commentKey = "comment"

    init?(_ dictionary:[String : AnyObject]?) {

        guard let dictionary = dictionary,
            let imageName = dictionary[imageNameKey] as? String,
            let aperture = dictionary[apertureKey] as? String,
            let shutterSpeed = dictionary[shutterSpeedKey] as? String,
            let iso = dictionary[isoKey] as? String,
            let comments = dictionary[commentKey]  as? String else {
                return nil
        }

        super.init()

        self.imageName = imageName
        self.aperture = aperture
        self.shutterSpeed = shutterSpeed
        self.iso = iso
        self.comments = comments
    }

}
```

The City Class

The City class contains properties that store the information on a city and the photos that were taken in that city. Table 6-3 lists the desired properties and methods of the City class.

Table 6-3. *City Properties and Methods*

Item	Type	Description
var cityName:String?	Variable	The name of a city. No validation is applied to this field.
var photos:[Photo]?	Variable	Array of Photo objects. Each of these photos was taken in the same city.
init?(_ dictionary: [String : AnyObject]?)	Method	Allows other code to create City instances. Requires a dictionary with certain mandatory keys as input.

The init method will require a dictionary with all of the following mandatory keys to be present:

- city
- photos

The complete City class is presented in Listing 6-4. If you would like to examine the code for the tests, download the finished project anonymously from github using the following URL:

https://github.com/asmtechnology/Lesson06.iOSTesting.2017.Apress.git

Listing 6-4. City.swift

```
import Foundation

class City: NSObject {

    var cityName:String?
    var photos:[Photo]?

    let cityKey = "city"
    let photosKey = "photos"

    init?(_ dictionary:[String:AnyObject]?) {
        guard let dictionary = dictionary,
            let cityName = dictionary[cityKey] as? String,
            let array = dictionary[photosKey] as? [AnyObject] else {
                return nil
        }
```

```
    super.init()

    self.cityName = cityName
    self.photos = [Photo]()

    for item in array {
        guard let dictionary = item as? [String : AnyObject] else {
            continue
        }

        if let photo = Photo(dictionary) {
            photos?.append(photo)
        }
    }
  }

}
```

The Album Class

The Album class contains properties that store the information on a collection of city instances. The album is the top-level model object for this project. Table 6-4 lists the desired properties and methods of the Album class.

Table 6-4. City Properties and Methods

Item	Type	Description
var cities:[City]?	Variable	Array of City objects.
init()	Method	Allows other code to create Album instances.
func load(filePath:String?) -> Void	Method	Used to load a plist file and recursively create model layer objects.

The load method is provided to allow your app to load the Albums.plist file and create City objects from the contents of the plist file.

The complete Album class is presented in Listing 6-5. If you would like to examine the code for the tests, download the finished project anonymously from github using the following URL:

```
https://github.com/asmtechnology/Lesson06.iOSTesting.2017.Apress.git
```

Listing 6-5. Album.swift

```swift
import Foundation

class Album: NSObject {

    var cities:[City]?

    override init() {
        super.init()

        if cities == nil {
            cities = [City]()
        }
    }

    func load(filePath:String?) -> Void {

        guard let filePath = filePath,
            let array = NSArray(contentsOfFile: filePath) as? [AnyObject]
            else {
                return
        }

        for item in array {
            guard let dictionary = item as? [String : AnyObject] else {
                continue
            }

            if let city = City(dictionary) {
                cities?.append(city)
            }
        }

    }
}
```

Building the ViewModel Layer

There are three view model classes that we need to build:

- CollectionViewModel,
- CollectionViewCellViewModel, and
- CollectionViewSectionHeaderViewModel.

These correspond to the CollectionViewController, CollectionViewCell, and CollectionViewSectionHeader classes respectively.

The view models will use protocols to establish an interface through which they can communicate with their respective view controllers.

The CollectionViewModel Class

The CollectionViewModel class represents the view model between the CollectionViewController class and the Album model object.

Create a new iOS Unit Test Case class called CollectionViewModelTests under the PhotoBookTests group of the project explorer. Ensure this new file is part of the PhotoBookTests target only.

Delete the testExample and testPerformanceExample methods from CollectionViewModelTests.swift. Create a new unit test method called the following:

testInit_ValidView_InstantiatesObject()in a separate extension and add following code to the method body:

```swift
func testInit_ValidView_InstantiatesObject() {
    let viewModel = CollectionViewModel(view:mockCollectionViewController!)
    XCTAssertNotNil(viewModel)
}
```

Add the following variable declaration to the top of the CollectionViewModelTests class:

```swift
fileprivate var mockCollectionViewController:MockCollectionViewController?
```

You will notice that this code fails to compile; this is because the CollectionViewModel class has not been created yet. To fix this failure, create a new class called CollectionViewModel under the ViewModel group in the project navigator. In the file location dialog box, ensure both the PhotoBook and PhotoBookTests targets are checked (see Figure 6-21).

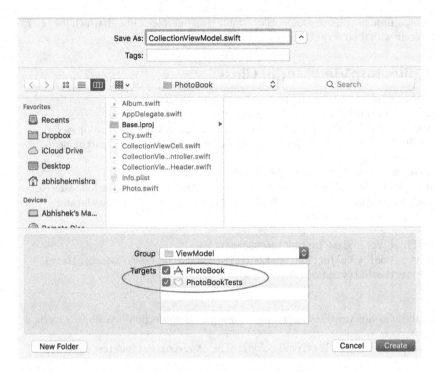

Figure 6-21. *CollectionViewModel.swift Target Membership*

Update the contents of the CollectionViewModel.swift file to match the following code snippet:

```
import Foundation

class CollectionViewModel : NSObject {

    init(view:CollectionViewControllerProtocol) {
        super.init()
    }
}
```

The initializer for the CollectionViewModel class takes a reference to the view. Note that the type of the view parameter is CollectionViewControllerProtocol and not CollectionViewController.

The view model makes use of a protocol to create a loosely coupled relationship with the view. As far as the view model is concerned, any class that implements the CollectionViewControllerProtocol protocol can be used as the view. This loose coupling with the view makes the view model easy to instantiate in a unit test, independent of a view controller.

Create a new Swift file called CollectionViewControllerProtocol under the Protocols group of the project explorer, and ensure the new file is a member of both the PhotoBook and PhotoBookTests targets. Update the code in CollectionViewControllerProtocol .swift to resemble the following:

```
import Foundation

protocol CollectionViewControllerProtocol : class {

}
```

Create a new group called Mocks under the PhotoBookTests group, and create a new Swift class called MockCollectionViewController under the Mocks group. Ensure the MockCollectionViewController.swift file is only a member of the PhotoBookTests target.
Update the code in MockCollectionViewController.swift to resemble the following:

```
import UIKit
import XCTest

class MockCollectionViewController : CollectionViewControllerProtocol {

}
```

Open the CollectionViewModelTests.swift file and update the setUp() method to resemble the following:

```
override func setUp() {
    super.setUp()
    mockCollectionViewController = MockCollectionViewController()
}
```

The updated setup() method instantiates a MockCollectionViewController object and saves a reference to this new instance in the mockCollectionViewController private variable. The code in CollectionViewModelTests.swift should now resemble Listing 6-6.

Listing 6-6. CollectionViewModelTests.swift

```
import XCTest

class CollectionViewModelTests: XCTestCase {

    fileprivate var mockCollectionViewController:MockCollectionViewController?

    override func setUp() {
        super.setUp()
        mockCollectionViewController = MockCollectionViewController()
    }
```

```
override func tearDown() {
    // Put teardown code here. This method is called after the
    invocation of each test method in the class.
    super.tearDown()
}

}

// MARK: initialization tests
extension CollectionViewModelTests {

    func testInit_ValidView_InstantiatesObject() {
        let viewModel = CollectionViewModel(view:mockCollectionViewController!)
        XCTAssertNotNil(viewModel)
    }

}
```

Save the file and run all unit tests using the Product ➤ Test menu item. You will see that the unit test you have added in CollectionViewModelTests.swift has passed (see Figure 6-22).

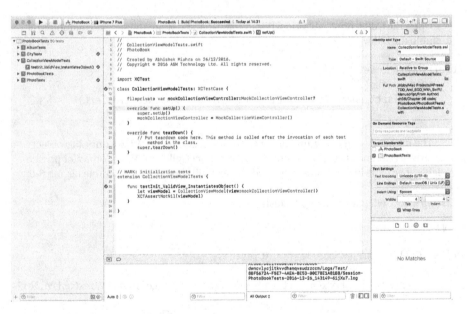

Figure 6-22. *CollectionViewModel Tests are Passing*

The view model test created so far verifies that a view model can be instantiated, and in order to make this test pass you created a view model class, a protocol, and a mock class.

The next test you will write will verify that the view model saves a reference to the view that was injected into the initializer, in an instance variable. Create a new unit test method called the following:

testInit_ValidView_CopiesViewToIvar() under the previous test method and add following code to the method body:

```
func testInit_ValidView_CopiesViewToIvar() {

        let viewModel = CollectionViewModel(view:mockCollectionViewController!)

        if let lhs = mockCollectionViewController, let rhs = viewModel.view
        as? MockCollectionViewController {
            XCTAssertTrue(lhs === rhs)
        }
}
```

Add the following variable declaration to the CollectionViewModel class:

```
weak var view:CollectionViewControllerProtocol?
```

Add the following line to the end of the init() method of the CollectionViewModel class:

```
self.view = view
```

Save the file and run all unit tests using the Product ➤ Test menu item. You will notice that all tests written so far continue to pass.

The next test you will write will verify that the view model de-serializes the Albums. plist file into an Album object and stores a reference to this Album object in an instance variable. Create a new unit test method called the following:

testInit_ValidView_AlbumIVarIsNotNil() under the previous test method and add following code to the method body:

```
func testInit_ValidView_AlbumIVarIsNotNil() {
    let viewModel = CollectionViewModel(view:mockCollectionViewController!)
    XCTAssertNotNil(viewModel.photoAlbum)
}
```

Add the following variable declaration to the CollectionViewModel class:

```
var photoAlbum:Album?
```

Add the following code to the end of the init() method of the CollectionViewModel class:

```
if photoAlbum == nil {
    photoAlbum = Album()
}

let path = Bundle.main.path(forResource: "Albums", ofType: "plist")
photoAlbum?.load(filePath:path)
```

187

The above snippet creates an Album object and calls the load() method on the Album object with the path to the Albums.plist file.

Save the file and run all unit tests using the Product ➤ Test menu item. You will notice that all tests written so far continue to pass.

View Model – View Controller Binding

Table 6-5 lists the methods we will add to the CollectionViewModel class. Most of these methods will be called from the collection view delegate and data source methods of the view controller.

Table 6-5. *CollectionViewModel Methods*

Item	Description
func performInitialViewSetup()	Should be called from the viewDidLoad() method of the collection view controller class. Resets user interface elements to their initial states.
func numberOfSections() -> Int	Called from the numberOfSections(in collectionView: UICollectionView) -> Int collection view data source method. Returns the number of City object in the Album.
func numberOfItemsInSection (_ section: Int) -> Int	Called from the collectionView (_ collectionView: UICollectionView, numberOfItemsInSection section: Int) -> Int collection view data source method. Returns the number of Photo objects in a given City object.
func cellViewModel(in dexPath:IndexPath) -> CellViewModelProtocol?	Called from the collectionView (_ collectionView: UICollectionView, cellForItemAt indexPath: IndexPath) -> UICollectionViewCell collection view data source method. Returns a view model that can be used by a collection view cell.
func headerViewModel (indexPath:IndexPath) -> HeaderViewModelProtocol?	Called from the collectionView (_ collectionView: UICollectionView, viewForSupplementaryElementOfKind kind: String, at indexPath: IndexPath) -> UICollectionReusableView collection view data source method. Returns a view model that can be used by a collection view cell.

It is worth noting that both the collection view cell and collection view section header use their own view models. Both these view models can be instantiated by calling the appropriate method on a CollectionViewModel object.

We haven't discussed the view models for the collection view cell and section header yet. For the purposes of building the CollectionViewModel object first, you will create a bare-bones version of the other view model objects. Once the CollectionViewModel class has been built, you will build other view model objects in subsequent sections of this chapter.

Since the collection view model uses a protocol to bind with the collection view controller, you will need to add methods to the protocol that will allow the view model to request the view controller to update user interface elements. Table 6-6 lists the methods that will be added to CollectionViewControllerProtocol.

Table 6-6. CollectionViewControllerProtocol Methods

Item	Description
func setNavigationTitle (_ title:String) -> Void	Called by the view model. The collection view controller should set up for the appropriate title for the navigation controller.
func setSectionInset(top:Float, left:Float, bottom:Float, right:Float) -> Void	Called by the view model. The collection view controller should set up the section insets for the collection view.
func setupCollectionViewCellToUseMaxWidth() -> Void	Called by the view model. The collection view controller should ensure that each cell occupies all of the available screen width.

You will now develop the methods of the CollectionViewModel class using TDD techniques.

Testing the performInitialViewSetup Method

The performInitialViewSetupMethod method should perform the following tasks:

- Set the text displayed in the navigation bar.
- Set up the UICollectionView object's section insets.
- Setup the cell size of the UICollectionView object to ensure it is as wide as possible.

Add the following code snippet to the bottom of the CollectionViewModelTests.swift file:

```
// MARK: performInitialViewSetup tests
extension CollectionViewModelTests {
```

```
func testPerformInitialViewSetup_Calls_SetNavigationTitle_
OnCollectionViewController() {
    let expectation = self.expectation(description: "expected
    setNavigationTitle() to be called")
    mockCollectionViewController!.expectationForSetNavigationTitle =
    expectation

    let viewModel = CollectionViewModel(view:mockCollectionViewController!)
    viewModel.performInitialViewSetup()

    self.waitForExpectations(timeout: 1.0, handler: nil)

}

func testPerformInitialViewSetup_Calls_SetSectionInset_
OnCollectionViewController() {
    let expectation = self.expectation(description: "expected
    setSectionInset() to be called")
    mockCollectionViewController!.expectationForSetSectionInset =
    expectation

    let viewModel = CollectionViewModel(view:mockCollectionViewController!)
    viewModel.performInitialViewSetup()

    self.waitForExpectations(timeout: 1.0, handler: nil)

}

func testPerformInitialViewSetup_Calls_
SetupCollectionViewCellToUseMaxWidth_OnCollectionViewController() {
    let expectation = self.expectation(description: "expected
    setupCollectionViewCellToUseMaxWidth() to be called")
    mockCollectionViewController!.
    expectationForSetupCollectionViewCellToUseMaxWidth = expectation

    let viewModel = CollectionViewModel(view:mockCollectionViewController!)
    viewModel.performInitialViewSetup()

    self.waitForExpectations(timeout: 1.0, handler: nil)
}

}
```

This code snippet adds three new test cases, one for each task that must be performed by performInitialViewSetup(). Since all three test cases test parts of a single method, I have grouped them into in a class extension; however you can add all four test methods to the class definition instead of a separate extension.

To get this code to compile, you will need to make a few code changes to the project:

Add a few variable declarations and method implementations to the MockCollectionViewController.swift file:

```
var expectationForSetNavigationTitle:XCTestExpectation?
var expectationForSetSectionInset:XCTestExpectation?
var expectationForSetupCollectionViewCellToUseMaxWidth:XCTestExpectation?

func setNavigationTitle(_ title:String) -> Void {
    expectationForSetNavigationTitle?.fulfill()
}

func setSectionInset(top:Float, left:Float, bottom:Float, right:Float) ->
Void {
    expectationForSetSectionInset?.fulfill()
}

func setupCollectionViewCellToUseMaxWidth() -> Void {
    expectationForSetupCollectionViewCellToUseMaxWidth?.fulfill()
}
```

Add the following method implementation to the CollectionViewModel.swift file:

```
func performInitialViewSetup() {
    view?.setNavigationTitle("Photo Album")
    view?.setSectionInset(top: 20, left: 0, bottom: 0, right: 0)
    view?.setupCollectionViewCellToUseMaxWidth()
}
```

Add the following method definitions to the CollectionViewControllerProtocol.swift file:

```
func setNavigationTitle(_ title:String) -> Void
func setSectionInset(top:Float, left:Float, bottom:Float, right:Float) -> Void
func setupCollectionViewCellToUseMaxWidth() -> Void
```

Add the following method implementations to the CollectionViewController.swift file in a class extension:

```
extension CollectionViewController : CollectionViewControllerProtocol {

    func setNavigationTitle(_ title:String) -> Void {
        self.title = title
    }

    func setSectionInset(top:Float, left:Float, bottom:Float, right:Float)
    -> Void {
```

```
    if let collectionView = self.collectionView,
        let collectionViewLayout = collectionView.collectionViewLayout
        as? UICollectionViewFlowLayout {
        collectionViewLayout.sectionInset = UIEdgeInsetsMake(20, 0, 20, 0)
    }
}

func setupCollectionViewCellToUseMaxWidth() -> Void {

    if let collectionView = self.collectionView,
        let collectionViewLayout = collectionView.collectionViewLayout
        as? UICollectionViewFlowLayout {
        collectionViewLayout.itemSize = CGSize(width: collectionView.
        bounds.width, height: collectionView.bounds.width * 0.6)
    }
  }
}
```

Save the file and run all unit tests using the Product ➤ Test menu item. You will see that the unit tests you have added in LoginViewModelTests.swift have passed (see Figure 6-23).

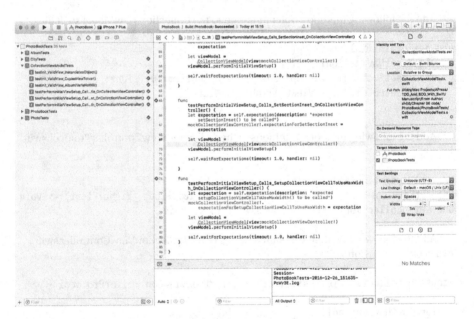

Figure 6-23. LoginViewModel Tests are all Passing

Testing the numberOfSections Method

The numberOfSections() method of the view model is called by the collection view controller's numberOfSections(in collectionView: UICollectionView) -> Int method. When this method is called, the view model returns the number of City objects in the Album.

Add the following code snippet to the bottom of the CollectionViewModelTests.swift file:

```
// MARK: numberOfSections  tests
extension CollectionViewModelTests {

    func testNumberOfSections_ValidViewModelWithAlbum_
    ReturnsNumberOfCitiesInAlbum() {
        let viewModel = CollectionViewModel(view:mockCollectionViewController!)
        XCTAssertEqual(viewModel.numberOfSections(), viewModel.photoAlbum!.
        cities!.count)
    }

    func testNumberOfSections_ValidViewModelNilAlbum_ReturnsZero() {
        let viewModel = CollectionViewModel(view:mockCollectionViewController!)
        viewModel.photoAlbum = nil

        XCTAssertEqual(viewModel.numberOfSections(), 0)
    }
}
```

Add the following method implementation to the CollectionViewModel.swift file:

```
func numberOfSections() -> Int {
    guard let photoAlbum = photoAlbum,
        let cities = photoAlbum.cities else {
            return 0
    }

    return cities.count
}
```

Save the file and run all unit tests using the Product > Test menu item. You will see that the unit tests you have added in CollectionViewModelTests.swift have passed.

Testing the numberOfItemsInSection Method

The numberOfItemsInSection(_ section: Int) method of the view model is called by the collection view controller's collectionView(_ collectionView: UICollectionView, numberOfItemsInSection section: Int) -> Int method. When this method is called, the view model returns the number of Photo objects in the City object identified by the section parameter. If the section parameter is invalid the method returns 0.

Add the following code snippet to the bottom of the CollectionViewModelTests.swift file:

```
// MARK: numberOfItemsInSection tests
extension CollectionViewModelTests {

    func testNumberOfItemsInSection_ValidViewModelNilAlbum_ReturnsZero() {
        let viewModel = CollectionViewModel(view:mockCollectionViewController!)
        viewModel.photoAlbum = nil

        XCTAssertEqual(viewModel.numberOfItemsInSection(0), 0)
    }

    func testNumberOfItemsInSection_ValidViewModelNilCities_ReturnsZero() {
        let viewModel = CollectionViewModel(view:mockCollectionViewController!)
        viewModel.photoAlbum!.cities = nil

        XCTAssertEqual(viewModel.numberOfItemsInSection(0), 0)
    }

    func testNumberOfItemsInSection_NegtiveSectionIndex_ReturnsZero() {
        let viewModel = CollectionViewModel(view:mockCollectionViewController!)

        XCTAssertEqual(viewModel.numberOfItemsInSection(-1), 0)
    }

    func testNumberOfItemsInSection_OutOfBoundsSectionIndex_ReturnsZero() {
        let viewModel = CollectionViewModel(view:mockCollectionViewController!)

        XCTAssertEqual(viewModel.numberOfItemsInSection(1000), 0)
    }

    func testNumberOfItemsInSection_ValidSectionIndex_ReturnsExpectedValue() {
        let viewModel = CollectionViewModel(view:mockCollectionViewController!)

        XCTAssertEqual(viewModel.numberOfItemsInSection(0), viewModel.
        photoAlbum!.cities![0].photos!.count)
    }

}
```

Add the following method implementation to the CollectionViewModel.swift file:

```
func numberOfItemsInSection(_ section: Int) -> Int {
    guard let photoAlbum = photoAlbum,
        let cities = photoAlbum.cities else {
            return 0
    }
```

```
if ((section < 0) || (section >= cities.count)) {
    return 0
}

guard let photos = cities[section].photos else {
    return 0
}

return photos.count
}
```

Save the file and run all unit tests using the Product ➤ Test menu item. You will see that the unit tests you have added in CollectionViewModelTests.swift have passed.

Testing the cellViewModel Method

The cellViewModel(indexPath:IndexPath) method of the view model is called by the collection view controller's collectionView(_ collectionView: UICollectionView, cellForItemAt indexPath: IndexPath) -> UICollectionViewCell method. When this method is called, the view model returns a view model for the collection view cell at the specified index path. If the indexPath parameter is invalid the method returns nil.

Add the following code snippet to the bottom of the CollectionViewModelTests.swift file:

```
// MARK: cellViewModel tests
extension CollectionViewModelTests {

    func testCellViewModel_ValidViewModelNilAlbum_ReturnsNil() {
        let viewModel = CollectionViewModel(view:mockCollectionViewController!)
        viewModel.photoAlbum = nil

        XCTAssertNil(viewModel.cellViewModel(indexPath:IndexPath(row: 0,
        section: 0)))
    }

    func testCellViewModel_ValidViewModelNilCities_ReturnsNil() {
        let viewModel = CollectionViewModel(view:mockCollectionViewController!)
        viewModel.photoAlbum!.cities = nil

        XCTAssertNil(viewModel.cellViewModel(indexPath:IndexPath(row: 0,
        section: 0)))
    }

    func testCellViewModel_ValidViewModelNilPhotos_ReturnsNil() {
        let viewModel = CollectionViewModel(view:mockCollectionViewController!)
        viewModel.photoAlbum!.cities![0].photos = nil
```

```
        XCTAssertNil(viewModel.cellViewModel(indexPath:IndexPath(row: 0,
        section: 0)))
    }

    func testCellViewModel_NegtiveRowIndex_ReturnsNil() {
        let viewModel = CollectionViewModel(view:mockCollectionViewController!)

        XCTAssertNil(viewModel.cellViewModel(indexPath:IndexPath(row: -1,
        section: 0)))
    }

    func testCellViewModel_NegtiveSectionIndex_ReturnsNil() {
        let viewModel = CollectionViewModel(view:mockCollectionViewController!)

        XCTAssertNil(viewModel.cellViewModel(indexPath:IndexPath(row: 0,
        section: -1)))
    }

    func testCellViewModel_OutOfBoundsRowIndex_ReturnsNil() {
        let viewModel = CollectionViewModel(view:mockCollectionViewController!)

        XCTAssertNil(viewModel.cellViewModel(indexPath:IndexPath(row: 1000,
        section: 0)))
    }

    func testCellViewModel_OutOfBoundsSectionIndex_ReturnsNil() {
        let viewModel = CollectionViewModel(view:mockCollectionViewController!)

        XCTAssertNil(viewModel.cellViewModel(indexPath:IndexPath(row: 0,
        section: 1000)))
    }

    func testCellViewModel_ValidSectionIndex_DoesNotReturnNil() {
        let viewModel = CollectionViewModel(view:mockCollectionViewController!)

        XCTAssertNotNil(viewModel.cellViewModel(indexPath:IndexPath(row: 0,
        section: 0)))
    }

    func testCellViewModel_ValidSectionIndex_
    ReturnsViewModelWithExpectedModelObject() {
        let viewModel = CollectionViewModel(view:mockCollectionViewController!)

        let rowIndex = 0
        let sectionIndex = 0

        let cellViewModel = viewModel.cellViewModel(indexPath:IndexPath(row:
        rowIndex, section: sectionIndex))
```

```
        let expectedModelObject = viewModel.photoAlbum!.
        cities![sectionIndex].photos![rowIndex]

        XCTAssertEqual(cellViewModel!.photo, expectedModelObject)

    }

}
```

Add the following method implementation to the CollectionViewModel.swift file:

```
func cellViewModel(indexPath:IndexPath) -> CellViewModelProtocol? {

    guard let photoAlbum = photoAlbum,
        let cities = photoAlbum.cities else {
            return nil
    }

    if ((indexPath.section < 0) || (indexPath.section >= cities.count)) {
        return nil
    }

        guard let photos = cities[indexPath.section].photos else {
        return nil
    }

    if ((indexPath.row < 0) || (indexPath.row >= photos.count)) {
        return nil
    }

    return CollectionViewCellViewModel(model:photos[indexPath.row])
}
```

Create a new Swift file called CollectionViewCellViewModel.swift under the ViewModel group of the project explorer, and ensure the new file is a member of both the PhotoBook and PhotoBookTests targets. Update the code in CollectionViewCellViewModel.swift to resemble the following:

```
import Foundation

class CollectionViewCellViewModel : NSObject {

    weak var photo:Photo?

    init?(model:Photo?) {

        guard let model = model else {
            return nil
        }
```

```
            super.init()
            self.photo = model
    }
}
```

The CollectionViewCellViewModel class will act as the view model for the collection view cell. Although this class has not been discussed in detail just yet, you will need a bare-bones implementation in order to get the tests to compile.

Save the file and run all unit tests using the Product ➤ Test menu item. You will see that the unit tests you have added in CollectionViewModelTests.swift have passed.

Testing the headerViewModel Method

The headerViewModel(indexPath: IndexPath) method of the view model is called by the collection view controller's collectionView(_ collectionView: UICollectionView, viewForSupplementaryElementOfKind kind: String, at indexPath: IndexPath) -> UICollectionReusableView method. When this method is called, the view model returns a view model for the collection view section header at the specified index path. If the indexPath parameter is invalid the method returns nil.

Add the following code snippet to the bottom of the CollectionViewModelTests.swift file:

```
// MARK: headerViewModel tests
extension CollectionViewModelTests {

    func testHeaderViewModel_ValidViewModelNilAlbum_ReturnsNil() {
        let viewModel = CollectionViewModel(view:mockCollectionViewController!)
        viewModel.photoAlbum = nil

        XCTAssertNil(viewModel.headerViewModel(indexPath:IndexPath(row: 0,
        section: 0)))
    }

    func testHeaderViewModel_ValidViewModelNilCities_ReturnsNil() {
        let viewModel = CollectionViewModel(view:mockCollectionViewController!)
        viewModel.photoAlbum!.cities = nil

        XCTAssertNil(viewModel.headerViewModel(indexPath:IndexPath(row: 0,
        section: 0)))
    }

    func testHeaderViewModel_NegtiveSectionIndex_ReturnsNil() {
        let viewModel = CollectionViewModel(view:mockCollectionViewController!)

        XCTAssertNil(viewModel.headerViewModel(indexPath:IndexPath(row: 0,
        section: -1)))
    }
```

```swift
func testHeaderViewModel_OutOfBoundsSectionIndex_ReturnsNil() {
    let viewModel = CollectionViewModel(view:mockCollectionViewController!)

    XCTAssertNil(viewModel.headerViewModel(indexPath:IndexPath(row: 0,
    section: 1000)))
}

func testHeaderViewModel_ValidSectionIndex_DoesNotReturnNil() {
    let viewModel = CollectionViewModel(view:mockCollectionViewController!)

    XCTAssertNotNil(viewModel.headerViewModel(indexPath:IndexPath(row:
    0, section: 0)))
}

func testHeaderViewModel_ValidSectionIndex_
ReturnsViewModelWithExpectedSectionTitle() {
    let viewModel = CollectionViewModel(view:mockCollectionViewController!)

    let rowIndex = 0
    let sectionIndex = 0

    let headerViewModel = viewModel.headerViewModel(indexPath:IndexPath
    (row: rowIndex, section: sectionIndex))

    let expectedSectionTitle = viewModel.photoAlbum!.
    cities![sectionIndex].cityName!

    XCTAssertEqual(headerViewModel!.sectionTitle, expectedSectionTitle)

}

}
```

Add the following method implementation to the CollectionViewModel.swift file:

```swift
func headerViewModel(indexPath:IndexPath) ->
CollectionViewSectionHeaderViewModel? {
    guard let photoAlbum = photoAlbum,
        let cities = photoAlbum.cities else {
            return nil
    }

    if ((indexPath.section < 0) || (indexPath.section >= cities.count)) {
        return nil
    }

    return CollectionViewSectionHeaderViewModel(model:cities[indexPath.
    section].cityName)
}
```

Create a new Swift file called CollectionViewSectionHeaderViewModel.swift under the ViewModel group of the project explorer, and ensure the new file is a member of both the PhotoBook and PhotoBookTests targets. Update the code in CollectionViewSectionHeaderViewModel.swift to resemble the following:

```
import Foundation

class CollectionViewSectionHeaderViewModel : NSObject {

    var sectionTitle:String?

    init?(model:String?) {

        guard let model = model else {
            return nil
        }

        super.init()
        self.sectionTitle = model
    }

}
```

The CollectionViewSectionHeaderViewModel class will act as the view model for the collection view section header. Although this class has not been discussed in detail just yet, you will need a bare-bones implementation in order to get the tests to compile.

Save the file and run all unit tests using the Product ➤ Test menu item. You will see that the unit tests you have added in CollectionViewModelTests.swift have passed.

The CollectionViewCellViewModel Class

The CollectionViewCellViewModel class represents the view model for the collection view cell. The process of building the CollectionViewCellViewModel class is similar to that of the CollectionViewModel class.

The complete CollectionViewCellViewModel class is shown in Listing 6-7. If you would like to examine the code for the tests and related mock objects, download the finished project anonymously from github using the following URL:

```
https://github.com/asmtechnology/Lesson06.iOSTesting.2017.Apress.git
```

Listing 6-7. CollectionViewCellViewModel.swift

```
import Foundation

class CollectionViewCellViewModel : NSObject {

    weak var photo:Photo?
    var collectionViewCell:CollectionViewCellProtocol?
```

```swift
init?(model:Photo?) {

    guard let model = model else {
        return nil
    }

    super.init()
    self.photo = model
}

func setView(_ view:CollectionViewCellProtocol) {
    self.collectionViewCell = view
}

func setup() {

    guard let collectionViewCell = collectionViewCell ,
        let photo = photo,
        let imageName = photo.imageName,
        let aperture = photo.aperture,
        let shutterSpeed = photo.shutterSpeed,
        let iso = photo.iso,
        let comments = photo.comments else {
            return
    }

    collectionViewCell.loadImage(resourceName: imageName)
    collectionViewCell.setCaption(captionText: comments)
    collectionViewCell.setShotDetails(shotDetailsText: "\(aperture), \
    (shutterSpeed), ISO \(iso)")
    }
}
```

It is worth noting that the view model has a reference to the collection view cell and the type of this reference is CollectionViewCellProtocol. The CollectionViewCell protocol contains a small number of methods that allow the view model to update the contents of the collection view cell. The complete definition for this protocol is shown in Listing 6-8.

Listing 6-8. CollectionViewCellProtocol.swift

```swift
import Foundation

protocol CollectionViewCellProtocol : class {
    func loadImage(resourceName:String)
    func setCaption(captionText:String)
    func setShotDetails(shotDetailsText:String)
}
```

The CollectionViewSectionHeaderViewModel Class

The CollectionViewSectionHeaderViewModel class represents the view model for the collection view section header. The complete class is shown in Listing 6-9. If you would like to examine the code for the tests and related mock objects, download the finished project anonymously from github using the following URL:

```
https://github.com/asmtechnology/Lesson06.iOSTesting.2017.Apress.git
```

Listing 6-9. CollectionViewSectionHeaderViewModel.swift

```swift
import Foundation

class CollectionViewSectionHeaderViewModel : NSObject {

    var sectionTitle:String?
    var collectionViewSectionHeader:CollectionViewSectionHeaderProtocol?

    init?(model:String?) {

        guard let model = model else {
            return nil
        }

        super.init()
        self.sectionTitle = model
    }

    func setView(_ view:CollectionViewSectionHeaderProtocol) {
        self.collectionViewSectionHeader = view
    }

    func setup() {

        guard let collectionViewSectionHeader = collectionViewSectionHeader,
            let sectionTitle = sectionTitle else {
                return
        }

        collectionViewSectionHeader.setHeaderText(text: sectionTitle)
    }

}
```

It is worth noting that the view model has a reference to the collection view section header, and the type of this reference is CollectionViewSectionHeaderProtocol. The CollectionView CollectionViewSectionHeaderProtocol protocol contains a single method to allow the view model to update the text displayed in the section header. The complete definition for this protocol is shown in Listing 6-10.

Listing 6-10. CollectionViewSectionHeaderProtocol.swift

```
import Foundation

protocol CollectionViewSectionHeaderProtocol : class {
    func setHeaderText(text:String)
}
```

Binding the View Layer to the View Model

So far in this chapter, we have used a test-driven approach to build the model and view model layers. The view model objects have made use of protocols to describe an interface to the view layer, and for the purposes of testing the view model objects, you have used mock objects for the view layer.

The tests have all passed, which indicates the view model and model layers are working as expected, using mock view layer objects. It is now time to implement the view layer protocols on the actual view layer classes. Table 6-7 lists the view layer classes and the corresponding protocols that we need to implement.

Table 6-7. *View Layer Protocols*

View Layer Class	Protocol
CollectionViewController	CollectionViewControllerProtocol
CollectionViewCell	CollectionViewCellProtocol
CollectionViewSectionHeader	CollectionViewSectionHeaderProtocol

While implementing these protocols in the view layer, we are not going to use a test-driven approach as UI tests will be better suited to testing visual changes on the view layer.

Previously in this chapter, you have implemented the methods defined in CollectionViewControllerProtocol in the CollectionViewController class; therefore there is no need to make any changes to the CollectionViewController class in this section.

Add the following code to the end of the CollectionViewCell class to implement the methods of the CollectionViewCellProtocol protocol.

```
extension CollectionViewCell : CollectionViewCellProtocol {

    func loadImage(resourceName:String) {
        imageView.image = UIImage(named: resourceName)
    }

    func setCaption(captionText:String) {
        captionLabel.text = captionText
    }

    func setShotDetails(shotDetailsText:String) {
        shotDetailsLabel.text = shotDetailsText
    }

}
```

Add the following code to the end of the CollectionViewSectionHeader class to implement the methods of the CollectionViewSectionHeaderProtocol protocol.

```
extension CollectionViewSectionHeader : CollectionViewSectionHeaderProtocol {

    func setHeaderText(text:String) {
        title?.text = text
    }

}
```

Now all that is remaining is to bind the view controller classes to their respective view models; this will involve instantiating a view model (if one is not being passed in the initializer) and calling out to methods on the view model.

The process of using a test-driven approach to binding a view controller class to a view model has been covered in Chapter 5. The rest of the sections in this chapter will list the bindings and present the final code for the view controller class.

Binding the Collection View Controller Class to the View Model

Table 6-8 lists the methods in the CollectionViewController class along with their associated view model bindings.

Table 6-8. Collection view controller and view model bindings

Collection View Controller Method	Collection View Model Method
func viewDidLoad()	func performInitialViewSetup()
func numberOfSections(in collectionView: UICollectionView) -> Int	func numberOfSections() -> Int
func collectionView(_ collectionView: UICollectionView, numberOfItemsInSection section: Int) -> Int	func numberOfItemsInSection (_ section: Int) -> Int
func collectionView(_ collectionView: UICollectionView, cellForItemAt indexPath: IndexPath) -> UICollectionViewCell	func cellViewModel(indexPath:Index Path) -> CellViewModelProtocol?
func collectionView(_ collectionView: UICollectionView, viewForSupplementaryElementOfKind kind: String, at indexPath: IndexPath) -> UICollectionReusableView	func headerViewModel(indexPath:Index Path) -> HeaderViewModelProtocol?

The finished CollectionViewController class is provided in Listing 6-11. If you would like to examine the code for the tests and related mock objects, download the finished project anonymously from github using the following URL:

```
https://github.com/asmtechnology/Lesson06.iOSTesting.2017.Apress.git
```

Listing 6-11. CollectionViewController.swift

```swift
import UIKit

private let cellReuseIdentifier = "CollectionViewCell"
private let headerReuseIdentifier = "CollectionViewSectionHeader"

class CollectionViewController: UICollectionViewController {

    var viewModel:CollectionViewModel?

    override func viewDidLoad() {
        super.viewDidLoad()

        if self.viewModel == nil {
            self.viewModel = CollectionViewModel(view: self)
        }

        self.viewModel?.performInitialViewSetup()
    }

    override func didReceiveMemoryWarning() {
        super.didReceiveMemoryWarning()
        // Dispose of any resources that can be recreated.
    }

    // MARK: UICollectionViewDataSource
    override func numberOfSections(in collectionView: UICollectionView) -> Int {
        guard let viewModel = viewModel else {
            return 0
        }

        return viewModel.numberOfSections()
    }

    override func collectionView(_ collectionView: UICollectionView,
    numberOfItemsInSection section: Int) -> Int {
        guard let viewModel = viewModel else {
            return 0
        }

        return viewModel.numberOfItemsInSection(section)
    }
```

```swift
    override func collectionView(_ collectionView: UICollectionView,
    cellForItemAt indexPath: IndexPath) -> UICollectionViewCell {

        let cell = collectionView.dequeueReusableCell(withReuseIdentifier:
        cellReuseIdentifier, for: indexPath)

        guard let viewModel = viewModel,
            let collectionViewCell = cell as? CollectionViewCell,
            let cellViewModel = viewModel.cellViewModel(indexPath:indexPath)
            else {
                return cell
        }

        collectionViewCell.viewModel = cellViewModel
        cellViewModel.setView(collectionViewCell)

        collectionViewCell.setup()
        return collectionViewCell
    }

    override func collectionView(_ collectionView: UICollectionView,
    viewForSupplementaryElementOfKind kind: String, at indexPath: IndexPath)
    -> UICollectionReusableView {

        let header = collectionView.dequeueReusableSupplementaryView(ofKind:
        kind, withReuseIdentifier: headerReuseIdentifier, for: indexPath)

        guard let viewModel = viewModel,
            let sectionHeader = header as? CollectionViewSectionHeader,
            let sectionHeaderViewModel = viewModel.headerViewModel(indexPath
            :indexPath) else {
                return header
        }

        sectionHeader.viewModel = sectionHeaderViewModel
        sectionHeaderViewModel.setView(sectionHeader)

        sectionHeader.setup()
        return sectionHeader
    }
}

extension CollectionViewController : CollectionViewControllerProtocol {

    func setNavigationTitle(_ title:String) -> Void {
        self.title = title
    }
```

```swift
func setSectionInset(top:Float, left:Float, bottom:Float, right:Float)
-> Void {

    if let collectionView = self.collectionView,
        let collectionViewLayout = collectionView.collectionViewLayout
        as? UICollectionViewFlowLayout {
        collectionViewLayout.sectionInset = UIEdgeInsetsMake(20, 0, 20, 0)
    }
}

func setupCollectionViewCellToUseMaxWidth() -> Void {

    if let collectionView = self.collectionView,
        let collectionViewLayout = collectionView.collectionViewLayout
        as? UICollectionViewFlowLayout {
        collectionViewLayout.itemSize = CGSize(width: collectionView.
        bounds.width, height: collectionView.bounds.width * 0.6)
    }
}
}
}
```

Binding the CollectionViewCell Class to the View Model

Table 6-9 lists the methods in the CollectionViewCell class along with their associated view model bindings.

Table 6-9. *Collection view cell and view model bindings*

Collection View Cell Method	Cell View Model Method
func setup()	func setup()

The finished CollectionViewCell class is provided in Listing 6-12. If you would like to examine the code for the tests and related mock objects, download the finished project anonymously from github using the following URL:

https://github.com/asmtechnology/Lesson06.iOSTesting.2017.Apress.git

Listing 6-12. CollectionViewCell.swift

```swift
import UIKit

class CollectionViewCell: UICollectionViewCell {

    @IBOutlet weak var imageView: UIImageView!
    @IBOutlet weak var captionLabel: UILabel!
    @IBOutlet weak var shotDetailsLabel: UILabel!
```

```swift
    var viewModel:CollectionViewCellViewModel?

    func setup() {
        viewModel?.setup()
    }
}

extension CollectionViewCell : CollectionViewCellProtocol {

    func loadImage(resourceName:String) {
        imageView.image = UIImage(named: resourceName)
    }

    func setCaption(captionText:String) {
        captionLabel.text = captionText
    }

    func setShotDetails(shotDetailsText:String) {
        shotDetailsLabel.text = shotDetailsText
    }

}
```

Binding the CollectionViewSectionHeader Class to the View Model

Table 6-10 lists the methods in the CollectionViewSectionHeader class along with their associated view model bindings.

Table 6-10. *Collection view section header and view model bindings*

Collection View Section Header Method	Section Header View Model Method
func setup()	func setup()

The finished CollectionViewSectionHeader class is provided in Listing 6-13. If you would like to examine the code for the tests and related mock objects, download the finished project anonymously from github using the following URL:

https://github.com/asmtechnology/Lesson06.iOSTesting.2017.Apress.git

Listing 6-13. CollectionViewSectionHeader.swift

```swift
import UIKit

class CollectionViewSectionHeader: UICollectionReusableView {

    @IBOutlet weak var title: UILabel!
```

```swift
    var viewModel:CollectionViewSectionHeaderViewModel?

    func setup() {
        viewModel?.setup()
    }
}

extension CollectionViewSectionHeader : CollectionViewSectionHeaderProtocol {

    func setHeaderText(text:String) {
        title?.text = text
    }

}
```

This concludes the development of this collection view controller-based photo browser app.

Summary

In this chapter you have created a collection view controller-based application using TDD techniques and the MVVM application architecture. The app that you have built loads photos from the application bundle and displays the photos in collection view cells.

In the next chapter you will modify this example to download images over a network connection, instead of reading them from a property list file.

CHAPTER 7

■ ■ ■

Testing URLSession

This chapter will examine the process of applying TDD techniques to the networking layer of your application. There are various types of networking technologies available to iOS developers. This chapter will only cover networking with the URLSession class. The URLSession connection allows you to conveniently download resources over HTTP connections.

This chapter will modify the PhotoBook app that was built in Chapter 6. The modified version of the app will download images and metadata from a server on the Internet, as opposed to using bundled assets and .plist files.

There are no changes to the user interface of the application. Figure 7-1 depicts the user interface of the finished application (which is the same as the PhotoBook app at the end of Chapter 6).

© Abhishek Mishra 2017
A. Mishra, *iOS Code Testing*, DOI 10.1007/978-1-4842-2689-6_7

Figure 7-1. *User Interface of the PhotoBook Application*

The complete source code for the app can be downloaded anonymously from github using the following URL:

`https://github.com/asmtechnology/Lesson07.iOSTesting.2017.Apress.git`

The modified application architecture consists of an additional networking layer (see Figure 7-2).

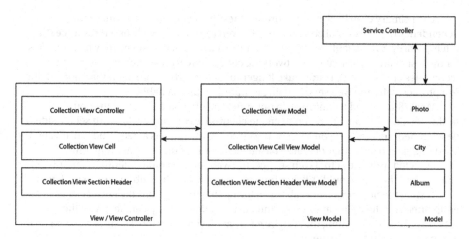

Figure 7-2. Modified Application Architecture with Networking Layer

A brief description of the layers and the component classes follows:

- **Model Layer:** Consists of the Photo, City, and Album classes.

- **View Model Layer:** Consists of the CollectionViewModel, CollectionViewCellViewModel, and CollectionViewSectionHeaderViewModel classes.

- **View/View Controller Layer:** Consists of the CollectionViewController, CollectionViewCell, and CollectionViewSectionHeader classes.

- **Networking Layer:** Consists of the ServiceController class, which provides convenient methods that can be used to download images and metadata asynchronously from back-end RESTful JSON web services.

Strategies for Testing the Networking Layer

There are two common approaches to testing networking code:

- **Asynchronous testing techniques:** These rely on making actual network calls to a server and using the waitForExpectations(timeout) method of XCTest to wait a few seconds for the network service to respond.

- **Mock/Stub based testing techniques:** These rely on creating mock or stub objects that replace HTTP calls altogether.

The primary drawback of asynchronous testing techniques is the inherent dependency on an external component (the web resource). A web-based resource that is temporarily unreachable, or a poorer-than-usual connection speed may be all it takes for the test to fail. Tests that test networking code and rely on asynchronous testing techniques are extremely brittle, take longer to execute, and more often than not fail due to a problem with the web service being temporarily unreachable.

Mock/Stub based techniques do not suffer the drawbacks of asynchronous testing techniques, and allow you to create client-side code in parallel with server-side development so long as a common web service specification is agreed upon in advance. The main drawback with mock/stub based techniques is that they are inherently disconnected from the actual web service, the web service could potentially completely change, and the tests would still continue to pass because the stubs were not updated.

Testing the network layer is about ensuring that the app calls the correct API endpoints with the right parameters, and ensuring that the app can deal with the response. This is something that can be easily achieved using mocks/stubs and will be the approach taken in this chapter.

Preparing the PhotoBook Project

Duplicate the PhotoBook Xcode project created in Chapter 6 and open the duplicate project in Xcode.

Locate the following files in the project navigator and delete them (see Figure 7-3).

- Albums.plist
- ValidAlbum.plist
- InvalidAlbum.plist
- InvalidAlbum2.plist
- EmptyAlbum.plist

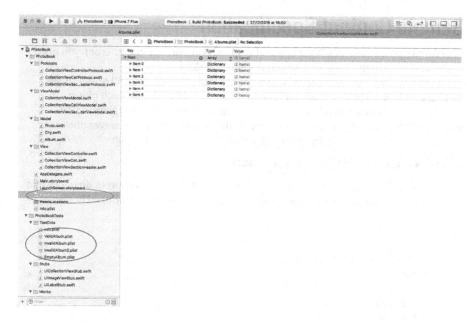

Figure 7-3. *Files to be Deleted from the Project*

Delete all the assets from the project's asset bundle, but do not delete the asset bundle itself. The asset bundle is called Assets.xcassets in the project navigator (see Figure 7-4).

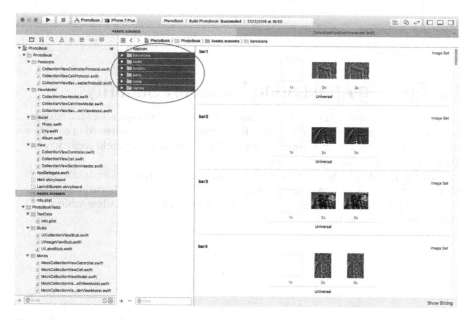

Figure 7-4. *Assets to be Deleted from the Project*

Remote Content Specification

In order to update the PhotoBook app to download content from the Internet, you need to know what form this content takes, and where it resides.

Let us assume that your server-side team has told you that they will host a single JSON file with metadata for cities and photos as well as JPEG files for each photo.

The JSON file will be called albumlist.json, and it, along with the relevant JPEG images, will be stored in the same directory on the remote server. The server does not support SSL and the URL to this directory on the server is the following:

http://www.asmtechnology.com/apress2017/

A sample JSON file with valid data has been included in the Resources directory that accompany this chapter's code downloads, a portion of which is reproduced below:

```
[
  {
    "city": "Vienna (Austria)",
    "photos": [
      {
        "imageName": "v1.jpg",
        "aperture": "f2.8",
        "shutterSpeed": "400",
        "iso": "100",
        "comment": "HDR image of a weekend market in Vienna."
      }
    ]
  }
]
```

Configuring Application Transport Security

The server that is used to host the images and metadata for this project does not support HTTPS connections. To allow plain vanilla HTTP connections, you will need to configure the project's Application Transport Security (ATS) settings. In a real-world scenario you should always use HTTPS connections.

Locate the Info.plist file under the PhotoBook group in the project navigator and click on it. Add a new dictionary key to this plist called App Transport Security Settings (see Figure 7-5). In this new dictionary, add a new Boolean key called Allow Arbitrary Loads with the value of Yes.

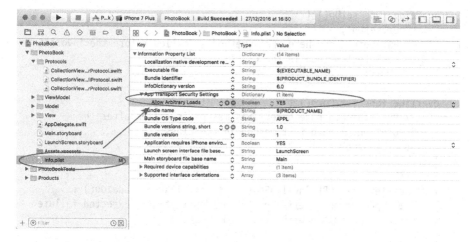

Figure 7-5. Application Transport Settings

Building the Networking Layer

The networking layer of this app consists of a single class called ServiceController that implements the following method:

```
func fetchFromURL(urlString:String?,
     success:@escaping (Data) -> Void,
     failure:@escaping (NSError) -> Void)
     -> Void
```

The fetchFromURL method requires three parameters:

- urlString: A string that contains the URL to download.

- success: A closure that will be called if the download succeeded.

- failure: A closure that will be called if the download did not succeed.

Create a new unit test case class called ServiceControllerTests and update its contents to match Listing 7-1.

Listing 7-1. ServiceControllerTests.swift

```
import XCTest

class ServiceControllerTests: XCTestCase {

    let invalidURL:String = ""
    let validAlbumListURL:String = "http://www.asmtechnology.com/apress2017/
    albumlist.json"
```

```swift
override func setUp() {
    super.setUp()
    // Put setup code here. This method is called before the invocation
    of each test method in the class.
}

override func tearDown() {
    // Put teardown code here. This method is called after the
    invocation of each test method in the class.
    super.tearDown()
}

func testfetchFromURL_invalidSession_fails_WithErrorCode100() {
    let expectation = self.expectation(description: "Expected failure
    block to be called with error code = 100")

    let serviceController =
                    ServiceController()
    serviceController.session = nil

        serviceController.fetchFromURL(
        urlString: validAlbumListURL,
        success: { (data) in
                    // do nothing
        },
        failure:{ (error) in
                    if error.code == 100 {
                            expectation.fulfill()
                    }
        })

    self.waitForExpectations(timeout: 1.0,
                            handler: nil)
}

func testfetchFromURL_nilURL_fails_WithErrorCode101() {
    let expectation = self.expectation(description: "Expected failure
    block to be called with error code = 101")

    let serviceController =
                    ServiceController()

        serviceController.fetchFromURL(
        urlString: nil,
    success: { (data) in
            // do nothing
        },
```

```
                failure:{ (error) in
                        if error.code == 101 {
                            expectation.fulfill()
                    }
            })

    self.waitForExpectations(timeout: 1.0,
                                handler: nil)
}

func testfetchFromURL_invalidURL_fails_WithErrorCode101() {
    let expectation = self.expectation(description: "Expected failure
    block to be called with error code = 101")

    let serviceController =
                    ServiceController()

        serviceController.fetchFromURL(
        urlString: invalidURL,
      success: { (data) in
            // do nothing
        },
        failure:{ (error) in
                    if error.code == 101 {
                        expectation.fulfill()
                }
            })

    self.waitForExpectations(timeout: 1.0,
                                handler: nil)
}

func testfetchFromURL_validURL_callsDataTask_onURLSession_
withTheSameURL() {

    guard let expectedURL = URL(string: validAlbumListURL) else {
        return
    }

    let expectation = self.expectation(description: "Expected dataTask
    to be called on URLSession")

    let mockURLSession = MockURLSession()
    mockURLSession.dataTaskExpectation =
                    (expectation, expectedURL)

    let serviceController =
                        ServiceController()
```

```
        serviceController.session =
                                    mockURLSession

        serviceController.fetchFromURL(

urlString: validAlbumListURL,
                success: { (data) in
                            // do nothing
                },
                failure:{ (error) in
                            // do nothing
        })

        self.waitForExpectations(timeout: 1.0,
                                    handler: nil)
    }

    func testfetchFromURL_validURL_validDataTask_callsResume_onDataTask() {

        let expectation = self.expectation(description: "Expected dataTask
        block to be called on URLSession")

        let mockURLSession = MockURLSession()
        mockURLSession.dataTaskToReturn?.resumeExpectation = expectation

            let serviceController =
                        ServiceController()
            serviceController.session =
                        mockURLSession

            serviceController.fetchFromURL(
            urlString: validAlbumListURL,
            success: { (data) in
                            // do nothing
            },

            failure:{(error) in
                    // do nothing
            })

        self.waitForExpectations(timeout: 1.0,
                                    handler: nil)
    }

}
```

There are five unit tests in this class; each of these is briefly described below:

`testfetchFromURL_invalidSession_fails_WithErrorCode100()`

This test calls the fetchFromURL(urlString, success, failure) method of the ServiceController class. The ServiceController class is set up to have a nil URLSession, and the test expects the failure closure will be called with a specific error code.

`testfetchFromURL_nilURL_fails_WithErrorCode101()`

This test calls the fetchFromURL(urlString, success, failure) method of the ServiceController class with a nil value for the urlString parameter. The test expects the failure closure will be called with a specific error code.

`testfetchFromURL_invalidURL_fails_WithErrorCode101()`

This test calls the fetchFromURL(urlString, success, failure) method of the ServiceController class with an invalid value for the urlString parameter. The test expects the failure closure will be called with a specific error code.

This project does not have a dedicated URL validator object, and instead relies on the Swift URL class's failable initializer to fail if the string supplied cannot be converted into a valid URL.

`testfetchFromURL_validURL_callsDataTask_onURLSession_withTheSameURL()`

This test calls the fetchFromURL(urlString, success, failure) method of the ServiceController class with a valid URL. The test expects that the fetchFromURL method will call the dataTask(with, completionHandler) method on the URLSession object within the ServiceController class to retrieve a URLSessionDataTask instance.

`testfetchFromURL_validURL_validDataTask_callsResume_onDataTask()`

This test calls the fetchFromURL(urlString, success, failure) method of the ServiceController class with a valid URL. The test expects that the fetchFromURL method will call the resume method on the URLSessionDataTask instance that it has retrieved from the URL session.

These tests will not compile as they require the following classes to be defined:

- ServiceController
- MockURLSession
- MockURLSessionDataTask

Creating the ServiceController Class

Create a new group in the project navigator called Controllers, and ensure this group is under the PhotoBook group. Create a new Swift class called ServiceController under the Controllers group. Ensure that the new class is included in both the build as well as the test target. (See Figure 7-6.)

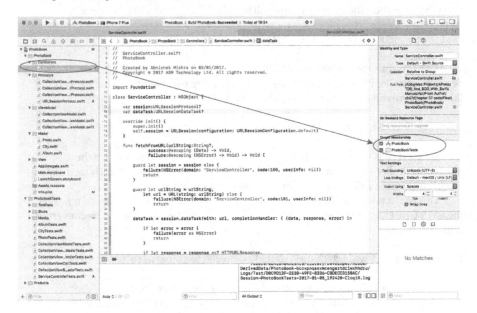

Figure 7-6. *Target Membership for the ServiceController.swift File*

Update the contents of ServiceController.swift to resemble Listing 7-2.

Listing 7-2. ServiceController.swift

```
import Foundation

class ServiceController : NSObject {

        var session:URLSessionProtocol?
        private var dataTask:URLSessionDataTask?

        override init() {
                super.init()
                self.session =

                URLSession(configuration:
                        URLSessionConfiguration.default)
        }

        func fetchFromURL(urlString:String?,
                success:@escaping (Data) -> Void,
```

```
        failure:@escaping (NSError) -> Void)
    -> Void {

        guard let session = session else {
            failure(NSError(
                domain: "ServiceController",
                code:100,
                userInfo: nil))
        return
        }

        guard let urlString = urlString,
        let url = URL(string: urlString)
        else {
            failure(NSError(
domain: "ServiceController",
                code:101,
                userInfo: nil))
            return
        }

        dataTask = session.dataTask(
                    with: url,
                    completionHandler: {
                    (data, response, error) in

        if let error = error {
            failure(error as NSError)
            return
        }

        if let response = response as?
                              HTTPURLResponse,
            let data = data {
            if response.statusCode == 200 {
                success(data)
                return
            }
        }

        failure(NSError(
            domain: "ServiceController", code:102,
            userInfo: nil))
        return
        })

        dataTask?.resume()
    }

}
```

This class has an init method, the fetchFromURL method, and a couple of instance variables. I would like to draw your attention to the session variable, which is declared as:

```
var session:URLSessionProtocol?
```

In most apps you may have built in the past, the session variable would be of type URLSession and not URLSessionProtocol. In fact there is no protocol provided by Apple by that name. The reason for using a protocol instead of a concrete type is to facilitate injecting a mock/stub object from a unit test.

Create a new Swift file called URLSessionProtocol.swift under the Protocols group and ensure the file is a member of both the build and test targets. Update the contents of the new file to resemble Listing 7-3.

Listing 7-3. URLSessionProtocol.swift

```
import Foundation

protocol URLSessionProtocol : class {
    func dataTask(with url: URL,
      completionHandler: @escaping (Data?,
          URLResponse?, Error?) -> Swift.Void) -> URLSessionDataTask
}

extension URLSession : URLSessionProtocol {

}
```

Creating the MockURLSession Class

Create a new Swift class under the Mocks group of the project explorer. Name the class MockURLSession and ensure that the new file is only included in the test target (see Figure 7-7).

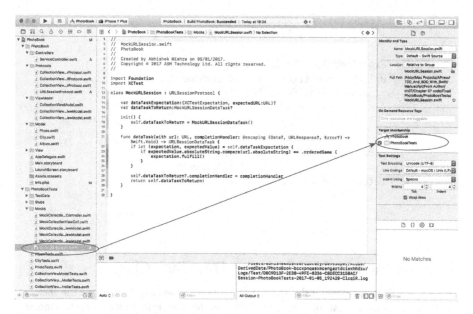

Figure 7-7. *Target Membership for the MockURLSession.swift File*

Update the contents of MockURLSession.swift to resemble Listing 7-4.

Listing 7-4. MockURLSession.swift

```swift
import Foundation
import XCTest

class MockURLSession : URLSessionProtocol {

    var dataTaskExpectation:
            (XCTestExpectation, expectedURL:URL)?
    var dataTaskToReturn:MockURLSessionDataTask?

    init() {
        self.dataTaskToReturn =
                        MockURLSessionDataTask()
    }

    func dataTask(with url: URL,
            completionHandler: @escaping (Data?,

                                URLResponse?,
                                Error?) -> Swift.Void)
        -> URLSessionDataTask {
```

```
        if let (expectation, expectedValue) =
                         self.dataTaskExpectation {

    if    expectedValue.absoluteString.compare(
          url.absoluteString) == .orderedSame {
             expectation.fulfill()
          }
    }

          self.dataTaskToReturn?.completionHandler =
                              completionHandler
          return self.dataTaskToReturn!
    }

}
```

Creating the MockURLSessionDataTask Class

Create a new Swift class under the Mocks group of the project explorer. Name the class
MockURLSessionDataTask and ensure that the new file is only included in the test target.
   Update the contents of MockURLSessionDataTask.swift to resemble Listing 7-5.

Listing 7-5. MockURLSessionDataTask.swift

```
import Foundation
import XCTest

class MockURLSessionDataTask : URLSessionDataTask {

    var resumeExpectation: XCTestExpectation?

    var completionHandler:((Data?, URLResponse?, Error?) -> Swift.Void)?
    var dataToReturn:Data?
    var urlResponseToReturn:URLResponse?
    var errorToReturn:Error?

    override func resume() {
        resumeExpectation?.fulfill()

        if let
            completionHandler = completionHandler
            {
            DispatchQueue.main.asyncAfter(
                    deadline: .now() + 0.1) {
                completionHandler(
                            self.dataToReturn,
                            self.urlResponseToReturn,
                            self.errorToReturn)
```

```
          }
        }
      }
    }
```

Save the file and use the Test Navigator to run all the tests in the ServiceController test case (see Figure 7-8). You should see all the tests in ServiceControllerTests.swift pass. However, if you try to run all tests using the Product ➤ Test menu item, you will see that some of other tests that were previously passing at the end of Chapter 6 now crash altogether.

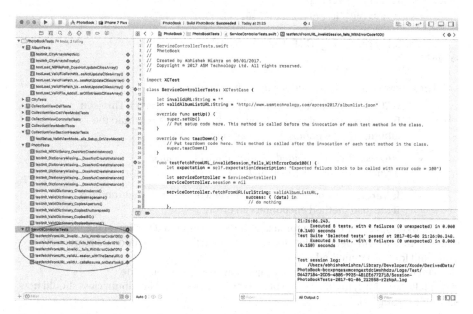

Figure 7-8. *All Test Cases in ServiceControllerTests.swift are Passing*

Over the rest of this chapter, you will fix/replace these broken tests to accommodate the fact that the app will now use the new ServiceController class to download content from the Internet.

Updating the Model Layer

The model layer of this app consists of three classes: Album, City, and Photo. The Album and the Photo class will need to be updated to use the new ServiceController class instead of the old method of loading a local .plist file and reading images from a local asset bundle.

Updating the Album Class

The current version of Album class has a method called

```
func load(filePath:String?) -> Void
```

When the Album class has been updated, this method will be replaced by a new method that has the same name, but accepts different parameters:

```
func load(urlString:String?,
    success:@escaping (Void) -> Void,

        failure:@escaping (NSError) -> Void)
-> Void
```

These new parameters are briefly described below:

- **urlString:** A URL that identifies a json file on the server. This json file will contain all metadata on an album, the cities within the album, and the photos within each city.

- **success:** A user-provided closure that will be called asynchronously if the load method succeeds.

- **failure:** A user-provide closure that will be called asynchronously if the load method encounters an error.

Let us adopt a test-driven approach to build the modified version of the load method. To start with, let us delete the old version of the load method and any tests that were built for the old method.

Open the Album.swift file in the project navigator and delete the load(filePath:String?) method as it will no longer be needed. The Album class should now resemble Listing 7-6.

Listing 7-6. Album.swift

```
import Foundation

class Album: NSObject {

    var cities:[City]?

    override init() {
        super.init()

        if cities == nil {
            cities = [City]()
        }
    }
}
```

Open the AlbumTests.swift file in the project navigator and delete the following test methods, as these tests are not relevant anymore:

- `testLoad_NilFilePath_DoesNotUpdateCitiesArray()`

- `testLoad_ValidFilePathWithNoCities_DoesNotUpdateCitiesArray()`

- `testLoad_ValidFilePath_InvalidRootElementType_DoesNotUpdateCitiesArray()`

- `testLoad_ValidFilePath_ValidRootElementType_InvalidChildElementType_DoesNotUpdateCitiesArray()`

- `testLoad_ValidFile_AddsExpectedNumberOfEntriestoCitiesArray()`

Delete the following instance variable declarations:

- `var emptyAlbumPlistFile: String?`

- `var invalidAlbumPlistFile: String?`

- `var invalidAlbumPlistFile2: String?`

- `var validAlbumPlistFile: String?`

Delete the following lines from the setUp() method:

```
let bundle = Bundle(for: type(of:self))

emptyAlbumPlistFile = bundle.path(
                forResource: "EmptyAlbum",
                ofType: "plist")

invalidAlbumPlistFile = bundle.path(
                forResource: "InvalidAlbum",
            ofType: "plist")

invalidAlbumPlistFile2 = bundle.path(
                forResource: "InvalidAlbum2",
            ofType: "plist")

validAlbumPlistFile = bundle.path(
                forResource: "ValidAlbum",
            ofType: "plist")
```

The AlbumTests class should now resemble Listing 7-7.

Listing 7-7. AlbumTests.swift

```
import XCTest

class AlbumTests: XCTestCase {

    override func setUp() {
        super.setUp()
    }

    override func tearDown() {
        // Put teardown code here. This method is called after the
        invocation of each test method in the class.
        super.tearDown()
    }

    func testInit_CityArrayIsNotNil() {
        let album = Album()
        XCTAssertNotNil(album.cities)
    }

    func testInit_CityArrayIsEmpty() {
        let album = Album()
        XCTAssertEqual(album.cities?.count, 0)
    }
}
```

Writing New Tests for the load() Method

Add the following tests to the AlbumTests.swift file:

```
func testLoad_nilURL_fails_withErrorCode101() {

    let expectation = self.expectation(description: "Expected failure
    block to be called with error code = 101")

            let album = Album()
            album.load(urlString: nil,
            success: { (Void) in
        // do nothing
            }, failure: { (error) in
        if error.code == 101 {
            expectation.fulfill()
        }
            })

        self.waitForExpectations(timeout: 1.0,
                                     handler: nil)
    }
```

```
func testLoad_invalidURL_fails_withErrorCode101() {

    let expectation = self.expectation(description: "Expected failure
    block to be called with error code = 101")

    let album = Album()
    album.load(
        urlString: invalidURL,
        success: { (Void) in
        // do nothing
    }, failure: { (error) in
        if error.code == 101 {
            expectation.fulfill()
        }

        })

    self.waitForExpectations(timeout: 1.0,
                                    handler: nil)
}

func testLoad_validURL_callsFromFetchURLonServiceController_
withExpectedURL() {

    let expectation = self.expectation(description: "Expected fetchURL
    to be called")

    let mockServiceController =
                        MockServiceController()
    mockServiceController.
                fetchFromURLExpectation =
                (expectation, validAlbumListURL)

    let album = Album()
    album.serviceController =
                mockServiceController

    album.load(
        urlString: validAlbumListURL,
        success: { (Void) in
        // do nothing
    }, failure: { (error) in
        // do nothing
    })

    self.waitForExpectations(timeout: 1.0,
                                    handler: nil)
}
```

```
func testLoad_validURL_failsWhenServiceControllerFails() {
        let expectation =
                self.expectation(description:
                "Expected fetchURL to be called")

        let mockServiceController =
            MockServiceController()
        mockServiceController.
            shouldFailOnFetch = true

        let album = Album()
        album.serviceController =
            mockServiceController

        album.load(
            urlString: validAlbumListURL,
            success: { (Void) in
            // do nothing
        }, failure: { (error) in
            expectation.fulfill()
        })

        self.waitForExpectations(timeout: 1.0,
                                 handler: nil)
    }

    func testLoad_onServiceControllerFailure_doesNotUpdateCityArray() {

        let mockServiceController =
                    MockServiceController()
        mockServiceController.
shouldFailOnFetch = true

        let album = Album()
        album.serviceController =
                    mockServiceController

        album.load(
            urlString: validAlbumListURL,
            success: { (Void) in
            // do nothing
        }, failure: { (error) in
            // do nothing
        })

        XCTAssertEqual(album.cities?.count, 0)
    }
```

```swift
func testLoad_validURL_serviceControllerReturnsValidData_
citiesArrayHasExpectedCount() {

    let bundle = Bundle(for: type(of:self))
    let filePath = bundle.path(
                forResource: "ValidAlbumList",
                ofType: "json")
    let stubResponseData = try!
            Data(contentsOf: URL(fileURLWithPath:
                                    filePath!))

    let mockServiceController =
                MockServiceController()
    mockServiceController.
                shouldFailOnFetch = false
    mockServiceController.
                dataToReturnOnSuccess =
                stubResponseData

    let album = Album()
        album.serviceController =
        mockServiceController

    album.load(
        urlString: validAlbumListURL,
        success: { (Void) in
        // do nothing
    }, failure: { (error) in
        // do nothing
    })

    XCTAssertEqual(album.cities?.count, 6)
}
```

There are six unit tests in the preceding snippet, and each of them are briefly described below:

```
testLoad_nilURL_fails_withErrorCode101()
```

This test calls the load(urlString, success, failure) method of the Album class with nil for the urlString parameter. The test expects that the failure closure will be called with a specific error code.

```
testLoad_invalidURL_fails_withErrorCode101()
```

This test calls the load(urlString, success, failure) method of the Album class with an invalid vlaue for the urlString parameter. The test expects that the failure closure will be called with a specific error code.

```
testLoad_validURL_callsFromFetchURLonServiceController_withExpectedURL()
```

This test calls the load(urlString, success, failure) method of the Album class with a valid URL. The test expects that the load method of the Album class will call the fetchFromURL method of the ServiceController class with the same URL that was provided to the load method.

```
testLoad_validURL_failsWhenServiceControllerFails()
```

This test calls the load(urlString, success, failure) method of the Album class with a valid URL and simulates a failure in the service controller class. The test expects that the failure closure that was provided to the load method will be called.

```
testLoad_onServiceControllerFailure_doesNotUpdateCityArray()
```

This test calls the load(urlString, success, failure) method of the Album class with a valid URL and simulates a failure in the service controller class. The test expects that the number of elements in the city array of the Album class have not changed.

Simulating a failure in the service controller class is achieved by injecting a MockServiceController object into the Album class:

```
let mockServiceController =
            MockServiceController()
mockServiceController.
            shouldFailOnFetch = true

let album = Album()
album.serviceController =
            mockServiceController
```

The MockServiceController class hasn't been built yet, but will have a Boolean instance variable called shouldFailOnFetch that will be used to simulate a failure within the fetchFromURL method.

```
testLoad_validURL_serviceControllerReturnsValidData_
citiesArrayHasExpectedCount()
```

This test calls the load(urlString, success, failure) method of the Album class with a valid URL and simulates a successfull download operation in the service controller class. The test expects a specific number of elements in the city array of the Album class.

Simulating a successful download operation in the service controller class is achieved by, once again, injecting a MockServiceController object into the Album class:

```
let bundle = Bundle(for: type(of:self))
let filePath = bundle.path(
            forResource: "ValidAlbumList",
            ofType: "json")
```

```
let stubResponseData = try!
        Data(contentsOf: URL(fileURLWithPath:
                                    filePath!))

let mockServiceController =
            MockServiceController()
mockServiceController.
            shouldFailOnFetch = false
mockServiceController.
            dataToReturnOnSuccess =
            stubResponseData
```

The MockServiceController will have an instance variable called dataToReturnOnSuccess that can be preloaded with a stub response.

Let us now make a few changes to get these new tests to compile. Add the following instance variables to the AlbumTests.swift file:

```
let invalidURL:String = ""
let validAlbumListURL:String = http://www.asmtechnology.com/apress2017/
                                    albumlist.json
```

Add the ValidAlbumList.json file into the TestData group. Ensure the file is included with the test target only. You can get this file from the resource directory provided with the downloadable code that accompanies this chapter (see Figure 7-9).

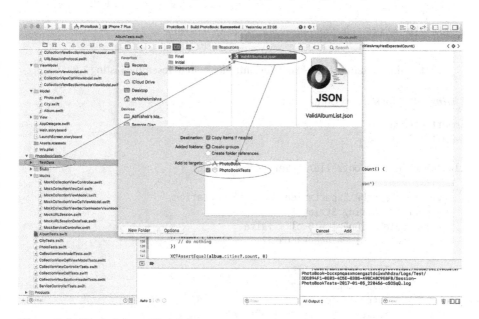

Figure 7-9. Xcode Import File Dialog

Creating the MockServiceController Class

Create a new Swift class called MockServiceController under the Mocks group. Ensure the file is included with the test target only (see Figure 7-10).

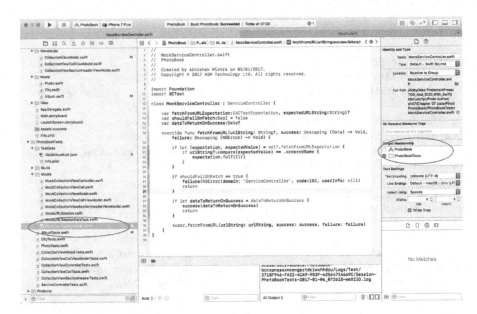

Figure 7-10. *MockServiceController.swift Target Membership*

Update the contents of MockServiceController.swift to resemble Listing 7-8.

Listing 7-8. MockServiceController.swift

```swift
import Foundation
import XCTest

class MockServiceController : ServiceController {

    var fetchFromURLExpectation:(XCTestExpectation,
    expectedURLString:String)?
    var shouldFailOnFetch:Bool = false
    var dataToReturnOnSuccess:Data?

    override func fetchFromURL(
            urlString: String?,
            success: @escaping (Data) -> Void,
            failure: @escaping (NSError) -> Void)
            {
```

```
            if let
            (expectation, expectedValue) =
            self.fetchFromURLExpectation {
            if urlString?.
                        compare(expectedValue)
                        == .orderedSame {
            expectation.fulfill()
        }
        }

        if shouldFailOnFetch == true {
        failure(NSError(
                domain: "ServiceController",
                code:102,
                userInfo: nil))
        return
         }

            if let
            dataToReturnOnSuccess = dataToReturnOnSuccess {
        success(dataToReturnOnSuccess)
        return
            }

    super.fetchFromURL(
                urlString: urlString,
                success: success,
                failure: failure)
    }
}
```

Add the following updated version of the load() method to the Album class:

```
func load(urlString:String?,
    success:@escaping (Void) -> Void,
        failure:@escaping (NSError) -> Void)
-> Void {

    serviceController.fetchFromURL(
        urlString: urlString,
        success: { (receivedData) in

            guard
            let array = try?
                    JSONSerialization.jsonObject(
                    with: receivedData,
            options: JSONSerialization.
                            ReadingOptions.
                            mutableContainers) as?
```

237

```
        NSArray else {

            failure(NSError(
                        domain: "PhotoBook.Album",
                    code:200,
                    userInfo: nil))

                return
        }

    for item in array! {
        guard
            let dictionary = item as?
                    [String : AnyObject] else {
            continue
        }

        if let city = City(dictionary) {
            self.cities?.append(city)
        }
    }

    success()

},

failure: { (error) in
            failure(error)
})

}
```

Modifying the Album Class

Add the following instance variable declaration to the Album class:

```
var serviceController = ServiceController()
```

Save the file and use the Product ➤ Test menu item to run all tests. You will notice that the project fails to compile, this is because the CollectionViewModel class is using the old load() method of the Album class.

For now, comment out the following lines from the initializer of the CollectionViewModelClass:

```
let path = Bundle.main.path(
forResource: "Albums",
                        ofType: "plist")
photoAlbum?.load(filePath:path)
```

Save the file and use the Test Navigator to run all the tests in the AlbumTests test case (see Figure 7-11). You should see all the tests in AlbumTests.swift pass.

Figure 7-11. All Tests in AlbumTests.swift are now Passing

Updating the Photo Class

The Photo class will be updated to use the ServiceController to download an image from the Internet. The current version of the Photo class only stores the name of the image resource. Prior to the update of the Album class, this was the name of an image asset in the project's asset catalog. With the update of the Album class, this will now be the path of jpeg file on the server relative to the path of the albumlist.json file.

The new version of the Photo class will contain the following changes:

- The code to build an absolute URL of an image on the server given the base URL of the albumlist.json file and the filename of the image.

- A new method called downloadImage that will initiate the download of an image using a ServiceController instance.

- A UIImage instance that contains the image after it has been downloaded.

- A reference to a listener object that is notified when the image has finished downloading. The listener object will be an instance of CollectionViewCellViewModel.

- Call a method on the listener object once the image has finished downloading. The listener will, in turn, update the Collection view cell with the downloaded image.

239

Writing New Tests for the Photo Class

Open the PhotoTests.swift file in the project navigator and add the following test methods to the end of the class:

```swift
func testInit_ValidDictionary_downloadedImage_IsNil() {

    let mockServiceController =
                    MockServiceController()
    mockServiceController.
                    shouldFailOnFetch = true

    let photo =
                    Photo(validPhotoDictionary1)
    photo?.serviceController =
                    mockServiceController

    XCTAssertNil(photo?.downloadedImage)
}

func testInit_ValidDictionary_whenDownloadedImageIsCalled_
callsDownloadImage() {

            let expectation = self.expectation(
                    description: "Expected
                    downloadImage to be called")

    let mockServiceController =
                    MockServiceController()
    mockServiceController.
                    shouldFailOnFetch = true

    let photo =
                    MockPhoto(validPhotoDictionary1)
    photo?.downloadImageExpectation =
                    expectation
    photo?.imageName = "11.jpg"
    photo?.baseURL =
    "http://www.asmtechnology.com/apress2017/"
    photo?.serviceController =
                    mockServiceController

    let _ = photo?.downloadedImage
    self.waitForExpectations(timeout: 1.0,
                                    handler: nil)
}
```

```
func testBuildImageDownloadURL_nilImageName_returnsNil() {
    let photo =
                Photo(validPhotoDictionary1)
    photo?.imageName = nil

        XCTAssertNil(
            photo!.buildImageDownloadURL()
        )
}

func testBuildImageDownloadURL_validBaseURL_validImageName_
returnsCorrectImageURL() {
        let photo =
                Photo(validPhotoDictionary1)
    photo?.imageName = "11.jpg"
    photo?.baseURL = "http://www.asmtechnology.com/apress2017/"

    let expectedURL = "http://www.asmtechnology.com/apress2017/11.jpg"
    XCTAssertEqual(
        photo!.buildImageDownloadURL(),
        expectedURL)
}

func testDownloadImage_validImageURL_
callsFromFetchURLonServiceController_withExpectedURL() {

    let expectation = self.expectation(
                description: "Expected fetchURL
                to be called")
    let expectedURL = "http://www.asmtechnology.com/apress2017/11.jpg"

    let mockServiceController =
                MockServiceController()
    mockServiceController.
        fetchFromURLExpectation =
                (expectation, expectedURL)

        let photo =
                Photo(validPhotoDictionary1)
    photo?.imageName = "11.jpg"
    photo?.baseURL = "http://www.asmtechnology.com/apress2017/"
    photo?.serviceController = mockServiceController

    photo?.downloadImage()

    self.waitForExpectations(
                timeout: 1.0, handler: nil)
}
```

```
func testDownloadImage_validImageURL_serviceControllerReturnsValidData_
updatesImage() {

    let bundle = Bundle(for: type(of:self))
    let filePath = bundle.path(forResource: "bar1", ofType: "jpg")
    let stubResponseData = try!
                Data(contentsOf:
                URL(fileURLWithPath: filePath!))

    let mockServiceController =
                MockServiceController()
    mockServiceController.
                shouldFailOnFetch = false
    mockServiceController.
                dataToReturnOnSuccess =
                stubResponseData

    let photo =
                Photo(validPhotoDictionary1)
    photo?.imageName = "11.jpg"

    photo?.baseURL = "http://www.asmtechnology.com/apress2017/"
    photo?.serviceController =
                mockServiceController

    photo?.downloadImage()

    XCTAssertNotNil(photo?.downloadedImage)
}

func testDownloadImage_validImageURL_validListener_calls_
didDownloadImage_onListener() {

            let expectation =
            self.expectation(description:
            "Expected fetchURL to be called")

            let mockDownloadListener =
                        MockDownloadListener()
    mockDownloadListener.
                didDownloadImageExpectation =
                expectation

    let bundle = Bundle(for: type(of:self))
    let filePath = bundle.path(
        forResource: "bar1", ofType: "jpg")
    let stubResponseData = try!
```

```
            Data(contentsOf:
            URL(fileURLWithPath: filePath!))

    let mockServiceController =
            MockServiceController()
    mockServiceController.
            shouldFailOnFetch = false

        mockServiceController.
                dataToReturnOnSuccess =
                stubResponseData

    let photo =
            Photo(validPhotoDictionary1)
    photo?.imageName = "11.jpg"
    photo?.baseURL = "http://www.asmtechnology.com/apress2017/"
    photo?.serviceController =
            mockServiceController
    photo?.listener = mockDownloadListener

    photo?.downloadImage()

    self.waitForExpectations(
            timeout: 1.0, handler: nil)
}
```

There are seven unit tests in the preceding snippet, and each of them are briefly described below:

```
testInit_ValidDictionary_downloadedImage_IsNil()
```

This test creates a Photo instance with a valid dictionary and expects that the downloadedImage instance variable is nil. This is a new instance variable that will be added to the Photo class and will contain the image after it has been downloaded.

```
testInit_ValidDictionary_whenDownloadedImageIsCalled_callsDownloadImage()
```

This test creates a Photo instance with a valid dictionary and accesses the downloadedImage instance variable. The test expects that by trying to access this instance variable (which is nil as proven by the previous test), the downloadImage method will be called.

The downloadImage method is a new method that will be added to the Photo class and will contain the code to use a ServiceController instance to download an image.

```
testBuildImageDownloadURL_nilImageName_returnsNil()
```

This test calls the buildImageDownloadURL method on a Photo instance whose imageName instance variable is nil. The test expects that the buildImageDownloadURL method will return nil.

The buildImageDownloadURL method is a new method that will be added to the Photo class and will contain the code to compose the URL of the image on the server from a base URL and the filename of the image.

```
testBuildImageDownloadURL_validBaseURL_validImageName_
returnsCorrectImageURL()
```

This test calls the buildImageDownloadURL method on a Photo instance that has valid values for the baseURL and imageName instance variables. The test expects that the buildImageDownloadURL method will return a correctly formed URL.

The baseURL instance variable is a new addition to the Photo class and will contain the URL to a folder on the server where images are stored.

```
testDownloadImage_validImageURL_callsFromFetchURLonServiceController_
withExpectedURL()
```

This test calls the downloadImage method on a Photo instance and expects that the fetchURL method will be called on a ServiceController instance.

The downloadImage method is a new method that will be added to the Photo class. The photo class will also have a new ServiceController instance variable.

```
testDownloadImage_validImageURL_serviceControllerReturnsValidData_
updatesImage()
```

This test calls the downloadImage method on a Photo instance and simulates a successful download operation in the service controller class. The test expects the downloadedImage instance variable to be non-nil.

Simulating a successful download operation in the service controller class is achieved by injecting a MockServiceController object into the Photo class, and configuring the MockServiceController to return a stubbed response:

```
let bundle = Bundle(for: type(of:self))

let filePath = bundle.path(
            forResource: "bar1", ofType: "jpg")
let stubResponseData = try!
            Data(contentsOf:
            URL(fileURLWithPath: filePath!))

let mockServiceController =
            MockServiceController()
mockServiceController.shouldFailOnFetch = false
mockServiceController.dataToReturnOnSuccess =
            stubResponseData

let photo = Photo(validPhotoDictionary1)
photo?.serviceController =
            mockServiceController
```

As expected, these tests will not compile just yet as a few mock objects need to be created and a few instance variables and methods need to be added to the Photo class.

Add the bar1.jpg file into the TestData group. Ensure the file is included with the test target only. You can get this file from the resource directory provided with the downloadable code that accompanies this chapter (see Figure 7-12).

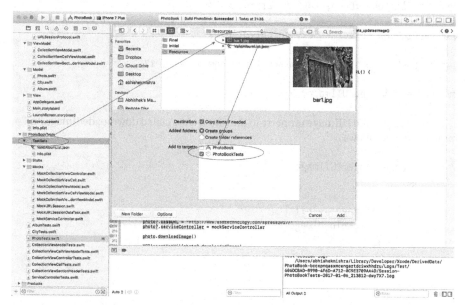

Figure 7-12. *Xcode File Import Dialog*

Creating the MockPhoto Class

Create a new class under the Mocks group called MockPhoto. Ensure that this new class is only included in the test target. Update the contents of MockPhoto.swift to resemble Listing 7-9.

Listing 7-9. MockPhoto.swift

```
import Foundation
import XCTest

class MockPhoto : Photo {

    var downloadImageExpectation: XCTestExpectation?

    override func downloadImage() -> Void {
        downloadImageExpectation?.fulfill()
        super.downloadImage()
    }

}
```

Modifying the Photo Class

Import the UIKit framework in the Photo.swift file and add the following instance variables to the Photo.swift class:

```
weak var listener:DownloadListenerProtocol?

var serviceController = ServiceController()

var baseURL = "http://www.asmtechnology.com/apress2017/"

private var image: UIImage?
```

Add a computed UIImage property to the Photo class called downloadedImage and implement it as follows:

```
var downloadedImage: UIImage? {
    get {

        if image == nil {
            downloadImage()
        }

        return image
    }
}
```

Add the following implementation for the buildImageDownloadURL method to the Photo class:

```
func buildImageDownloadURL() -> String? {
    guard let imageName = imageName else {
        return nil
    }

    return "\(baseURL)\(imageName)"
}
```

Add the following implementation of the downloadImage method to the Photo class:

```
func downloadImage() -> Void {

    guard let urlToFetch =
            buildImageDownloadURL() else {
        return
    }
```

```
    serviceController.fetchFromURL(
        urlString: urlToFetch,
        success: { (data) in
        self.image = UIImage(data: data)
                    self.listener?.didDownloadImage()
    }, failure: { (error) in
        // do nothing.
    })
}
```

Creating the DownloadListenerProtocol.swift File

Create a new file under the Protocols group called DownloadListenerProtocol. Ensure the file is included in both the build and test targets (see Figure 7-13).

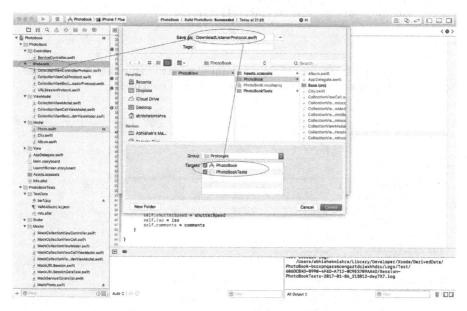

Figure 7-13. Xcode New File Options Dialog Showing Target Membership Settings for the DownloadListenterProtocol.swift File

Update the contents of the DownloadListenerProtocol.swift file to match Listing 7-10.

Listing 7-10. DownloadListenerProtocol.swift

```
import Foundation

protocol DownloadListenerProtocol : class {
    func didDownloadImage() -> Void
}
```

Creating the MockDownloadListener Class

Create a new class under the Mocks group called MockDownloadListener. Ensure that this new class is only included in the test target. Update the contents of MockDownloadListener.swift to resemble Listing 7-11.

Listing 7-11. MockDownloadListener.swift

```
import Foundation
import XCTest

class MockDownloadListener : DownloadListenerProtocol {

    var didDownloadImageExpectation:XCTestExpectation?

    func didDownloadImage() -> Void {
        didDownloadImageExpectation?.fulfill()
    }
}
```

Save the file and use the Test Navigator to run all the tests in the PhotoTests test case (see Figure 7-14). You should see all the tests in PhotoTests.swift pass.

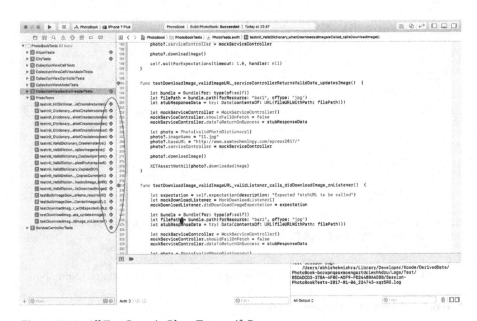

Figure 7-14. *All Test Cases in PhotoTests.swift Pass*

Updating the View Model Layer

Both the collection view model and the collection view cell view model classes require minor updates. As this chapter is about testing networking code, this section and the next one will not adopt a test-driven approach. Several examples of testing the view model and view controller layers have been presented in previous chapters.

Updates to the Collection View Model

Earlier in the chapter, you have commented out two lines from the initializer of the CollectionViewModel.swift class to get your test code to compile:

```
//let path = Bundle.main.path(
//     forResource:"Albums", ofType: "plist")
//photoAlbum?.load(filePath:path)
```

These lines were calling the load method on the album object with the path to a plist file bundled into the application.

The changes that have been made to the Album class now allow the album class to download album meta data from a JSON file on the Internet.

Replace the initializer of the CollectionViewModel class with the following updated version:

```
init(view:CollectionViewControllerProtocol,
     album:Album? = nil) {

    super.init()
    self.view = view

    photoAlbum = album ?? Album()

    photoAlbum?.load(urlString: "http://www.asmtechnology.com/apress2017/
    albumlist.json",
        success: { () in
            DispatchQueue.main.async {

                self.view?.
                reloadCollectionView()
            }
        },
    failure: { (error) in

            print(error.description)
        })
}
```

The updated initializer takes an optional Album parameter that can be used to inject a mock or stub object by a test if needed and calls the new load() method on the Album object.

Add the following method declaration to the CollectionViewControllerProtocol.swift file:

```
func reloadCollectionView() -> Void
```

Although we are not writing any new tests to cover this functionality in this chapter, we do need to delete obsolete tests and fix broken tests. Most of the old tests written for the collection view model will continue to pass; however, some will need updating.

The main reason the tests need updating is that the load() method of the photoAlbum class is now asynchronous, and the previous tests were written for a synchronous version of load().

To fix these tests, we will need to inject a modified Album instance into the CollectionViewModel that uses a stubbed service controller instance internally. Since this modified album instance is likely to be used in several tests, the code to create this instance will be placed in the setUp() method of the test case class:

```
let bundle = Bundle(for: type(of:self))
let filePath = bundle.path(
        forResource: "ValidAlbumList",
        ofType: "json")
stubResponseData = try!
                    Data(contentsOf:
                    URL(fileURLWithPath: filePath!))

stubServiceController = MockServiceController()
stubServiceController!.shouldFailOnFetch =
                                            false
stubServiceController!.dataToReturnOnSuccess =
                                    stubResponseData!

albumWithStubbedServiceController = Album()
albumWithStubbedServiceController!.
        serviceController = stubServiceController!
```

The rest of this section lists the tests that need to be updated; the updated versions of these tests can be found in the finished project that accompanies this chapter.

- testNumberOfItemsInSection_ValidSectionIndex_ReturnsExpectedValue()

- testCellViewModel_ValidViewModelNilPhotos_ReturnsNil ()

- testCellViewModel_ValidSectionIndex_DoesNotReturnNil ()

- testCellViewModel_ValidSectionIndex_ReturnsViewModelWithExpectedModelObject()

- testHeaderViewModel_ValidSectionIndex_DoesNotReturnNil()

Updates to the Collection View Cell View Model

The cell view model will be modified to act as a listener object for the Photo model class. By doing so, the cell view model call will be notified by the Photo class of the completion of an asynchronous image download.

Add the following line to the end of the initializer of the CollectionViewCellViewModel class:

```
photo?.listener = self
```

Delete the existing implementation of the setup() method and replace it with the following implementation:

```
func setup() {

        guard let collectionViewCell =
                        collectionViewCell ,
            let photo = photo,
            let aperture = photo.aperture,
            let shutterSpeed =
                photo.shutterSpeed,
            let iso = photo.iso,
            let comments =
                photo.comments else {
            return
        }

        collectionViewCell.updateImage(
                image: photo.downloadedImage)
        collectionViewCell.setCaption(
                captionText: comments)
        collectionViewCell.setShotDetails(
                shotDetailsText: "\(aperture),
                \(shutterSpeed), ISO \(iso)")
}
```

Add the following class extension to the CollectionViewCellViewModel.swift file:

```
extension CollectionViewCellViewModel : DownloadListenerProtocol {
    func didDownloadImage() -> Void {
        DispatchQueue.main.async {
            self.collectionViewCell?.
                updateImage(
                    image: self.photo?
                            .downloadedImage)
        }
    }
}
```

CHAPTER 7 ■ TESTING URLSESSION

This code will not compile just yet as it requires some changes to be made to the collection view cell class. You will make these changes in the next section.

You may have noticed that the modified version of the setup() method calls updateImage() on the collectionViewCell object, instead of loadImage(). In the previous chapter you have created a test that checks to ensure that a call to the setup() method calls the loadImage() method. This test is now obsolete and will have to be deleted.

Open the CollectionViewCellViewModelTests.swift file and delete the following test from the file:

```
testSetup_ValidPhoto_Calls_LoadImage_WithExpectedImageName()
```

You could alternately modify the test to check that updateImage() is being called; however this is left as an exercise for you and will not be addressed in this chapter.

Updating the View Layer

Both the collection view and the collection view cell classes require minor updates. Let us update the collection view controller class first.

Updates to the Collection View Controller

Earlier in this chapter you added a new method to the CollectionViewControllerProtocol. swift file:

```
func reloadCollectionView() -> Void
```

You will now need to implement this method in the collection view controller class. Modify the class extension in CollectionViewController.swift file by adding the following method implementation to the extension:

```
func reloadCollectionView() -> Void {
    self.collectionView?.reloadData()
}
```

Update the MockCollectionViewController.swift file by adding a stub implementation for the reloadCollectionView method. The modified MockCollectionViewController.swift file should resemble Listing 7-12.

Listing 7-12. MockCollectionViewController.swift

```
import UIKit

import XCTest

class MockCollectionViewController : CollectionViewControllerProtocol {
```

```
    var expectationForSetNavigationTitle:XCTestExpectation?
    var expectationForSetSectionInset:XCTestExpectation?
    var expectationForSetupCollectionViewCellToUseMaxWidth:XCTestExpectation?

    func setNavigationTitle(_ title:String) -> Void {
        expectationForSetNavigationTitle?.fulfill()
    }

    func setSectionInset(top:Float,
                         left:Float,
                         bottom:Float,
                         right:Float) -> Void {

        expectationForSetSectionInset?.fulfill()
    }

    func setupCollectionViewCellToUseMaxWidth()
        -> Void {
expectationForSetupCollectionViewCellToUseMaxWidth?.fulfill()
    }

    func reloadCollectionView() {

    }

}
```

Updates to the Collection View Cell

Open the CollectionViewCellProtocol.swift file from the project navigator, and add a statement to the top of the file to import the UIKit framework.

Remove the following method declaration from the protocol:

```
func loadImage(resourceName:String)
```

Add the following method declaration to the protocol:

```
func updateImage(image:UIImage?)
```

The contents of CollectionViewCellProtocol.swift should now resemble Listing 7-13.

Listing 7-13. CollectionViewCellProtocol.swift

```
import Foundation
import UIKit

protocol CollectionViewCellProtocol : class {
    func setCaption(captionText:String)
```

```
    func setShotDetails(shotDetailsText:String)
    func updateImage(image:UIImage?)
}
```

Open the CollectionViewCell.swift file in the project navigator and delete the implementation of the loadImage method.

Add the following code to the class to implement the updateImage method:

```
func updateImage(image:UIImage?) {
    imageView.image = image
    self.setNeedsLayout()
}
```

The contents of CollectionViewCell.swift should now resemble Listing 7-14.

Listing 7-14. CollectionViewCell.swift

```
import UIKit

class CollectionViewCell: UICollectionViewCell {

    @IBOutlet weak var imageView: UIImageView!
    @IBOutlet weak var captionLabel: UILabel!
    @IBOutlet weak var shotDetailsLabel: UILabel!

    var viewModel:CollectionViewCellViewModel?

    func setup() {
        viewModel?.setup()
    }
}

extension CollectionViewCell : CollectionViewCellProtocol {

    func setCaption(captionText:String) {
        captionLabel.text = captionText
    }

    func setShotDetails(shotDetailsText:String)
        {
        shotDetailsLabel.text = shotDetailsText
    }

    func updateImage(image:UIImage?) {
        imageView.image = image
        self.setNeedsLayout()
    }

}
```

Update the MockCollectionViewCell.swift file by removing the existing implementation of the loadImage method and adding a stub implementation for the new updateImage method. The modified MockCollectionViewCell.swift file should resemble Listing 7-15.

Listing 7-15. MockCollectionViewCell.swift

```swift
import Foundation
import XCTest

class MockCollectionViewCell : CollectionViewCellProtocol {

    var expectationForLoadImage:(XCTestExpectation, String?)?
    var expectationForSetCaption:(XCTestExpectation, String?)?
    var expectationForSetupShotDetails:(XCTestExpectation, String?)?

    func setCaption(captionText:String) {
        guard
          let (expectation, expectedValue) =
          self.expectationForSetCaption else {
            return
        }

        if let expectedValue = expectedValue {
            if (captionText.compare
                  (expectedValue) != .orderedSame)
              {
                return
              }
        }

            expectation.fulfill()
    }

    func setShotDetails(shotDetailsText:String)
      {
        guard
            let (expectation, expectedValue) =
            self.expectationForSetupShotDetails
            else {
            return
            }

        if
            let expectedValue = expectedValue {
            if (shotDetailsText.compare(
                    expectedValue) != .orderedSame)
                {
```

```
                return
        }
    }

    expectation.fulfill()
}

func updateImage(image: UIImage?) {

    }
}
```

Save the file and use the Product ➤ Test menu item to run all tests. You should see that all tests pass. Try out the modified app by running the app on the iOS Simulator.

This concludes the update of this collection view controller-based photo browser app to download content asynchronously over the Internet.

Summary

In this chapter you have learned to test network-related code in your app that uses URLSession using mocks and stubs. Testing network layer code using mocks and stubs allows you to build your application without having to explicitly connect to a server. For this technique to work the interface of the server-side APIs must be well defined. If the server-side APIs change, the tests in your iOS app will also need to be updated.

CHAPTER 8

■ ■ ■

Working with Legacy Code

If you have been developing iOS applications for a few years, chances are that you have been brought on to add new features to an existing app with a large code base that has been built over a few years and has been worked on by dozens of developers, most of whom have moved on to other projects.

There is little to no documentation, and there are either no unit tests at all, or just a handful of obsolete tests, some of which fail when run. This is an unfortunate reality on many projects in the industry. In some cases the developers involved may not have known of the benefits of testing, or what to test. In other cases there isn't sufficient buy-in from the business to invest into TDD or BDD techniques, and so developers only write tests when they have the time.

It is often not possible to spend months refactoring years of legacy code, and the best you can do as a new member of the team is to cover any new code you write with an appropriate level of tests.

This chapter will examine a few techniques that you can use to add new code to a large legacy code base, and, at the same time, write meaningful tests for the new code. It is not possible to cover every possible refactoring technique in a single chapter. There are entire books dedicated to the topic of refactoring. An excellent book on refactoring techniques (though not specific to iOS) is Working Effectively With Legacy Code by Michael C. Feathers.[1]

Splitting a Large Class

In many situations, the class in which you wish to make changes is already very large. The reason it may have become so large is probably that no one took the effort to refactor the class, and at some point it became so large that nobody quite knew where to begin.

When faced with this problem, an approach that you can apply is to split the class into smaller classes based on assigning a single responsibility to each of the fragment classes. This is also known as the single responsibility principle: it basically means that any given class should perform a discrete and well-defined function, and rely on other classes for other functions.

As an example, consider a large view controller class that makes a network request to download a JSON document from the Internet, parse the document, and update a few UI elements on the screen. Listing 8-1 presents the code for a class called LargeViewController.swift.

© Abhishek Mishra 2017
A. Mishra, *iOS Code Testing*, DOI 10.1007/978-1-4842-2689-6_8

Listing 8-1. LargeViewController.swift

```swift
import UIKit

class LargeViewController: UIViewController {

    @IBOutlet weak var userNameLabel: UILabel!
    @IBOutlet weak var emailAddressLabel: UILabel!

    private var session:URLSession?
    private var dataTask:URLSessionDataTask?

    override func viewDidLoad() {
        super.viewDidLoad()

        downloadUserProfile()
    }

    override func didReceiveMemoryWarning() {
        super.didReceiveMemoryWarning()
        // Dispose of any resources that can be recreated.
    }

    func downloadUserProfile() {

        self.session = URLSession(configuration: URLSessionConfiguration.default)

        guard let session = self.session,
            let url = URL(string: "http://someservice.com/getuser/") else {
            return
        }

        dataTask = session.dataTask(with: url,
                completionHandler: { (data, response, error) in

            if let _ = error {

                DispatchQueue.main.async {
                    let alertController = UIAlertController(title: "Error",
                                        message: "Unable to download user
                                                profile",
                                        preferredStyle: .alert)

                    let defaultAction = UIAlertAction(title: "OK",
                                        style: .default, handler: nil)

                    alertController.addAction(defaultAction)
```

```
            self.present(alertController, animated: true, completion: nil)
        }

        return
    }

    if let response = response as? HTTPURLResponse,
        let data = data {

        if response.statusCode != 200 {
            DispatchQueue.main.async {
                let alertController = UIAlertController(title: "Error",
                            message: "Unable to download user profile",
                            preferredStyle: .alert)

                let defaultAction = UIAlertAction(title: "OK",
                                style: .default, handler: nil)

                alertController.addAction(defaultAction)

                self.present(alertController, animated: true,
                completion: nil)
            }
        }

        guard let dictionary =
            try? JSONSerialization.jsonObject(with: data,
                options: JSONSerialization.ReadingOptions.
                    mutableContainers)
                as? [String : AnyObject] else {

                DispatchQueue.main.async {
                    let alertController =
                    UIAlertController(title: "Error",
                                message: "Unable to download user
                                        profile",
                                preferredStyle: .alert)

                    let defaultAction = UIAlertAction(title: "OK",
                                    style: .default, handler:
                                    nil)
                    alertController.addAction(defaultAction)

                    self.present(alertController,
                                    animated: true, completion: nil)
                }
            return
    }
```

```
            if let userName = dictionary?["username"] as? String,
                let emailAddress = dictionary?["emailAddress"] as? String {

                DispatchQueue.main.async {
                    self.userNameLabel.text = userName
                    self.emailAddressLabel.text = emailAddress
                }
            }

        }

        return
    })

    dataTask?.resume()
    }
}
```

The fundamental problem with this class is that it is doing too much. Its responsibilities currently include the following:

- Handling view lifecycle events.

- Making network requests.

- Handling network errors.

- Parsing data.

- Updating the user interface.

In order to split this class into smaller classes, you need to decide where to make the split, and how many smaller classes to create. You could base these decisions on the current responsibilities of the class.

Being a view controller, it can be expected to handle view life cycle events and contain the code to update the user interface. The other responsibilities can be farmed out to other objects. Using this line of reasoning, you can come up with the following classes:

- **LargeViewController.swift:** This is the view controller class and handles view lifecycle events and contains logic to update the UI.

- **NetworkController.swift:** This is a class dedicated to making network requests and handling relevant errors.

- **UserProfile.swift:** This class represents a user profile model object, and contains the logic to parse the contents of a dictionary into instance variables.

- **AlertFactory.swift:** This class handles the task of creating an alert controller.

Figure 8-1 represents the class diagram for this new approach.

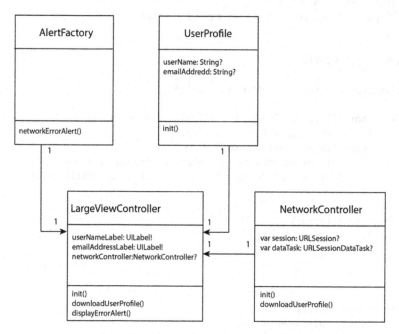

Figure 8-1. *Class Diagram of Refactored LargeViewController Class*

The revised LargeViewController.swift class is shown in Listing 8-2.

Listing 8-2. RefactoredLargeViewController.swift

```swift
import UIKit

class RefactoredLargeViewController: UIViewController {

    @IBOutlet weak var userNameLabel: UILabel!
    @IBOutlet weak var emailAddressLabel: UILabel!

    private var networkController:NetworkController?

    override func viewDidLoad() {
        super.viewDidLoad()

        downloadUserProfile()
    }
```

```swift
override func didReceiveMemoryWarning() {
    super.didReceiveMemoryWarning()
    // Dispose of any resources that can be recreated.
}

func downloadUserProfile() {

    self.networkController = NetworkController()

    networkController?.downloadUserProfile(success: { (data) in
        if let userProfile = UserProfile(data) {
            DispatchQueue.main.async {
                self.userNameLabel.text = userProfile.userName
                self.emailAddressLabel.text = userProfile.emailAddress
            }
        }
    }, failure: { (error) in
        self.displayErrorAlert()
    })

}

func displayErrorAlert() {
    DispatchQueue.main.async {
        self.present(AlertFactory.networkErrorAlert(), animated: true,
        completion: nil)
    }
}
}
```

The NetworkController.swift class is presented next in Listing 8-3.

Listing 8-3. NetworkController.swift

```swift
import Foundation

class NetworkController: NSObject {

    var session:URLSession?
    var dataTask:URLSessionDataTask?

    let userProfileURL = "http://someservice.com/getuser/"

    override init() {
        super.init()
        self.session = URLSession(configuration:
                    URLSessionConfiguration.default)
    }
```

```swift
func downloadUserProfile(success:@escaping (Data) -> Void,
                         failure:@escaping (NSError) -> Void) -> Void {

    guard let session = session else {
        failure(NSError(domain: "NetworkController",
                        code:100, userInfo: nil))
        return
    }

    guard let url = URL(string: userProfileURL) else {
        failure(NSError(domain: "NetworkController",
                code:101, userInfo: nil))
        return
    }

    dataTask = session.dataTask(with: url,
            completionHandler: { (data, response, error) in

        if let error = error {
            failure(error as NSError)
            return
        }

        if let response = response as? HTTPURLResponse,
            let data = data {
            if response.statusCode == 200 {
                success(data)
                return
            }
        }

        failure(NSError(domain: "ServiceController",
                code:102, userInfo: nil))
        return
    })

    dataTask?.resume()
}

}
```

The UserProfile.swift class is presented next in Listing 8-4.

Listing 8-4. UserProfile.swift

```swift
import Foundation

class UserProfile : NSObject {

    var userName:String?
    var emailAddress:String?

    init?(_ data:Data?) {

        guard let data = data,
            let dictionary = try? JSONSerialization.jsonObject(with: data,
             options: JSONSerialization.ReadingOptions.mutableContainers)
             as? [String : AnyObject],
            let userName = dictionary?["username"] as? String ,
            let emailAddress = dictionary?["emailAddress"] as? String else {
                return nil
        }

        self.userName = userName
        self.emailAddress = emailAddress

    }
}
```

The AlertFactory.swift class is presented next in Listing 8-5.

Listing 8-5. AlertFactory.swift

```swift
import UIKit

class AlertFactory : NSObject {

    static func networkErrorAlert() -> UIAlertController {

        let alertController = UIAlertController(title: "Error",
                            message: "Unable to download user profile",
                            preferredStyle: .alert)

        let defaultAction = UIAlertAction(title: "OK",
                            style: .default, handler: nil)
        alertController.addAction(defaultAction)

        return alertController
    }
}
```

Strictly speaking, LargeViewController.swift still has multiple responsibilities: that of managing lifecycle events, and that of updating the user interface. If you would like to refactor this class even further, you could use the MV-VM architectural pattern to introduce a view model object and move the responsibility of updating the user interface to the view model.

This exercise should give you an idea of how to approach the problem of splitting large classes into smaller, more focused, and more manageable classes.

Adding Functionality to an Existing Class

Refactoring a large class into smaller classes can in some cases involve a significant amount of time and effort. As a developer, you may be asked to add features to an existing legacy class without being given sufficient time to refactor the class first.

In this section we will look at techniques that will allow you to add functionality to existing classes in such a way that you could revisit the class in the future, when time permits, and move code into separate helper classes.

Encapsulate Using Classes and Methods

When adding code to an existing method in a legacy class, it is best to try and encapsulate your new code in a new method, and call the new method from the existing method. There are a few advantages to this approach:

- You could write tests for the new method.

- You would not be adding more code to a large untested legacy method.

- This technique may require you to inject some of the local variables from the source method as dependencies into the new method; this practice helps lay the foundation for more refactoring in the future.

In some situations, the class into which you are planning on adding a new method is very complex and is difficult to bring under test. This will typically occur when the class has a long list of dependencies and requires several parameters to be provided in its initializer.

In such a situation, you could encapsulate your new code within a method of a new class, and create an object of the new class within the legacy method. This technique is also known as Break Out Method Object.[1] Using new classes in this manner, however, should be treated as a stop-gap arrangement. You should aim to revisit the source method/class and refactor it properly in the near future. If you do not do so then you risk creating hundreds of small classes in your code base with no clearly defined purpose.

As an example, let us revisit the LargeViewController class from Listing 8-1. Let us assume you were asked to write some code to perform field-level validation on the email address of the downloaded user profile and reject profiles that contain invalid email addresses. Let us also assume that there are no tests for any of the current code in LargeViewController, and that you do not have the time to refactor the class.

One possible approach is to write the validation logic inside the downloadUserProfile() function, as shown in boldface in Listing 8-6.

Listing 8-6. Inline implementation within downloadUserProfile()

```
func downloadUserProfile() {

    self.session = URLSession(configuration:
                   URLSessionConfiguration.default)

    guard let session = self.session,
        let url = URL(string: "http://someservice.com/getuser/") else {
            return
    }

    dataTask = session.dataTask(with: url,
               completionHandler: { (data, response, error) in

        if let _ = error {

            DispatchQueue.main.async {
                let alertController = UIAlertController(title: "Error",
                              message: "Unable to download user profile",
                              preferredStyle: .alert)

                let defaultAction = UIAlertAction(title: "OK",
                     style: .default, handler: nil)
                alertController.addAction(defaultAction)

                self.present(alertController, animated: true,
                              completion: nil)
            }

            return
        }

        if let response = response as? HTTPURLResponse,
            let data = data {

            if response.statusCode != 200 {
                DispatchQueue.main.async {
                    let alertController = UIAlertController(title: "Error",
                                  message: "Unable to download user profile",
                                  preferredStyle: .alert)

                    let defaultAction = UIAlertAction(title: "OK",
                                   style: .default, handler: nil)
                    alertController.addAction(defaultAction)
```

```
            self.present(alertController,
                    animated: true, completion: nil)
        }
    }

    guard let dictionary =
        try? JSONSerialization.jsonObject(with: data,
        options: JSONSerialization.ReadingOptions.mutableContainers)
        as? [String : AnyObject] else {

        DispatchQueue.main.async {
            let alertController = UIAlertController(title: "Error",
                    message: "Unable to download user profile",
                    preferredStyle: .alert)

            let defaultAction = UIAlertAction(title: "OK",
                            style: .default, handler: nil)
            alertController.addAction(defaultAction)

            self.present(alertController,
                    animated: true, completion: nil)
        }

    }

    if let userName = dictionary?["username"] as? String,
        let emailAddress = dictionary?["emailAddress"] as? String {

        // validate email address
        if (emailAddress.characters.count < 6) {
            return
        }

        let whitespace = Set(" ".characters)
        if (emailAddress.characters.filter
            {whitespace.contains($0)}).count > 0 {
            return
        }

        let numbers = Set("0123456789".characters)
        if (emailAddress.characters.filter
            {numbers.contains($0)}).count > 0 {
            return
        }

        let specialCharacters =
            Set("+,!#$%^&*();\\/|<>\"".characters)
```

```
            if (emailAddress.characters.filter
                {specialCharacters.contains($0)}).count > 0 {
                return
            }

            guard let regexValidator = try? NSRegularExpression(pattern:
                            "([A-Z0-9._%+-]+@[A-Z0-9.-]+\\.[A-Z]{2,4})",
                            options: .caseInsensitive) else {
                return
            }

            if regexValidator.numberOfMatches(in: emailAddress,
                options:
                NSRegularExpression.MatchingOptions.reportCompletion,
                range: NSMakeRange(0, emailAddress.characters.count))> 0{
                return
            }

            DispatchQueue.main.async {
                self.userNameLabel.text = userName
                self.emailAddressLabel.text = emailAddress
            }
        }

    }

    return
})

    dataTask?.resume()
}
```

The drawback with this approach is that it adds more code to a method that not only already has a lot of code, but is also untested. An alternate approach would be to create a new class to handle email address validation with the validation logic encapsulated within a single method of this class. A class called EmailAddressValidator is presented in Listing 8-7.

Listing 8-7. EmailAddressValidator.swift

```
import Foundation

class EmailAddressValidator: NSObject {

    func validate(_ value:String) -> Bool {
        if (value.characters.count < 6) {
            return false
        }
```

```
let whitespace = Set(" ".characters)
if (value.characters.filter {whitespace.contains($0)}).count > 0 {
    return false
}

let numbers = Set("0123456789".characters)
if (value.characters.filter {numbers.contains($0)}).count > 0 {
    return false
}

let specialCharacters = Set("+,!#$%^&*();\\/|<>\"".characters)
if (value.characters.filter {specialCharacters.contains($0)}).count > 0 {
    return false
}

guard let regexValidator = try? NSRegularExpression(pattern: "([A-Z0-
9._%+-]+@[A-Z0-9.-]+\\.[A-Z]{2,4})", options: .caseInsensitive) else {
    return false
}

if regexValidator.numberOfMatches(in: value,
                                  options: NSRegularExpression.
                                           MatchingOptions.
                                           reportCompletion,
                                  range: NSMakeRange(0, value.
                                         characters.count)) > 0 {
    return true
}

    return false
  }

}
```

Since this class is new, and has no dependencies on any of the existing classes, it can easily be brought under test. With this class in place, adding email address validation to the downloadUserProfile() is a simple matter of adding three lines of code to the method:

```
if let userName = dictionary?["username"] as? String,
   let emailAddress = dictionary?["emailAddress"] as? String {

    let validator = EmailAddressValidator()
    if validator.validate(emailAddress) == false {
        return
    }
```

```
DispatchQueue.main.async {
    self.userNameLabel.text = userName
    self.emailAddressLabel.text = emailAddress
}
}
```

Rename and Replace

If the change you wish to make to a method is such that it adds either a precondition or a post condition, then instead of adding code to the beginning/end of the source method, you could rename the source method and create a new method with the same name as the source method. You can now add your code to this new method, and make a call to the original method from your new method. This technique is also known as Wrap Method.[1]

As an example, consider another scenario where you have been asked to initiate the process of downloading credentials only if an Internet connection is available, and save the credentials to the system keychain if valid credentials were downloaded.

These modifications will require you to add some code before you start the download, and then some code if the download was successful. If you were to use the strategy described in this section, then you would create a new private method called downloadProfileHelper() and move all the existing code from downloadProfile() into downloadProfileHelper().

As far as the public interface of the class is concerned, there are no changes. From the new (currently empty) downloadProfile() method, you would still make a call to downloadProfileHelper(); however, you would surround this call with calls to two new methods, one which contains the logic to check for an Internet connection, and the other that saves credentials to the keychain.

Your solution would resemble the following:

```
func downloadUserProfile() {
    if internetConnectionExists() {
        downloadUserProfileHelper()
        saveUserCredentialsToKeychain()
    }
}

func internetConnectionExists() -> Bool {
    // code to check if an internet connection exists
}

func saveUserCredentialsToKeychain() {
    // code to save user credentials to the keychain
}

func downloadUserProfileHelper() {
    // all the code that was previously present in downloadUserProfile
}
```

Decorators

Another neat trick when it comes to adding new code to a legacy code base is to make use of the decorator design pattern. The decorator design pattern allows you to add functionality to a class by wrapping that class within another class, with new functionality being provided by the wrapping class.

The decorator pattern is best explained using an example. Listing 8-8 presents the BankAccount class that was developed in Chapter 4.

Listing 8-8. BankAccount.swift

```swift
import Foundation

class BankAccount: NSObject {

    var accountName:String
    var accountNumber:String
    var sortingCode:String
    var accountType:AccountType
    var transactions:[Transaction]
    var owners:[AccountOwner]

    var accountBalance:Float {
        get {
            var balance:Float = 0.0
            for transaction in self.transactions {
                if let amount = Float(transaction.amount) {
                    if transaction.isIncoming {
                        balance += amount
                    } else {
                        balance -= amount
                    }
                }
            }
            return balance
        }
    }

    init?(accountName:String,
          accountNumber:String,
          sortingCode:String,
          accountType:AccountType,
          owners:[AccountOwner],
          accountNameValidator:AccountNameValidator? = nil,
          accountNumberValidator:AccountNumberValidator? = nil,
          sortingCodeValidator:SortingCodeValidator? = nil) {
```

```
        let validator1 = accountNameValidator ?? AccountNameValidator()
        if validator1.validate(accountName) == false {
            return nil
        }

        let validator2 = accountNumberValidator ?? AccountNumberValidator()
        if validator2.validate(accountNumber) == false {
            return nil
        }

        let validator3 = sortingCodeValidator ?? SortingCodeValidator()
        if validator3.validate(sortingCode) == false {
            return nil
        }

        if (owners.count == 0 || owners.count > 2) {
            return nil
        }

        self.accountName = accountName
        self.accountNumber = accountNumber
        self.sortingCode = sortingCode
        self.accountType = accountType
        self.owners = owners
        self.transactions = [Transaction]()
    }

    func setOpeningBalance(_ amount:Float) -> Void {
        if let openingBalanceTransaction = Transaction(txDescription: "Opening
        Balance", date: NSDate(), isIncoming: true, amount: "100.0") {
            self.transactions.removeAll()
            self.transactions.append(openingBalanceTransaction)
        }
    }

    func withdraw(_ amount:Float, _ person:AccountOwner?) -> Void {
        if let newTransaction = Transaction(txDescription: "ATM Withdrawal",
        date: NSDate(), isIncoming: false, amount: "\(amount)") {
            self.transactions.append(newTransaction)
        }
    }

    func deposit(_ amount:Float, _ person:AccountOwner?) -> Void {
        if let newTransaction = Transaction(txDescription: "Cash Deposit",
        date: NSDate(), isIncoming: true, amount: "\(amount)") {
            self.transactions.append(newTransaction)
        }
    }

}
```

This class has a very simple interface and can be used to represent a bank account, with a list of transactions in a banking system.

Now, let us assume that due to changing business needs, the banking system needs to be upgraded to differentiate between personal accounts and business accounts. Daily deposit and withdrawal limits are to be applied to both types of accounts. Additionally, all deposits and withdrawals for business accounts need to be logged into a special auditing system.

These requirements can easily be handled by creating decorator classes called PersonalBankAccount and BusinessBankAccount, which provide additional features over what currently exists in the BankAccount class, so that the needs of these specific account types can be met.

To start with, let us move the external interface of the BankAccount class to a protocol called BankAccountProtocol (see Listing 8-9), and have the BankAccount class implement this protocol.

Listing 8-9. BankAccountProtocol.swift

```swift
protocol BankAccountProtocol : class {

    var accountName:String {get set}
    var accountNumber:String {get set}
    var sortingCode:String {get set}
    var accountType:AccountType {get set}
    var transactions:[Transaction] {get set}
    var owners:[AccountOwner] {get set}

    func setOpeningBalance(_ amount:Float) -> Void
    func withdraw(_ amount:Float, _ person:AccountOwner?) -> Void
    func deposit(_ amount:Float, _ person:AccountOwner?) -> Void

}
```

The only change needed to ensure the BankAccount class implements this protocol is to add the name of the protocol to the class declaration:

```swift
class BankAccount: NSObject, BankAccountProtocol
```

With this change in place, we can use the decorator pattern to create the PersonalBankAccount class, which will impose daily deposit and withdrawal limits (Listing 8-10).

Listing 8-10. PersonalBankAccount.swift

```swift
import Foundation

class PersonalBankAccount : NSObject , BankAccountProtocol {

    var bankAccount:BankAccount

    var accountName:String {
        get {
            return bankAccount.accountName
        }

        set {
            bankAccount.accountName = newValue
        }
    }

    var accountNumber:String {
        get {
            return bankAccount.accountNumber
        }

        set {
            bankAccount.accountNumber = newValue
        }
    }

    var sortingCode:String {
        get {
            return bankAccount.sortingCode
        }

        set {
            bankAccount.sortingCode = newValue
        }
    }

    var accountType:AccountType {
        get {
            return bankAccount.accountType
        }

        set {
            bankAccount.accountType = newValue
        }
    }
```

```
var transactions:[Transaction] {
    get {
        return bankAccount.transactions
    }

    set {
        bankAccount.transactions = newValue
    }
}

var owners:[AccountOwner] {
    get {
        return bankAccount.owners
    }

    set {
        bankAccount.owners = newValue
    }
}

var accountBalance:Float {
    get {
        return bankAccount.accountBalance
    }
}

init(_ bankAccount:BankAccount) {
    self.bankAccount = bankAccount
    super.init()
}

func setOpeningBalance(_ amount:Float) -> Void {
    bankAccount.setOpeningBalance(amount)
}

func withdraw(_ amount:Float, _ person:AccountOwner?) -> Void {
    if withinDailyWithdrawalLimit(amount) {
        bankAccount.withdraw(amount, person)
    }
}

func deposit(_ amount:Float, _ person:AccountOwner?) -> Void {
    if withinDailyDepositlLimit(amount) {
        bankAccount.deposit(amount, person)
    }
}
}
```

```
extension PersonalBankAccount {
    func withinDailyWithdrawalLimit(_ amount:Float) -> Bool {
        // add code to ensure this transaction does not exceed daily
        // withrawal limits.
        return true
    }

    func withinDailyDepositlLimit(_ amount:Float) -> Bool {
        // add code to ensure this transaction does not exceed daily
        // deposit limits.
        return true
    }
}
```

Some of the key points to note about the PersonalBankAccount class are the following:

1. An instance variable of type BankAccount has been created, and the initializer accepts a BankAccount instance to be injected. The PersonalBankAccount class, in effect, wraps around a BankAccount class:

```
var bankAccount:BankAccount

init(_ bankAccount:BankAccount) {
    self.bankAccount = bankAccount
    super.init()
}
```

2. All the property declarations in the decorator class call the corresponding properties of the wrapped class:

```
var accountName:String {
    get {
        return bankAccount.accountName
    }

    set {
        bankAccount.accountName = newValue
    }
}
```

3. The deposit and withdraw methods implement additional logic before calling the corresponding methods of the wrapped class:

```
func withdraw(_ amount:Float, _ person:AccountOwner?) -> Void {
    if withinDailyWithdrawalLimit(amount) {
```

```
                    bankAccount.withdraw(amount, person)
            }
    }

    func deposit(_ amount:Float, _ person:AccountOwner?) -> Void {
            if withinDailyDepositlLimit(amount) {
                    bankAccount.deposit(amount, person)
            }
    }
```

This is the essence of the decorator pattern. The PersonalBankAccount class decorates the BankAccount class by adding some additional functionality on top of what is offered by BankAccount. You can use an instance of a PersonalBankAcccount anywhere in your code in place of a BankAccount instance. You could also implement this pattern by sub classing BankAccount, and modifying the methods implemented by the subclass.

Continuing with the approach used to create the PersonalBankAccount class, the BusinessBankAccount class will be very similar to the PersonalBankAccount class, with the only difference being the implementation of the deposit() and withdraw() methods:

```
    func withdraw(_ amount:Float, _ person:AccountOwner?) -> Void {
            if withinDailyWithdrawalLimit(amount) {
                    bankAccount.withdraw(amount, person)
                    logWidthdrawalForAudit(amount, person)
            }
    }

    func deposit(_ amount:Float, _ person:AccountOwner?) -> Void {
            if withinDailyDepositlLimit(amount) {
                    bankAccount.deposit(amount, person)
                    logDepositForAudit(amount, person)
            }
    }
```

Decoupling Classes Using Protocols

In the previous section we looked at techniques you can use to add code to legacy classes so as to be able to write tests for the new code, with minimal impact on the existing legacy code.

In time, when you decide to start writing tests for your legacy code, you are likely to try and write unit tests for one class at a time. However, classes in legacy code bases are often tightly coupled, and it is impossible to instantiate a single class in isolation.

This tight coupling manifests itself as a tree of of dependent classes, all of which need to be instantiated just in order to instantiate the one class you are truly interested in.

Managing the dependencies between classes will be one of the biggest challenges you will face when you bring legacy classes in to test. In this section we will look at using Protocols to break the tight coupling between classes often found in legacy code bases.

Consider for a moment, the instance variables of the BankAccount class, part of which is reproduced below:

```
class BankAccount: NSObject {

    var accountName:String
    var accountNumber:String
    var sortingCode:String
    var accountType:AccountType
    var transactions:[Transaction]
    var owners:[AccountOwner]


    ...
    ...
}
```

The 'transactions' and 'owners' variables create a strong coupling between the this class and the Transaction and AccountOwner classes. It is not possible to instantiate BankAccount under test without bringing in the other two classes as well.

You can break the tight coupling between these classes by using protocols as follows:

1.   Create two new protocols: TransactionProtocol and AccountOwnerProtocol.

2.   Declare all the methods and public instance variables of the Transaction class in the TransactionProtocol protocol.

3.   Declare all the methods and public instance variables of the AccountOwner class in the AccountOwnerProtocol protocol.

4.   Modify the declaration of the Transaction class to implement the TransactionProtocol protocol.

5.   Modify the declaration of the AccountOwner class to implement the AccountOwnerProtocol protocol.

6.   Modify the declaration of the BankAccount class to use protocols instead of the respective classes:

```
class BankAccount: NSObject {


    ...
    ...
```

```
    var transactions:[TransactionProtocol]
    var owners:[AccountOwnerProtocol]
        ...
        ...
}
```

By using protocols for instance variables, instead of concrete class names you have broken the tight coupling that previously existed in the BankAccount class. The BankAccount class can now easily be brought under test, without bringing in the Transaction and AccountOwner classes. You can use stub objects in place of the Transaction and AccountOwner classes.

Using Dependency Injection to Create More Testable Code

The idea behind dependency injection (DI) is to make dependencies between classes and methods more explicit. Consider the following seemingly innocent method added to the BankAccount class to provide the balance of the class at a particular instance in time.

```
func accountBalanceDescription() -> String {
    let dateFormatter = DateFormatter()
    dateFormatter.dateFormat = "MMMM dd yyyy"
    return "The balance in your account as of \(dateFormatter.string(from:
                                        Date())) is \(accountBalance)"
}
```

There are two problems with this method:

1. A new DateFormatter instance is created every time this method is called. This is very inefficient.

2. There is nothing in the method signature itself that suggests the method will create a date formatter, with a specific date format.

The method clearly has a dependency on a DateFormatter instance, and the dependency is hidden because you need to look into the implementation of the method to realize that it exists. In this case to make it more explicit, you could simply inject the date formatter as a parameter into the method:

```
func accountBalanceDescription(_ dateFormatter:DateFormatter) -> String {
    return "The balance in your account as of \(dateFormatter.string(from:
                                        Date())) is \(accountBalance)"
}
```

279

The problem is far worse if the hidden dependency is on a resource, or a data source that is shared between methods of the class. Consider, for example, the following pair of methods:

```
func deposit(_ amount:Float, _ person:AccountOwner) -> Void {

    let transactionDate = NSDate()

    if let newTransaction = Transaction(txDescription: "Cash Deposit",
                                        date: transactionDate,
                                        isIncoming: true,
                                        amount: "\(amount)") {

        self.transactions.append(newTransaction)

        UserDefaults.standard.set(transactionDate,
                        forKey: "lastDepositDate")
    }
}


func lastDepositDate() -> NSDate? {
    return UserDefaults.standard.object(forKey: "lastDepositDate")
    as? NSDate
}
```

The problem with these methods is the hidden dependency on a UserDefaults instance shared between the methods. This kind of code is very difficult to test. Once again, you could break the tight coupling between these methods and the UserDefaults class by exposing the dependency in the list of parameters provided as input to the methods:

```
func deposit(_ amount:Float, _ person:AccountOwner?,
            _ defaults:UserDefaults) -> Void {

    let transactionDate = NSDate()

    if let newTransaction = Transaction(txDescription: "Cash Deposit",
                                        date: transactionDate,
                                        isIncoming: true,
                                        amount: "\(amount)") {

        self.transactions.append(newTransaction)

        defaults.set(transactionDate, forKey: "lastDepositDate")
    }
}
```

```
func lastDepositDate(_ defaults:UserDefaults) -> NSDate? {
    return defaults.object(forKey: "lastDepositDate") as? NSDate
}
```

However, this solution presents us with a new problem - the two methods were designed to access the same UserDefaults instance. By exposing the UserDefaults instance in the parameter list, you are now allowing a user to potentially inject different UserDefaults instances into these methods.

A better solution in this situation would be to make the UserDefaults instance an instance variable of the class in which both these methods exist, and not expose the UserDefaults object in the method signatures:

```
class BankAccount: NSObject {

    var defaults:UserDefaults?

        ...
        ...
        ...


    func deposit(_ amount:Float, _ person:AccountOwner?) -> Void {

        let transactionDate = NSDate()

        if let newTransaction = Transaction(txDescription: "Cash Deposit",
                                            date: transactionDate,
                                            isIncoming: true,
                                            amount: "\(amount)") {

            self.transactions.append(newTransaction)

            self.defaults?.set(transactionDate, forKey: "lastDepositDate")
        }
    }

    func lastDepositDate() -> NSDate? {
        return self.defaults?.object(forKey: "lastDepositDate") as? NSDate
    }

        ...
        ...
        ...

}
```

Making dependencies explicit leads to looser coupling between objects, and makes it easier to test methods in isolation.

Summary

In this chapter you have looked at different ways to refactor legacy code, or add well-tested code to a legacy code base. You have learned to split large classes into smaller classes using the Single Responsibility Principle and encapsulate new code into methods or new classes.

You have also learned to use protocols as a way to decouple classes, use the decorator pattern, and inject dependencies to create more testable code.

Note

1. Refactoring Legacy Code, Michael C. Feathers, Prentice Hall Professional Technical Reference. ISBN 0-13-117705-2.

CHAPTER 9

■ ■ ■

Continuous Integration

Continuous Integration (CI) is an approach to software development that requires developers to push their code into a shared repository frequently, triggering an automated test and build cycle on a dedicated build computer. Build cycles can be triggered either periodically or after each code push.

When suites of unit (or user interface) tests are included in the build cycle, a CI system will only produce a build if all the tests pass. Failing tests usually send out email notifications to all members of the development team.

While a CI system does not mandate having a suite of automated tests run before as part of the build process, the key advantage to having the tests is the ability to catch issues early. If a developer on the team makes a change and the build breaks immediately after he pushes his change to the repository, chances are there is something in the files pushed that broke the build.

When a build is created successfully by a CI system, the build is stored on the CI system and is available for team members to download. Testers can always get the latest build straight from the CI system.

For a CI system to work, developers on the team must agree to the following principles:

- Push code frequently to the repository.

- Do Not push broken code to the repository.

- Do Not push to the repository before running a set of tests on their development machines.

Apple provides their own CI system called Xcode server, which integrates seamlessly with the Xcode development environment. Xcode server is part of macOS Server, and it is not installed automatically when you install Xcode. To use Xcode Server, you need to install and configure both the macOS Server application and Xcode on a Mac.

© Abhishek Mishra 2017
A. Mishra, *iOS Code Testing*, DOI 10.1007/978-1-4842-2689-6_9

■ **Note** A continuous integration workflow typically has developers use development Macs and a separate dedicated Mac called the build server. The build server has both Xcode installed as well as Xcode Server on it. The build computer can also host your source repositories, or it can connect to remote repositories hosted on GitHub/BitBucket. If you do not have a dedicated build computer, you can install the macOS Server app on your development Mac.

Installing macOS Server

Installing the macOS server is a straightforward process. As mentioned earlier in this chapter, it is quite common for companies to use a dedicated Mac on the network as the continuous integration server. The instructions in this chapter are agnostic to the Mac on which you install macOS server.

■ **Note** Before you install macOS server on your Mac, you must ensure the following:

- You have the latest version of Xcode installed on the Mac.

- You have downloaded and installed relevant provisioning profiles, simulators, and certificates.

- Have administrator credentials for the Mac.

- Have an iTunes account (for the Mac App Store).

- Have credentials to access a Git repository where your source code is staged.

To begin the installation process on the Mac on which you intend to use Xcode server, locate the macOS Server application in the Mac App Store and click Install (see Figure 9-1).

Figure 9-1. *macOS Server on the Mac App Store*

Launching macOS Server

Once macOS server has been installed on your Mac, launch it by launching the "Server. app" application from your Applications directory, or typing "Server" in spotlight, or clicking on the Launchpad icon in the dock and clicking on "Server." The first time you launch the macOS server application, you will be asked to configure it (see Figure 9-2).

Server

To set up Server on this Mac, click Continue.

Other Mac   Cancel   Continue   Help

Figure 9-2. macOS Server Configuration Screen

Clicking on Continue will ask you to accept the terms of a license agreement. Once you have accepted the license agreement, you will then be prompted to provide credentials for an Administrator account on the Mac. Once appropriate credentials are provided, macOS server will take a few minutes to install and configure various services on the Mac (See Figure 9-3).

● ◉ ◉

Server

Server is being set up on this Mac.

Getting host names

Figure 9-3. *macOS Server Set Up Procedure*

On subsequent launches, you will be asked to select a server instance to administer (see Figure 9-4). If you have installed macOS Server on both development Macs as well as a dedicated build Mac, then you can choose to administer the local server instance on the development Mac, or the server instance on the build Mac. Select the appropriate option and click Continue.

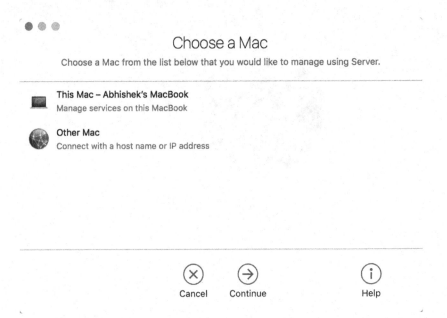

Figure 9-4. *Choose a Server Instance to Administer*

You can administer remote Macs only if the remote Mac has macOS Server installed and the "Using Server app on a remote computer" option is enabled in the settings tab of the Server app on the remote computer. (See Figure 9-5.)

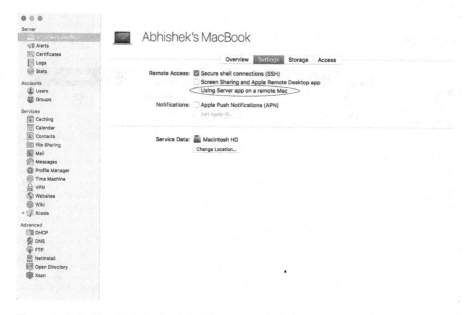

Figure 9-5. *Settings Required to Administer a macOS Server Instance Remotely*

Setting Up Access for Team Members

If you are running macOS Server on a dedicated Mac, you should create user accounts to allow other users on other Macs to connect to the server and access available services.

Click on Users under the Accounts section in the sidebar (see Figure 9-6). This will bring up a list of users who can access the macOS Server. Use the Add (+) button to create accounts for other Mac users on your network. The credentials you create here will be used by other users to connect to this server instance from their Macs, and are not related to the credentials they use to log in to their Macs.

Figure 9-6. Creating User Accounts for Other Team Members

Your team members will need to provide these credentials when connecting to Xcode Server from Xcode. This is covered later in this chapter under the topic "Adding Xcode Server Credentials to Xcode."

Starting Xcode Server

Launch the macOS server app and navigate to the Xcode option under the Services section in the sidebar. (See Figure 9-7.)

Figure 9-7. *Starting Xcode Server*

You can use the on/off switch on the top right corner of the window to start/stop the Xcode Server process. By default, all services provided by the macOS server app are turned off.

If this is the first time you are running Xcode Server on the computer, you will be asked to provide a path to Xcode on the local computer that can be used to create builds. If you have not installed Xcode, quit the macOS server app, install the latest version of Xcode from the Mac App Store, and resume the lesson from this point.

Click on the "Choose Xcode..." button and select the Xcode.app application in your "Applications" directory. You can, in the future, choose to use a different version of Xcode to create builds from the Xcode server settings page.

Xcode Server runs in its own user account. In previous versions this was a hidden user account created on the Mac. Since version 5.2 of Xcode Server, this account is just like any other account on your system and you can even log in to this account.

When asked to provide an account for Xcode Server (see Figure 9-8), you can choose to create a new account or use an existing one. It is best practice to keep a dedicated non-administrative account for Xcode server, and not use your everyday account.

Testing User
Xcode Server requires a logged-in user to integrate your projects. It is recommended that you use a dedicated, non-administrative user.

User Account:	New user account...
Full Name:	Xcode Server
Account Name:	xcodeserver
Password:	Required
Verify:	Verify

☐ Allow user to administer this server

Cancel   Create User

Figure 9-8. *Xcode Server User Account*

If you are using a single Mac setup that has Xcode server running on the same computer that you use for everyday development, you must log in to the dedicated user account that you have created for Xcode server .You can then use fast user switching to switch from the Xcode Server user account back to your everyday use account, and keep the Xcode Server process running in the background.

■ **Note**   Xcode server refers to "builds" as "integrations."

Once you provide a user account to the Xcode server that it can use, you will be prompted to log in as that user (See Figure 9-9).

You must log in as Xcode Server to run integrations.

Integrations will not start until you log in. If you use fast user switching to return to this user, integrations will continue to run in the background.

Don't Log In   Log In

Figure 9-9. *Log in using a Dedicated User Account*

You can either choose to log in now, or do so later. If you chose to log in later then you can do so in a number of ways, including using the Login option built into the Xcode Server configuration page (see Figure 9-10).

Figure 9-10. *Login Option Within the Xcode Server Configuration Page*

■ **Note**   You can still proceed to configure the Xcode server without logging in to the designated account. However, you will not be able to integrate until you log in to the dedicated user account you have provided.

Configuring Xcode Server

Xcode Server allows you to configure various parameters, through a settings page including the following:

- The Xcode version to use for integrations.
- Developer Teams
- Permissions
- Repositories

This settings page can be accessed using the View ➤ Xcode menu item. The settings page has two tabs labeled "Settings" and "Repositories" (see Figure 9-11).

Figure 9-11. *Xcode Server Configurtion Page*

Xcode versions, permissions, and developer teams can be configured under the tab labeled "Settings," and repositories can be configured under the tab labeled "Repositories."

Xcode Version

To change the Xcode version that will be used for subsequent integrations, click on the "Choose Xcode..." button in the Xcode service settings page and select the .app file corresponding to the version of Xcode that you would like to use.

Apple Developer Teams

If you would like to use Xcode Server to deploy builds and run tests on provisioned development devices, you will need to add the server to one of the development teams that you use with your Apple developer account.

Adding the server to a development team will allow Xcode Server to download the provisioning profiles and signing certificates it needs to prepare builds for your devices.

To add the server to your development team, click on the "Add Team..." button in the Xcode service settings page (see Figure 9-12).

Figure 9-12. *Adding Xcode Server to your Apple Developer Account*

You will be asked to log in to your iOS developer account and select a developer team. Enter your iOS developer account credentials and click on "Sign-In" (see Figure 9-13).

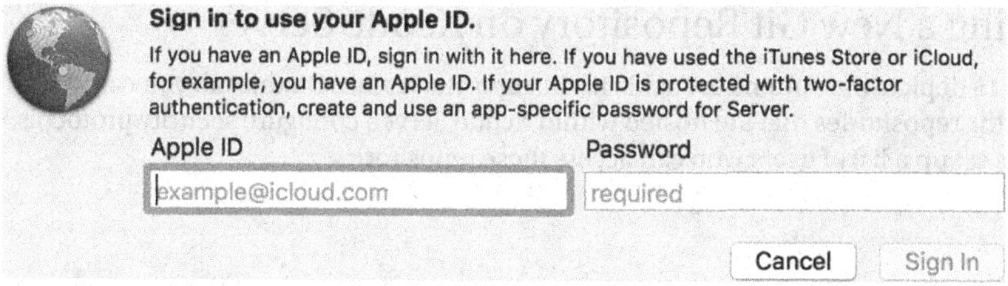

Sign in to use your Apple ID.

If you have an Apple ID, sign in with it here. If you have used the iTunes Store or iCloud, for example, you have an Apple ID. If your Apple ID is protected with two-factor authentication, create and use an app-specific password for Server.

Apple ID	Password
example@icloud.com	required

Cancel   Sign In

Figure 9-13. *Sign In With Apple Developer Credentials*

Development Devices

After having added a developer team to Xcode server, you can connect a provisioned development device to the Mac that is running Xcode Server. This device can be used to run automated tests. You will see all connected devices in the Development Devices list (see Figure 9-14). If you disconnect a device from the Mac, it will be removed from this list.

Developer Teams: Abhishek Mishra

Edit Teams...

Development Devices:

Name	Type	Status
Abhishek's iPhone	iPhone 6 Plus / 10.0.2	Abhishek Mishra

View bots ○   Q Search

Figure 9-14. *Connected Devices are Visible in the Development Devices Section*

Repositories

Xcode Server requires you to connect it to one or more source code repositories. The repositories themselves can be hosted remotely, or hosted within Xcode Server. For remotely hosted repositories, Xcode Server supports both Git and Subversion; however for locally hosted repositories, Xcode Server supports Git only.

If your repositories are hosted on a remote server (such as BitBucket or GitHub), then you do not need to use any of the options within the repositories tab. Instead you will need to configure appropriate access credentials within Xcode on your development machine and these credentials will also need to be provided when creating a build job (also known as a Bot) on Xcode server from within Xcode.

If your repositories are not hosted on a remote server, you can use the options in the repositories tab to create Git repositories that will be hosted within Xcode Server.

Creating a New Git Repository on Xcode Server

Figure 9-15 depicts the options available in the repositories tab. On this tab you can manage the repositories that are hosted within Xcode Server, configure security protocols, as well as set up a list of users who can access these repositories.

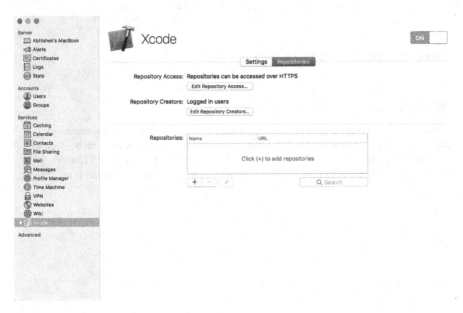

Figure 9-15. *Xcode Server Repositories Tab*

To configure the security protocols that can be used to authenticate users connecting to your repositories hosted within Xcode server, click on the "Edit Repository Access..." button. You will be presented with a dialog box that asks you to select the protocols to allow. Choices available are HTTPS and SSH (see Figure 9-16).

Figure 9-16. *Security Protocol Settings for Repositories Hosted Within Xcode Server*

To configure the list of users who can access your repositories hosted within Xcode Server, click on "Edit Repository Creators." By default, any users who have logged in to Xcode Server from within Xcode can access your repositories and create Bots.

Users who wish to connect to these repositories will need to add account credentials into Xcode on their development Mac so that Xocde can access these repositories. This is typically done using the Account preferences section within Xcode and is covered later in this chapter.

To create a new repository, click on the Add (+) button under the list of repositories (see Figure 9-17).

Figure 9-17. *Creating a New Repository Within Xcode Server*

Type in the name of the repository, and this name will appear in the Hosted Repositories list and will be part of the access URL.

Click the Edit button to specify the users that will be able to access the repository via SSH. To enable HTTPS access, select the "Allow logged in users to read and write" check box.

Click on Create to finish creating the new Git repository. The new repository will appear in the list of repositories. To make changes to who can access the repository, select the repository from the list of repositories, and click on the Edit button located below the list (see Figure 9-18).

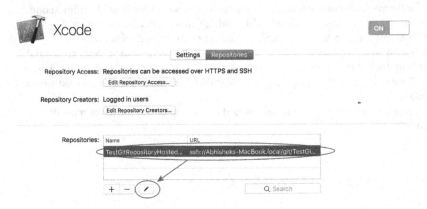

Figure 9-18. *Edit Who Can Access an Existing Repository*

Configuring Xcode

In this section we will look at connecting Xcode on a development Mac to an instance of Xcode server and cloning repositories.

Adding Xcode Server Credentials to Xcode

To access Git repositories hosted on Xcode Server on your development Mac, and to create bots on Xcode Server, you need to connect Xcode on your development Mac to Xcode Server.

Launch Xcode on your development Mac and select the Xcode ➤ Preferences menu item. Switch to the Accounts tab (see Figure 9-19).

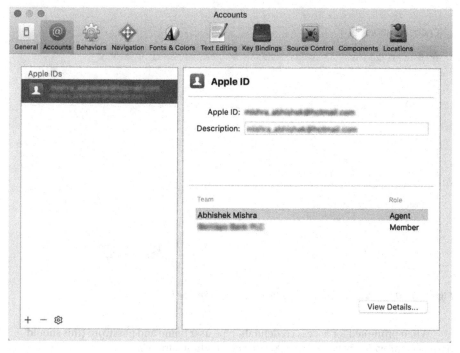

Figure 9-19. *Xcode Accounts Preferences*

This tab lists your development accounts, remotely hosted repositories, as well as Xcode server instances. To connect Xcode to your Xcode Server instance, click on the Add (+) button at the bottom of the list and select "Add Server..." from the list of options.

Choose a Xcode Server instance from the list of servers and click on Add (see Figure 9-20).

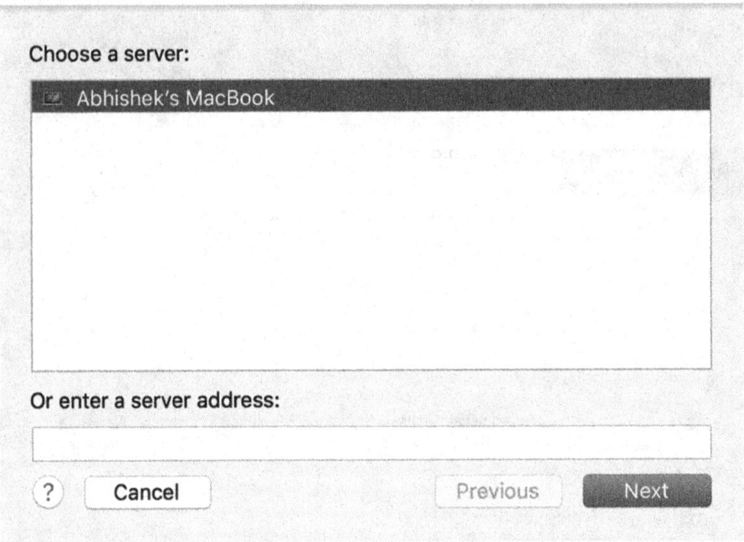

Choose a server:

☑ Abhishek's MacBook

Or enter a server address:

(?)   [Cancel]   [Previous]   [Next]

Figure 9-20. Add a Bookmark to a Remote Xcode Server Instance in Xcode

When prompted for access credentials, type user name and password (this should have been provided to you by your Xcode Server administrator).

You will now see the build server listed under the Servers section of the Accounts tab (see Figure 9-21).

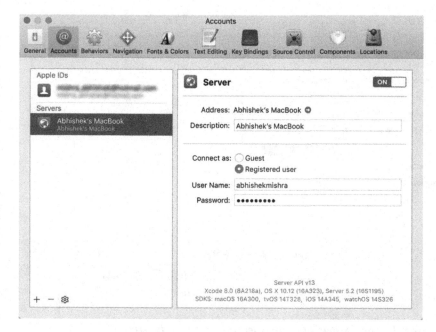

Figure 9-21. *Xcode Accounts Page Showing Xcode Server Instance*

Create a New Xcode Project and Host Its Repository on Xcode Server

Once you have added credentials into Xcode to access Xcode Server, you can host the repository for every new project you create on the server. To do this, enable the "Source control" check box when you are asked to select a location for the new project, and select the name of the server from the list of available options (see Figure 9-22).

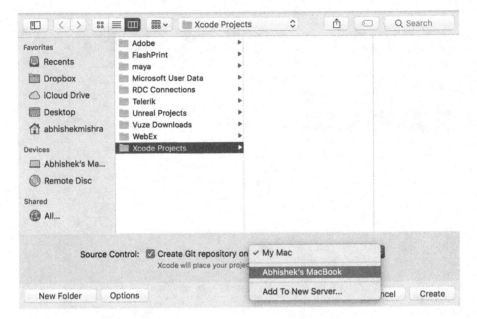

Figure 9-22. *Hosting the Repository for a new Project on Xcode Server*

If the server doesn't appear in the list, ensure you have added the server to Xcode, and that your user account has permission to create a repository on Xcode Server.

Clone an Existing Local Repository to Xcode Server

If you have an existing Xcode project within a Git repository on your development Mac and want to clone the repository to Xcode server, open the Xcode project and click on the Source Control ➤ *YourProjectName* ➤ Configure menu item. *YourProjectName* is a placeholder for the name of your Xcode project (see Figure 9-23).

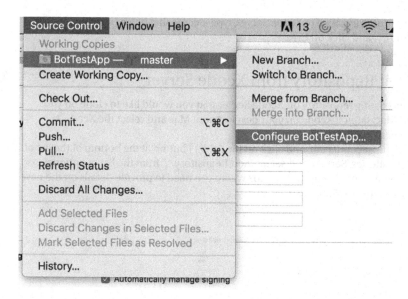

Figure 9-23. *Configuring Source Control Options for an Existing Xcode Project*

Switch to the Remotes tab and click on the Add (+) button and select "Create New Remote" from the context menu (see Figure 9-24).

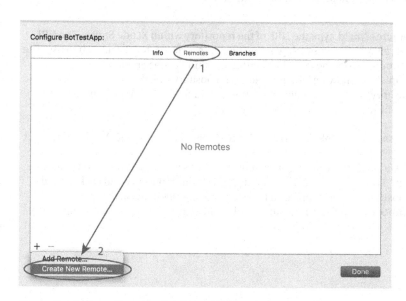

Figure 9-24. *Repository Configuration Dialog*

Select a running instance of Xcode Server, type a name that helps you identify the remote repository, and click on Create.

Clone a Git Repository from Xcode Server

If you have an existing repository on Xcode Server that you would like to clone on your development Mac, launch Xcode on your development Mac and select the Xcode ➤ Preferences menu item.

Switch to the Accounts tab, and click on the Add(+) button at the bottom of the list of Accounts/Repositories/Servers and select "Add Repository..." from the list of options.

You will be presented with a dialog box where you need to provide details on the new repository (see Figure 9-25).

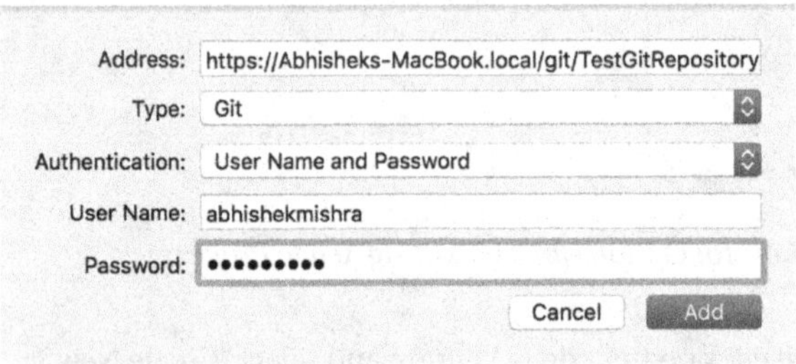

Address:	https://Abhisheks-MacBook.local/git/TestGitRepository
Type:	Git
Authentication:	User Name and Password
User Name:	abhishekmishra
Password:	•••••••••

Cancel   Add

Figure 9-25. *Cloning a Repository From Xcode Server*

In the "Address" field, type the URL of the repository within Xcode Server. The URL will begin with either https or ssh depending on the security protocol you wish to use. The URL can be obtained from the repository settings within Xcode Server.

For example the following URL represents a repository called "TestGitRepositoryHostedOnXcodeServer" hosted within Xcode Server running on the Mac called "Abhisheks-MacBook," accessed via HTTPS.

```
https://Abhisheks-MacBook.local/git/TestGitRepositoryHostedOnXcodeServer.git
```

Specify "Git" in the repository type combo box, and set authentication to "User Name and Password." Type the credentials required to access this repository and click on Add.

Your repository will now appear in the list of repositories in the accounts dialog box (see Figure 9-26). You have now successfully added a bookmark to the Git repository in Xcode.

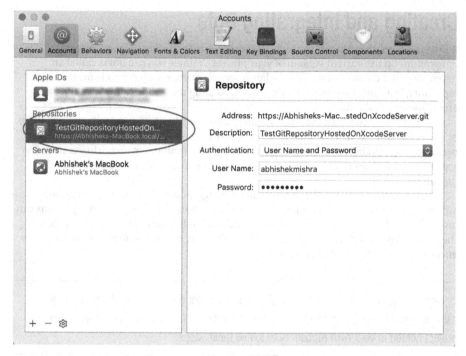

Figure 9-26. Remote Repository Listed in the Xcode Accounts Dialog Box

To check out the repository on your development Mac, close the accounts dialog box, and use the Source Control ➤ Check Out menu item. Select the repository from the list of available repository names and click on Next. Specify a location on your hard disk where you would like to save the repository clone and click Download.

Cloning a Git Repository from GitHub

If you have an existing repository hosted on GitHub/BitBucket that you would like to clone on your development Mac, launch Xcode on your development Mac and select the Xcode ➤ Preferences menu item.

Switch to the Accounts tab, and click on the Add(+) button at the bottom of the list of Accounts/Repositories/Servers and select "Add Repository…" from the list of options.

In the "Address" field, type the URL of the remote repository, Specify "Git" in the repository type combo box, and set authentication to "User Name and Password". Type the credentials required to access this repository and click on Add. The repository will now appear in the list of repositories in the accounts dialog box.

To check out the repository on your development Mac, close the accounts dialog box, and use the Source Control ➤ Check Out menu item. Select the repository from the list of available repository names and click on Next. Specify a location on your hard disk where you would like to save the repository clone and click Download.

Creating and Integrating Bots

A Bot is a server-side process (one which executes on Xcode Server) that performs integrations on the current version of your project. A single run of a bot is called an Integration and consists of pulling the latest version of your project's code from a repository, building the project, running tests, creating the build artifact (.ipa file), and archiving the build artifact.

You can configure a bot to perform integrations on-demand, or based on a schedule, or each time some code is pushed to the repository. The ability to create a bot that can perform an integration when any member of your development team pushes code to the repository make bots (and Xcode Server) a valuable tool in any continuous integration pipeline.

In addition to scheduled and on-demand integrations, a bot will also integrate automatically whenever you update the installed version of Xcode. These integrations run immediately, prior to running any normally scheduled integrations. You can compare these integrations with previous integrations to identify issues that may have been encountered as a result of the upgrade.

■ **Note** The screenshots in this section of the chapter are based on checking out an existing project from an existing repository from GitHub. You will need to use your own project hosted in your own repository to follow these steps.

Create a Bot

To create a bot on Xcode Server for a project, your project's code must be committed to a repository, and the repository must be added to Xcode or Xcode Server using one of the techniques listed earlier in this chapter.

In addition to having your project in a repository, you will also need to share the project's build scheme. A build scheme collates information about specific build configurations and targets. A shared scheme is one that is published to the repository, thus making it visible to Xcode Server.

When you create a new iOS project, Xcode creates a default scheme that performs the following actions:

- Analyze:Perform static code analysis.

- Test: Run unit and/or UI tests.

- Archive: Create a .ipa executable file.

■ **Note** The archive action in the debug scheme is set up by default to archive a release build. Creating a release build requires that appropriate provisioning profiles and certificates are setup in the project. You will also need to make sure these profiles and certificates are installed on the build Mac.

The default build scheme is, however, not shared. To share a build scheme, open the project that contains the build scheme in Xcode and use the Product ➤ Scheme ➤ Manage Schemes menu item. This will present a list of all build schemes defined for the project (see Figure 9-27).

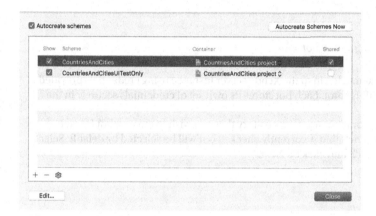

Figure 9-27. *Xcode Schemes*

Select the shared check box for the schemes you want to share, commit the changes, and push the commit (if you are using a Git repository.)

After sharing the scheme, you can create a bot using the Product ➤ Create Bot menu item. Type in a name that helps you identify the bot, select an instance of Xcode server (Figure 9-28), and click Next.

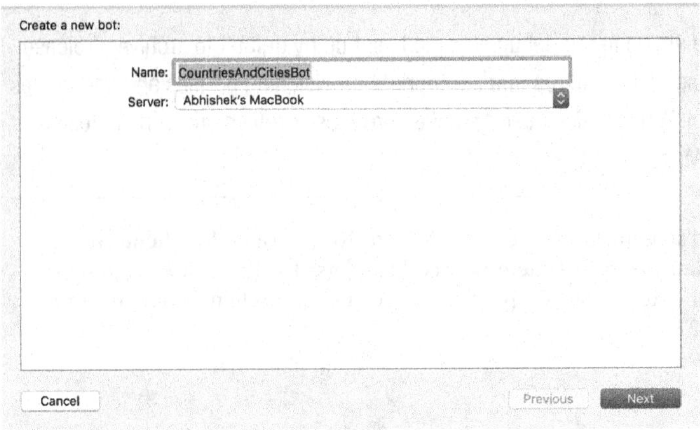

Figure 9-28. *Creating a New Bot*

You will be asked to log in to the Xcode server instance using credentials provided by your server administrator. Each bot stores its own set of credentials securely in the keychain

Next, select the branch in your repository that you wish to create a bot for (see Figure 9-29). The branch that is currently checked out will be selected by default. Select the appropriate branch and click on Next.

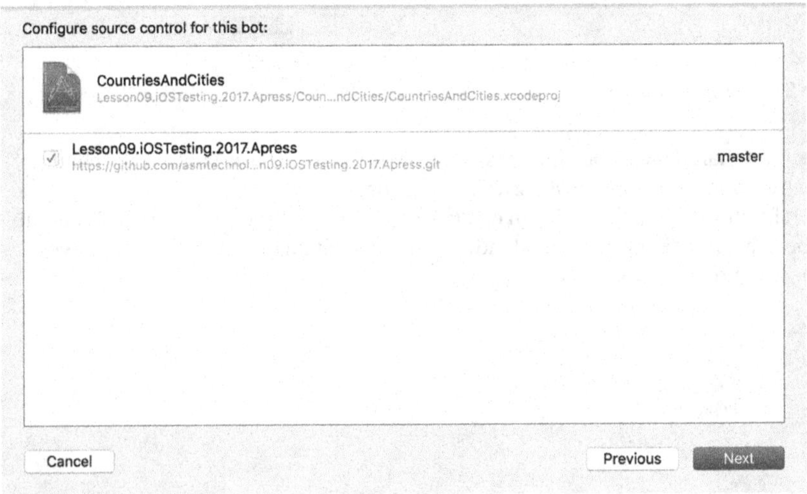

Figure 9-29. *Configuring Source Control for a Bot*

You will now be presented with the first of five configuration pages (see Figure 9-30). In the first configuration page, you specify the scheme, and build actions you wish to perform. Available choices for actions are Analyze, Test, and Archive.

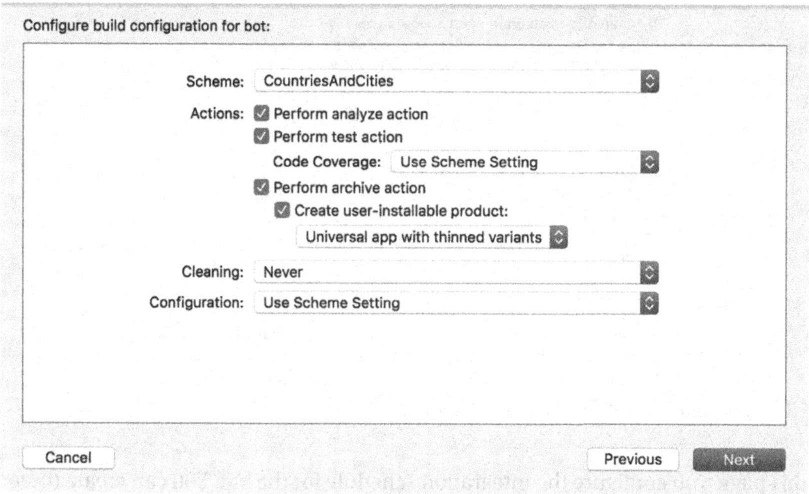

Figure 9-30. *Configuring Build Configuration for a Bot*

If you would like to perform a clean build, select the appropriate option under the Cleaning drop-down. Available options are:

- Always

- Once a day

- Once a week

- Never

A clean build involves a cleanup operation prior to the building operation. During the cleanup operation, temporary build files left over from previous builds are deleted.

If you would like to override the build configuration defined in the scheme, you can use the options in the Configuration drop-down. Available options are these:

- Use Scheme Setting

- Debug

- Release

When you have finished setting up the options on this page, click on next to go to the second configuration page (see Figure 9-31).

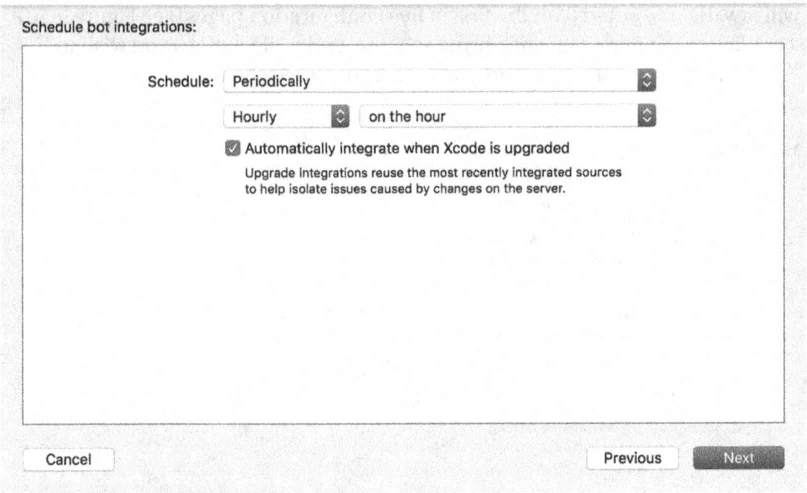

Figure 9-31. *Configuring an Integration Schedule*

On this page, you configure the integration schedule for the bot. You can create three types of schedules:

- Periodic: Xcode Server will integrate the bot as per a specific recurring schedule.

- On commit: Xcode Server will integrate the bot after each commit/push by any team member.

- Manual: The bot will only be integrated when you request it manually.

In addition to the specified schedule, if you would also like to have Xcode Server integrate the bot whenever Xcode is upgraded on the build Mac, ensure the "Automatically integrate when Xcode is upgraded" check box is selected.

When you have finished setting up the options on this page, click on next to go to the third configuration page (see Figure 9-32).

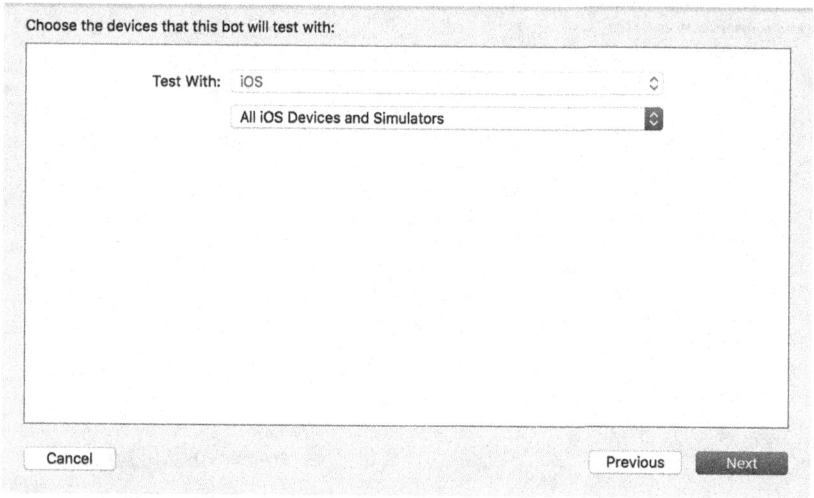

Figure 9-32. Configuring Test Devices

On this page, you configure the devices (or simulators) on which the test build action should be executed. You will only be presented with this page if you opted to enable the test action while creating the bot. Available options are the following:

- All iOS Devices and Simulators

- All iOS Devices

- All iOS Simulators

- Specific iOS Devices

■ **Note**   When you select a simulator, you must ensure the simulator is also installed on the build Mac.

When you have finished setting up the options on this page, click on next to go to the fourth configuration page (see Figure 9-33).

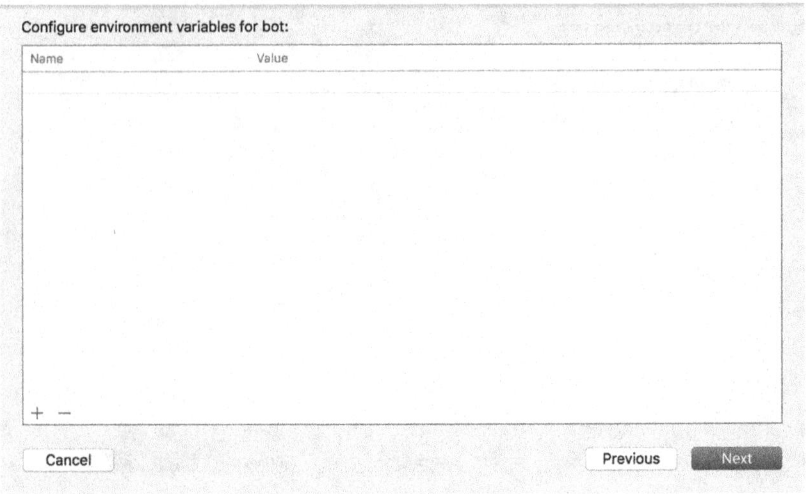

Figure 9-33. *Configuring Environment Variables*

On this page, you can provide a dictionary of environment variables that can be used by pre-integration and post-integration scripts. The scripts themselves, however, are defined in the next step.

Each environment variable consists of a key and a value. Both the key and the value are strings. To add an environment variable, use the Add(+) button.

When you have finished setting up environment variables on this page, click on next to go to the fifth configuration page (see Figure 9-34).

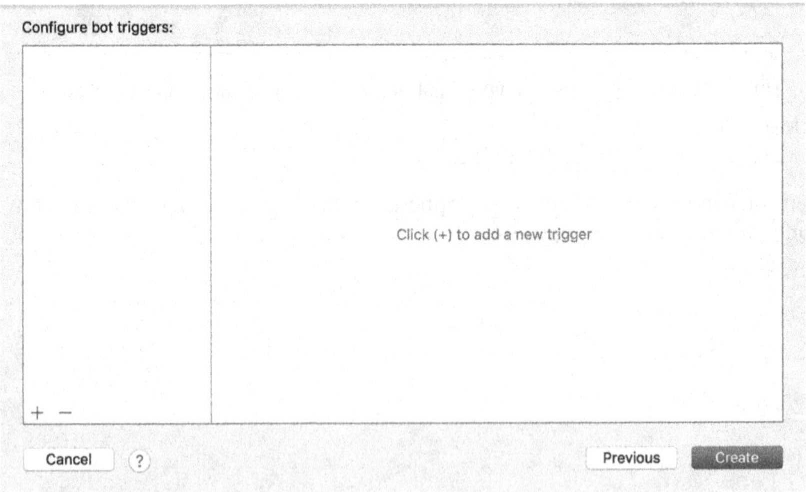

Figure 9-34. *Configuring Triggers*

On this page you can provide custom triggers for the bot. To create a trigger, click on the Add(+) button.

A trigger is an optional action that can be performed by a bot. By default no triggers are defined. You can define three types of triggers:

Pre-Integraton script: A bash shell script that is executed before the bot is integrated (see Figure 9-35). The most common task that some developers like to perform at this step is to remove any files from the project that they do not wish to ship with the app. Examples could be files with customer data, or files used to create client-side web service stubs. Any user-defined environment variables (defined in the previous step), as well as standard Xcode environment variables are accessible by the pre-integration script.

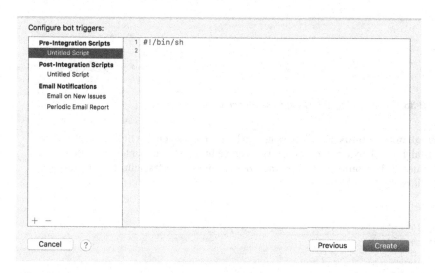

Figure 9-35. *Configuring a Pre-Integration Script*

Post-Integration script: A bash shell script that is executed after the application has been built successfully (see Figure 9-36). The most common tasks performed by developers at this step include submitting the app to a security audit service, or submitting the app to a third-party build repository. Any user-defined environment variables (defined in the previous step), as well as standard Xcode environment variables are accessible by the post-integration script. The post-integration script may be configured to run conditionally on success, test failures, build errors, build warnings, or static analysis warnings.

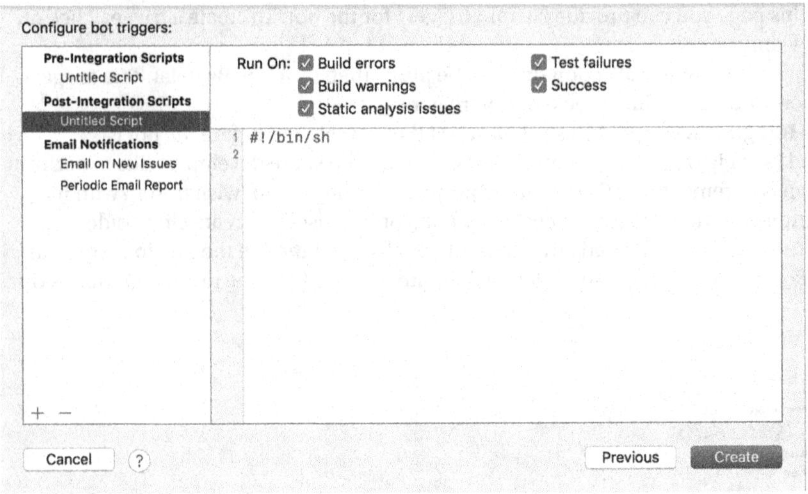

Figure 9-36. *Configuring a Post-Integration Script*

Email notifications: Email messages to be sent to a select list of recipients either periodically (regular summary reports) or when a build issue occurs (new issue reports). Build issues in this context are static analyzer warnings, unit test failures, and outright build failures (see Figure 9-37).

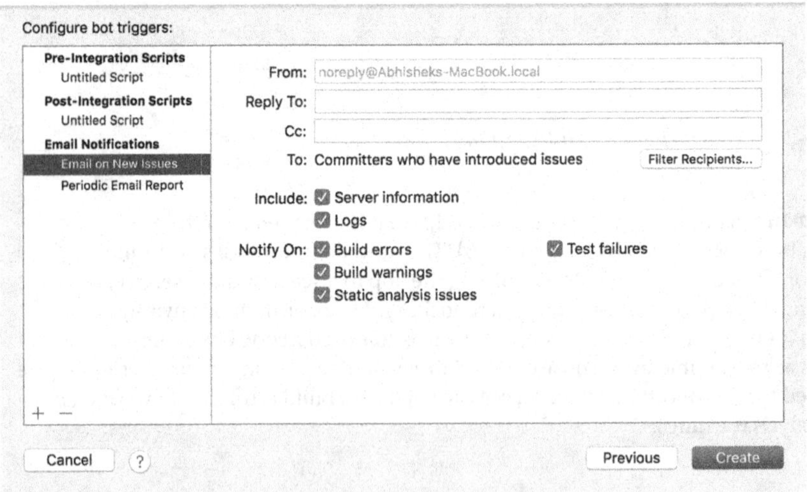

Figure 9-37. *Configuring Email Notifications*

When you have finished setting up appropriate triggers, click on the Create button to finish creating the bot.

Integrate a Bot

You can use the report navigator within Xcode to view a list of bots on connected server instances. To view the report navigator, launch Xcode and use the View ➤ Navigators ➤ Show Report Navigator menu item.

■ **Note** If you do not see your bots in the report navigator, ensure that you have connected Xcode to the Xcode Server instance.

Click on a bot within the report navigator to view details on the bot (see Figure 9-38). Click on "Edit Bot..." to edit some of the parameters that were set when the bot was created. Click on Integrate to integrate the bot manually.

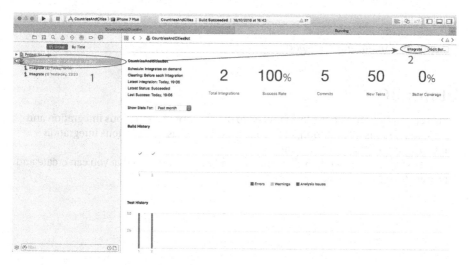

Figure 9-38. *Using Xcode to Integrate a Bot*

You do not need to integrate bots manually if the bot's schedule implies that Xcode Server will integrate the bot automatically at specific times, or due to a commit/push to the repository.

Click on the triangle beside the name of the bot to view a list of previous integrations (see Figure 9-39). For each integration you can access test logs, code coverage reports, build logs, and commit history. If the bot was created with the Archive action enabled, then you can access the build products through the summary tab.

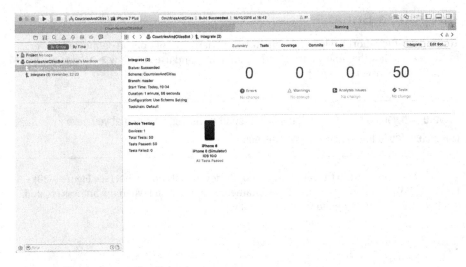

Figure 9-39. *An Integration Report*

Summary

In this chapter you have been introuduced to the concept of continuous integration and have learned to install and configure Xcode Server to act as a continuous integration server in your development pipeline.

You have also learned how to link Xcode and Xcode Server so that you can create and integrate Bots using Xcode.

■ ■ ■

CHAPTER 10

Introduction to Behavior-Driven Development

Behavior-Driven Development (BDD) is an approach to software development that was built with the aim of formalizing the best practices followed by Test-Driven Development practitioners. BDD as we know it today is the result of the efforts of Dan North and numerous others over the years. To read a detailed introduction to BDD, visit Dan North's website at https://dannorth.net/introducing-bdd/. This chapter will introduce you to BDD concepts and techniques.

What Is Behavior Driven Development

One of the key issues faced by people who are new to TDD is deciding what to test. Unfortunately TDD leaves this aspect open to the practitioner to decide. While experienced TDD practitioners know from experience what to test (and what not to), newcomers to TDD often do not know and, in some cases, give up on TDD altogether.

Behavior-driven development is about testing the behavior of a system, and not the implementation details. A system could be either an individual class or a group of classes that make up an aggregate unit of functionality.

As an example, consider the bank account project discussed in Chapter 4 with three key classes – BankAccount, AccountOwner, and Transaction. In terms of relationships, a BankAccount can have up to two AccountOwners and a variable number of Transactions (Figure 10-1).

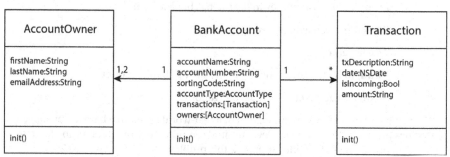

Figure 10-1. *Relationship Between Model Layer Objects*

© Abhishek Mishra 2017
A. Mishra, *iOS Code Testing*, DOI 10.1007/978-1-4842-2689-6_10

These model objects in isolation are not very useful from a business perspective. We have followed a rigid test-driven approach to developing these components in Chapter 4. The tests that we wrote verified that a number of validator objects worked as expected, and that creating a Model layer object makes calls to a number of validator objects. These tests, however, are of little value to a product owner as they don't directly tell him whether a business requirement is met.

The business requirement could, for instance, be something like this: As a joint account customer, I want to be able to withdraw money from my account if there is money in the account, so that I can use the cash to make a purchase.

To put it another way, the tests that we have written while following a test-driven approach are too detailed to be useful for a product owner to be able to verify that the developers have built the system that was asked of them.

The Difference between BDD and TDD

The key difference between behavior-driven development and test-driven development is that BDD tests are written at a different level of detail than TDD tests.

BDD-style tests system behavior is where the acceptable behavior of the system is defined by a set of scenarios, which are, in turn, derived from business requirements.

BDD-style tests are generally more descriptive and meaningful to the business. They are described in a language called Domain Specific Language (DSL) that contains terms and concepts encountered in the business domain.

BDD-style tests could, in theory, be written using the existing XCTest framework with cleverly thought of method names, and a fair bit of mocking and stubbing. In practice, BDD-style tests are written using a special framework. One such framework for iOS developers using Swift is called Quick.

Business Requirements and User Scenarios

The best way to understand how BDD works is to examine a concrete example. Let us assume that your company has been contracted to build a new banking system for retail operations, and after a few weeks of analysis, the business analyst has documented the following two requirements:

> **As a** [customer]
>
> **I want to** [deposit money in my savings bank account]
>
> **So that** [I can reach my savings goals]
>
> **As a** [customer].
>
> **I want to** [withdraw money from my savings bank account].
>
> **So that** [I can meet a financial obligation].

This is obviously an oversimplification of a real-world scenario where the business analyst has probably documented a few hundred requirements, but it serves to illustrate how a team practicing BDD would approach this problem.

A developer would then sit with the business analyst and a member of the QA team to agree on a set of user scenarios. Let us assume the team has been able to come up with the following two scenarios (again an oversimplification; in real life each requirement would expand into multiple scenarios):

Given [A joint savings account has a credit balance of $100]

When [An account holder withdraws $50 from the account]

Then [The account should have a credit balance of $50]

Given [A joint savings account has a credit balance of $100]

When [An account holder deposits $50 into the account]

Then [The account should have a credit balance of $150]

Once a set of user scenarios has been mutually agreed upon, the QA team will proceed to write QA scripts to test the scenarios when the system is testable using either automated testing techniques or manual testing techniques.

From User Scenarios to BDD Tests

The developer will then create a Swift class in the test target and write BDD-style tests using Quick. The name of the class will have the word "Specification" (or Spec) in it, as BDD tests are written to a specification provided by the business. Listing 10-1 presents a BDD-style test class called BankAccountSpecification.swift.

Listing 10-1. BankAccountSpecification.swift

```
import Foundation
import Quick
import Nimble

class BankAccountSpecification : QuickSpec {

    override func spec() {
        var mary:AccountOwner?
        var phil:AccountOwner?
        var maryAndPhil:[AccountOwner] = [AccountOwner]()
        var jointSavingsAccount:BankAccount?

        beforeEach {

            mary = AccountOwner(firstName: "Mary",
                                lastName: "Daniels",
                                emailAddress: "mdaniels@domain.com")

            phil = AccountOwner(firstName: "Phil",
                                lastName: "Burlington",
                                emailAddress: "p.burlington@domain.com")
```

```
            maryAndPhil.removeAll()
            maryAndPhil.append(mary!)
            maryAndPhil.append(phil!)

            jointSavingsAccount =
            BankAccount(accountName: "Savings Account",
            accountNumber: "87548390",
            sortingCode: "498711",
            accountType: .savingsAccount,
            owners: maryAndPhil)
        }

        describe("A joint savings account has a credit balance of $100") {
            context("An account holder withdraws $50 from the account") {
                it("The account should have a credit balance of $50") {

                    jointSavingsAccount?.setOpeningBalance(100)
                    jointSavingsAccount?.withdraw(50, mary)
                    expect(jointSavingsAccount!.accountBalance).to(equal(50))
                }
            }
        }

        describe("A joint savings account has a credit balance of $100") {
            context("An account holder deposits $50 into the account") {
                it("The account should have a credit balance of $150") {

                    jointSavingsAccount?.setOpeningBalance(100)
                    jointSavingsAccount?.deposit(50, mary)
                    expect(jointSavingsAccount!.accountBalance).to(equal(150))
                }
            }
        }

    }
}
```

The test case file starts out by importing the Quick and Nimble frameworks:

```
import Foundation
import Quick
import Nimble
```

Quick is a framework that allows you to write BDD-style tests in Swift. Nimble is a framework that lets you create assertions that are more verbose than the standard XCTAssert macros provide by Xcode.

Anatomy of a Quick Test Case

A Quick test case class is always a subclass of QuickSpec, and must have a method called spec in it. Tests for all user scenarios that define the specification are placed within the body of the spec() method:

```
class BankAccountSpecification : QuickSpec {

    override func spec() {

        // All test code goes here.

    }
}
```

Inside the spec() method, you will find call to a function called beforeEach with a single closure as the function argument:

```
class BankAccountSpecification : QuickSpec {

    override func spec() {

        beforeEach {

            // Setup code goes here

        }
    }
}
```

The beforeEach method of a Quick test case is equivalent to the setUp() method of an XCTestCase. Quick test cases can also have an afterEach method that would be the equivalent of the teardown() method of a unit test.

After the call to the beforeEach method (and before the call to the afterEach method if the test class has one), a number of BDD-style tests are written using nested calls to three functions: describe(), context(), it():

```
override func spec() {

    beforeEach {
    }

    describe(/* the "Given" part of a scenario statement*/) {
        context(/* the "When" part of a scenario statement*/){
            it(/* the "Then" part of a scenario statement */) {
                // test logic goes here
            }
        }
    }
}
```

The describe() function takes a string argument that corresponds to the "Given" part of the scenario that you are testing and a trailing closure that contains statements to be executed by Quick when testing the scenario.

The context() function takes a string argument that corresponds to the "When" part of the scenario you are testing and a trailing closure that contains statements to be executed by Quick when testing the scenario.

The it() function also takes a string argument that corresponds to the "Then" part of the scenario you are testing and a trailing closure that contains the actual statements that will test your production code.

There is a one-to-one correspondence between a user scenario and a Quick BDD test. To make things easier to understand, Listing 10-2 presents a user scenario and its corresponding BDD test, written using Quick.

> **Given** [A joint savings account has a credit balance of $100]
>
> **When** [An account holder withdraws $50 from the account]
>
> **Then** [The account should have a credit balance of $50]

Listing 10-2. User Scenario and Corresponding Quick BDD Test

```
describe("A joint savings account has a credit balance of $100") {
  context("An account holder withdraws $50 from the account") {
    it("The account should have a credit balance of $50") {

        jointSavingsAccount?.setOpeningBalance(100)
        jointSavingsAccount?.withdraw(50, mary)
        expect(jointSavingsAccount!.accountBalance).to(equal(50))
    }
  }
}
```

From a business perspective, if this test passes it means that some tangible unit of functionality has been built – something that a customer can relate to.

Your test statements go in the it() block of a Quick BDD test. In the case of Listing 10-1, the test statements are the following:

```
jointSavingsAccount?.setOpeningBalance(100)
jointSavingsAccount?.withdraw(50, mary)
expect(jointSavingsAccount!.accountBalance).to(equal(50))
```

These tests are built assuming that a BankAccount object has methods called setOpeningBalance, withdraw(), and a computed property called accountBalance, which will behave in a manner consistent with the scenario being described.

To ensure that the BankAccount class behaves as expected, a test expectation statement is used:

```
expect(jointSavingsAccount!.accountBalance).to(equal(50))
```

The expectation statement is expressed using constructs available in the Nimble framework. Nimble is included with Quick and provides a more verbose method of creating an expectation.

However, there is nothing stopping you from using XCTest assert macros to make these expectations; the equivalent statement using the XCTAssertEqual macro would be this:

```
XCTAssertEqual(jointSavingsAccount!.accountBalance, 50)
```

Whether you choose to use Nimble over XCTest assert macros is a matter of personal preference. If you would like more information on Nimble assertions, visit the following URL:

```
https://github.com/Quick/Nimble
```

If you compare the BDD-style test with TDD-style tests, you should see that BDD style tests are more verbose, and focus on the what and not the how. There is nothing in these BDD tests that focuses on the details of the underlying implementation of the BankAccount class, just how it should behave in different scenarios.

The BankAccount class as developed in chapter 4 does not contain methods called setOpeningBalance(), withdraw(), deposit() or a computed property called accountBalance. Therefore, as with any test code, these tests will not compile just yet.

To get these tests to compile, the BankAccount class will have to be modified to resemble Listing 10-3.

Listing 10-3. Modified BankAccount.swift

```
import Foundation

enum AccountType {
    case currentAccount
    case savingsAccount
}

class BankAccount: NSObject {

    var accountName:String
    var accountNumber:String
    var sortingCode:String
    var accountType:AccountType
    var transactions:[Transaction]
    var owners:[AccountOwner]

    var accountBalance:Float {
        get {
            var balance:Float = 0.0
            for transaction in self.transactions {
                if let amount = Float(transaction.amount) {
```

```
                if transaction.isIncoming {
                    balance += amount
                } else {
                    balance -= amount
                }
            }
        }
        return balance
    }
}

init?(accountName:String,
      accountNumber:String,
      sortingCode:String,
      accountType:AccountType,
      owners:[AccountOwner],
      accountNameValidator:AccountNameValidator? = nil,
      accountNumberValidator:AccountNumberValidator? = nil,
      sortingCodeValidator:SortingCodeValidator? = nil) {

    let validator1 = accountNameValidator ?? AccountNameValidator()
    if validator1.validate(accountName) == false {
        return nil
    }

    let validator2 = accountNumberValidator ?? AccountNumberValidator()
    if validator2.validate(accountNumber) == false {
        return nil
    }

    let validator3 = sortingCodeValidator ?? SortingCodeValidator()
    if validator3.validate(sortingCode) == false {
        return nil
    }

    if (owners.count == 0 || owners.count > 2) {
        return nil
    }

    self.accountName = accountName
    self.accountNumber = accountNumber
    self.sortingCode = sortingCode
    self.accountType = accountType
    self.owners = owners
    self.transactions = [Transaction]()
}
```

```
func setOpeningBalance(_ amount:Float) -> Void {
    if let openingBalanceTransaction =
        Transaction(txDescription: "Opening Balance",
        date: NSDate(),
        isIncoming: true,
        amount: "100.0") {
            self.transactions.removeAll()
            self.transactions.append(openingBalanceTransaction)
    }
}


func withdraw(_ amount:Float, _ person:AccountOwner?) -> Void {
    if let newTransaction =
        Transaction(txDescription: "ATM Withdrawal",
        date: NSDate(),
        isIncoming: false,
        amount: "\(amount)") {
            self.transactions.append(newTransaction)
    }
}


func deposit(_ amount:Float, _ person:AccountOwner?) -> Void {
    if let newTransaction =
        Transaction(txDescription: "Cash Deposit",
        date: NSDate(),
        isIncoming: true,
        amount: "\(amount)") {
            self.transactions.append(newTransaction)
    }
}

}
```

You can execute Quick BDD-style tests just as you do any other test, using the Product ➤ Test menu item. After executing the tests, if you were to look at the test navigator for a test report, you would see that BDD style tests appear alongside regular unit tests, but are more human readable (Figure 10-2).

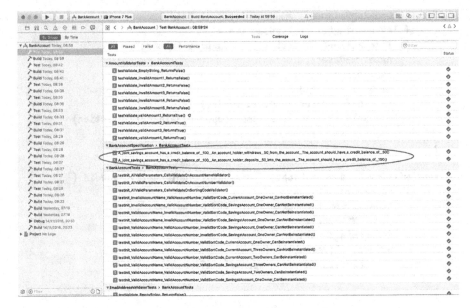

Figure 10-2. *BDD Tests Have More Verbose Names Than TDD Tests*

In the next two chapters, you will learn to integrate Quick and Nimble into a Swift project and try out a few Quick tests.

Advantages and Disadvantages of BDD

After having being introduced to behavior-driven development, you might be wondering whether BDD is a replacement for TDD. Both TDD and BDD have their own uses: test-driven development focuses on how your code is structured and operates at a lower level than BDD. Behavior-driven development helps ensure that the code you are writing fulfills business objectives.

As with any technique, behavior-driven development has its own advantages and disadvantages. Some of the advantages of BDD over TDD are the following:

- Tests are more verbose.

- Each passing test proves that the product is closer to what the customer wants.

- BDD tests are useful to business analysts and product owners as well as developers.

- BDD tests are not as fragile as TDD tests. If you change the manner in which a scenario is implemented, BDD tests are less likely to break.

Some of the disadvantages of BDD are the following:

- BDD requires product owners, testers, and business analysts to buy into the process. All too often teams start out with good intentions, but after a few weeks the business loses interest in writing specifications, and it becomes the responsibility to the developer to write the scenarios as well as the code to make those scenarios pass.

- User requirements change as the project evolves, and BDD requires that user requirements are documented in a usable format before the developers start developing. For this to work, the project has a well-defined road map of upcoming features. Having up-front, well-defined requirements before development does not necessarily mean that the project has to follow the waterfall model. BDD can be used in Agile Scrum projects, but the business will need to commit to making sure those requirements for all the stories that are picked up in a sprint are well defined before the sprint begins.

- BDD works best in a team where iterative development is practiced.

- BDD requires collaboration between the business and the development team. The business has to factor the technical constraints of the current system before creating new user stories. All too often the business analysts and product owners work in their own camps and hand over their requirements to the developers in a sprint planning session.

Summary

In this chapter you have learned about the core concepts involved in Behavior-Driven Development. Using a hypothetical example of a development team that has been contracted to build a simple banking solution, you have examined the process of business requirement analysis and user story creation.

You have also been introduced to two popular open source frameworks called Quick and Nimble. These frameworks are commonly used to develop BDD-style tests for iOS projects.

CHAPTER 11

■ ■ ■

Installing Quick

In the previous chapter you learned about the Behavior-Driven Development and its relationship with Test-Driven development. In this chapter you will download a popular Swift BDD testing framework, called Quick, and set up an Xcode project to use it.

Quick includes a framework called Nimble that provides better replacements for XCTAssert() statements. Nimble will be examined in a little more detail in this chapter, but from an installation perspective you need to be aware that the version of Quick and Nimble you install will depend on the Swift version you intend to use.

Table 11-1 provides information on the versions of Swift and compatible versions of Quick and Nimble respectively. This book is written for Swift 3 users; hence, all examples will be using Quick version 1.0.0 and Nimble version 5.0.0

Table 11-1. *Swift, Quick, Nimble version compatibility matrix*

Swift Version	Quick Version	Nimble Version
2.2 / 2.3	0.9.3	4.1.0
3	1.0.0 (or newer)	5.0.0 (or newer)

Adding Quick to an Xcode Project

In this section you will learn of three alternate ways to include Quick in an Xcode project:

- Using CocoaPods
- Using Carthage
- Using Git Submodules

Adding Quick to an Xcode Project Using CocoaPods

CocoaPods is a dependency management solution for Swift and Objective-C projects. It simplifies the task of adding third-party frameworks in your project along with their dependencies.

© Abhishek Mishra 2017
A. Mishra, *iOS Code Testing*, DOI 10.1007/978-1-4842-2689-6_11

If you have never used CocoaPods on your Mac, you will need to first install it. Installing CocoaPods will require that you have administrative privileges on your Mac.

Launch the Terminal app on your Mac and type the following at the shell prompt:

```
$ sudo gem install cocoapods
```

You will be asked to enter your password. The download process can take a few minutes after which installation will kick off automatically. During the installation process, numerous status messages will be displayed (Figure 11-1).

Figure 11-1. *Cocoapods Installation in Terminal*

At the end of the installation process, you should see a line in your Terminal window that is similar to this:

```
13 gems installed
```

To test your CocoaPods installation, type the following command into the Terminal window, and the output should resemble Figure 11-2.

```
$ pod
```

```
● ● ●                          ⬆ abhishekmishra — -bash — 99×41
[Abhisheks-MacBook:~ abhishekmishra$ pod                                              ]
Usage:

    $ pod COMMAND

    CocoaPods, the Cocoa library package manager.

Commands:

    + cache         Manipulate the CocoaPods cache
    + deintegrate   Deintegrate CocoaPods from your project
    + env           Display pod environment
    + init          Generate a Podfile for the current directory
    + install       Install project dependencies according to versions from a
                    Podfile.lock
    + ipc           Inter-process communication
    + lib           Develop pods
    + list          List pods
    + outdated      Show outdated project dependencies
    + plugins       Show available CocoaPods plugins
    + repo          Manage spec-repositories
    + search        Search for pods
    + setup         Setup the CocoaPods environment
    + spec          Manage pod specs
    + trunk         Interact with the CocoaPods API (e.g. publishing new specs)
    + try           Try a Pod!
    + update        Update outdated project dependencies and create new Podfile.lock

Options:

    --silent        Show nothing
    --version       Show the version of the tool
    --verbose       Show more debugging information
    --no-ansi       Show output without ANSI codes
    --help          Show help banner of specified command
Abhisheks-MacBook:~ abhishekmishra$ ▊
```

Figure 11-2. *Testing the Cocoapods Installation*

Now that you have verified your CocoaPods installation, you can proceed with creating a new Xcode project and using CocoaPods to add the Quick library and its dependencies to the project.

Launch Xcode and create a new iOS project based on the Single View Application template. Use the following options while creating the new project (see Figure 11-3):

- **Product Name:** TryQuickWithCocoaPods

- **Team:** None

- **Organization Name:** *Provide a suitable name*

- **Organization Identifier:** *Provide a suitable identifier*

- **Language:** Swift

- **Devices:** iPhone

- **Use Core Data:** Unchecked

- **Include Unit Tests:** Checked

- **Include UI Tests:** Unchecked

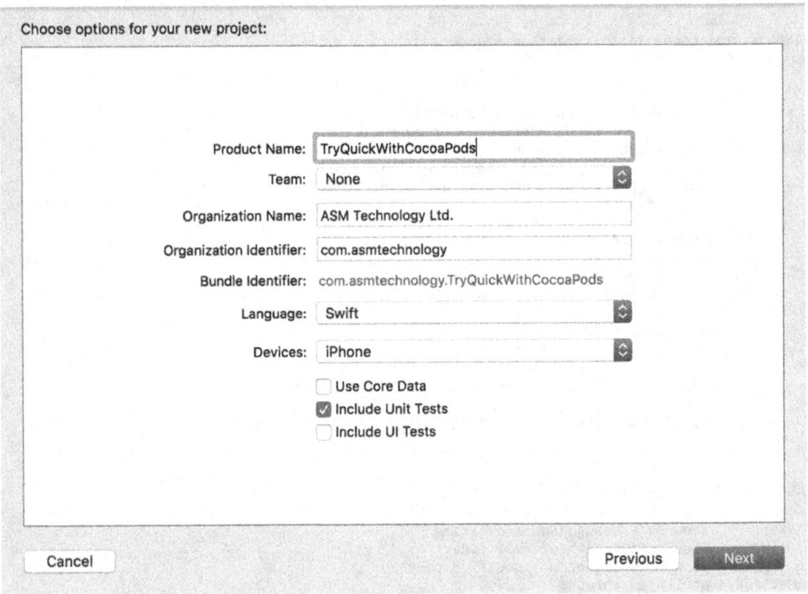

Choose options for your new project:

Product Name: TryQuickWithCocoaPods

Team: None

Organization Name: ASM Technology Ltd.

Organization Identifier: com.asmtechnology

Bundle Identifier: com.asmtechnology.TryQuickWithCocoaPods

Language: Swift

Devices: iPhone

☐ Use Core Data
☑ Include Unit Tests
☐ Include UI Tests

Cancel   Previous   Next

Figure 11-3. *Xcode Project Options Dialog*

Once the project is created, quit Xcode and go back to the Terminal window and navigate to the folder on your Mac where you have created the new Xcode project. Create a new file called Podfile in this directory (with no extension) using the following command:

```
$ touch Podfile
```

Open the new file in TextEdit by typing the following command in the Terminal window and hitting Enter.

```
$ open -e Podfile
```

Using TextEdit, add the following lines to the Podfile, and save the file. Close TextEdit when you are finished making the changes.

```
# Podfile

use_frameworks!
```

```
def testing_pods
    pod 'Quick'
    pod 'Nimble'
end

target 'TryQuickWithCocoaPodsTests' do
    testing_pods
end
```

Return to the Terminal window and type the following command, and hit Enter:

```
$ pod install
```

After a few minutes, you will see a message similar to the following indicating that the installation and setup is complete (Figure 11-4).

```
Pod installation complete! There are two dependencies from the Podfile and
two total pods installed.
```

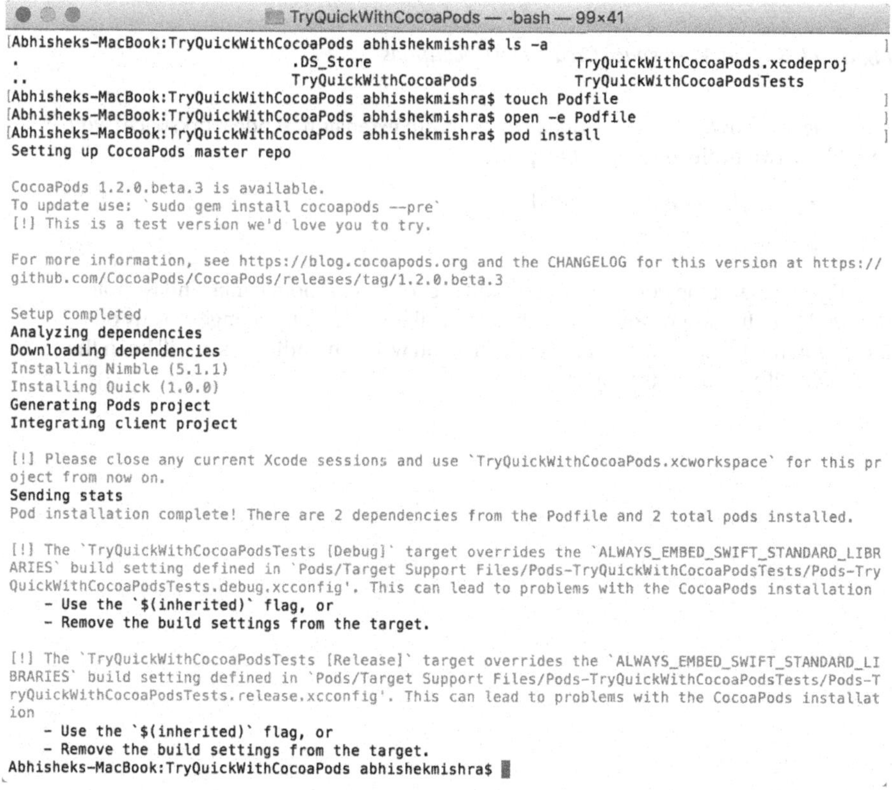

Figure 11-4. *Result of the Pod Install Command*

Look in the project directory for a new workspace file that has been created by CocoaPods. From now on you will have to use this workspace file and not the original .xcodeproj file (Figure 11-5).

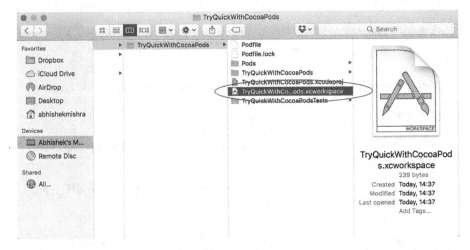

Figure 11-5. *New Workspace Created by Cocoapods*

When you open the new workspace file (with extension .xcode workspace), you should see two projects in the workspace:

- TryQuickWithCocoaPods

- Pods

If you expand the Pods project you will see folders for both Quick and Nimble (Figure 11-6). It is important to note that you will not make any changes to any of the files in the Pods project. All the code that you write, including tests, will be in the TryQuickWithCocoaPods project.

Figure 11-6. *The Pods Project with Quick and Nimble*

At this point you have added Quick (and Nimble) to your Xcode project, and your project should be able to build and run on the iOS Simulator without any issues.

Adding Quick to an Xcode Project Using Carthage

Carthage is another dependency management solution that is designed to simplify the process of adding third-party frameworks and their dependencies into an iOS project.

The merits of using one dependency management solution over the other are beyond the scope of this chapter. Often it comes down to individual preference. One of the key differences between CocoaPods and Carthage is that Carthage downloads and builds frameworks for you, but you need to add the frameworks to your project manually.

If you do not have Carthage installed on your Mac, the easiest way to install it is by visiting the following URL and downloading the latest Carthage.pkg file (Figure 11-7).

```
https://github.com/Carthage/Carthage/releases
```

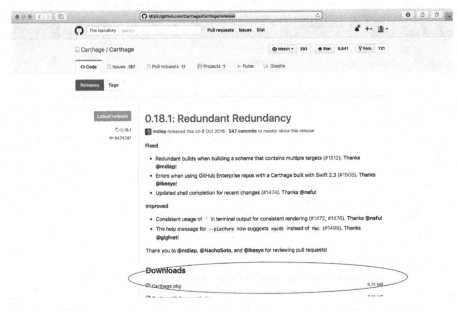

Figure 11-7. Downloading the Carthage Installer

Once the file has downloaded, locate it in your Downloads folder and double-click it to launch the installer. Follow the on-screen instructions to install Carthage (Figure 11-8).

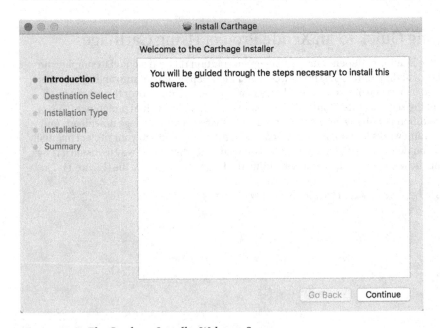

Figure 11-8. The Carthage Installer Welcome Screen

You will need administrative access on your Mac to finish the installation process.

To test your Carthage installation, type the following command into the Terminal window, and the output should resemble Figure 11-9.

```
$ carthage
```

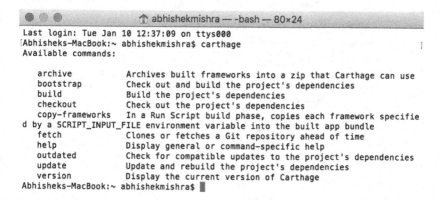

```
● ● ●                🏠 abhishekmishra — -bash — 80×24
Last login: Tue Jan 10 12:37:09 on ttys000
[Abhisheks-MacBook:~ abhishekmishra$ carthage                                  ]
Available commands:

    archive         Archives built frameworks into a zip that Carthage can use
    bootstrap       Check out and build the project's dependencies
    build           Build the project's dependencies
    checkout        Check out the project's dependencies
    copy-frameworks In a Run Script build phase, copies each framework specifie
d by a SCRIPT_INPUT_FILE environment variable into the built app bundle
    fetch           Clones or fetches a Git repository ahead of time
    help            Display general or command-specific help
    outdated        Check for compatible updates to the project's dependencies
    update          Update and rebuild the project's dependencies
    version         Display the current version of Carthage
Abhisheks-MacBook:~ abhishekmishra$ █
```

Figure 11-9. *Testing Your Carthage Installation*

Now that you have verified your Carthage installation, you can proceed with creating a new Xcode project and using Carthage to add the Quick library and its dependencies to the project.

Launch Xcode and create a new iOS project based on the Single View Application template. Use the following options while creating the new project (see Figure 11-10):

- **Product Name:** TryQuickWithCarthage

- **Team:** None

- **Organization Name:** *Provide a suitable name*

- **Organization Identifier:** *Provide a suitable identifier*

- **Language:** Swift

- **Devices:** iPhone

- **Use Core Data:** Unchecked

- **Include Unit Tests:** Checked

- **Include UI Tests:** Unchecked

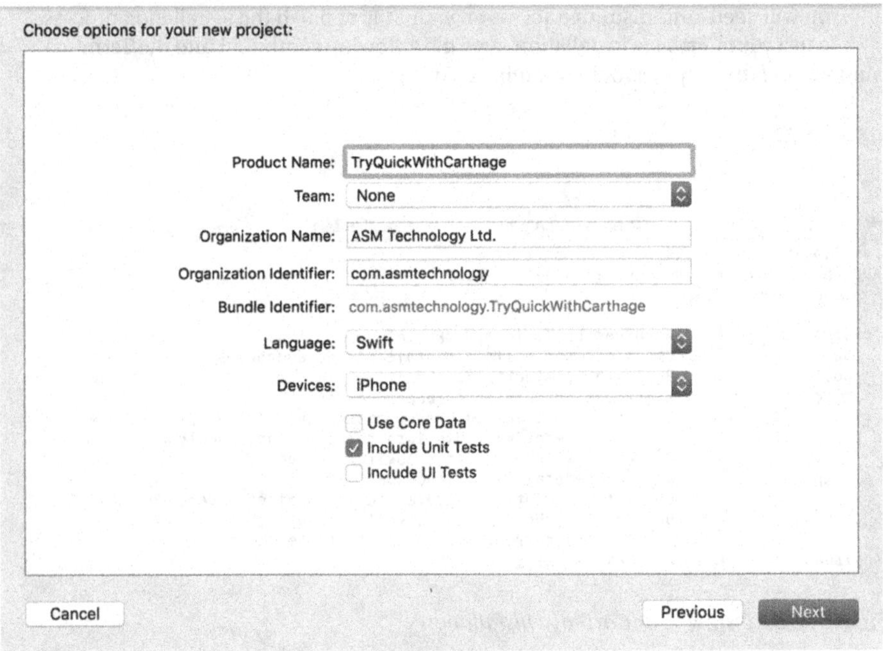

Figure 11-10. *Xcode Project Options Dialog Box*

Once the project is created, quit Xcode and go back to the Terminal window and navigate to the folder on your Mac where you have created the new Xcode project. Create a new file called Cartfile in this directory (with no extension) using the following command:

```
$ touch Cartfile
```

Open the new file in TextEdit by typing the following command in the Terminal window and hitting Enter.

```
$ open -e Carfile
```

Using TextEdit, add the following lines to the Podfile, and save the file. Close TextEdit when you are finished making the changes.

```
github "Quick/Quick"
github "Quick/Nimble"
```

The content of a Cartfile is somewhat simpler than that of Podfile. Each line is just the name of the repository in which the framework resides and the path to the framework on that repository.

Return to the Terminal window and type the following command, and hit Enter:

```
$ carthage update --platform iOS
```

After a few minutes, you will see status messages similar to the following indicating that both the Nimble and Quick source files have been downloaded and built into frameworks (Figure 11-11).

```
*** Cloning Nimble
*** Cloning Quick
*** Checking out Nimble at "v5.1.1"
*** Checking out Quick at "v1.0.0"
*** xcodebuild output can be found in /var/folders/zz/40885yyd4sj5y_1c4d4q8d
n40000gn/T/carthage-xcodebuild.x01qbs.log
*** Building scheme "Nimble-iOS" in Nimble.xcodeproj
*** Building scheme "Quick-iOS" in Quick.xcworkspace
```

Figure 11-11. *Successful Build of Quick and Nimble*

When Carthage finishes, you will find a new folder called Carthage created alongside your Xcode project in finder (Figure 11-12).

Figure 11-12. *Carthage Folder in Your Project Directory*

Inside the Carthage folder, you will find two additional folders:

- **Checkouts:** This is where Carthage checks out the source code for each library that you added into the Cartfile.

- **Build:** This folder contains the frameworks built from the sources in the Checkouts folder.

Unlike CocoaPods, Carthage does not modify the Xcode project. You will need to add the frameworks into your project manually.

Open the TryQuickWithCarthage project that you have created earlier and add both the Quick.framework and Nimble.framework files from the Build directory into your project's test target (Figure 11-13).

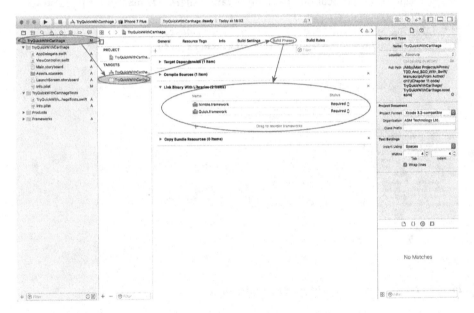

Figure 11-13. *Ensure the Quick and Nimble Frameworks are Added to the Test Target*

Add a new Copy Files Phase to the test target by clicking on the + button and selecting New Copy File Phase from the drop-down menu (Figure 11-14).

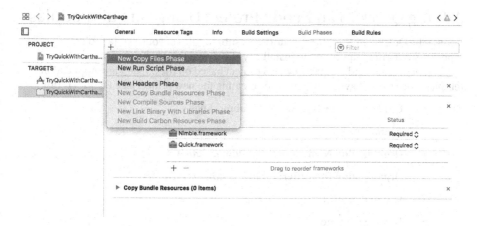

Figure 11-14. *Adding a New Copy Files Phase*

Set the value of the Destination combo box of the new build phase to Frameworks and add both frameworks to the list (Figure 11-15).

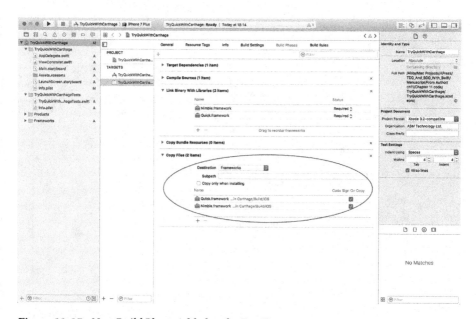

Figure 11-15. *New Build Phase Added to the Test Target*

At this point you have added Quick and Nimble to your Xcode project using Carthage, and your project should be able to build and run on the iOS Simulator without any issues.

Adding Quick to an Xcode Project Using Git Submodules

Adding the Quick and Nimble repositories as submodules of your Xcode project's repository does not require you to install any additional tools beforehand.

Launch Xcode and create a new iOS project based on the Single View Application template. Use the following options while creating the new project (see Figure 11-16):

- **Product Name:** TryQuickWithSubmodules
- **Team:** None
- **Organization Name:** *Provide a suitable name*
- **Organization Identifier:** *Provide a suitable identifier*
- **Language:** Swift
- **Devices:** iPhone
- **Use Core Data:** Unchecked
- **Include Unit Tests:** Checked
- **Include UI Tests:** Unchecked

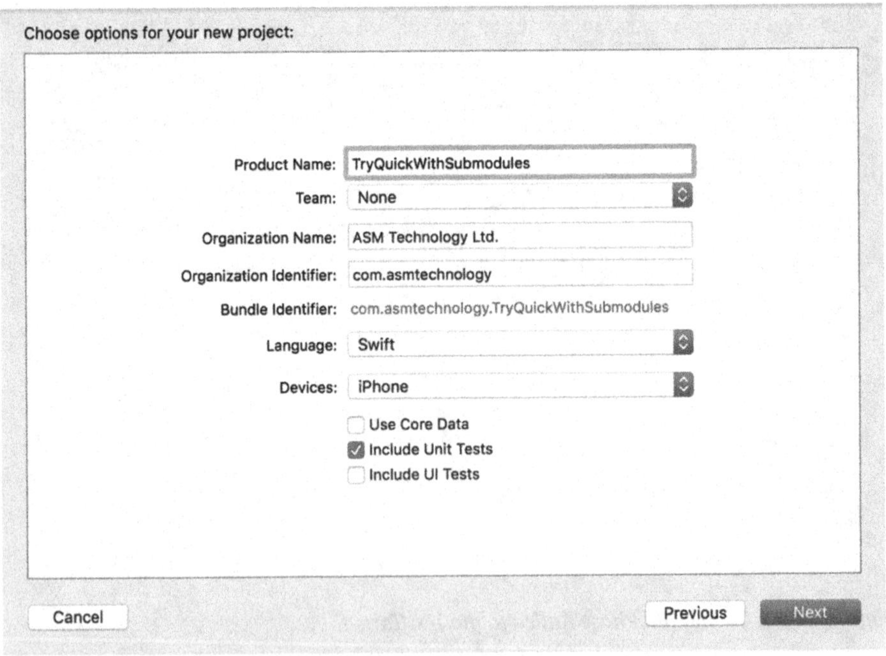

Figure 11-16. Xcode Project Options Dialog

In the Project location dialog box, select an empty folder and ensure you have checked the Create Git repository option (Figure 11-17).

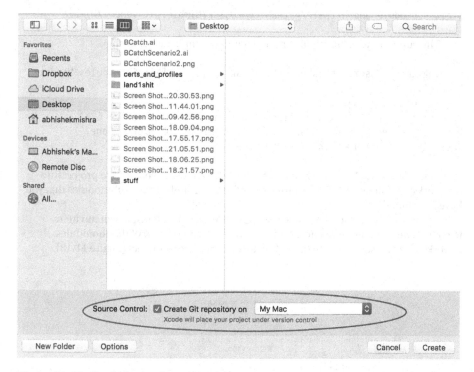

Figure 11-17. *Xcode Project Location Dialog Box*

Once the project is created, quit Xcode and go back to the Terminal window and navigate to the folder on your Mac where you have created the new Xcode project.

Type the following command into the Terminal window and press Enter to add the Quick Git repository as a submodule of your project's Git repository:

```
$ git submodule add https://github.com/Quick/Quick.git Vendor/Quick
```

The output in your Terminal window should resemble the following:

```
Cloning into '/Users/abhishekmishra/Desktop/TryQuickWithSubmodules/Vendor/
Quick'...
remote: Counting objects: 6736, done.
remote: Compressing objects: 100% (71/71), done.
remote: Total 6736 (delta 23), reused 0 (delta 0), pack-reused 6664
Receiving objects: 100% (6736/6736), 1.93 MiB | 1.74 MiB/s, done.
Resolving deltas: 100% (4026/4026), done.
```

Type the following command into the Terminal window and press Enter to add the Nimble Git repository as a submodule of your project's Git repository:

```
$ git submodule add https://github.com/Quick/Nimble.git Vendor/Nimble
```

The output in your Terminal window should resemble the following:

```
Cloning into '/Users/abhishekmishra/Desktop/TryQuickWithSubmodules/Vendor/
Nimble'...
remote: Counting objects: 6782, done.
remote: Total 6782 (delta 0), reused 0 (delta 0), pack-reused 6782
Receiving objects: 100% (6782/6782), 1.39 MiB | 1.03 MiB/s, done.
Resolving deltas: 100% (4575/4575), done.
```

You will now create a new Xcode workspace, and include your Xcode project into this workspace along with Xcode projects for the Quick and Nimble submodules that you have just cloned.

Open your project in Xcode and use the File ➤ New ➤ Workspace menu item to create a new Xcode workspace. Name the workspace TryQuickWithSubmodules. xcworkspace and save it in the same directory as your Xcode project (Figure 11-18).

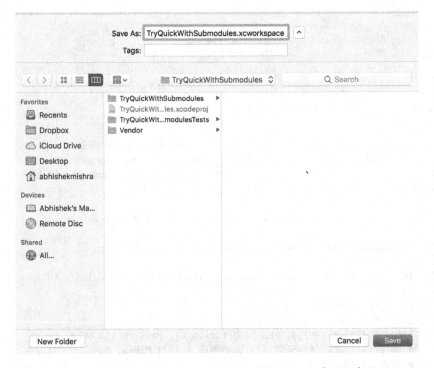

Figure 11-18. *Saving the Workspace to the Same Directory as the Xcode Project*

Xcode will create an empty workspace for you. Close the TryQuickWithSubmodule Xcode project window (not the empty workspace) if it is open, and use the File ➤ Add Files to "TryQuickWithSubmodules"... menu item (Figure 11-19).

Figure 11-19. *Adding a Project to a Workspace*

Navigate to the TryQuickWithSubmodules.xcodeproj file to add the Xcode project to the workspace (Figure 11-20).

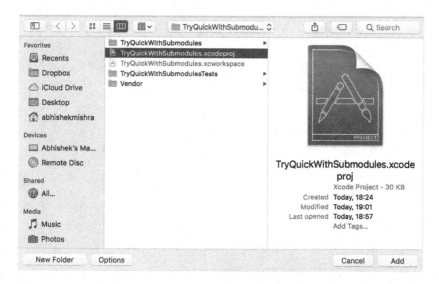

Figure 11-20. *Locating the Xcode Project That Will be Added to the Workspace*

345

You will see a new node appear in the Project Navigator that contains the entire TryQuickWithSubmodules project under the workspace (Figure 11-21).

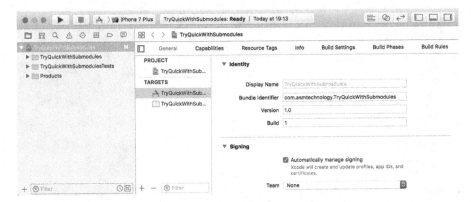

Figure 11-21. *TryQuickWithSubmodules Project in the Xcode Workspace*

Drag and drop the Quick.xcodeproj file onto the Project Navigator. The Quick. xcodeproj file will be located in the Vendor/Quick subdirectory of your project's directory in Finder. While dropping the .xcodeproj file onto the Project Nsvigator, make sure to drop it above the TryQuickWithSubmodules node so as to make the new node a sibling node and not a child node (Figure 11-22).

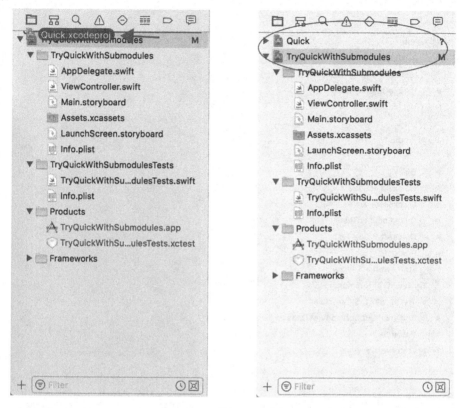

Figure 11-22. *Using Drag-and-Drop Operations to Add the Quick Xcode Project to the Workspace*

Using drag-and-drop operations, add the Nimble.xcodeproj file into the Project Navigator make sure to drop it above the TryQuickWithSubmodules node so as to make the new node a sibling node and not a child node. The Project Navigator should now contain nodes for each project in the workspace (Figure 11-23).

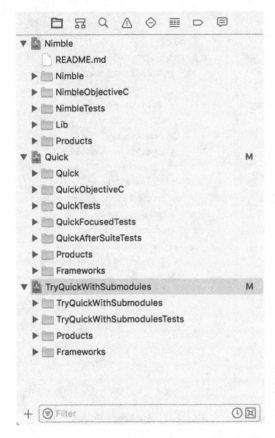

Figure 11-23. *Xcode Project Navigator Showing the Workspace with Three Projects*

Open the Poject settings page for the TryQuickWithSubmodules project, select the test target, and add the Quick.framework and Nimble.framework files to the Link Binaries with Libraries list (Figure 11-24).

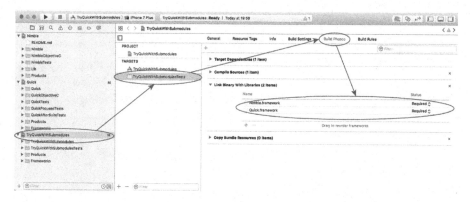

Figure 11-24. Adding the Quick and Nimble Framewok Files to the Test Target

At this point you have added Quick and Nimble to your Xcode project using Git submodules, and your project should be able to build and run on the iOS Simulator without any issues.

Summary

In this chapter you have learned three different ways by which you can add the Quick and Nimble frameworks to an Xcode project. You have learned to use two popular dependency management frameworks – CocoaPods and Carthage. You have also learned to include the Quick and Nimble frameworks using Git submodules.

CHAPTER 12

■ ■ ■

Applying TDD and BDD Techniques

In the previous chapter you learned how to add Quick and Nimble to an Xcode project. In this chapter you will build an app using a combination of TDD and BDD techniques.

You will build a simple app that lets users browse restaurant listings in London. Users will be able to select from a list of locations within London, and the app will present a list of restaurants in the selected locations. The app will have the data for all the restaurants included within the app bundle and will not need to make calls to a web service to fetch this data.

Reviewing the Business Requirements

While building this app, your business has decided to try a behavior-driven approach. The product owners and business analyst have interviewed various users groups and studied reports on user trends in the target demographic. After a few weeks of collective analysis and documentation, they have come up with a set of business requirements listed in Table 12-1.

© Abhishek Mishra 2017
A. Mishra, *iOS Code Testing*, DOI 10.1007/978-1-4842-2689-6_12

Table 12-1. RestaurantDirectory Application Requirements

Number	Requirement
1	**As a** [customer], **I want to** [view a list of restaurants near my chosen area within London], **So that** [I can plan my next meal].
2	**As a** [customer], **I want to** [get an idea of the distance between my chosen restaurant and the closest underground station], **So that** [I can make my travel plans].
3	**As a** [customer], **I want to** [get an idea of the quality of food served at a restaurant], **So that** [I can make a well informed decision to eat there].
4	**As a** [customer], **I want to** [know the type of cuisine served at a restaurant], **So that** [I can make a well informed decision to eat there].

These requirements were then handed over to the development team. The business analyst who documented these requirements then sat down with a developer and a tester and prepared a set of user scenarios based on these requirements. The user scenarios are listed in Table 12-2.

Table 12-2. RestaurantDirectory User Scenarios

Number	User Scenario
1	**Given** [the app is launched], **When** [the main screen of the app is loaded], **Then** [there is an option in the user interface to select an area of London from a list].
2	**Given** [the app is launched], **When** [the main screen of the app is loaded], **Then** [there is a Next button in the user interface].
3	**Given** [the main screen of the app is loaded], **When** [no area has been selected], **Then** [the Next button is not enabled].
4	**Given** [the main screen of the app is loaded], **When** [an area in London has been selected], **Then** [the Next button is enabled].
5	**Given** [the user has selected a location], **When** [the Next button is tapped], **Then** [a new screen appears with a list of restaurants in that location].

(*continued*)

Table 12-2. (*continued*)

Number	User Scenario
6	**Given** [the list of restaurants is visible on the screen], **When** [a restaurant's name is displayed in that list], **Then** [the listing should be accompanied by the name of the nearest tube station].
7	**Given** [the list of restaurants is visible on the screen], **When** [a restaurant's name is displayed in that list], **Then** [the listing should be accompanied by the approximate distance in miles to the nearest tube station].
8	**Given** [the list of restaurants is visible on the screen], **When** [a restaurant's name is displayed in that list], **Then** [the listing should be accompanied by an integer between 1 to 5 that indicates the quality of the restaurant, with 1 being the poorest and 5 the best].
9	**Given** [the list of restaurants is visible on the screen], **When** [a restaurant's name is displayed in that list], **Then** [the listing should be accompanied by the cuisine served at the restaurant].

From the perspective of the QA team, each of these user stories is testable by running the app and inspecting the results visually. However, from the perspective of an app developer, many of these requirements are visual in nature and cannot be tested using TDD or BDD techniques.

Take, for instance, Scenario 1, which requires a UI element, is visible on the screen. This scenario is easy to test using visual inspection, but is not easy to test programmatically.

Therefore, while the QA team will test each of these scenarios using a variety of techniques available to them, the developers will only be able to create Quick tests for a subset of the scenarios. Table 12-3 lists the subset of scenarios that will be tested by the developers using Quick.

Table 12-3. *RestaurantDirectory User Scenarios Testable with Quick*

Number	User Scenario	Notes
1	**Given** [the app is launched], **When** [the main screen of the app is loaded], **Then** [there is an option in the user interface to select an area of London from a list].	Not testable using Quick as it requires visual verification.
2	**Given** [the app is launched], **When** [the main screen of the app is loaded], **Then** [there is a Next button in the user interface].	Not testable using Quick as it requires visual verification.
3	**Given** [the main screen of the app is loaded], **When** [no area has been selected], **Then** [the Next button is not enabled].	
4	**Given** [the main screen of the app is loaded], **When** [an area in London has been selected], **Then** [the Next button is enabled].	
5	**Given** [the user has selected a location], **When** [the Next button is tapped], **Then** [a new screen appears with a list of restaurants in that location].	Partially testable. The developer can test that tapping the button initiates the process of displaying a new screen, but cannot test that the new screen has actually appeared.
6	**Given** [the list of restaurants is visible on the screen], **When** [a restaurant's name is displayed in that list], **Then** [the listing should be accompanied by the name of the nearest tube station].	Partially testable. The developer can test that a specific method is being called on the view controller with an expected value. The developer, however, cannot test that the text has actually updated on the screen without visual inspection of the results.
7	**Given** [the list of restaurants is visible on the screen], **When** [a restaurant's name is displayed in that list], **Then** [the listing should be accompanied by the approximate distance in miles to the nearest tube station].	Partially testable. The developer can test that a specific method is being called on the view controller with an expected value. The developer, however, cannot test that the text has actually updated on the screen without visual inspection of the results.

(continued)

Table 12-3. (*continued*)

Number	User Scenario	Notes
8	**Given** [the list of restaurants is visible on the screen], **When** [a restaurant's name is displayed in that list], **Then** [the listing should be accompanied by an integer between 1 to 5 that indicates the quality of the restaurant, with 1 being the poorest and 5 the best].	Partially testable. The developer can test that a specific method is being called on the view controller with an expected value. The developer, however, cannot test that the text has actually updated on the screen without visual inspection of the results.
9	**Given** [the list of restaurants is visible on the screen], **When** [a restaurant's name is displayed in that list], **Then** [the listing should be accompanied by the cuisine served at the restaurant].	Partially testable. The developer can test that a specific method is being called on the view controller with an expected value. The developer, however, cannot test that the text has actually updated on the screen without visual inspection of the results.

The contents of Table 12-3 are clearly communicated across the team so that all parties have clear expectations on who will test what aspects of the system. In addition to that, it has been agreed that the following field validation criteria will apply to restaurant listings:

- **Restaurant name:** Between 2 to 30 characters in length, cannot have numbers or special characters. The ampersand (&) character is allowed.

- **Cuisine type:** Between 4 to 10 characters in length, cannot have numbers, special characters, or white space. A restaurant can have up only one cuisine.

- **Nearest Tube station name:** Between 4 to 30 characters in length, cannot contain numbers or special characters. The ampersand (&) character is allowed.

- **Rating:** A number between 0 and 5 inclusive. Cannot contain white space, alphanumeric, or special characters.

High-Level Application Architecture

The application architecture consists of three distinct layers (see Figure 12-1).

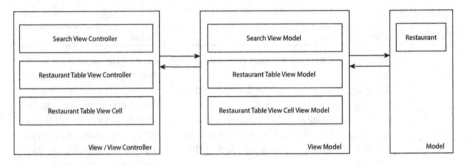

Figure 12-1. *High-Level Application Architecture*

A brief description of the layers and the component classes follows:

- **Model Layer:** Consists of the Restaurant class, instances of which are used to hold the data that will be displayed to the user. The model layer also contains validator objects that encapsulate the validation logic for the fields of the Restaurant object.

- **View Model Layer:** Consists of the SearchViewModel, RestaurantTableViewModel, RestaurantTableViewCellViewModel classes.

- **View/View Controller Layer:** Consists of the SearchViewController, RestaurantTableViewController. and classes.

Figure 12-2 depicts the user interface of the finished application.

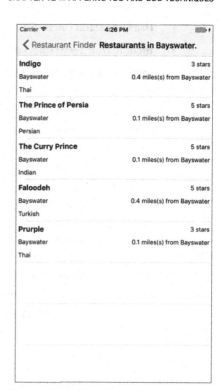

Figure 12-2. *User Interface of the RestaurantFinder Application*

The complete source code for the app can be downloaded anonymously from github using the following URL:

`https://github.com/asmtechnology/Lesson12.iOSTesting.2017.Apress.git`

Creating the Xcode Project

Launch Xcode and create a new iOS project based on the Single View Application template. Use the following options while creating the new project (see Figure 12-3):

- **Product Name:** RestaurantDirectory
- **Team:** None
- **Organization Name:** Provide a suitable name
- **Organization Identifier:** Provide a suitable identifier
- **Language:** Swift
- **Devices:** iPhone

- **Use Core Data:** Unchecked

- **Include Unit Tests:** Checked

- **Include UI Tests:** Unchecked

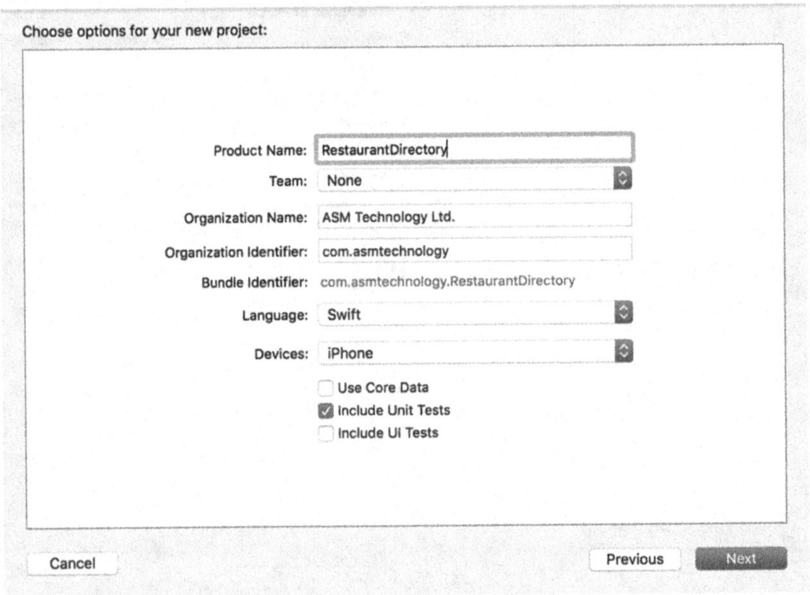

Choose options for your new project:

Product Name:	RestaurantDirectory
Team:	None
Organization Name:	ASM Technology Ltd.
Organization Identifier:	com.asmtechnology
Bundle Identifier:	com.asmtechnology.RestaurantDirectory
Language:	Swift
Devices:	iPhone

☐ Use Core Data
☑ Include Unit Tests
☐ Include UI Tests

Cancel   Previous   Next

Figure 12-3. *Xcode Project Options Dialog*

■ **Note** The project being created in this chapter does not include user interface (UI) tests. If you wish, you can add UI tests to a project retrospectively. Chapter 13 covers the topic of user interface testing.

Save the project to a suitable location on your computer and click Create. Since this project will contain several new classes, it will be a good idea to place class files under appropriate groups within the project navigator.

Create the following groups in the Xcode project navigator, nested under the RestaurantDirectory folder:

- View

- Model

- ViewModel

- Protocols

Adding Resources to the Project

Add the RestaurantData.json file included with this lesson's downloads into the project. While adding this file, ensure the "Copy Items if Needed" option is checked in the import dialog box (see Figure 12-4).

Figure 12-4. *Xcode File Import Dialog*

The JSON file you have imported contains data on restaurants, and a sample of the contents of the JSON file is presented in Listing 12-1.

Listing 12-1. RestaurantData.json

```
[
  {
    "area": "Notting Hill",
    "rating": "4",
    "cuisine": "Persian",
    "distance": "0.3",
    "tubeStation": "Notting Hill Gate",
    "restaurantName": "Alibaba's"
  }
]
```

Building the User Interface Layer

The user interface for this application consists of two storyboard scenes embedded within a navigation controller (see Figure 12-5).

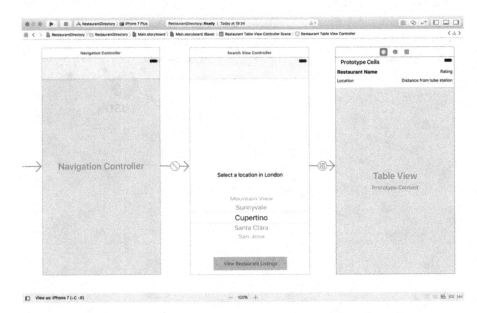

Figure 12-5. *Storyboard Layout for the RestaurantFinder Application*

Delete the ViewController.swift file from the project navigator, and create the following Swift classes under the View group:

- A UIViewController subclass called SearchViewController.

- A UITableViewController subclass called RestaurantTableViewController.

- A UITableViewCell subclass called RestaurantTableViewCell.

Ensure these classes are included in both the RestaurantDirectory and RestaurantDirectoryTests targets. The project navigator should resemble Figure 12-6.

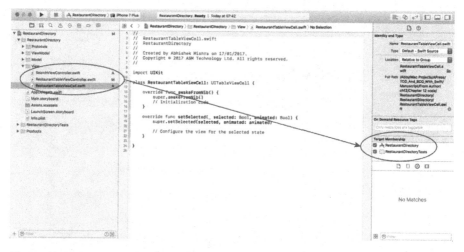

Figure 12-6. *Target Membership for New Classes Added to the Project*

Open the Main.storyboard file and select the default scene in the storyboard. Switch to the Identity Inspector and change the class associated with the scene to SearchViewController (see Figure 12-7).

Figure 12-7. *Using the Identity Inspector to Change the Class Associated with a Stroyboard Scene*

Drag and drop a label, picker view, and button from the Object Library onto the search view controller scene. Set the text displayed in the label to "Select a location in London" and the font size of the text in the label to 14 points. Set the text displayed in the button to "View Restaurant Listings" and the background color to a shade of gray. Position the objects on the scene to resemble Figure 12-8. Use appropriate constraints for the object to maintain their relative position on different screen sizes.

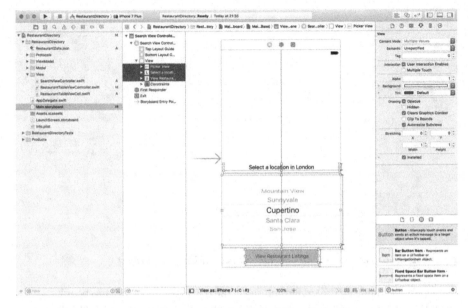

Figure 12-8. *User Interface Elements Added to Default Storyboard Scene*

Using the storyboard, set up the SearchViewController class to act as the delegate and data source for the picker view. Table 12-4 lists the outlets and action methods that you need to create in the SearchViewController class along with their associated user interface elements.

Table 12-4. *Search view controller outlets and actions*

Name	Type	Description
@IBOutlet weak var locationPicker: UIPickerView!	IB Outlet	Connect this outlet to the picker view in the storyboard scene.
@IBOutlet weak var viewRestaurantButton: UIButton!	IB Outlet	Connect this outlet to the View Restaurant Listings button of the storyboard scene.
@IBAction func onViewListings (_ sender: Any)	IB Action	Connect this method to the Touch Up Inside event of the View Restaurant Listings button.

Implement the UIPickerViewDelegate protocol in a separate class extension on SearchViewController by adding the following code to the end of the SearchViewController.swift file:

```swift
extension SearchViewController : UIPickerViewDelegate {

    func pickerView(_ pickerView: UIPickerView,
                    titleForRow row: Int,
                    forComponent component: Int) -> String? {

        return nil
    }

    func pickerView(_ pickerView: UIPickerView,
                    didSelectRow row: Int, inComponent component: Int) {

    }
}
```

Implement the UIPickerViewDataSource protocol in a separate class extension on SearchViewController by adding the following code to the end of the SearchViewController.swift file:

```swift
extension SearchViewController : UIPickerViewDataSource {

    func numberOfComponents(in pickerView: UIPickerView) -> Int {

        return 0
    }

    func pickerView(_ pickerView: UIPickerView,
                    numberOfRowsInComponent component: Int) -> Int {

        return 0
    }

}
```

The above snippets contain bare-bones implementations of the picker view delegate and data source methods. The code in SearchViewController.swift should now resemble Listing 12-2.

Listing 12-2. SearchViewController.swift

```swift
import UIKit

class SearchViewController: UIViewController {

    @IBOutlet weak var locationPicker: UIPickerView!
    @IBOutlet weak var viewRestaurantButton: UIButton!
```

```swift
    override func viewDidLoad() {
        super.viewDidLoad()

        // Do any additional setup after loading the view.
    }

    override func didReceiveMemoryWarning() {
        super.didReceiveMemoryWarning()
        // Dispose of any resources that can be recreated.
    }

    @IBAction func onViewListings(_ sender: Any) {
    }
}

extension SearchViewController : UIPickerViewDelegate {

    func pickerView(_ pickerView: UIPickerView,
                    titleForRow row: Int,
                    forComponent component: Int) -> String? {

        return nil
    }

    func pickerView(_ pickerView: UIPickerView,
                    didSelectRow row: Int,
                    inComponent component: Int) {

    }
}

extension SearchViewController : UIPickerViewDataSource {

    func numberOfComponents(in pickerView: UIPickerView) -> Int {

        return 0
    }

    func pickerView(_ pickerView: UIPickerView,
                    numberOfRowsInComponent component: Int) -> Int {

        return 0
    }

}
```

Drag and drop a Table View Controller from the Object Library onto the storyboard scene. With the Table View Controller scene selected, switch to the Identity Inspector and change the class associated with the scene to be RestaurantTableViewController (see Figure 12-9).

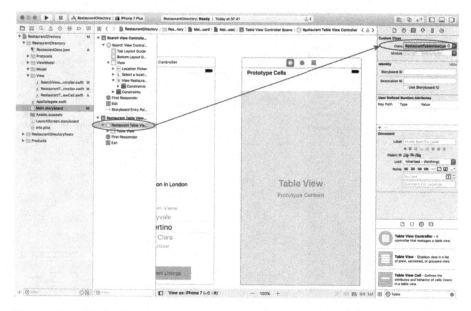

Figure 12-9. *Xcode Identity Inspector*

Select the table view cell and use the Identity Inspector to change the class associated with the cell to be RestaurantTableViewCell (see Figure 12-10).

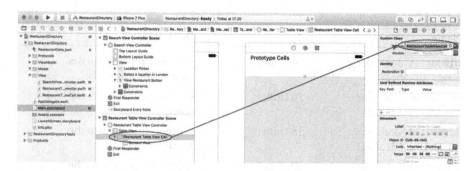

Figure 12-10. *Using the Identity Inspector to Change the Class Associated with a UITableViewCell*

With the table view cell still selected, switch to the Attributes Inspector and set the value of the Identitifier attribute to RestaurantTableViewCellIdentifier.

Drag and drop five labels from the Object library onto the prototype cell of the table view. Name and arrange the labels to resemble Figure 12-11. Create appropriate layout constraints to maintain this arrangement on different screen sizes.

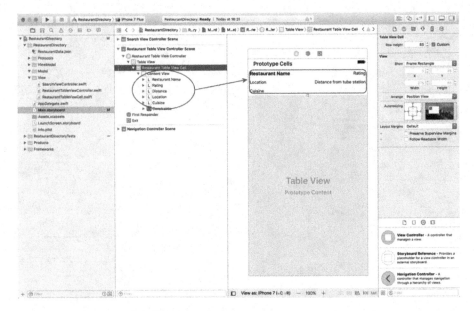

Figure 12-11. *Prototype Cell Layout*

Table 12-5 lists the outlets and action methods that you need to create in the RestaurantTableViewCell class along with their associated user interface elements.

Table 12-5. *Restaurant table view cell outlets and actions.*

Name	Type	Description
@IBOutlet weak var name: UILabel!	IB Outlet	Connect this outlet to the Restaurant Name label.
@IBOutlet weak var rating: UILabel!	IB Outlet	Connect this outlet to the Rating label.
@IBOutlet weak var location: UILabel!	IB Outlet	Connect this outlet to the Location label.
@IBOutlet weak var distance: UILabel!	IB Outlet	Connect this outlet to the Distance label.
@IBOutlet weak var cuisine: UILabel!	IB Outlet	Connect this outlet to the Cuisine label.

Select the Search View Controller scene in the storyboard and use the Editor ➤ Embed In ➤ Navigation Controller menu item to add a navigation controller to the beginning of the storyboard (Figure 12-12).

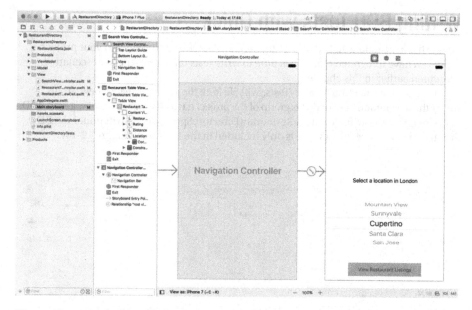

Figure 12-12. Embedding the Default Storyboard Scene in a Navigation Controller

Create a Show Detail segue from the search view controller scene to the restaurant list view controller scene of the storyboard. With the segue selected, switch to the Attributes Inspector and set the value of the Identifier attribute to presentSearchResults (Figure 12-13).

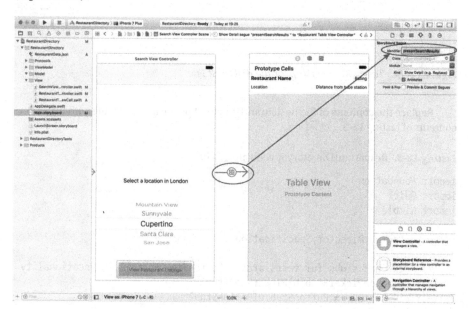

Figure 12-13. Using the Identity Inspector to Specify a Segue Identifier

Writing BDD Tests with Quick

Follow the instructions in Chapter 11 to integrate Quick and Nimble into your project. Once you have integrated Quick, it is time to write tests for each of the user scenarios presented earlier in this chapter.

Delete the RestaurantDirectoryTests.swift file from the project. Create a new Group under the RestaurantDirectoryTests group of the project navigator. Name the new group BDD.

Create a new Swift file called RestaurantDirectorySpecificaton.swift under the BDD group and make sure the new file is only included in the test target (Figure 12-14).

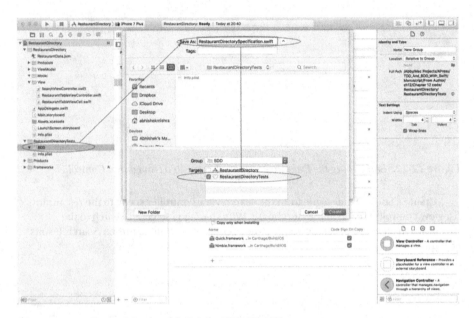

Figure 12-14. *Target Membership for the BDD Test File*

Replace the contents of the RestaurantDirectorySpecificaton.swift file with the contents of Listing 12-3.

Listing 12-3. RestaurantDirectorySpecificaton.swift

```swift
import Foundation
import Quick
import Nimble

class RestaurantDirectorySpecification : QuickSpec {

    // mocks and stubs for tests around SearchViewController funcationality
    var locationPickerStub:UIPickerViewStub?
    var viewRestaurantButtonStub:UIButtonStub?
```

```
var searchViewController:MockSearchViewController?
var searchViewModel:SearchViewModel?

// mocks and stubs for tests around RestaurantTableViewCell
// funcationality
var restaurantNameLabelStub:UILabelStub?
var restaurantRatingLabelStub:UILabelStub?
var restaurantDistanceLabelStub:UILabelStub?
var restaurantLocationLabelStub:UILabelStub?
var restaurantCuisineLabelStub:UILabelStub?
var restaurantTableViewCell:MockRestaurantTableViewCell?

var validRestaurantDataFile1:String?
var validRestaurant: Restaurant?
var cellViewModel: RestaurantTableViewCellViewModel?

func prepareForSearchViewControllerTests() {
    let bundle = Bundle(for: type(of:self))
    validRestaurantDataFile1 = bundle.path(forResource:
    "ValidRestaurantDataFile1",
    ofType: "json")

    locationPickerStub = UIPickerViewStub()
    viewRestaurantButtonStub = UIButtonStub()

    searchViewController = MockSearchViewController()
    searchViewController!.locationPicker = locationPickerStub!
    searchViewController!.viewRestaurantButton =
    viewRestaurantButtonStub!

    searchViewModel = SearchViewModel(view: searchViewController!)
    searchViewModel!.loadRestaurantData(filePath:
    validRestaurantDataFile1!)

    searchViewController!.viewModel = searchViewModel!
}

func prepareForRestaurantTableViewCellTests() {

    restaurantNameLabelStub = UILabelStub()
    restaurantRatingLabelStub = UILabelStub()
    restaurantDistanceLabelStub = UILabelStub()
    restaurantLocationLabelStub = UILabelStub()
    restaurantCuisineLabelStub = UILabelStub()

    restaurantTableViewCell = MockRestaurantTableViewCell()
    restaurantTableViewCell!.name = restaurantNameLabelStub!
    restaurantTableViewCell!.rating = restaurantRatingLabelStub!
```

369

```
            restaurantTableViewCell!.distance = restaurantDistanceLabelStub!
            restaurantTableViewCell!.location = restaurantLocationLabelStub!
            restaurantTableViewCell!.cuisine = restaurantCuisineLabelStub!

            var validDictionary = [String : AnyObject]()
            validDictionary["area"] = "Oxford Street" as AnyObject
            validDictionary["rating"] = "5" as AnyObject
            validDictionary["cuisine"] = "Indian" as AnyObject
            validDictionary["distance"] = "0.05" as AnyObject
            validDictionary["tubeStation"] = "Bayswater" as AnyObject
            validDictionary["restaurantName"] = "Curry King" as AnyObject

            validRestaurant = Restaurant(validDictionary)

            cellViewModel = RestaurantTableViewCellViewModel(model:
            validRestaurant!)
            cellViewModel!.view = restaurantTableViewCell!

            restaurantTableViewCell!.viewModel = cellViewModel!
    }

    override func spec() {

        beforeEach {

        }

        describe("the main screen of the app is loaded") {
            context("no area has been selected") {
                it("the Next button is not enabled") {

                    self.prepareForSearchViewControllerTests()
                    self.searchViewController!.viewDidLoad()

                    expect(self.viewRestaurantButtonStub!.isEnabled).
                    to(equal(false))

                }
            }
        }

        describe("the main screen of the app is loaded") {
            context("an area in London has been selected") {
                it("the Next button is enabled") {

                    self.prepareForSearchViewControllerTests()
```

```
                self.searchViewController!.pickerView(
                self.locationPickerStub!, didSelectRow: 0,
                inComponent: 0)

                expect(self.viewRestaurantButtonStub!.isEnabled).
                to(equal(true))
            }
        }
    }

    describe("the user has selected a location") {
        context("the Next button is tapped") {
            it("a new screen appears with a list of restaurants in
                that location") {

                self.prepareForSearchViewControllerTests()

                self.searchViewController!.pickerView(
                self.locationPickerStub!,
                didSelectRow: 0, inComponent: 0)

                self.searchViewController!.onViewListings(self)

                expect(self.searchViewController!.
                displayResultsScreenCalled).to(equal(true))
            }
        }
    }

    describe("the list of restaurants is visible on the screen") {
        context("a restaurant's name is displayed in that list") {
            it("the listing should be accompanied with the name
                of the nearest tube station") {

                self.prepareForRestaurantTableViewCellTests()

                self.restaurantTableViewCell!.setup()

                let expectedValue = "\(self.validRestaurant!.distance!)
                miles(s) from \(self.validRestaurant!.tubeStation!)"

                expect(self.restaurantDistanceLabelStub!.text).
                to(equal(expectedValue))
            }
        }
    }
```

```
describe("the list of restaurants is visible on the screen") {
    context("a restaurant's name is displayed in that list") {
        it("the listing should be accompanied by the approximate
            distance in miles to the nearest tube station") {

            self.prepareForRestaurantTableViewCellTests()

            self.restaurantTableViewCell!.setup()

            let expectedValue = "\(self.validRestaurant!.distance!)
            miles(s) from \(self.validRestaurant!.tubeStation!)"

            expect(self.restaurantDistanceLabelStub!.text).
            to(equal(expectedValue))
        }
    }
}


describe("the list of restaurants is visible on the screen") {
    context("a restaurant's name is displayed in that list") {
        it("the listing should be accompanied by an integer between
            1 to 5 that indicates the quality of the restaurant,
            with 1 being the poorest and 5 the best") {

            self.prepareForRestaurantTableViewCellTests()

            self.restaurantTableViewCell!.setup()

            let expectedValue = "\(self.validRestaurant!.rating!)
                            stars"
            expect(self.restaurantRatingLabelStub!.text).
            to(equal(expectedValue))
        }
    }
}

describe("the list of restaurants is visible on the screen") {
    context("a restaurant's name is displayed in that list") {
        it("the listing should be accompanied by the cuisine served
            at the restaurant") {

            self.prepareForRestaurantTableViewCellTests()

            self.restaurantTableViewCell!.setup()

            let expectedValue = self.validRestaurant!.cuisine!

            expect(self.restaurantCuisineLabelStub!.text).
            to(equal(expectedValue))
```

```
                }
            }
        }

    }
}
```

The code in Listing 12-3 defines a BDD specification class called RestaurantDirectorySpecification that is a subclass of QuickSpec and has a number of BDD-style tests, one for each user scenario described in Table 12-3, which we saw earlier. An analysis of the contents of the file is presented next.

At the top of the file are three import statements that import the Foundation, Quick, and Nimble frameworks:

```
import Foundation
import Quick
import Nimble
```

The RestaurantDirectorySpecification class is declared as a subclass of QuickSpec (and not XCTest) as we intend to write BDD-style tests:

```
class RestaurantDirectorySpecification : QuickSpec
```

The class contains a number of Ivars that are used to create stubbed versions of the SearchViewController and the RestaurantTableViewCell classes:

```
// mocks and stubs for tests around SearchViewController funcationality
var locationPickerStub:UIPickerViewStub?
var viewRestaurantButtonStub:UIButtonStub?
var searchViewController:MockSearchViewController?
var searchViewModel:SearchViewModel?

// mocks and stubs for tests around RestaurantTableViewCell funcationality
var restaurantNameLabelStub:UILabelStub?
var restaurantRatingLabelStub:UILabelStub?
var restaurantDistanceLabelStub:UILabelStub?
var restaurantLocationLabelStub:UILabelStub?
var restaurantCuisineLabelStub:UILabelStub?
var restaurantTableViewCell:MockRestaurantTableViewCell?

var validRestaurantDataFile1:String?
var validRestaurant: Restaurant?
var cellViewModel: RestaurantTableViewCellViewModel?
```

Immediately following the instance variable declarations are a couple of methods that perform the necessary object instantiation and assignment into the instance variables. These methods are named the following:

- prepareForSearchViewControllerTests(), and

- prepareForRestaurantTableViewCellTests()

The class has one other method called spec(), which is where the Quick tests are written. As described in Chapter 10, each BDD test is written in the following format:

```
override func spec() {

    beforeEach {
    }

    describe(/* the "Given" part of a scenario statement*/) {
        context(/* the "When" part of a scenario statement*/){
            it(/* the "Then" part of a scenario statement */) {
                // test logic goes here
            }
        }
    }
}
```

The beforeEach() method of a Quick test case is equivalent to the setUp() method of an XCTestCase. After the call to the beforeEach() method, a number of BDD-style tests are written using nested calls to three functions: describe(), context(), it().

Let us examine each testable BDD scenario listed in Table 12-3 and the corresponding BDD test code (scenarios 1 and 2 are not testable using Quick as they rely on visual inspection of the user interface).

Examining the BDD Test for Scenario Number 3

Let us examine Scenario number 3, which is the first test scenario that can be tested using BDD techniques:

> **Given** [the main screen of the app is loaded],
>
> **When** [no area has been selected],
>
> **Then** [the Next button is not enabled].

The BDD-style test case to test this scenario is presented below:

```
describe("the main screen of the app is loaded") {
    context("no area has been selected") {
        it("the Next button is not enabled") {

            self.prepareForSearchViewControllerTests()
            self.searchViewController!.viewDidLoad()

            expect(self.viewRestaurantButtonStub!.isEnabled).
            to(equal(false))

        }
    }
}
```

The main screen of this app is represented by an instance of the SearchViewController class, which has a picker with a list of locations, and a button that will allow a user to view a list of restaurants in the location selected in the picker.

The aim of this scenario is to ensure that the button is not enabled before the user has selected a location in the picker.

In order to test that the criteria defined in this scenario are met, all you need to do is call the viewDidLoad method on a SearchViewController instance, and check that the isEnabled property of the button is false.

Instantiating the view controller within a test requires that stub objects are assigned to the outlets defined in the view controller. This is achieved using a call to prepareForSearchViewControllerTests() at the beginning of the test.

Examining the BDD Test for Scenario Number 4

Let us examine Scenario number 4, which is the next test scenario that can be tested using BDD techniques:

> **Given** [the main screen of the app is loaded],
>
> **When** [an area in London has been selected],
>
> **Then** [the Next button is enabled].

The BDD-style test case to test this scenario is presented below:

```
describe("the main screen of the app is loaded") {
    context("an area in London has been selected") {
        it("the Next button is enabled") {

            self.prepareForSearchViewControllerTests()

            self.searchViewController!.pickerView(
            self.locationPickerStub!, didSelectRow: 0,
            inComponent: 0)

            expect(self.viewRestaurantButtonStub!.isEnabled).
            to(equal(true))
        }
    }
}
```

This scenario also describes the behavior of the SearchViewController class. The aim of this scenario is to ensure that the button on the view controller is enabled when the user has selected a location in the picker.

In order to test that the criteria defined in this scenario are met, all you need to do is call the pickerView(picker, didSelectRow, inComponent) method on a SearchViewController instance, and check that the isEnabled property of the button is true.

Examining the BDD Test for Scenario Number 5

Let us examine Scenario number 5, which is the next test scenario that can be tested using BDD techniques:

Given [the user has selected a location],

When [the Next button is tapped],

Then [a new screen appears with a list of restaurants in that location].

The BDD-style test case to test this scenario is presented below:

```
describe("the user has selected a location") {
    context("the Next button is tapped") {
        it("a new screen appears with a list of restaurants in that
        location") {

            self.prepareForSearchViewControllerTests()

            self.searchViewController!.pickerView(
            self.locationPickerStub!, didSelectRow: 0,
            inComponent: 0)

            self.searchViewController!.onViewListings(self)

            expect(self.searchViewController!.displayResultsScreenCalled).
            to(equal(true))
        }
    }
}
```

This scenario describes what happens after the user taps on the View Restaurant Listings button in the SearchViewController. The expected behavior is that the results screen appears with a list of restaurants. The result screen is represented by an instance of the RestaurantListTableViewController class.

Trying to confirm that the result screen has visually appeared would be a user interface test and will be better suited to tools used by the QA team. From a code perspective, we could test that tapping on the button will call a method, which, in turn, would have the logic to display the next screen.

This project will be built using the MV-VM architectural pattern; therefore the SearchViewController class will have an associated view model class called SearchViewModel. The view model class will contain the presentation logic, and to support this logic, the view controller class will provide a method called displayResultsScreen() that the view model can call.

In order to test that the criteria defined in this scenario are met, all you need to do is select a row in the picker, then call the onViewListings() action method, and check that the displayResultsScreen() method is called on the view controller.

But how do you check if the displayResultsScreen() is called? In this project I will create a subclass of SearchViewController called MockSearchViewController that will contain a Boolean instance variable that will be set to true when the displayResultsScreen() method is called.

Examining the BDD Test for Scenario Number 6

Let us examine Scenario number 6, which is the next test scenario that can be tested using BDD techniques:

Given [the list of restaurants is visible on the screen],

When [a restaurant's name is displayed in that list],

Then [the listing should be accompanied by the name of the nearest tube station].

The BDD-style test case to test this scenario is presented below:

```
describe("the list of restaurants is visible on the screen") {
    context("a restaurant's name is displayed in that list") {
        it("the listing should be accompanied with the name of the nearest
        tube station") {

            self.prepareForRestaurantTableViewCellTests()
            self.restaurantTableViewCell!.setup()

            let expectedValue = "\(self.validRestaurant!.distance!)
            miles(s) from \(self.validRestaurant!.tubeStation!)"

            expect(self.restaurantDistanceLabelStub!.text).
            to(equal(expectedValue))
        }
    }
}
```

This scenario describes the behavior of the RestaurantListTableViewCell class and can be tested by ensuring that a given cell of the table view has some specific text in the restaurantDistanceLabel.

The test code requires that an instance of RestaurantListTableViewCell is instantiated with stub objects for the outlets. This is achieved by a call to prepareForRestaurantTableViewCellTests() at the beginning of the test.

The test code also assumes that the table view cell will have a method called setup() that will be called by the table view controller before presenting the cell.

Examining the BDD Test for Scenario Number 7

Let us examine Scenario number 7, which is the next test scenario that can be tested using BDD techniques:

> **Given** [the list of restaurants is visible on the screen],
>
> **When** [a restaurant's name is displayed in that list],
>
> **Then** [the listing should be accompanied by the approximate distance in miles to the nearest tube station].

The BDD-style test case to test this scenario is presented below:

```
describe("the list of restaurants is visible on the screen") {
    context("a restaurant's name is displayed in that list") {
        it("the listing should be accompanied by the approximate distance in
            miles to the nearest tube station") {

            self.prepareForRestaurantTableViewCellTests()
            self.restaurantTableViewCell!.setup()

            let expectedValue = "\(self.validRestaurant!.distance!)
            miles(s) from \(self.validRestaurant!.tubeStation!)"

            expect(self.restaurantDistanceLabelStub!.text).
            to(equal(expectedValue))
        }
    }
}
```

This scenario is similar to the previous one, and can also be tested by ensuring that a given cell of the table view has some specific text in the restaurantDistanceLabel.

Examining the BDD Test for Scenario Number 8

Let us examine Scenario number 8, which is the next test scenario that can be tested using BDD techniques:

> **Given** [the list of restaurants is visible on the screen],
>
> **When** [a restaurant's name is displayed in that list],
>
> **Then** [the listing should be accompanied by an integer between 1 to 5 that indicates the quality of the restaurant, with 1 being the poorest and 5 the best].

The BDD-style test case to test this scenario is presented below:

```
describe("the list of restaurants is visible on the screen") {
    context("a restaurant's name is displayed in that list") {
        it("the listing should be accompanied by an integer between 1 to 5
            that indicates the quality of the restaurant, with 1 being the
            poorest and 5 the best") {
```

```
                self.prepareForRestaurantTableViewCellTests()
                self.restaurantTableViewCell!.setup()

                let expectedValue = "\(self.validRestaurant!.rating!) stars"

                expect(self.restaurantRatingLabelStub!.text).
                to(equal(expectedValue))
            }
        }
    }
}
```

This scenario also describes the behavior of the RestaurantListTableViewCell class and can be tested by ensuring that a given cell of the table view has some specific text in the restaurantRatingLabel.

Examining the BDD Test for Scenario Number 9

Let us examine Scenario number 9, which is the next test scenario that can be tested using BDD techniques:

> **Given** [the list of restaurants is visible on the screen],
>
> **When** [a restaurant's name is displayed in that list],
>
> **Then** [the listing should be accompanied by the cuisine served at the restaurant].

The BDD-style test case to test this scenario is presented below:

```
describe("the list of restaurants is visible on the screen") {
    context("a restaurant's name is displayed in that list") {
        it("the listing should be accompanied by the cuisine served at the
        restaurant") {

                self.prepareForRestaurantTableViewCellTests()
                self.restaurantTableViewCell!.setup()

                let expectedValue = self.validRestaurant!.cuisine!

                expect(self.restaurantCuisineLabelStub!.text).
                to(equal(expectedValue))
            }
        }
    }
}
```

This scenario also describes the behavior of the RestaurantListTableViewCell class and can be tested by ensuring that a given cell of the table view has some specific text in the restaurantCuisineLabel UILabel.

Creating Stub Objects

At this point, your project will have several code compilation issues as these tests rely on many objects that have not been created. The stub text fields, labels, and pickers are straightforward to create using subclassing techniques.

Create a new group called Stubs under the RestaurantDirectoryTests group in the Project Navigator, and create a new Swift file called UILabelStub.swift under this group. Ensure the file is only included in the test target (Figure 12-15).

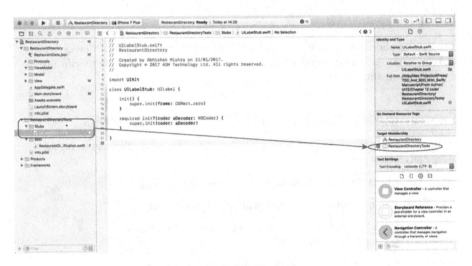

Figure 12-15. *Target Membership for the UILabelStub Class*

Update the code in UILabelStub.swift to match the contents of Listing 12-4.

Listing 12-4. UILabelStub.swift

```swift
import UIKit

class UILabelStub: UILabel {

    init() {
        super.init(frame: CGRect.zero)
    }

    required init?(coder aDecoder: NSCoder) {
        super.init(coder: aDecoder)
    }

}
```

Create a new Swift file called UIButtonStub.swift under the Stubs group, ensuring the file is only included in the test target and update the contents of the new file to match the contents of Listing 12-5.

Listing 12-5. UIButtonStub.swift

```swift
import UIKit

class UILabelStub: UILabel {

    init() {
        super.init(frame: CGRect.zero)
    }

    required init?(coder aDecoder: NSCoder) {
        super.init(coder: aDecoder)
    }

}
```

Create a new Swift file called UITextFieldStub.swift under the Stubs group, ensuring the file is only included in the test target, and update the contents of the new file to match the contents of Listing 12-6.

Listing 12-6. UITextFieldStub.swift

```swift
import UIKit

class UITextFieldStub : UITextField {

    init(text:String) {
        super.init(frame: CGRect.zero)
        super.text = text
    }

    required init?(coder aDecoder: NSCoder) {
        super.init(coder: aDecoder)
    }
}
```

Create a new Swift file called UITableViewStub.swift under the Stubs group, ensuring the file is only included in the test target, and update the contents of the new file to match the contents of Listing 12-7.

Listing 12-7. UITableViewStub.swift

```swift
import UIKit

class UITableViewStub: UITableView {
```

```
init() {
    super.init(frame: CGRect.zero, style: UITableViewStyle.plain)
}

required init?(coder aDecoder: NSCoder) {
    super.init(coder: aDecoder)
}

override func dequeueReusableCell(withIdentifier identifier: String) ->
UITableViewCell? {
    return RestaurantTableViewCell()
}
}
```

Create a new Swift file called UIPickerViewStub.swift under the Stubs group, ensuring the file is only included in the test target, and update the contents of the new file to match the contents of Listing 12-8.

Listing 12-8. UIPickerViewStub.swift

```
import UIKit

class UIPickerViewStub : UIPickerView {

    init() {
        super.init(frame: CGRect.zero)
    }

    required init?(coder aDecoder: NSCoder) {
        super.init(coder: aDecoder)
    }

}
```

Adding The Restaurant Data File to the Project

Create a new group called TestData under the RestaurantDirectoryTests group in the Project Navigator, and add the ValidRestaurantDataFile1.json file included with this lesson's downloads into the project. While adding this file, ensure the "Copy Items if Needed" option is checked in the import dialog box and that the file is only included in the test target (Figure 12-16).

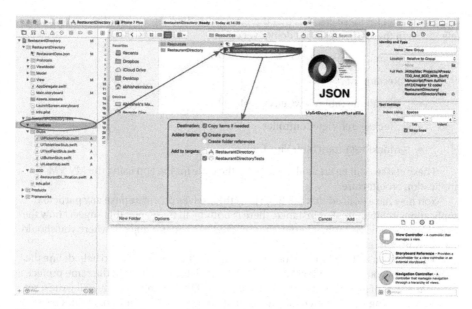

Figure 12-16. Xcode File Import Dialog

Examining the Remaining Compilation Errors

If you switch to the RestaurantDirectorySpecification.swift file, you will notice that several compilation error messages that were previously visible have disappeared; however, there are still 10 errors remaining (Figure 12-17).

Figure 12-17. RestaurantDirectorySpecification.Swift Compilation Errors

The reason for these errors is that there are still quite a few classes that are being referenced in these BDD tests but do not yet exist:

- SearchViewModel

- Restaurant

- RestaurantTableViewCellViewModel

- MockSearchViewController

- MockRestaurantTableViewCell

These classes will be created as we build the code for the app using the MV-VM application architecture.

You may have noticed that the BDD tests themselves do not impose any particular application architecture. For instance, there is nothing in these tests that suggest how the model layer should be built, whether there should be validator objects, where you should use view models, etc.

This is because BDD tests operate at a higher level of abstraction. To help define the architecture of your code, you will need to revert to TDD techniques in the same project.

At the start of a project that uses both BDD and TDD techniques, you will write a set of BDD tests using Quick, which may not initially compile, and if they do, will not pass.

You will then move on to develop your application's code using TDD techniques, while at the same time keeping an eye on the BDD tests. If initially your BDD tests were not compiling, you will need to temporarily comment out the portions of the test code that do not compile so that you can focus on building your application's code.

Periodically, you will need to uncomment the BDD tests and execute the BDD tests. Doing so frequently will ensure that the code you are writing using TDD techniques is moving toward satisfying the requirements provided by the business. In time, as more of your application's code is built along with their associated unit tests, your BDD tests will begin to pass as well.

The rest of this chapter will describe the characteristics of the model, view model, and view controller layers of the application, and then we will build these using standard TDD techniques that have been covered in earlier chapters.

Building the Model Layer

There is only one model class that we need to build – Restaurant. The Restaurant class contains properties that store the information for a single restaurant. Table 12-6 lists the desired properties and methods of the Photo class.

Table 12-6. *Properties and Methods of the Photo Class*

Item	Type	Description
`var area:String?`	Variable	The location in London where the restaurant is based.
`var rating:String?`	Variable	A number between 0 and 5, which represented the average rating received by the restaurant.
`var cuisine:String?`	Variable	The cuisine served at the restaurant.
`var distance:String?`	Variable	The distance between the restaurant and the nearest tube station.
`var tubeStation:String?`	Variable	The name of the nearest London underground station.
`var restaurantName:String?`	Variable	The name of the restaurant.
`init? (_ dictionary:[String : AnyObject]?)`	Method	Allows other code to create Restaurant instances. Requires a dictionary with certain mandatory keys as input.

The init() method will require a dictionary with all of the following mandatory keys to be present:

- restaurantName
- rating
- cuisine
- area
- distance
- tubeStation

The complete Restaurant class is shown in Listing 12-9. If you would like to examine the code for the validator objects and associated tests, download the finished project anonymously from github using the following URL:

https://github.com/asmtechnology/Lesson12.iOSTesting.2017.Apress.git

Listing 12-9. Restaurant.swift

```
import Foundation

class Restaurant : NSObject {

    var area:String?
    var rating:String?
    var cuisine:String?
```

```swift
var distance:String?
var tubeStation:String?
var restaurantName:String?

var restaurantNameValidator:RestaurantNameValidator?
var tubeStationValidator:TubeStationValidator?
var cuisineValidator:CuisineValidator?
var ratingValidator:RatingValidator?

let areaKey = "area"
let ratingKey = "rating"
let cuisineKey = "cuisine"
let distanceKey = "distance"
let tubeStationKey = "tubeStation"
let restaurantNameKey = "restaurantName"

init?(_ dictionary:[String : AnyObject]?) {

    guard let dictionary = dictionary,
        let area = dictionary[areaKey] as? String,
        let rating = dictionary[ratingKey] as? String,
        let cuisine = dictionary[cuisineKey] as? String,
        let distance = dictionary[distanceKey] as? String,
        let tubeStation = dictionary[tubeStationKey] as? String,
        let restaurantName = dictionary[restaurantNameKey]  as? String
        else {
            return nil
    }

    super.init()

    let restaurantNameValidator = self.restaurantNameValidator ??
    RestaurantNameValidator()
    if restaurantNameValidator.validate(restaurantName) == false {
        return nil
    }

    let tubeStationValidator = self.tubeStationValidator ??
    TubeStationValidator()
    if tubeStationValidator.validate(tubeStation) == false {
        return nil
    }
```

```
let cuisineValidator = self.cuisineValidator ?? CuisineValidator()
if cuisineValidator.validate(cuisine) == false {
    return nil
}

let ratingValidator = self.ratingValidator ?? RatingValidator()
if ratingValidator.validate(rating) == false {
    return nil
}

self.area = area
self.rating = rating
self.cuisine = cuisine
self.distance = distance
self.tubeStation = tubeStation
self.restaurantName = restaurantName
    }

}
```

Building the ViewModel Layer

There are three view model classes that we need to build - SearchViewModel,
RestaurantTableViewModel, and RestaurantTableViewCellViewModel. These
correspond to the SearchViewController, RestaurantTableViewController, and
RestaurantTableViewCell classes respectively.

The view models will use protocols to establish an interface through which they can
communicate with their respective view controllers.

The SearchViewModel Class

The SearchViewModel class represents the view model between the
SearchViewController class and the Restaurant model object. The desired instance
variables and methods of the view model class are described in Table 12-7.

Table 12-7. SearchViewModel instance variables and methods

Name	Type	Description
weak var view:SearchViewContr ollerProtocol?	Ivar	Reference to the view controller, uses a protocol to define a list of methods that the view model can use.
var selectedArea:String?	Ivar	Represents the location within London selected by the user by interacting with the picker view.
var restaurants: [String: [Restaurant]]	Ivar	A dictionary of restaurants, with one entry for each location of London.
func performInitialViewSetup()	Method	Called from the viewDidLoad() method of the view controller.
func numberOfComponents() -> Int	Method	Called from the numberOfComponents(in pickerView: UIPickerView) method of the view controller.
func numberOfRowsInComponent(_ component:Int) -> Int	Method	Called from the pickerView (_ pickerView: UIPickerView, numberOfRowsInComponent component: Int) method of the view controller.
func titleForRow(_ row:Int, component:Int) -> String?	Method	Called from the pickerView (_ pickerView: UIPickerView, titleForRow row: Int, forComponent component: Int) method of the view controller.
func didSelectRow(_ row:Int, component:Int) -> Void	Method	Called from the pickerView (_ pickerView: UIPickerView, didSelectRow row: Int, inComponent component: Int) method of the view controller.
func onViewListings() -> Void	Method	Called from the onViewListings (_ sender: Any) method of the view controller.
func viewModelForSelectedArea() -> RestaurantTableViewModel?	Method	Called from the prepare(for segue: UIStoryboardSegue, sender: Any?) method of the view controller.
func loadRestaurantData(fileP ath:String?) -> Void	Method	Called from the init() method of the view model class.
init(view:SearchViewControlle rProtocol)	Method	Called from the viewDidLoad() method of the view controller.

The SearchViewModel class requires that a protocol called SearchViewControllerProtocol is defined and implemented by the SearchViewController class. Listing 12-10 decribes the protocol.

Listing 12-10. SearchViewControllerProtocol.swift

```
import Foundation

protocol SearchViewControllerProtocol : class {
    func setNavigationTitle(_ title:String)
    func enableRestaurantListingsButton(_ state:Bool)
    func displayResultsScreen()
}
```

These methods are implemented in SearchViewController.swift by adding the following class extension to the end of the file:

```
extension SearchViewController : SearchViewControllerProtocol {
    func setNavigationTitle(_ title:String) {
        self.title = title
    }

    func enableRestaurantListingsButton(_ state:Bool) {
        self.viewRestaurantButton.isEnabled = state
    }

    func displayResultsScreen() {
        self.performSegue(withIdentifier: "presentSearchResults", sender:
        self)
    }
}
```

The complete SearchViewModel class is provided in Listing 12-11. If you would like to examine the code for the associated tests, download the finished project anonymously from github using the following URL:

https://github.com/asmtechnology/Lesson12.iOSTesting.2017.Apress.git

Listing 12-11. SearchViewModel.swift

```
import Foundation

class SearchViewModel : NSObject {

    var restaurants: [String: [Restaurant]]
    var selectedArea:String?

    weak var view:SearchViewControllerProtocol?

    init(view:SearchViewControllerProtocol) {
```

```
    self.view = view
    self.restaurants = [String: [Restaurant]]()

    super.init()

    let path = Bundle.main.path(forResource: "RestaurantData", ofType:
    "json")
    loadRestaurantData(filePath:path)
}

func loadRestaurantData(filePath:String?) -> Void {

    guard let filePath = filePath,
        let fileData = try? Data(contentsOf: URL(fileURLWithPath:
        filePath)),
        let array = try? JSONSerialization.jsonObject(with: fileData,
        options: JSONSerialization.ReadingOptions.mutableContainers) as?
        NSArray else {
            return
    }

    for item in array! {
        guard let dictionary = item as? [String : AnyObject] else {
            continue
        }

        if let restaurant = Restaurant(dictionary),
            let area = restaurant.area {

            if self.restaurants[area] == nil {
                self.restaurants[area] = [Restaurant]()
            }

            self.restaurants[area]?.append(restaurant)
        }
    }
}

func performInitialViewSetup() {
    view?.setNavigationTitle("Restaurant Finder")
    view?.enableRestaurantListingsButton(false)
}

func numberOfComponents() -> Int {
    return 1
}
```

```swift
func numberOfRowsInComponent(_ component:Int) -> Int {
    return self.restaurants.count
}

func titleForRow(_ row:Int, component:Int) -> String? {
    let keys = [String](self.restaurants.keys)

    if row < 0 || row >= keys.count {
        return nil
    }

    return keys[row]
}

func didSelectRow(_ row:Int, component:Int) -> Void {
    let keys = [String](self.restaurants.keys)

    if row < 0 || row >= keys.count {
        return
    }

    self.selectedArea = keys[row]

    self.view?.enableRestaurantListingsButton(true)
}

func onViewListings() -> Void {
    self.view?.displayResultsScreen()
}

func viewModelForSelectedArea() -> RestaurantTableViewModel? {
    guard let selectedArea = self.selectedArea else {
        return nil
    }

    let keys = [String](self.restaurants.keys)
    if keys.contains(selectedArea) == false {
        return nil
    }

    return RestaurantTableViewModel(selectedArea, restaurantList:self.
    restaurants[selectedArea])
}

}
```

While building the SearchViewModel class using a test-driven approach, you will need to create a mock view controller object to instantiate the view model, and to test the binding between the view model and the view controller.

As it turns out, a mock search view controller class was also one of the missing classes needed to make the Quick BDD tests compile. Listing 12-12 contains the code in a class called MockSearchViewController that will be used by both unit tests and Quick BDD tests.

Listing 12-12. MockSearchViewController.swift

```
import Foundation
import XCTest

class MockSearchViewController : SearchViewController {

    var expectationForSetNavigationTitle:XCTestExpectation?
    var expectationForEnableRestaurantListingsButton:(XCTestExpectation,
    Bool)?
    var expectationForDisplayResultsScreen:XCTestExpectation?

    var displayResultsScreenCalled:Bool

    init() {
        displayResultsScreenCalled = false
        super.init(nibName: nil, bundle: nil)
    }

    required init?(coder aDecoder: NSCoder) {
        displayResultsScreenCalled = false
        super.init(coder: aDecoder)
    }

    override func setNavigationTitle(_ title:String) {
        expectationForSetNavigationTitle?.fulfill()
        super.setNavigationTitle(title)
    }

    override func enableRestaurantListingsButton(_ state:Bool) {
        guard let (expectation, expectedValue) = self.
        expectationForEnableRestaurantListingsButton else {
            super.enableRestaurantListingsButton(state)
            return
        }

        if state == expectedValue {
            expectation.fulfill()
        }
```

```
        super.enableRestaurantListingsButton(state)
    }

    override func displayResultsScreen() {
        expectationForDisplayResultsScreen?.fulfill()
        displayResultsScreenCalled = true
    }
}
```

The RestaurantTableViewModel Class

The RestaurantTableViewModel class represents the view model between the RestaurantTableViewController class and an array of Restaurant model objects. The desired instance variables and methods of the view model class are described in Table 12-8.

Table 12-8. RestaurantTableViewModel instance variables and methods

Name	Type	Description
var view:RestaurantTableViewContr ollerProtocol?	Ivar	Reference to the view controller, uses a protocol to define a list of methods that the view model can use.
var area:String	Ivar	Represents the location within London selected by the user. This will be displayed as the title in the navigation bar.
var restaurantList:[Restaurant]	Ivar	An array of Restaurant objects.
func performInitialViewSetup()	Method	Called from the viewDidLoad() method of the view controller.
func numberOfSections() -> Int	Method	Called from the numberOfSections(in tableView: UITableView) -> Int method of the view controller.
func numberOfRowsInSection(_ section:Int) -> Int	Method	Called from the tableView (_ tableView: UITableView, numberOfRowsInSection section: Int) -> Int method of the view controller.
func cellViewModel(forIndexPath indexPath:IndexPath) -> RestaurantTableViewCellViewModel?	Method	Called from the tableView (_ tableView: UITableView, cellForRowAt indexPath: IndexPath) -> UITableViewCell method of the view controller.
init? (_ area:String, restaurantList:[Restaurant]?)	Method	Called from the viewDidLoad() method of the view controller.

The RestaurantTableViewModel class requires that a protocol called RestaurantTableViewControllerProtocol is defined in the project, and implemented by the RestaurantTableViewController class. Listing 12-13 decribes the protocol:

Listing 12-13. RestaurantTableViewControllerProtocol.swift

```
import Foundation

protocol RestaurantTableViewControllerProtocol : class {
    func setNavigationTitle(_ title:String)
}
```

These methods are implemented in RestaurantTableViewController.swift by adding the following class extension to the end of the file:

```
extension RestaurantTableViewController :
RestaurantTableViewControllerProtocol {
    func setNavigationTitle(_ title:String) {
        self.title = title
    }
}
```

Listing 12-14 provides the complete RestaurantTableViewModel class and is listed below. If you would like to examine the code for the associated tests, download the finished project anonymously from github using the following URL:

```
https://github.com/asmtechnology/Lesson12.iOSTesting.2017.Apress.git
```

Listing 12-14. RestaurantTableViewModel.swift

```
import Foundation

class RestaurantTableViewModel : NSObject {

    var area:String
    var restaurantList:[Restaurant]
    var view:RestaurantTableViewControllerProtocol?

    init? (_ area:String, restaurantList:[Restaurant]?) {
        guard let restaurantList = restaurantList else {
            return nil
        }
```

```
        self.area = area
        self.restaurantList = restaurantList

        super.init()
    }

    func performInitialViewSetup() {
        view?.setNavigationTitle("Restaurants in \(area).")
    }

    func numberOfSections() -> Int {
        return 1
    }

    func numberOfRowsInSection(_ section:Int) -> Int {
        return restaurantList.count
    }

    func cellViewModel(forIndexPath indexPath:IndexPath) ->
    RestaurantTableViewCellViewModel? {
        let row = indexPath.row
        if row < 0 || row >= self.restaurantList.count {
            return nil
        }

        let restaurant = restaurantList[row]
        return RestaurantTableViewCellViewModel(model:restaurant)
    }
}
```

The RestaurantTableViewCellViewModel Class

The RestaurantTableViewCellViewModel class represents the view model between the RestaurantTableViewCell class and a single Restaurant model object. The desired instance variables and methods of the view model class are described in Table 12-9.

Table 12-9. *RestaurantTableViewCellViewModel instance variables and methods*

Name	Type	Description
`var view:RestaurantTable ViewCellProtocol?`	Ivar	Reference to the view controller, uses a protocol to define a list of methods that the view model can use.
`var model:Restaurant?`	Ivar	Represents the data for a restaurant in London.
`func setup()`	Method	Called from the `setup ()` method of the table view cell, which in turn is called from the `tableView(_ tableView: UITableView, cellForRowAt indexPath: IndexPath) -> UITableViewCell` method of the table view controller.
`init(model:Restaurant?)`	Method	Used to create an instance of the view model.

The RestaurantTableViewCellViewModel class requires that a protocol called RestaurantTableViewCellProtocol is defined in the project, and implemented by the RestaurantTableViewCellr class. Listing 12-15 describes the protocol.

Listing 12-15. RestaurantTableViewCellProtocol.swift

```
import Foundation

protocol RestaurantTableViewCellProtocol : class {
    func setRestaurantLocation(_ location:String)
    func setRestaurantRating(_ rating:String)
    func setRestaurantCuisine(_ cuisine:String)
    func setRestarantDistance(_ distance:String)
    func setRestaurantName(_ restaurantName:String)
}
```

These methods are implemented in RestaurantTableViewCellr.swift by adding the following class extension to the end of the file:

```
extension RestaurantTableViewCell : RestaurantTableViewCellProtocol {

    func setRestaurantLocation(_ location:String) {
        self.location.text = location
    }

    func setRestaurantRating(_ rating:String) {
        self.rating.text = rating
    }
```

```
func setRestaurantCuisine(_ cuisine:String) {
    self.cuisine.text = cuisine
}

func setRestarantDistance(_ distance:String) {
    self.distance.text = distance
}

func setRestaurantName(_ restaurantName:String) {
    self.name.text = restaurantName
}
}
```

The complete RestaurantTableViewCellViewModel class is provided in Listing 12-16.
If you would like to examine the code for the associated tests, download the finished project
anonymously from github using the following URL:

```
https://github.com/asmtechnology/Lesson12.iOSTesting.2017.Apress.git
```

Listing 12-16. RestaurantTableViewCellViewModel.swift

```
import Foundation

class RestaurantTableViewCellViewModel : NSObject {

    var model:Restaurant?
    var view:RestaurantTableViewCellProtocol?

    init(model:Restaurant?) {
        self.model = model
        super.init()
    }

    func setup() {

        guard let view = view ,
            let model = model,
            let area = model.area,
            let rating = model.rating,
            let cuisine = model.cuisine,
            let distance = model.distance,
            let tubeStation = model.tubeStation,
            let restaurantName = model.restaurantName else {
                return
        }

        view.setRestaurantLocation(area)
        view.setRestaurantRating("\(rating) stars")
        view.setRestaurantCuisine(cuisine)
```

```
        view.setRestarantDistance("\(distance) miles(s) from \(tubeStation)")
        view.setRestaurantName(restaurantName)
    }
}
```

While building the RestaurantTableViewCellViewModel class using a test-driven approach, you will need to create a mock table view cell object to test the binding between the view model and the cell.

As it turns out a mock table view cell class was one of the missing classes needed to make the Quick BDD tests compile. Listing 12-17 contains the code in a class called MockRestaurantTableViewCell that will be used by both unit tests and Quick BDD tests.

Listing 12-17. MockRestaurantTableViewCell.swift

```swift
import Foundation
import XCTest

class MockRestaurantTableViewCell : RestaurantTableViewCell {

    var expectationForSetRestaurantLocation:(XCTestExpectation, String)?
    var expectationForSetRestaurantRating:(XCTestExpectation, String)?
    var expectationForSetRestaurantCuisine:(XCTestExpectation, String)?
    var expectationForSetRestaurantDistance:(XCTestExpectation, String)?
    var expectationForSetRestaurantName:(XCTestExpectation, String)?

    override func setRestaurantLocation(_ location:String) {
        guard let (expectation, expectedValue) = self.
        expectationForSetRestaurantLocation else {
            super.setRestaurantLocation(location)
            return
        }

        if location.compare(expectedValue) == .orderedSame {
            expectation.fulfill()
        }

        super.setRestaurantLocation(location)
    }

    override func setRestaurantRating(_ rating:String) {
        guard let (expectation, expectedValue) = self.
        expectationForSetRestaurantRating else {
            super.setRestaurantRating(rating)
            return
        }

        if rating.compare(expectedValue) == .orderedSame {
            expectation.fulfill()
        }
```

```
        super.setRestaurantRating(rating)
    }

    override func setRestaurantCuisine(_ cuisine:String) {
        guard let (expectation, expectedValue) = self.
        expectationForSetRestaurantCuisine else {
            super.setRestaurantCuisine(cuisine)
            return
        }

        if cuisine.compare(expectedValue) == .orderedSame {
            expectation.fulfill()
        }

        super.setRestaurantCuisine(cuisine)
    }

    override func setRestarantDistance(_ distance:String) {
        guard let (expectation, expectedValue) = self.
        expectationForSetRestaurantDistance else {
            super.setRestarantDistance(distance)
            return
        }

        if distance.compare(expectedValue) == .orderedSame {
            expectation.fulfill()
        }

        super.setRestarantDistance(distance)
    }

    override func setRestaurantName(_ restaurantName:String) {
        guard let (expectation, expectedValue) = self.
        expectationForSetRestaurantName else {
            super.setRestaurantName(restaurantName)
            return
        }

        if restaurantName.compare(expectedValue) == .orderedSame {
            expectation.fulfill()
        }

        super.setRestaurantName(restaurantName)
    }

}
```

View Controller to View Model Bindings

The model and view model layers are now ready. All that remains is to instatiate view model objects and integrate calls to these view model objects from their corresponding view controllers.

Listing 12-18 presents the final SearchViewController class, fully integrated with the SearchViewModel class.

Listing 12-18. SearchViewController.swift

```
import UIKit

class SearchViewController: UIViewController {

    @IBOutlet weak var locationPicker: UIPickerView!
    @IBOutlet weak var viewRestaurantButton: UIButton!

    var viewModel:SearchViewModel?

    override func viewDidLoad() {
        super.viewDidLoad()

        if self.viewModel == nil {
            self.viewModel = SearchViewModel(view: self)
        }

        self.viewModel?.performInitialViewSetup()
    }

    override func didReceiveMemoryWarning() {
        super.didReceiveMemoryWarning()
        // Dispose of any resources that can be recreated.
    }

    @IBAction func onViewListings(_ sender: Any) {
        self.viewModel?.onViewListings()
    }

    override func prepare(for segue: UIStoryboardSegue, sender: Any?) {
        guard let identifier = segue.identifier,
            let destination = segue.destination as?
            RestaurantTableViewController,
            let viewModel = self.viewModel else {
                return
        }

        if identifier.compare("presentSearchResults") != .orderedSame {
            return
        }
```

```
        let detailViewModel = viewModel.viewModelForSelectedArea()
        detailViewModel?.view = destination as
        RestaurantTableViewControllerProtocol
        destination.viewModel = detailViewModel
    }

}

extension SearchViewController : UIPickerViewDelegate {

    func pickerView(_ pickerView: UIPickerView, titleForRow row: Int,
    forComponent component: Int) -> String? {

        guard let viewModel = self.viewModel else {
            return nil
        }

        return viewModel.titleForRow(row, component:component)
    }

    func pickerView(_ pickerView: UIPickerView, didSelectRow row: Int,
    inComponent component: Int) {
        guard let viewModel = self.viewModel else {
            return
        }

        return viewModel.didSelectRow(row, component:component)
    }
}

extension SearchViewController : UIPickerViewDataSource {

    func numberOfComponents(in pickerView: UIPickerView) -> Int {
        guard let viewModel = self.viewModel else {
            return 0
        }

        return viewModel.numberOfComponents()
    }

    func pickerView(_ pickerView: UIPickerView, numberOfRowsInComponent
    component: Int) -> Int {

        guard let viewModel = self.viewModel else {
            return 0
        }
```

```
        return viewModel.numberOfRowsInComponent(component)
    }

}

extension SearchViewController : SearchViewControllerProtocol {
    func setNavigationTitle(_ title:String) {
        self.title = title
    }

    func enableRestaurantListingsButton(_ state:Bool) {
        self.viewRestaurantButton.isEnabled = state
    }

    func displayResultsScreen() {
        self.performSegue(withIdentifier: "presentSearchResults", sender:
        self)
    }
}
```

Listing 12-19 presents the final RestaurantListTableViewController class, fully integrated with the RestaurantTableViewModel class.

Listing 12-19. RestaurantListTableViewController.swift

```swift
import UIKit

class RestaurantTableViewController: UITableViewController {

    var viewModel: RestaurantTableViewModel?

    override func viewDidLoad() {
        super.viewDidLoad()
        viewModel?.performInitialViewSetup()
    }

    override func didReceiveMemoryWarning() {
        super.didReceiveMemoryWarning()
        // Dispose of any resources that can be recreated.
    }

    // MARK: - Table view data source

    override func numberOfSections(in tableView: UITableView) -> Int {
        guard let viewModel = self.viewModel else {
            return 0
        }
```

```
        return viewModel.numberOfSections()
    }

    override func tableView(_ tableView: UITableView, numberOfRowsInSection
    section: Int) -> Int {
        guard let viewModel = self.viewModel else {
            return 0
        }

        return viewModel.numberOfRowsInSection(section)
    }

    override func tableView(_ tableView: UITableView, cellForRowAt
    indexPath: IndexPath) -> UITableViewCell {
        let cell = tableView.dequeueReusableCell(withIdentifier:
        "RestaurantTableViewCellIdentifier", for: indexPath) as?
        RestaurantTableViewCell

        guard let viewModel = viewModel,
            let restaurantTableViewCell = cell else {
                return UITableViewCell()
        }

        let detailViewModel = viewModel.cellViewModel(forIndexPath:
        indexPath)
        detailViewModel?.view = restaurantTableViewCell

        restaurantTableViewCell.viewModel = detailViewModel
        restaurantTableViewCell.setup()

        return restaurantTableViewCell
    }
}

extension RestaurantTableViewController :
RestaurantTableViewControllerProtocol {
    func setNavigationTitle(_ title:String) {
        self.title = title
    }
}
```

Listing 12-20 presents the final RestaurantListTableViewCell class, fully integrated with the RestaurantTableViewCellViewModel class.

Listing 12-20. RestaurantListTableViewCell.swift

```swift
import UIKit

class RestaurantTableViewCell: UITableViewCell {

    @IBOutlet weak var name: UILabel!
    @IBOutlet weak var rating: UILabel!
    @IBOutlet weak var distance: UILabel!
    @IBOutlet weak var location: UILabel!
    @IBOutlet weak var cuisine: UILabel!

    var viewModel:RestaurantTableViewCellViewModel?

    override func awakeFromNib() {
        super.awakeFromNib()
        // Initialization code
    }

    override func setSelected(_ selected: Bool, animated: Bool) {
        super.setSelected(selected, animated: animated)

        // Configure the view for the selected state
    }

    func setup() {
        viewModel?.setup()
    }

}

extension RestaurantTableViewCell : RestaurantTableViewCellProtocol {

    func setRestaurantLocation(_ location:String) {
        self.location.text = location
    }

    func setRestaurantRating(_ rating:String) {
        self.rating.text = rating
    }

    func setRestaurantCuisine(_ cuisine:String) {
        self.cuisine.text = cuisine
    }

    func setRestarantDistance(_ distance:String) {
        self.distance.text = distance
    }
```

```
func setRestaurantName(_ restaurantName:String) {
    self.name.text = restaurantName
}
}
```

You can download the finished project anonymously from github using the following URL:

```
https://github.com/asmtechnology/Lesson12.iOSTesting.2017.Apress.git
```

If you execute all tests using the Product > Test menu item, you will see that all BDD and TDD tests pass.

Summary

In this chapter you have learned to combine BDD and TDD techniques while building an iOS App. You started by reviewing the business reuirements and creating a set of user stories to cover the requirements. You then determined that not all user stories were testable by BDD techniques; some scenarios would be better tested using visual inspection techniques.

For the scenarios that could be tested using BDD techniques, you learned to create BDD tests using Quick. The BDD tests were failing initially, and you determined that you will need to create the required application functionality to make the BDD tests pass.

Since BDD tests do not dictate the manner in which you write the underlying code, you opted to use TDD techniques and the application architecture to build the underlying application functionality.

By doing so, you used a combination of both BDD and TDD techniques to build the application.

CHAPTER 13

■ ■ ■

Testing the User Interface

User Interface (UI) tests allow you to test your application from the outside, just as your users would see the application. Every time you decide to run your application on the simulator or device, you are, in effect, testing the UI of your application. Since Xcode 7, Apple has provided the ability to create automated UI tests. These automated UI tests are great at finding regression defects, and used correctly can reduce the regression testing effort for your apps.

UI tests are built using a set of classes in XCTest. Unlike unit tests that derive from XCTest, UI tests derive from XCUITest. UI tests are typically assigned their own group and build target in an Xcode project as shown in Figure 13-1.

Figure 13-1. Separate Folder Group and Build Targets for UI Tests

As you can see from Figure 13-1, the code that makes your app, its associated unit tests, and user interface tests is part of the same Xcode project. However, unlike unit tests, UI tests are packaged and deployed into a separate application called the Test Runner.

© Abhishek Mishra 2017
A. Mishra, *iOS Code Testing*, DOI 10.1007/978-1-4842-2689-6_13

The code that makes up your UI test cases executes within the test runner app and not the main app being tested (subject under test). Naturally, the first order of business for the test runner is to launch an instance of the app to be tested.

How does the test runner app interact with the UI of the subject under test programmatically? The answer is through the use of proxy user interface elements that are set up by Xcode during the test session. This is depicted in Figure 13-2.

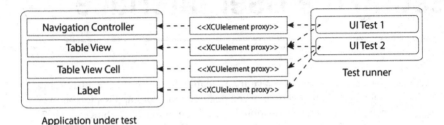

Application under test

Figure 13-2. *The Test Runner and the Application Under Test*

The code in a typical UI test case attempts to find a proxy user interface element in the subject under test, and creates assertions based on the state of the proxy element. Proxy elements are instances of XCUIElement and have a very limited list of properties and methods that you can use within your UI test.

Xcode also provides a related feature called UI recording. UI recording is a tool to help you create UI tests. When UI recording is enabled, an instance of the subject under test is launched in the iOS simulator and you can interact with it as you normally would. Xcode records your interaction with the app and builds a user interface test that can perform the same sequence of interactions for you.

Adding Support for UI Testing to Your Project

Adding support for UI testing involves linking XCTest, making a new file group in the Xcode project, and creating a new build target.

New Projects

The process is slightly simpler if you are creating a new project. Simply ensure the Include UI Tests check box is selected in the project options dialog box (see Figure 13-3).

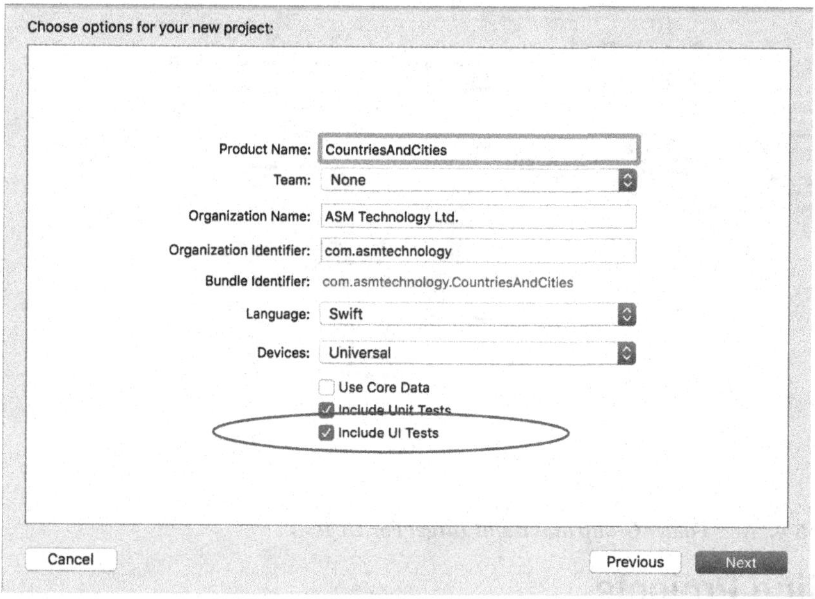

Figure 13-3. *Xcode Project Options Dialog Box*

When you do this, you will notice a few changes:

- A new group has been added to the Xcode project. This group will be used to contain your UI test files.

- A new build target, also known as the UI test target, is added to the project.

- The test target is preconfigured to test the host application.

All of these points are visible in Figure 13-4.

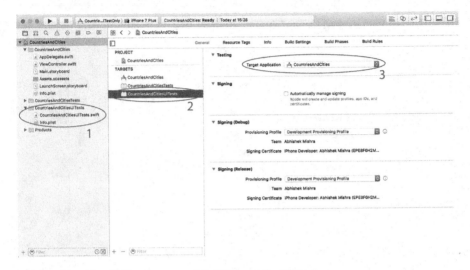

Figure 13-4. New Folder Group and Build Target For UI Tests

Existing Projects

Adding support for UI testing to an existing project requires that you add a new test target to your Xcode project by selecting File ➤ New ➤ Target.

In the target template dialog box, select iOS UI Testing Bundle under the Test category (Figure 13-5).

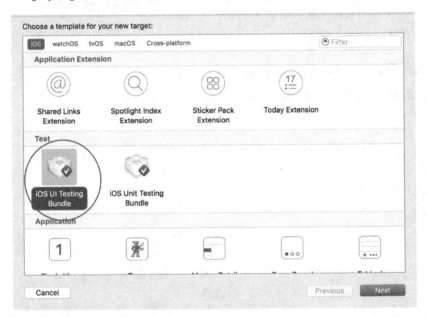

Figure 13-5. Xcode Target Template Dialog Box

Accept the default values in the target options dialog box and click Finish (Figure 13-6).

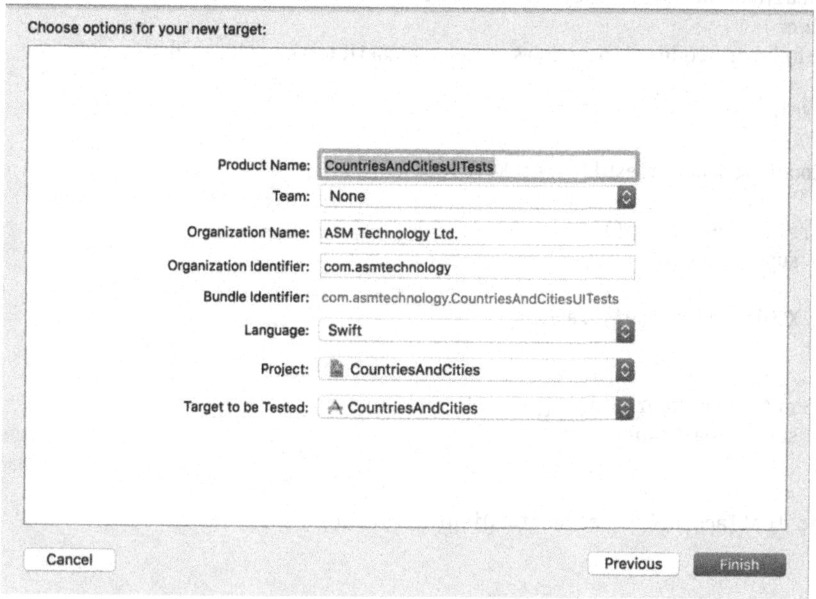

Figure 13-6. *Xcode Target Options Dialog Box*

UI Test Classes

A UI test class is just a Swift class that inherits from XCUITestCase. Similar in many respects to unit test classes, UI test classes also contain setup, teardown, and test methods.

Setup method: There is only one setup method in a UI test class. The signature of the setup method is this:

```
override func setUp()
```

The setup is called before each UI test method is executed in the UI test class. Note the use of the override keyword to indicate that the base method definition is in the super class (XCUITestCase).

Teardown method: There is only one teardown method in a UI test class. The signature of the setup method is this:

```
override func tearDown()
```

The teardown method is also prefixed with the override keyword, and is called after each UI test method has finished executing in the UI test class.

Test methods: A UI test class usually has multiple test methods, and each method contains a single UI test. The names of Test methods all begin with the word test, for example:

```
func testTappingOnDeleteButtonDisplaysAlert() {

}
```

The names of test methods should describe the user interaction they intend to test, and the length of the user journey being tested in a single method should be kept as short as possible.

The following code snippet shows what a typical UI test class looks like:

```
import XCTest

class CountriesAndCitiesUITests: XCTestCase {

    override func setUp() {
        super.setUp()

        XCUIApplication().launch()
    }

    override func tearDown() {
        super.tearDown()
    }

    func testTappingOnDeleteButtonDisplaysAlert() {

    }

    func testCountryListAppearsOnAppLaunch() {

    }

}
```

■ **Note** You may choose to create a single UI test class per view controller of your app, but sometimes it may be better to create UI test classes that represent user journeys. View controllers seldom exist in isolation; usually your users will start on an initial view controller and move on to other view controllers by interacting with your app. If your UI tests involve multiple view controllers, it may be better to name them based on the user journeys they represent.

To execute all tests (in all test classes) in a project, use the Product ➤ Test menu item. This will launch the app on the iOS Simulator (or device) and execute all test cases sequentially.

If your project has both unit tests and UI tests, then the unit tests will execute first and the UI tests will be executed only after all unit tests finish. If you want to execute UI tests without waiting for unit tests, you need to create a new build scheme that does not include unit tests.

The most common approach when it comes to creating new build schemes is to duplicate an existing one, and make changes on the copy. To duplicate an existing build scheme, begin by selecting the Product ➤ Schemes ➤ Manage Schemes menu item.

You will be presented with a list of build schemes in your project. Ensure that the scheme you wish to duplicate is selected, and click on the settings icon at the bottom-left corner of the scheme list (Figure 13-7).

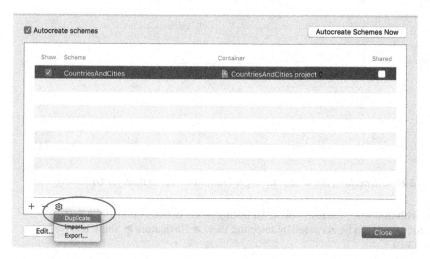

Figure 13-7. *Duplicating an Existing Build Scheme*

Selecting the "Duplicate" option from the context menu that appears when you click on the settings icon will create a copy of the scheme, and open the scheme properties dialog box. Specify a meaningful name for the new scheme and then ensure the unit test target is unchecked under the Test section of the scheme properties dialog box (Figure 13-8).

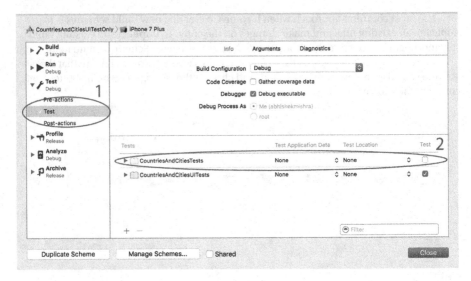

Figure 13-8. *Unchecking the Unit Test Target From the Scheme Built for UI Testing*

As with unit tests, the result of the UI testing phase is also visible in the Test Navigator, which can be accessed by selecting View ➤ Navigators ➤ Show Test Navigator (Figure 13-9).

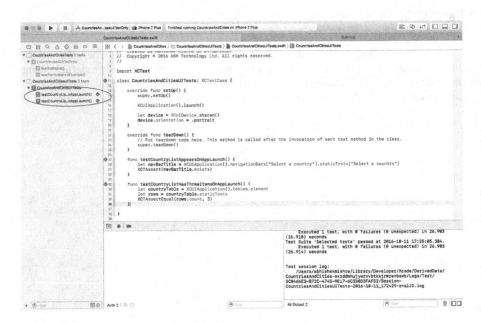

Figure 13-9. *Results of UI Tests are Visible in the Test Navigator*

Tests that have passed have a green tick box next to their names. A Red tick box beside the name of a test means that the test did not pass. Keep in mind that Xcode needs to compile your test code before it can run the tests, so this means that you will need to fix any compilation errors in your project before any tests can run.

Creating New Test Classes

You can add new UI test classes to your project in one of two ways:

1. Command-Click on the UI test group in the project navigator and select the "New File..." option from the context menu. This will present a dialog box with a list of file templates to choose from. Select the "UI Test Case class" template under the iOS Category (Figure 13-10).

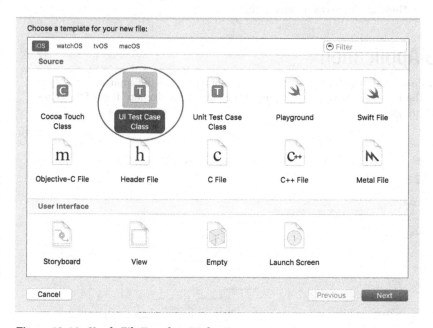

Figure 13-10. Xcode File Template Dialog Box

2. With the Test Navigator visible, click on the Add button (+) at the bottom of the navigator and select the "New UI Test Class" menu item from the context menu (Figure 13-11).

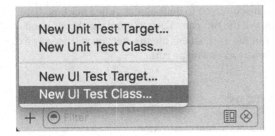

Figure 13-11. *Creating a New UI Test Class*

Changes to XCTest to Support UI Testing

In order to support UI testing, four new classes and two new protocols have been added to XCTest. These are discussed in this section.

XCUIApplication

An XCUIApplication instance is a proxy object that represents the application being tested. The Target application is specified in the "Target Application" field of the UI test target settings (Figure 13-12).

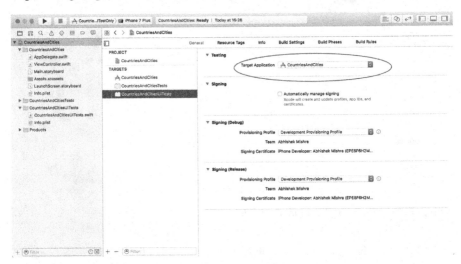

Figure 13-12. *The Target Application Setting Within the UI Test Target*

Recall that UI tests are run within the context of a separate app from the one you are testing, and they communicate with the subject under test using proxy opbjects.

The two most commonly used methods of XCUIApplication are launch() and terminate(). Typically, you instantiate an XCUIApplication instance in your test class's setup() method and call the launch method:

```
override func setUp() {
    super.setUp()

    XCUIApplication().launch()
}
```

The call to launch is synchronous, and returns when the application to be tested is launched and ready for user interaction. If the application to be tested could not be launched, then a test failure will be generated.

You can optionally pass an array of launch arguments by setting the launchArguments properties. For example, the following snippet passes a launch argument ENABLE_CLIENT_SIDE_MOCKS to the UIApplication instance, via the XCUIApplication proxy.

```
override func setUp() {
    super.setUp()

    let application = XCUIApplication()
    application.launchArguments = ["ENABLE_CLIENT_SIDE_MOCKS"]
    application.launch()
}
```

It is up to the application under test to look out for these arguments and do something meaningful with them. The array of values you provide to XCUIApplication.launchArguments can be accessed in the application under test using CommandLine.arguments.

The following code snippet demonstrates how to retrieve launch arguments in the application under test by calling CommandLine.arguments. The first element in this array is always the full path to the application, which is why it examines elements from index 1 onward:

```
func application(_ application: UIApplication, didFinishLaunchingWithOptions
launchOptions: [UIApplicationLaunchOptionsKey: Any]?) -> Bool {

    let launchArguments = CommandLine.arguments

    for index in 1...launchArguments.count {
        let argument = launchArguments[index] as String
        if argument.compare("ENABLE_CLIENT_SIDE_MOCKS") == .orderedSame {
            // do something here to enable client side mocks.
        }
    }

    return true
}
```

To terminate an app, you could call the terminate() method on the XCUIApplication proxy object. This is not strictly necessary as XCTest will terminate the application instance automatically every time a UI test finishes executing.

XCUIDevice

An instance of this class represents the device on which the UI test is running. XCUIDevice is a singleton, and there is always only one instance of this class, which can be accessed as follows:

```
let device = XCUIDevice.shared()
```

XCUIDevice has one property called orientation that can be used to get or set the orientation of the device on which UI tests are executing. Table 13-1 lists the most commonly used values of the orientation property.

Table 13-1. Orientation values

Value	Description
portrait	The device is oriented vertically with the home button at the bottom.
portraitUpsideDown	The device is oriented vertically with the home button at the top.
landscapeLeft	The device is oriented horizontally with the home button on the right.
landscapeRight	The device is oriented horizontally with the home button on the left.

It is a good idea to set the orientation of the device explicitly in the setUp() method before running a UI test. This is demonstrated in the following code snippet where the device orientation is set to portrait after the application under test is launched:

```
override func setUp() {
    super.setUp()

    XCUIApplication().launch()

    let device = XCUIDevice.shared()
    device.orientation = .portrait
}
```

XCUIElement, XCUIElementAttributes

An XCUIElement instance is a proxy for a user interface element in the application under test. It is almost always obtained by calling one of the methods on an XCUIElementQuery instance.

It is possible to create proxies for elements that do not yet exist on the user interface of the application under test. This is because an XCUIElement is only evaluated when a method is called on it. At the time of evaluation, if the XCUIElement does not resolve into an actual element, a test failure will be generated.

It is important to keep in mind that the XCUIElement is just a proxy and provides a very limited set of methods. XCUIElement instances do not let you access the underlying user element directly. For instance, if you had an XCUIElement proxy that represents a button instance on a view, you cannot dereference the XCUIElement to arrive at the underlying UIButton object.

Table 13-2 lists some of the methods available to call on XCUIElement instances. These methods are designed to provide the ability to interact with the underlying user interface element in a manner similar to how the end user of your app would.

Table 13-2. XCUIElement Methods

Property/Method Name	Description
var exists: Bool { get }	Returns true if the XCUIElement proxy resolves into an actual UI element in the application being tested.
func tap()	Sends a tap event to the underlying UI element in the application being tested.
func doubleTap()	Sends a double tap event to the underlying UI element in the application being tested.
func press(forDuration duration: TimeInterval)	Sends a long press gesture event to the underlying UI element in the application being tested, holding for the specified duration.
func press(forDuration duration: TimeInterval, thenDragTo otherElement: XCUIElement)	Sends a press and hold gesture to the underlying UI element in the application being tested that then drags to another element. Useful for table cell reordering tests.
func swipeUp()	Sends a swipe up gesture to the underlying UI element in the application being tested.
func swipeDown()	Sends a swipe down gesture to the underlying UI element in the application being tested.
func swipeLeft()	Sends a swipe left gesture to the underlying UI element in the application being tested.
func swipeRight()	Sends a swipe left gesture to the underlying UI element in the application being tested.
func pinch(withScale scale: CGFloat, velocity: CGFloat)	Sends a pinch gesture to the underlying UI element in the application being tested.
func rotate(_ rotation: CGFloat, withVelocity velocity: CGFloat)	Sends a rotate gesture to the underlying UI element in the application being tested.
func adjust(toNormalizedSliderPosition normalizedSliderPosition: CGFloat)	Adjusts the value of a slider in the application being tested. The desired slider position is sent as a normalized value [0.0, 1.0].
func adjust(toPickerWheelValue pickerWheelValue: String)	Adjusts the value of a picker wheel in the application being tested.

XCUIElement conforms to the XCUIElementAttributes protocol. This protocol defines several properties that return the values of commonly used attributes of UI elements, and is discussed next.

■ **Note**   XCUIElement also conforms to the XCUIElementTypeQueryProvider protocols, which are discussed later in this chapter.

XCUIElementAttributes

The XCUIElementAttributes protocol defines several properties that return commonly used attributes. Table 13-3 lists some of the commonly used properties defined in XCUIElementAttributes.

Table 13-3. XCUIElementAttribute Properties

Property Name	Description
var identifier: String { get }	Returns the accessibility identifier of the element.
var frame: CGRect { get }	Returns the frame property of the element in screen coordinate space.
var title: String { get }	Returns the accessibility title of the element.
var label: String { get }	Returns the caption of the element (if applicable).
var elementType: XCUIElementType	Returns an enumeration value that represents the type of the element.
var isEnabled: Bool { get }	Returns true if the element is enabled for user interaction.
var placeholderValue: String? { get }	Returns the placeholder value that is displayed when the element has no value. Commonly used when the proxy element refers to a UITextField.

The elementType property is of type XCUIElementType and is a large enumeration of values. Some of the more commonly used values are listed here:

- XCUIElementType.Alert
- XCUIElementType.Button
- XCUIElementType.NavigationBar
- XCUIElementType.TabBar

- XCUIElementType.ToolBar

- XCUIElementType.ActivityIndicator

- XCUIElementType.SegmentedControl

- XCUIElementType.Picker

- XCUIElementType.Image

- XCUIElementType.StaticText

- XCUIElementType.TextField

- XCUIElementType.DatePicker

- XCUIElementType.TextView

- XCUIElementType.WebView

- XCUIElementTypeQueryProvider

XCUIElementQuery and XCUIElementTypeQueryProvider

Unlike the other classes discussed so far, an XCUIElementQuery does not represent a proxy user interface element. Instead, an instance of this class represents a query used to obtain a XCUIElement proxy.

Table 13-4 lists some of the properties and methods provided by XCUIElementQuery. Some of these methods return an XCUIElement, while others return yet another XCUIElementQuery instance. In the latter case, the returned XCUIElementQuery instance is usually used to obtain a smaller subset of elements.

Table 13-4. XCUIElementQuery Methods

Property/Method Name	Description
var count: UInt { get }	Evaluates the query at the time this property is called and returns the number of matches found.
func element(boundBy index: UInt) -> XCUIElement	Resolves the query at the time this method is called and returns an element at the specified index.
func element(matching elementType: XCUIElementType, identifier: String?) -> XCUIElement	Resolves the query at the time this method is called and returns an element that matches a specific type and accessibility identifier.
func children(matching type: XCUIElementType) -> XCUIElementQuery	Returns a new query that can be used to extract children of a specific type.

You do not instantiate an XCUIElementQuery directly; instead you use one of the methods defined by the XCUIElementTypeQueryProvider protocol on an object that implements it to get a suitable query. The following objects implement XCUIElementTypeQueryProvider:

- XCUIApplication,

- XCUIElement, and

- XCUIElementQuery.

Table 13-5 lists some of the commonly used methods of the XCUIElementTypeQueryProvider protocol. Typically, you will use one of these methods on the XCUIApplication instance to return an initial XCUIElementQuery, and you will then use the methods defined in XCUIElementQuery to recursively filter down to a specific user interface element.

Table 13-5. *XCUIElementTypeQueryProvider Methods*

Property/Method name	Description
`var windows: XCUIElementQuery { get }`	Returns a query that provides access to all windows that are currently visible in app. iOS applications have just a single window.
`var alerts: XCUIElementQuery { get }`	Returns a query that provides access to all alerts that are currently visible in app. Usually there is only one alert visible in an app at a time.
`var buttons: XCUIElementQuery { get }`	Returns an query that provides access to all buttons that are currently visible in app.
`var navigationBars: XCUIElementQuery { get }`	Returns a query that provides access to all navigation bars that are currently visible in app.
`tables: XCUIElementQuery { get }`	Returns a query that provides access to all table views that are currently visible in app.
`var collectionViews: XCUIElementQuery { get }`	Returns a query that provides access to all collection views that are currently visible in app.
`var staticTexts: XCUIElementQuery { get }`	Returns a query that provides access to all labels that are currently visible in app.
`var textFields: XCUIElementQuery { get }`	Returns a query that provides access to all text fields that are currently visible in app.
`textViews: XCUIElementQuery { get }`	Returns a query that provides access to all text views that are currently visible in app.
`var maps: XCUIElementQuery { get }`	Returns a query that provides access to all map views that are currently visible in app.
`var otherElements: XCUIElementQuery { get }`	Returns a query that provides access to all view controllers that are currently visible in app.

The following snippet uses application.staticTexts to create a query that can return all the visible static labels on the device's screen.

```
let allLabels = XCUIApplication().staticTexts
print (allLabels.count)
```

If you want to retrieve a XCUIElement proxy for the second static label (assuming it exists), you can use the element(boundBy:) method of the query as shown in the following statement:

```
let secondLabel = allLabels.element(boundBy: 1)
```

To retrieve the actual text displayed on the static label, you can use the label property on the proxy as follows:

```
let caption = secondLabel.label
```

Using the element(boundBy:) method is sensitive to the layout of the user interface. A better approach would be to set up accessibility identifiers for the user interface elements that you wish to access in your UI tests and retrieve proxies to these elements regardless of how they are laid out on the screen.

To set up an accessibility identifier for a user interface element, select the user interface element in the storyboard and use the Identity Inspector (Figure 13-13).

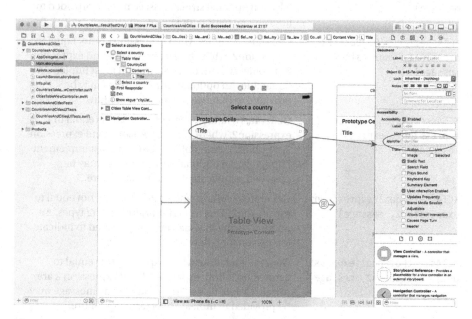

Figure 13-13. Setting Up an Accessibility Identifier

After setting up accessibility identifiers, you can use the element(matching:, identifier:) method to locate a particular user interface element, regardless of how the user interface is laid out.

```
let application = XCUIApplication()
let query = application.staticTexts
let welcomeLabel = query.element(matching: .staticText, identifier:
"WelcomeMessage")
```

Assertions

Once you have located the user interface element of interest in your UI test, you will either inspect one of its attributes and compare the results to an expected value, or interact with the user interface element to display a new view and inspect one of the attributes of the new view.

Just like unit tests, UI tests also use assertions to compare the state of an object with an expected value. Table 13-6 lists some of these assertion functions used within UI tests.

Table 13-6. *XCTest Assertion Macros*

Macro	Description
XCTAssert(expression, message)	Generates a failure if the expression evaluates to false. An optional string message may be provided to indicate the reason for failure.
XCTAssertEqualObjects(expression1, expression2, message)	Generates a failure when expression1 is not equal to expression2, where both expression 1 and expression 2 are objects. Both objects involved must implement Equatable. An optional string message may be provided to indicate the reason for failure.
XCTAssertNotEqualObjects(expression1, expression2, message)	Generates a failure when expression1 is equal to expression2, where both expression 1 and expression 2 are objects. Both objects involved must implement Equatable. An optional string message may be provided to indicate the reason for failure.
XCTAssertEqual(expression1, expression2, message)	Generates a failure when expression1 is not equal to expression2. This test is for primitive data types. An optional string message may be provided to indicate the reason for failure.
XCTAssertNotEqual(expression1, expression2, message)	Generates a failure when expression1 is equal to expression2. Both expression1 and expression 2 are primitive data types. An optional string message may be provided to indicate the reason for failure.
XCTAssertNil (expression, message)	Generates a failure when the expression is not nil. An optional string message may be provided to indicate the reason for failure.

(continued)

Table 13-6. (*continued*)

Macro	Description
XCTAssertNotNil(expression, message)	Generates a failure when the expression is nil. An optional string message may be provided to indicate the reason for failure.
XCTAssertTrue (expression, message)	Generates a failure when the expression evaluates to false. Identical to XCTAssert(), provided to create more readable tests. An optional string message may be provided to indicate the reason for failure.
XCTAssertFalse (expression, message)	Generates a failure when the expression evaluates to true. An optional string message may be provided to indicate the reason for failure.

The following code snippet lists a UI test case that will try to locate a button with the accessibility identifier "FacebookLoginButton" and assert if the button was not found:

```
func testFacebookLoginButtonExists() {
    let application = XCUIApplication()
    let query = application.buttons
    let button = query.element(matching: .button, identifier:
    "FacebookLoginButton")
    XCTAssert(button.exists)
}
```

Note that XCTAssert was used instead of XCTAssertNotNil. This is because button is an instance of XCUIElement, which is just a proxy object. Proxy objects just contain the information needed by the test runner to try and locate a user interface element.

Only when you try to access the underlying element (by calling exists() on the XCUIElement) will the test runner try to resolve the XCUIElement into an actual user interface element.

The following snippet builds on the previous test and asserts if the text displayed on the button does not match a specific value. The text displayed on the button is not the same as its accessibility identifier.

```
func testFacebookLoginButtonDisplaysCorrectLabel(){
    let application = XCUIApplication()
    let query = application.buttons
    let button = query.element(matching: .button, identifier:
    "FacebookLoginButton")
    let buttonLabel = button.label

    XCTAssertEqual(buttonLabel, "Login With Facebook")
}
```

UI Recording

Composing UI test scripts one line at a time is not something you would like to do if the user journey was long and involved and consisted of several interactions to bring up the object you want to test.

The good news is that you do not have to create UI test scripts one line at a time. Xcode provides a feature called UI recording, which can be used to help create UI test scripts. With UI recording, you can launch an instance of your application and interact with it as normal. While you interact with your app, Xcode records your taps, gestures, selections, and key strokes and generates an appropriate UI test script.

UI recording is tightly coupled with UI testing. To begin UI recording, simply place the text cursor within a UI test case and tap the red record button at the bottom of the Xcode editor (see Figure 13-14).

Figure 13-14. *The UI Recording Button*

To stop recording, simply tap the stop button, which replaces the record button during a recording session. UI recording is not foolproof, and often you may find that you can generate a more efficient script to achieve the same objective. However, UI recording can be used as a starting point to build UI tests that you can fine-tune and add appropriate test assertions.

Waiting Before Asserting

Sometimes it is necessary to wait for an operation to complete before you can use your assertion. This is usually the case when an animation is involved and you need to wait for the animation to complete before the UI element you are interested in appears on the screen. Take, for instance, a simple table view-based application in which the user taps on a row to drill down to the next screen.

You could easily simulate a tap on a row using a simple statement such as this:

```
XCUIApplication().tables.cells.staticTexts["United Kingdom"].tap()
```

However, you will need to wait for the next screen to appear before you can create any assertions that are based on UI elements of that screen. Fortunately, XCTest has just the thing in the form of test expectations.

A test expectation is an instance of XCTestExpectation and represents an expected result. For example, to set up an expectation that indicates a text label with the caption "Hello World!" exists, you could use the following snippet:

```
let label = XCUIApplication().staticTexts["Hello World!"]
let predicate = NSPredicate(format: "exists == 1", argumentArray: nil)
self.expectation(for: predicate, evaluatedWith: label, handler: nil)
```

The preceding snippet starts out by retrieving an XCUIElement proxy object for a label with text "Hello World!"

```
let label = XCUIApplication().staticTexts["Hello World!"]
```

Recall that XCUIElement is a proxy object and just represents the information needed to locate a UI element in the app being tested. It is therefore possible to create XCUIElement instances even when the user interface elements are not on screen. Only when you call a method on the XCUIElement instance does the test runner check to see if the proxy can be resolved to an existing object on the screen.

Once an XCUIElement instance has been obtained, an expectation is set up using the expectation (for:, evaluatedWith:, handler:) method of the XCTestCase class.

```
let predicate = NSPredicate(format: "exists == 1", argumentArray: nil)
self.expectation(for: predicate, evaluatedWith: label, handler: nil)
```

The expectation is expressed as a predicate that is evaluated on an object. The object in this case is the label, and the predicate is set up to call the exists() method and ensure the result is 1.

The net result is that the expectation represents a situation where a label with the caption "Hello World!" exists.

Once an expectation has been set up, you need to call the waitForExpectations (timeout:, handler:) method on an XCTestCase instance:

```
self.waitForExpectations(timeout: 5, handler: nil)
```

The waitForExpectations (timeout:, handler:) method waits a specified amount of time (in seconds) and fails the test if one or more expectations are unfulfilled. XCTestExpectation objects have an internal timer-based mechanism by which they periodically check if they can be moved to the fulfilled state. This is a built-in mechanism in an expectation object and you do not need to do anything to kick off the timer.

Putting It All Together

In this section you will write a few user interface tests for an existing application. The application is called CountriesAndCities and can be downloaded from this book's website.

Download the project, open it in Xcode, and try it out on a simulator. As you can see, the app is a master-detail type app with two simple screens: the first lists three countries, and when you select a country from this list, a list of cities in that country are displayed in the second screen (see Figure 13-15).

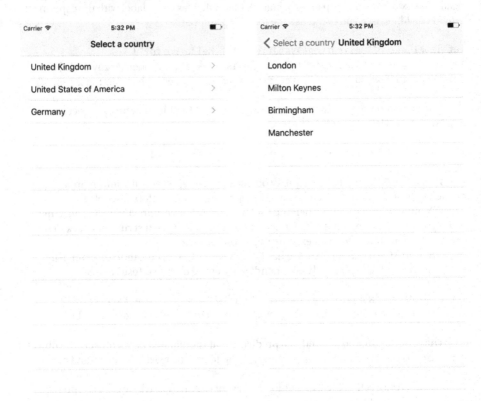

Figure 13-15. *Finished User Interface of Sample Application*

To begin writing a few UI tests, open the project in Xcode and open the CountriesAndCitiesUITests.swift file in the project explorer (see Figure 13-16).

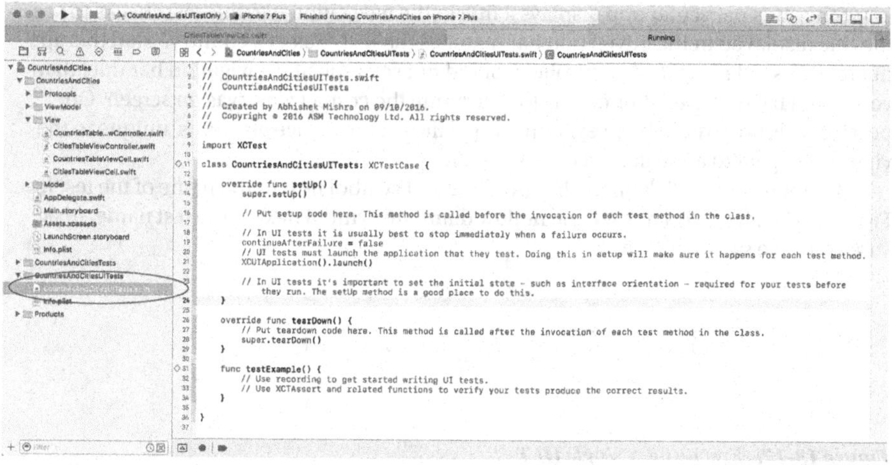

Figure 13-16. *CountriesAndCitiesUITests.swift File in the Project Explorer*

Modify the setUp() method to resemble the following snippet:

```
override func setUp() {
    super.setUp()

    continueAfterFailure = false
    XCUIApplication().launch()

    let device = XCUIDevice.shared()
    device.orientation = .portrait
}
```

This snippet first calls the setUp() method of the superclass, and then sets the continueAfterFailure variable (inheritied from XCTestCase) to false. Setting this variable to false will ensure that UI testing will stop immediately when a test fails. The default behavior is to skip over the failed test and continue with the next test .

The next line in the snippet calls the launch() method of XCUIApplication, thereby launching the subject under test. Finally, the snippet sets the device orientation to portrait. It is a good idea to specify device orientation in the setUp() method of UI tests.

The first test you will create will ensure that the list of countries view controller is visible onscreen after the app is launched. To do so, add a test method called testCountryListAppearsOnAppLaunch and implement it as shown in the following snippet:

```
func testCountryListAppearsOnAppLaunch() {
    let navBarTitle = XCUIApplication().navigationBars["Select a country"].
    staticTexts["Select a country"]
    XCTAssert(navBarTitle.exists)
}
```

Since this particular app displays a title in the navigation bar, this test checks to see if the title displayed in the navigation bar matches the text "Select a country." Had this app not made use of navigation controllers, or did not set a specific navigation bar title, then you would have to use other means to determine the correct view was on screen. One possible solution would be to examine if specific user interface elements, unique to the view you expect to appear, exist on the screen.

To run this test, click on the hollow diamond symbol next to the name of the test (see Figure 13-17). If you do not see the hollow diamond symbol next to the test name, make sure you have saved the file.

```
func testCountryListAppearsOnAppLaunch() {
    let navBarTitle = XCUIApplication().navigationBars["Select a
        country"].staticTexts["Select a country"]
    XCTAssert(navBarTitle.exists)
}
```

Figure 13-17. *Executing a Single UI Test*

Another useful test would be one that counts the number of countries displayed in the app when it is launched. The following code snippet shows how such a test could be written:

```
func testCountryListHasThreeItemsOnAppLaunch() {
    let countryTable = XCUIApplication().tables.element
    let rows = countryTable.staticTexts
    XCTAssertEqual(rows.count, 3)
}
```

This test makes use of some internal knowledge of the way the app has been built. For instance, it assumes there is only one table on the screen. This test will be labeled "too specific" by most people, and to be honest, it is. Counting the number of items makes it very specific, and somewhat fragile.

This test could, for instance, easily break if an extra row was added to the table, or if the test was run on a device with a smaller screen size. The later situation can be of particular importance if your test is counting the number of rows that are visible on a full-screen table view on a plus-sized iPhone. Running such a test on a device with a smaller screen implies fewer rows will be visible, and the test will break.

■ **Note** You can use UIDevice and UIScreen methods within the test to work out what type of device you are running the test on, and use that information to work out the number of rows you can expect to find onscreen.

Whether this type has business value depends on how critical is the number of initial items that are visible on screen. This is something you will need to decide, keeping in mind the needs of the business, and the inherent fragility of the test.

The final test for this example will involve verifying that tapping on a country name from the list of countries will drill down to a list of cities within that country. The following code snippet shows how such a test could be written:

```
func testTappingOnCountryDisplaysDetailViewWithExpectedTitle() {

    let app = XCUIApplication()
    app.tables.staticTexts["United Kingdom"].tap()

    let label = app.navigationBars["United Kingdom"].staticTexts["United
    Kingdom"]
    let predicate = NSPredicate(format: "exists == 1", argumentArray: nil)

    self.expectation(for: predicate, evaluatedWith: label.exists, handler:
    nil)
    self.waitForExpectations(timeout: 5, handler: nil)
}
```

There are quite a few things going on in this test. The tests starts by simulating a tap on one of the countries in the list of countries shown when the app is launched:

```
let app = XCUIApplication()
app.tables.staticTexts["United Kingdom"].tap()
```

Tapping on a row in a table will result in the list of cities being animated on screen (sliding in from the right). This is standard behavior in a master-detail type of app build with table view controllers and navigation controllers.

The slide-from-right animation implies that the list of countries will not be visible instantly, and the test will need to wait for a few milliseconds before if can proceed to inspect the view that has been animated on screen.

The code in the test achieves the wait, using expectations. An expectation is set up to expect the existence of a navigation bar with the title of the country that was tapped on the first screen.

```
let label = app.navigationBars["United Kingdom"].staticTexts["United Kingdom"]
let predicate = NSPredicate(format: "exists == 1", argumentArray: nil)
self.expectation(for: predicate, evaluatedWith: label.exists, handler: nil)
```

This expectation will be fulfilled when the slide-from-right animation finishes animating the list of cities on screen. This expectation also makes use of a subtle design fact of the application: the name of the country that was selected on the first screen becomes the title of the second screen.

With the expectation set up, the test uses the waitForExpectation(timeout:, handler:) method to wait up to 5 seconds for the animation to complete, and the expectation to be fulfilled.

```
self.waitForExpectations(timeout: 5, handler: nil)
```

To try all units and tests, select the Product ➤ Test menu item.

Summary

In this chapter you have learned how to add support for UI Testing to new and existing Xcode projects. You have also learned how to write UI tests using the XCUITest framework and how to use the UI Recording tool to help create UI Tests.

Index

◼ A

AccountOwner class
  AccountOwnerTests, 64
  create additional tests, 68
  create unit test method, 66–67
  integrating validator classes
    into, 85–94
  nine test case, 69
  parameters, 85
  test case file, 66
  variables and methods, 64
AccountOwnerTests, 65
addChocolateChipCookie(), 37
addGingerbreadCookie(), 37
addShortbreadCookie(), 37
Album class, 228
Album.swift, 228–229
AlertFactory.swift, 264
Apple developer teams, 294–295
Application Transport Security (ATS), 216
Assertions, 7–9
Asynchronous testing techniques, 213

◼ B

BankAccount class
  swift, 96–97
  transaction variables and
    methods, 96
BankAccountProtocol.swift, 273
BankAccountSpecification.swift, 319–320
BankAccount.swift, 271–273
Behavior-driven development
  (BDD), 1, 329
  advantages and
    disadvantages, 326–327

bank account project, 317
BankAccountSpecification.
  swift, 319–320
business requirements and user
  scenarios, 318–319
description, 317
Quick test case class, 322–323
Relationship Between Model Layer
  Objects, 317
Behavior verification tests, 3
BitBucket, 295
Bots, 295, 306
  configuring build configuration, 309
  configuring source control, 308
  configuring test devices, 311
  creating, 306–308, 312–313
  environment variables, 312
  integrating, 315–316
  integration schedule, 310
  triggers, 313
    email notifications, 314
    post-integration script, 313–314
    pre-integraton script, 313
BusinessBankAccount, 273
Business requirements, 351–355

◼ C

Carthage, 335
  creating new project, 337–338
  dependency management
    solution, 335
  folder, 339–340
  installer, 336–337
  repository, 338
  testing, 337
  test target, 340–341

CocoaPods, 329, 332
  creating new project, 331–332
  installation in terminal, 330
  new workspace file, 334
  pod install command, 333
  pods project, 335
  testing, 330–331
  verification, 331
Code coverage report, 25
CollectionViewCellProtocol.swift, 253
CollectionViewCell.swift, 254
Collection view controller, TDD
  application architecture, 162
  model layer, building, 177
    Album class, 181–182
    City class, 180
    Photo class, 178–179
  user interface layer
    application storyboard, 165–166
    collection view cell, 172–177
    creating new classes, 166
    scene, 167–169
    section header accessory
      view, 169–172
  ViewModel layer, building, 182
    cellViewModel method, 195–198
    CollectionViewCellViewModel
      class, 200–201
    CollectionViewModel class,
      183–185, 187–188
    CollectionViewSectionHeader
      ViewModel class, 202
    headerViewModel
      method, 198–200
    numberOfItemsInSection
      method, 193–195
    numberOfSections() method, 193
    performInitialViewSetup
      method, 189–192
    view controller binding, 188–189
    view layer to, 203–209
  Xcode project, 162
    adding resources, 164–165
    navigator, 163
ColorDetailViewController, 51, 55
ColorDetailViewModel, 51, 58
ColorListTableViewController, 51–54
ColorTableViewModel, 51, 56–57
context() function, 322
Continuous integration (CI), 283
  bots, 306

configuring build
  configuration, 309
configuring source control, 308
configuring test devices, 311
creating, 306–308, 312–313
environment variables, 312
integrating, 315–316
integration schedule, 310
triggers, 313–314
macOS server, installing, 284
  Apple developer
    teams, 294–295
  configuring Xcode
    server, 293–294
  development devices, 295
  launching, 285–288
  new Git repository on Xcode
    server, 296–297
  repositories, 295
  setting up access for team
    members, 289–290
  starting Xcode server, 290–292
  Xcode version, 294
Xcode server
  clone Git repository
    from, 304–305
  clone existing local repository
    to, 302–304
  cloning Git repository from
    GitHub, 305
  credentials to Xcode, 298–301
  hosting repository for new
    project, 301–302
Controller component, 44
CookieController class
  characteristics, 36–37
  CookieController swift, 37
  CookieControllerTests
    swift, 32–36
CookieFactory app
  iOS simulator, 13
  project navigator, 18–19
Cookie factory app
  code coverage data, 40–41
  Cookie class, 28–32
  CookieController class, 32–38
  model layer, 28
  View Controller class, 27, 39–40
Core Data, 98–99
CountriesAndCitiesUITests.swift
  file, 428–429

■ D

dataToReturnOnSuccess, 235
Decorators
    BankAccountProtocol.swift, 273
    BankAccount.swift, 271–273
    PersonalBankAccount.swift, 274–277
Dependency injection (DI), 279–281
describe(), 322
displayResultsScreen()
    method, 376
Domain Specific Language
    (DSL), 318
DownloadListenerProtocol, 247
downloadProfileHelper(), 270

■ E

element(boundBy:) method, 423
Email address validator
    class, 82–84, 268–269

■ F

Factory method, 49–50
Fake objects, 9
FirstNameValidator class, 70
    compile, 74–75
    failing tests, 76
    swift file, 71, 73–74
    Unit Test Case, 71
    validate(), 74

■ G

GitHub, 295
    cloning Git repository from, 305
Git submodules, 342–349
Green stage, 10

■ H

High-level application
    architecture, 355–357

■ I, J, K

Include unit tests, 16
Instantiating class, 9
Interaction test, 3

■ L

LargeViewController.swift, 258–261
Last name validator class, 76–81
launch() method, 429
Legacy code
    AlertFactory.swift, 264
    developing iOS applications, 257
    DI, 279–281
    downloadUserProfile(), 266–268
    EmailAddressValidator.swift, 268–269
    LargeViewController.swift, 258–261
    NetworkController.swift, 262–263
    protocols, 277–278
    RefactoredLargeViewController.
        swift, 261–262
    rename and replace, 270
    UserProfile.swift, 264
Login view controller
    Identifier attribute, 114
    Identity Inspector, 106–107
    UI Components, 107
    UITextFieldDelegate, 108–109
LoginViewControllerProtocol, 126

■ M

Mac App Store, 14
macOS server, installing, 284
    Apple developer teams, 294–295
    development devices, 295
    launching, 285–288
    repositories, 295
    setting up access for team
        members, 289–290
    Xcode server
        configuring, 293–294
        new Git repository on, 296–297
        starting, 290–292
        version, 294
Massive view controllers, 45
Master-detail apps, 50
Master view model, 50
Mock, 46
    object, 9, 245
MockCollectionViewCell.swift, 255
MockCollectionViewController.
    swift, 252–253
MockDownloadListener class, 248
MockPhoto class, 245

MockServiceController
    class, 234, 236–238
Mock/Stub based testing
    techniques, 213
MockURLSession class, 224–225
MockURLSessionDataTask
    class, 226–227
MockURLSession.swift, 225
Mock validator, 86–87, 90–91
Model component, 44
Model layer, 162, 356
    AccountOwner class, 64–67, 69–70
    bank account class, 61
    building, 177, 384–386
        Album class, 181–182
        City class, 180
        Photo class, 178–179
    complex apps, 61
    email address validator class, 82–84
    first name validator class, 70, 72–76
    last name validator class, 76–81
    LoginModel class, 115–116
    SignupModel class, 116–118
    simple app, 61
Model layer, updation
    Album class
        AlbumTests.swift, 229–233
        instance variables, 235
        load method, 233, 234
        MockServiceController class,
           creation, 236–238
        MockServiceController
           object, 234
        modification, 238
        parameters, 228
        setUp() method, 229
        Xcode import file dialog, 235
    Photo class
        baseURL instance variable, 244
        buildImageDownloadURL
           method, 243
        downloadedImage instance
           variable, 243
        DownloadListenerProtocol.
           swift, 247
        MockDownloadListener
           class, 248
        MockPhoto class, creation, 245
        MockServiceController
           object, 244
        modification, 246–247

        PhotoTests.swift file, 240–243
        version, 239
Model-View-Controller (MVC), 44
    architectural pattern, 44–45
    controller component, 44
    iOS apps, 44
    model component, 44
    testability issues, 45
Model, View, ViewModel
    (MVVM), 48
    advantages, 47–48
    application architecture, 384
    architectural pattern, 46
    instantiation, 48
    on iOS, 46
    navigation controller-based
        apps, 50–59
    ReactiveCocoa, 47
    RxSwift, 47
    swift protocols, 47
    table view controllers, 49
Modified BankAccount.
    swift, 323–325

▓ N

Navigation controller-based apps
    challenges, 50
    color, 51, 59
    ColorDetailViewController, 51, 55
    ColorDetailViewModel, 51, 58
    ColorList app, 51
    ColorListTableViewController, 51–54
    ColorTableViewModel, 51, 56–57
    master view model, 50
    MVVM pattern, 50
Negative unit test, 4–6
NetworkController.swift, 262–263
Networking layer, PhotoBook app
    fetchFromURL method, 217, 221
    MockURLSession class, 224–225
    MockURLSessionDataTask
        class, 226–227
    ServiceController, 217, 221–224
    ServiceControllerTests, 217–220
Nimble, 329

▓ O

Object-oriented system, 3
onViewListings() action method, 376

■ P

Performance testing methods, 21
PersonalBankAccount, 273–277
PhotoBook application
   layers and component classes, 213
   model layer (*see* Model layer, updation)
   modified application architecture, 213
   network layer (*see* Networking layer, PhotoBook app)
   remote content specification, 216
   source code, 212
   user interface, 212
Photo class, 239
Project navigator, 18–19

■ Q

Quick
   BDD tests with, 368
   beforeEach() method, 374
   creating stub objects, 380–382
   examining, 374–379
   instance variables, 373
   remaining compilation errors, 383–384
   restaurant data file to project, 382
   RestaurantDirectorySpecificaton. swift, 368–373
   spec(), 374
Quick framework, 329
   compatible versions of Nimble and, 329
   to Xcode project
      using Carthage, 335–341
      using CocoaPods, 329–332, 334–335
      using Git submodules, 342–349
Quick test case class
   BDD tests, 326
   context() function, 322
   modified BankAccount. swift, 323–325
   spec() method, 321
   user scenario and corresponding Quick BDD test, 322–323
   XCTestCase, 321

■ R

ReactiveCocoa, 47
Red-green-refactor approach, 10–11
RefactoredLargeViewController. swift, 261–262
Remote content specification, 216
reset(), 37
RestaurantDirectorySpecification, 373
RxSwift, 47

■ S

Segue identifier, 367
ServiceController class, 221–224
ServiceControllerTests, 217
setUp() method, 21, 411, 429
Signup view controller
   Identifier attribute, 114
   UITextFieldDelegate, 112–113
spec(), 374
State verification test, 3
Stub, 9, 380
   based testing techniques, 213
Subject under test, 2
Swift methods, 21
Swift protocols, 47

■ T

Table view controllers, 49
TDD and BDD techniques
   adding resources to project, 359
   BDD tests with Quick, 368
      beforeEach() method, 374
      creating stub objects, 380–382
      examining, 374–379
      instance variables, 373
      remaining compilation errors, 383–384
      restaurant data file to project, 382
      RestaurantDirectorySpecificaton. swift, 368–373
      spec(), 374
   business requirements, reviewing, 351–353, 355
   high-level application architecture, 355–357
   model layer, building, 384–386

TDD and BDD techniques (*cont.*)
   RestaurantDirectory application
      requirements, 352
   RestaurantDirectory user
      scenarios, 352–355
   restaurant table view cell, 366
   search view controller, 362
   user interface layer, 360–367
   view controller to view model
      bindings, 400–405
   ViewModel layer, building, 387
      RestaurantTableViewCellView
         Model class, 395–399
      RestaurantTableViewModel
         class, 393–395
      SearchViewModel
         class, 387, 389–392
   Xcode project, creating, 357–358
Teardown method, 21, 411
Test case. *See* unit test
Test case class
   performance testing
      methods, 21
   setup method, 21
   swift methods, 21
   teardown method, 21
   test methods, 21
testCountryListAppearsOnApp
   Launch, 429
Test-Driven Development
   (TDD), 329
   assertions, 7–9
   defined, 1
   instantiating class, 9
   interaction test, 3–4
   negative test, 4–6
   principles of
      minimum amount of
         code, 11
      red-green-refactor
         approach, 10
      remove duplication, 11
      test first, 10
   state verification test, 3
   subject under test, 2
   test suite, 6
   unit test, 2–3
   writing test, 2
TestGitRepositoryHostedOnXcode
   Server, 304
Testing networking layer, strategies

asynchronous testing
   techniques, 213
mock/stub based testing
   techniques, 213
Test methods, 21, 411
Test navigator, 23–24
Test suite, 6
Transaction class
   swift, 95
   validator objects, 94
   variables and methods, 94

■ U

Unit tests, 2–3, 66
   add support for, 16, 18
   assertions, 7–9
   case class, 20, 22
   create project, 15–16
   first, 10
   interaction test, 3
   negative test, 4–5
   state verification test, 3
   UI layer, 46
URLSessionProtocol.swift, 224
User interface (UI), 360–367
   application storyboard, 165–166
   assertions, 424–425
   collection view cell
      adding labels, 175
      image view, 172
      navigation controller, 177
      outlets, 176
      Pin constraints button, 175
      translucent view, 174
   collection view controller
      scene, 167–169
   CountriesAndCitiesUITests.
      swift file, 428–429
   creating new classes, 166
   login view controller, 106–109
   recording, 408, 426
   sample application, 428
   section header accessory
      view, 169–172
   separate folder group and build
      targets, 407
   signup view
      controller, 110, 112–113
   slide-from-right animation, 431
   Test class

creation, 415
duplicate option, 413
navigator, 414
setup method, 411
teardown method, 411
unchecking unit test
target, 414
XCUIApplication, 416–417
testCountryListAppearsOnApp
Launch, 429
testing
existing projects, 410
new projects, 408–410
test runner and application
under test, 408
UI recording, 408, 426
waiting before asserting, 426–427
XCTest, 407
XCUIDevice, 418
XCUIElement, 408, 418–419
XCUIElementAttributes, 420–421
XCUIElementQuery, 421–423
XCUIElementTypeQuery
Provider, 421–423
UserProfile.swift, 264

■ V, W

View component, 44
View controllers class, 39–40, 44–45.
    See also Collection view
    controller, TDD
application architecture, 102
finished application, 101
user interface (*see* User
    interface (UI))
view model (*see* View model)
Xcode project, 103–104
View controller to view model
    bindings, 400–405
viewDidLoad() method, 48–49
View layer updation
collection view cell, 253–256
collection view controller, 252–253
View model, 46–51, 53–55, 57–58, 162, 356
login view controller
LoginViewControllerTests,
153–154
passwordDidEndOnExit, 152
passwordUpdated, 155–156
performInitialSetup, 148–149, 151

UITextFieldStub, 154
userNameDidEndOnExit, 151
userNameUpdated, 155–156
signup view controller, 157–159
test-driven approach, 147
ViewModel layer
login method
login controller, 138, 140
LoginViewModel, 142–143
MockLoginController, 140–141
tests, 137–138
login view controller
LoginViewControllerProtocol, 126
LoginViewModel methods, 125
passwordDidEndOnExit, 131
passwordUpdated, 134–136
performInitialViewSetup, 126–129
user interface, 123–124
userNameDidEndOnExit, 129–130
userNameUpdated, 131–134
LoginViewModel
LoginViewController
Protocol, 120–121
LoginViewModelTests, 118–119,
122–123
SignupViewModel, 143–146
ViewModel layer, building, 182, 387
cellViewModel method, 195–198
CollectionViewCellViewModel
class, 200–201
CollectionViewModel
class, 183–185, 187–188
CollectionViewSectionHeader
ViewModel class, 202
headerViewModel method, 198–200
numberOfItemsInSection
method, 193–195
numberOfSections() method, 193
performInitialViewSetup
method, testing, 189–192
RestaurantTableViewCellView
Model class, 395–399
RestaurantTableViewModel
class, 393–395
SearchViewModel class, 387, 389–392
view controller binding, 188–189
view layer to, 203
CollectionViewCell
class, 207–208
CollectionViewController
class, 204–207

ViewModel layer, building (*cont.*)
    CollectionViewSectionHeader
      class, 208–209
View Model layer, updation
    collection view cell view
      model, 251
    collection view model, 249–250
View/view controller layer, 162, 356

■ X, Y, Z

Xcode
    code coverage report, 25
    download and install, 14
    project navigator, 18–19
    report navigator, 25
    test case classes, 20–22
    test navigator, 23–24
    test suite, 6
    unit test, 15–16
Xcode 8, 15, 25
Xcode project, 162
    adding resources, 164–165
    creating, 357–358
    navigator, 163
    Quick to

    using Carthage, 335–341
    using CocoaPods, 329–332,
      334–335
    using Git submodules, 342–349
    size inspector, 170
Xcode server
    clone existing local repository
      to, 302–304
    clone Git repository from, 304–305
    cloning Git repository from
      GitHub, 305
    configuring, 293–294
    credentials to Xcode, 298–301
    hosting repository for new
      project, 301–302
    new Git repository on, 296–297
    repositories, 295
    starting, 290–292
    version, 294
XCTest, 407
    assertion macros, 7
XCUIApplication, 416–417
XCUIDevice, 418
XCUIElement, 408, 418–419
XCUIElementAttributes, 420–421
XCUIElementQuery, 421–423

Get the eBook for only $5!

Why limit yourself?

With most of our titles available in both PDF and ePUB format, you can access your content wherever and however you wish—on your PC, phone, tablet, or reader.

Since you've purchased this print book, we are happy to offer you the eBook for just $5.

To learn more, go to http://www.apress.com/companion or contact support@apress.com.

Apress®

Printed in the United States
By Bookmasters